THE DICTIONARY
OF DRINK AND DRINKING

Lexington College

310 S. Peoria St. Ste. 512
Chicago, Il 60607 3534

Phone 312-226-6294
Fax   312-226-6405

THE DICTIONARY
OF DRINK AND
DRINKING

by

OSCAR A. MENDELSOHN
B.Sc., F.R.I.C., F.R.A.C.I.

*Sometime Missioner Abroad for Commonwealth and Victorian
Governments
Registered Public Analyst for the States of Victoria,
New South Wales and Queensland*

Line-drawings by T. Paul

HAWTHORN BOOKS, INC.
Publishers, New York

First American Edition, November 1965

PRINTED IN GREAT BRITAIN
H–3108

To

THE FELLOWSHIP OF TRENCHERMEN

Good men all of that
Melbourne group of
citizens of the fork

By Way of Introduction

SURELY there are few educated and balanced people of the Western Civilization who are not pleasantly interested in some phase of drinks and drinking. So far as I can discover, this is the first attempt in English to gather up the general information on the subject and put it into easily referable form. Of course there have been many excellent specialized collections published — dictionaries of wine, word-books of beer, collections of cocktail recipes and so forth, but this book is not limited to any single group of beverages and it attempts to cover the whole field. It also includes simple definitions of technical terms, brief outlines of processes and indications (not complete recipes) of hundreds of mixed drinks. There will be found, I hope with interest, digressions and quotations and also translations of classical allusions. In short, I have drawn no rigid line and have not hesitated to use any item that bears on the large, wide and handsome subject of the nature and use of alcoholic beverages. Naturally enough, bias, personal preference and prejudice have had full play!

I can claim confidently that this book contains errors and omissions sufficiently large in number and flagrant in nature to satisfy the most enthusiastic of my enemies. The plain fact is that the subject is too vast for any person to be its full master. *Gaffes* are inevitable.

Alcoholic beverages are almost universal. I think Australia, Patagonia and the Northern Arctic Region are the only settled areas of the world without indigenous examples. This absence is no reflection, of course, upon the mental capabilities of the aboriginal inhabitants of these places but merely indicates a lack of fermentable carbohydrate in the native flora. The named and defined varieties of alcoholic drinks far exceed ten thousand (France alone having wines in one region, the Bordeaux, beyond that number) and no man could possibly write of all of them from first-hand knowledge.[1] The aspiring lexicographer of alcoholica must therefore rely upon specialist authors for much of his material, for example the grades of armagnac brandy, the criteria of South African dry white wines, the technology of bourbon whiskey, the significance of controlled appellation in Portugal, the nomenclature of mead, the black grape varieties of Switzerland, the meaning of *gruit* and the nature of Marchiafava's disease. Such a list could be multiplied greatly.

Very well, then, says your hypercritical one, choose your authorities wisely and you automatically cancel the chance of error — or almost so.

---

[1] Consider. Germany is reported to possess over 50,000 registered vineyards along the Rhine. Certainly some of these are but 2 or 3 acres in area but a few of the pocket-handkerchief plots produce wine of world fame.

Yes, you reply meekly, of course that is true, but what happens when two apparently equally eminent specialists make startlingly disparate statements about the same thing? In the end you necessarily take refuge in an intelligent guess — and nobody but a gambling addict deludes himself that he can always guess right.

I hope that even though the total number of errors may be large, the proportion will prove to be low. I should in fairness point out that I have had the text read by a number of experts in specialized fields with the object of reducing errors. Corrections and amendments will be gratefully received *provided the authority is quoted.*

Names and descriptions of proprietary beverages have been excluded with the exception of a few which have acquired some special significance or importance or are prime examples of types. The inclusion of a representative collection of these proprietary drinks and named brands might well have had some utility but the difficulties of choice are too formidable and proprietary brands appear and disappear with kaleidoscopic speed. Moreover, to describe the actual composition of a proprietary beverage would usually be impossible and anything less would have small virtue.

It is not a contradiction that there will be found included a representative collection of names of wine and spirit shippers and of some of the distilleries and breweries of the United Kingdom and Dominions. It seems to me these are equally worthy of inclusion as the hundreds of wine estates. The criterion of selection has been age and celebrity and I accept mournfully that anybody who attempts such a task cannot avoid making enemies.

To save space I have omitted titles such as Clos and Château from hundreds of French wine names and also, in most cases, the definite article. I have used also the bare geographical names of German wine parishes and towns for the relevant wines. Thus Enkirch is listed but not Enkircher. I am sure there will be no confusion. I have tried to be consistent in the spelling of European names, especially German, but some alternatives may have insinuated themselves.

A large number of grape varieties have been noted, but the list is not complete. Many wine grapes are of small importance because they are of strictly local use for the production of a wine of mediocre or lesser quality. Another difficulty is the unfortunate proliferation of names for the same vine. An identical variety of grape growing in France, Germany, Italy, Spain, Australia, South Africa, California, Hungary and Russia may bear nine different names. This confusion is increasing and there is a real need for an international standard nomenclature of grape sorts.

As to the relative space allotted to entries, especially those of individual European wines, I recognize that despite anything I may claim, I shall be soundly blamed for making no more than bare mention of some especially loved wines or wine estates. Example: A knowledgeable wine-lover, an expert on one type of the wines of Bordeaux, looked at this book in typescript, and promptly complained to me that Château Frisson (shall we say?)

was worth more than my single line. Had he not actually spent many happy hours on that lovely estate? Was it not producing a charming wine at a most reasonable price? I answered that I had given full measure of space to the world-famous wine of the class of which Frisson was admittedly a worthy fellow-member but there were over thirty other members, each no doubt with its loyal band of followers. Moreover, as fully ventilated under various entries (see, for example, Médoc), reputation and classification are by no means always reliable. Many an obscure wine is a finer thing than a celebrity of the same type and in any case wine from the one vineyard in Europe may vary radically in quality in successive years. Indeed, it was with considerable hesitation that I finally decided to use qualifications such as 'fine', 'celebrated', 'noted' and 'mediocre' for some of the wines which have long borne those reputations. Even the mention of an individual vineyard in this book is an indication that it has achieved *some* degree of importance.

I have consulted so many books, journals and other material that the customary acknowledgments are inappropriate or even impossible. Moreover, one source may have generated many entries while another may have been limited in utility to a single item. Nevertheless, grateful I am to the many and varied writers on general or specific alcoholic beverages and their technology. I do, however, especially thank Messrs. Allen & Unwin for permission to repeat some of the entries from the short glossary in my own book *The Earnest Drinker* (London, 1950). I am also grateful to M. André Simon, that combination of the best of two worlds who has put the whole citizenry of fine gastronomy in his debt. I also thank Arthur Cridland, B.Sc., of Sydney, my friend from early schooldays and a keen judge of wine and words.

This book is a glossary, not an encyclopaedia. It aims at nothing more than concise definition; those who need fuller information should consult an appropriately focused book. There are admirable specialized books available for almost every group of alcoholic beverages. I emphasize that the work is intended for laymen and no knowledge of science is assumed.

Everybody who uses this collection is sure to be irritated or angered, sooner or later, by the absence of some item which he feels is worthier of a place than many other duly installed. But somewhere one must cry halt. I assert here and now that I make no claim to have exhausted the field. New vineyards, new combinations of flavours, new alcoholic aphorisms happily arise almost continuously.

I thank my secretaries, Roma Wilson and Gillian White, for their skill and patience.

OSCAR A. MENDELSOHN

Heidelberg, Victoria,
Australia, 1964

PS. Hawk-eyed readers who detect a seeming inconsistency in the spellings *whisky* and *whiskey* are respectfully but firmly informed that this is no accident. The accepted spelling of Scotch is *whisky* and of Irish *whiskey*. The American whiskies usually take the Irish spelling.

Aargauer: Swiss white table wine, mainly from Villingen, Wettingen, and Schinznach.

A.B.: Mixture of equal parts mild and bitter ale.

Abbaye-Skinner: Red table wine from Médoc.

Abbé-Gorsse-de-Gorsse: Red table wine from Margaux, Médoc.

Abboccato: Sweetish white wine mainly from Orvieto, Italy. In Italian slang the word means 'taken in' or 'defrauded'. It has become a general term for a semi-sweet wine.

A.B.C.: Cocktail of apricot liqueur, whisky, vermouth.

Abel-Laurent, Ch.: Red table wine from Margaux, Médoc.

Aberdeen: Scottish centre for production of Highland malt whisky.

Abfüllung: German wine-container term meaning 'bottled by', the equivalent of the French *mise du Château*.

Abiet-Landat: Red table wine from Cissac, Médoc.

Ablagern: German term for maturing, either in wood or bottle.

Abocado: Spanish wine term for 'slightly sweetened'.

A bon vin point d'enseigne: French for 'good wine needs no bush'.

Abrau: Crimean white table wine, perhaps the best known of the Russian growths.

Abrau-Durso: Russian (Crimean) sparkling wine of champagne (q.v.) type.

Abricotine: Liqueur made from ripe apricots. The same liqueur appears under several names. The flavour, if entirely natural, is a rare delight but unfortunately cream of apricot or the like is sometimes pointed up with crude synthetic essence.

Absinthe: Technically a gin (q.v.) because it is an unsweetened alcoholic solution of flavouring agents. The characteristic flavour is that of aniseed and wormwood (*Artemisia absinthium*) but most brands also contain cinnamon, cloves, angelica, nutmeg, lemon, cardamon and more. Oil of wormwood is poisonous. Some countries such as Switzerland and France forbid the manufacture of absinthe, others merely limit the wormwood content. The drinking of absinthe, especially in the Latin Quarter of Paris, has always been associated with extreme Bohemianism. The dramatic effect of turning the liquid milky or opalescent by the addition of water merely depends upon the precipitation from solution of the flavorous gums, resins and oils. The same simple trick can be worked with ouzo (q.v.) and similar gins. There are numerous modern absinthe substitutes, presumably harmless.

Absinthe Suissesse: An elaborate mixed drink of the gaudy past made with egg white, anisette, crème de menthe, orange flower water and, of course, absinthe, all beaten with ice in a shaker.

Absolute Alcohol: In theory, chemically pure ethyl alcohol and therefore containing no water. In practice it is exceedingly difficult, perhaps impossible without elaborate precautions, to remove the last traces of water from a hygroscopic substance such as ethyl alcohol.

Abstberg: German (Graach, q.v.) white wine.

Abteilikor: German term for any liqueur produced in a monastery.

Abtswind: German (Franconian) wine parish. Mainly white wines said by one authority to be 'very dry and possessing a gun-flint bouquet all their own'. There are also some reds of fair quality.

Aburdaham: Old-established shippers of madeira (q.v.).

A.C.: Common abbreviation for *appellation contrôlée* (q.v.).

Acco: Wine-growing region mentioned in the Bible.

Acerbe: Harsh, bitter, sour. A term applied by the French to poor wine, especially if made from unripe grapes.

Acetaldehyde: The organic compound largely responsible (with diethyl acetal) for the characteristic flavour of flor (q.v.) sherries.

Acetification: The process of converting ethyl alcohol (q.v.) to vinegar (acetic acid). It is the defect of souring that takes place in light alcoholic beverages when they are exposed to air, whereby acetic-forming bacteria gain entrance. The process is also termed 'pricking'. See also Acidity. The volatile acidity of wine and other beverages represents spoilage and is to be sharply distinguished from the fixed acidity of wine, cider and a number of other beverages. Fixed acidity is a measure of the presence of tartaric, malic, citric and/or other non-volatile acids which are essential to flavour and longevity. The addition of wholesome acid to a deficient wine is permissible in most countries.

Acetobacter: The micro-organism which turns alcohol to acetic acid (vinegar) and is thus an enemy of the wine-maker. By exclusion of air (oxygen) the organism can be restrained.

Achaia: Greek wine district, the main source of mavrodaphne (q.v.).

Achkarren: German white wine from Kaiserstuhl (q.v.).

Achtel: A German and Austrian liquid measure, an eighth of an eimer. The eimer varies with locality from about 12½ to 15 gallons. Cf. the English octave (q.v.).

Achtmorgen: German (Ruppertsberg, q.v.) white wine.

Acidity: The quality of tart flavour in wine, cider and numerous other alcoholic beverages. An acid content is natural, agreeable and desirable. The main acid of wine is tartaric. If the must (q.v.) is deficient in acidity, tartaric acid is added, a quite laudable process. Acidity must be distinguished from sourness. See also Acetification. A sufficient wholesome acid content is essential for longevity. The acid of cider and perry is malic, of oranges and lemons citric.

Acidity, volatile: The acid of a wine which can be distilled. It is almost always the undesirable acetic acid (vinegar).

Ackerman: Bessarabian wine region.

Acquit Régional Blanc: French official certificate for export alcohol.

Acquit Régional Jaune d'Or: French official export certificate for cognac and armagnac, printed on golden paper, hence the name.

Acrospire: The plumule developed in the germination of a grain, especially in malting.

Adam: Cocktail of rum, grenadine, lemon.

Adam and Eve: Cocktail of gin, curaçao, yellow chartreuse.

Adega: Portuguese version of *bodega* (q.v.), a wine storehouse.

Adlersberg: Hungarian red wine from Ofen-Pest. See also Ofen.

Adom-Atic: Israeli red wine bottled in accordance with Mosaic law.

Adonis: Appetizer of sherry, sweet vermouth and bitters.

Advocaat: Dutch (originally) liqueur (q.v.) made from sweetened brandy mixed with egg yolk and flavoured with vanilla and coffee. The name means 'barrister' and the terminal 't' is sounded. The legal implication is a mystery.

Aeolian Islands: These, also known as the Lipari or Eolic group, include Lipari, Stromboli, Salina and Filoudi, all known for wine production for thousands of years and more recently for malmsey (q.v.). The islands are romantic but, in candour, the wines are so-so.

Afen-Pest: Hungarian wine centre. The good red Adlersberg is often sold as Afen-Adlersberg.

Affenthaler: German (Baden) red table wine of good quality.

Afile: Italian white table wine from Latium.

Africa: Great wine-producing country and destined to be greater. Growth is concentrated in the extreme north (Mediterranean areas of Algeria, Tunis and Morocco) and extreme south (Cape Province).

Afuera: Spanish term for sherry made from grapes grown on *albariza* soil.

Aga Khan: The spiritual head of the Moslems of the Ismaili sect. Moslems eschew alcohol but by a merciful dispensation of Allah it has been ordained that as soon as liquor passes the Aga Khan's lips (but not those of lesser breed) it turns to pure water.

Agave: The cactus-like plant native to Mexico upon which is based an interesting and important native alcoholic beverage industry. The agave (the name means 'admirable', and refers to the beautiful appearance of the plants in flower) is a member of the *Amaryllidaceae* and is a slow-growing palm-like plant also known as the *maguey* or *pita*. It used to be called the century plant because it was believed to take 100 years to flower, but the *Oxford Dictionary of Horticulture* exposes the error by pointing out dryly that the large varieties take only 40 years! The Mexican national drink, pulque (q.v.), is made by cutting out the inflorescence at an early stage and collecting and fermenting sugar-containing sap that will flow for nearly six months. See also Mezcal and Tequila.

Age: It is common knowledge and experience that many alcoholic beverages improve on keeping, but in most cases the underlying causes and the route of the chemistry involved are still obscure. There have been many attempts to accelerate the expensive and tedious method of maturing by mere natural storage. These include exposure to heat (rancio), mechanical agitation, electrical discharge, addition of traces of oxidizing and other agents, exposure to radiation and more, but apparently little success has been achieved.

The changes that occur vary with the nature of the beverage and the conditions of storage. Some, e.g. spirits and fortified wines, seem to require a minute and slow ingress of air to oxidize or otherwise change displeasing 'fusel-oil' into fragrant, characteristic esters. Others, such as dry wines, are harmed by even limited access to oxygen.

Beer and ale need only comparatively short maturation. See also Lager. White beverage wines mature more rapidly than red. Both are stored in oaken vessels for a period varying from a year to five or more ('cask age') and are then bottled and stored for a further one to ten years before use ('bottle age'). Some red beverage wines, e.g. some bordeaux, are said to need 20 years to attain their optimum quality.

Sherry is already aged when bottled and there is no benefit in further storage. Spirits do not improve in bottle and the extravagant price paid for parcels of old brandy, whisky or rum is a waste of money. Gin actually declines in quality on long storage.

The prejudice against young beverage wines is often misplaced. Some of these never improve materially on keeping and may, indeed, soon go downhill.

Fortified sweet wines usually respond nobly to ageing in both wood and glass. There is no substitute for an aged port. Madeira is said to be the longest-lived of all wines and to be drinkable after a century. However, whether this is true of the modern wine of Madeira is arguable.

The meanings of the stars and other cabbalistic signs on spirit labels is discussed in alphabetical place.

Agios Georgios: Greek very sweet and dark dessert wine from Nemea.

Aglianico del Vulture: Italian dark red table wine from Mount Vulture, near Naples.

Agly: Wine centre near Roussillon for *vins doux naturels* (q.v.).

Agqueria, D': One of the best growths of Tavel (q.v.).

Agrafe: A steel clamp placed over the cork of the bottle during the manufacture of champagne or other sparkling wine.

Agresto: Italian unripe grape juice used in place of vinegar. Syn. 'verjuice'.

Agros: Cyprian dessert wine.

Agua Bianca: 'White water', liqueur of bergamot flavour containing fragments of silver leaf.

Aguachirle: Spanish term for inferior wine. See also Piquette and Tresterwein.

Aguapié: The Portuguese equivalent of the Spanish aguachirle (q.v.).

Aguardiente: 'Burning water', brandy or similar spirit of Spain, Portugal and South America.

Aguardiente de Bagaço: Portuguese brandy distilled from marc. See also Grappa.

Aguardiente de Cana: 'Cane spirit', the common Spanish and South American term for rum.

Aguardiente de Palma: Spirit made in the Philippines from fermented juice of the nipa palm. Also known as aguardiente de nipa.

Ahm: See Aum.

Ahmchen: German wine measure, about 6¼ gallons.

Ahner Riesling: White table wine of Luxembourg.

Ahornwein: German term for beverage made from maple sugar or sap of sugar maple tree.

Ahr: German wine region. The River Ahr is a left-bank tributary of the Rhine. Wine has been grown here since the Roman occupation. One of the few Rhenish areas specializing in reds. Amongst the best vineyards are those at Heimersheim, Landskrone, Berg, Ahrweiler, Rosenthal, Dabhaus, Walporzheim, Marienthal, Trotzenberg, Dernau, Haardtberg, Rech, Herrenberg, Mayschoss, Monochberg, Laacherberg, Altenahr and Eckenberg.

Ahrbleichert: The German term for the pale ('bleached') red wines of Ahr (q.v.).

Ahsis: A Biblical name apparently equivalent to flavoured wine. Also asis. See also Bible.

Aiche: German (Rheinhessen) cask, about 64 litres.

Aidanil: Russian (Crimean) red and white wines.

Aiglerie, Ch.: French (Anjou) white wine.

Aiglon, Ch.: French (Médoc) white wine.

Aigrots, Les: French (Beaune) table wine.

Aiguebelle: French liqueur (q.v.). The yellow is about 42%, and the green 46% alcohol.

Aiguilhe, Ch.: French (St. Émilion) red and white wines.

Aime: French (Alsatian) cask, about 114 litres.

Ainé: French for 'senior' and sometimes used of wine to indicate superiority.

Ajaccio: Corsican red and white table wines.

Ajenjo: Spanish spirit of absinthe (q.v.) type.

Akavit, Akvavit: See Aquavit.

Alambic du Gers Système Verdier: French name of the special type of pot-still (q.v.) used to make armagnac (q.v.) brandy. This differs from a cognac still in being one of continuous type.

Alambrado: Spanish white table wine.

Alaska: Cocktail of gin, lemon juice and orange marmalade.

Alba: Italian (Piedmont) red Barolo wine.

Alba Flora: Spanish (Minorca) white wine.

Alban: The name of the wine region south of Rome of great antiquity, and mentioned with approval by Horace.

Albana di Bertinoto: Italian white table wine from the Bologna region. There are several other Italian wines which bear the name Albana.

Albanello: Sicilian white table wine.

Albariza: The Spanish name for the chalky soil around Jerez on which the vines flourish that yield sherry. See also Barros and Arenas.

Albersweiler: German (Palatinate) dry wines.

Alberts: French (Blayais) red wine.

Albig: German (Rheinhessen) dry white wine (hock).

Albillo: One of the lesser grapes used in Spain for sherry.

Albillo Castellano: Spanish white wine grape.

Albtrauf: German wine centre of Württemberg.

Albury: Australian wine district on Murray River, border of Victoria and New South Wales. Importance has declined.

Alcamo: Italian white table wine from Sicily.

Alcohol, Diuretic Action of: The belief is widespread that alcohol is a somewhat powerful diuretic but the pharmacology of the subject is still obscure. It is undoubted that some alcoholic beverages are actively diuretic, for example, gin and beer. However, gin contains an appreciable quantity of oil of juniper, which is a well-recognized diuretic while the hop extract of beer also has a diuretic action. Further, beer is usually drunk in large volume, inevitably resulting in diuresis.

There seems no evidence that other spirits and wine, taken in moderation, have any marked diuretic action beyond that of fluid quantity. The fact that alcohol is a vasodilator probably involves some small increase in kidney permeability.

Alcohol, Ethyl: The liquid substance of chemical formula C_2H_5OH on whose presence the effect of alcoholic beverages primarily depends. The name is derived from the Arabic *al kohl*, the fine powder (probably antimony sulphide) used by Arabian women for painting the eyelids. Later, by some process never explained to the satisfaction of this writer, the word came to be applied both to fine powder in general and to the liquid we know today. That liquid for a long period was also known as 'burning wine', *aqua vitae* or 'water of life'.

Alcohol is a colourless, mobile liquid, considerably lighter than water, with a specific gravity of about 0·8 at room temperature, water being 1. (In other words an imperial gallon of water weighs 10 lb. and a gallon of alcohol only about 8 lb.) As everybody knows, it readily burns in air, with an almost colourless flame. It is exceedingly difficult to prepare pure alcohol, owing to its strong affinity (vague word, although still used by the chemist) for water; and to certain other technical reasons relating to the physical chemistry of distillation. When pure, dry alcohol is prepared it must be put into an airtight receptacle immediately or it will at once commence to absorb water vapour from the air, and be no longer pure alcohol. Really pure alcohol is actually only a chemical curiosity, and even so-called 'absolute' alcohol very rarely conforms to the description. Pure alcohol probably has no definable odour. The smell of all ordinary specimens is perhaps due to the presence of tiny quantities of impurities called the 'congenerics'.

Contrary to general belief, alcohol is not a stimulant but actually the pharmacological opposite, a depressant. Technically, it is a volatile anaesthetic. It acts by dulling the higher nerve centres and removing the inhibitions that act as a restraining influence. In some people these inhibitions are too potent and a moderate amount of alcohol will produce a healthy normality. The subject is too large for discussion here.

Alcohol, Methyl: The simplest of all alcohols (q.v.), of chemical formula CH_3OH. Unlike common ethyl or beverage alcohol, methyl alcohol or methanol is distinctly poisonous, even causing total and permanent blindness or death. Wood spirit (formed by the destructive distillation of wood) is an impure form which used to be employed as a denaturant, hence the name methylated spirit.

Alcohol, Physiological and Pharmacological Action of: Alcohol is a true foodstuff able to supply a part of the calorific or energy needs of the human being, but it is also an active drug because it has a marked and prompt action upon living tissue. Men have been close observers for thousands of years of the results of ingesting alcohol, yet the continued ignorance of the facts is astonishing. This applies not only to laymen but to a segment of the medical and scientific ranks. The subject is so large that here it is only possible to set out a few bald statements.

1. Contrary to general belief, alcohol is not a stimulant but the pharmacological opposite, a depressant. It acts by inhibiting or depressing various restraining influences which normally operate. Thus a person who has over-indulged may become garrulous, reckless, boastful, belligerent and so on, contrary to his usual behaviour and his seemingly normal character. Similarly, another person may become generous, courageous, tolerant and so forth. According to this writer's observation,

one effect of alcohol is to heighten the mood in which it is taken. The genial become more so (often tediously) while the gloomy become bullies. Drowning one's sorrows may often be a myth.

2. In a general way, alcohol diminishes skill and judgement but it is familiar knowledge that a very moderate intake may actually improve performance, both physical and mental.

3. Modern medicine teaches that most or perhaps all the diseases, even *delirium tremens*, previously attributable to alcohol are in fact only indirect results, the direct cause being lack of vitamins and other nutritional essentials. This stems from the familiar fact that drunkards often neglect their diet. (Admittedly the patient suffers just as much whether alcohol is the direct or indirect cause!)

4. Pharmacologically, alcohol is a volatile anaesthetic and we no longer remember that until a century ago, with all its limitations, it was an extremely valuable aid to surgery.

5. It is a vasodilator (a drug which dilates the arteries and therefore lowers blood-pressure). For this reason it is bad policy to drink before exposure to great cold. When the blood-vessels are dilated there is an increased loss of bodily heat from the skin. Even to this day drunken persons arrested by police and put into cold cells are not infrequently found dead in the morning. Alcohol still has a valued place in the treatment of certain cardiac conditions.

6. Alcohol is a true food. A limited amount can be burnt in the body and replace other energy-foods.

A suitable specialized text should be consulted for an account of the fate (utilization and excretion) of alcohol in the body. See also Drunk, Sex and Alcohol, and Shakespeare.

Alcoholic Fallacies: See Fallacies, Drinking.

Alcoholic Strength: See Strength.

Alcoholism: The excessive consumption of alcoholic beverages. It is a deplorable business, but no worse than gluttony.

Alcoholometry: The operation of ascertaining the alcoholic strength of a mixture of alcohol and water, and in particular of alcoholic beverages. See also Strength.

Alcohols: A class of organic chemical substances characterized by the presence of the group —OH, combined in a particular way. In common speech, the unadorned word 'alcohol' always means ethyl alcohol. In chemistry, however, there are known literally hundreds of alcohols, some of great complexity, with a wide range of commercial, scientific and medical uses. Traces of more complex alcohols than ethyl are often found in alcoholic beverages, and some of these contribute to bouquet, fragrance and character. Others again, some of which occur in fusel-oil (q.v.), are of a harsh flavour and are removed partly by ageing. See also Alcohol, Ethyl.

Alcools Blancs: French term for brandies which are colourless because not aged in wood. The name is especially applied to fruit brandies such as quetsch, mirabelle, fraise and kirsch (q.v.).

Aldabo: Cuban liqueur of rum base and citrus flavour.

Aldegrund: German (Lower Moselle) wine region.

Aldehydes: A class of chemical compounds that may be regarded as oxidation products of alcohols. Some of the aldehydes, like the esters (q.v.), are of pleasing aroma, and contribute to the characteristic flavours of alcoholic beverages.

Aldrich, Henry (1648–1710): I know nothing of him except (and this is enough) that he wrote:

> If all be true that I do think,
> There are five reasons we should drink;
> Good wine — a friend — or being dry —
> Or lest we should be by and by —
> Or any other reason why.

Ale: An obsolete term for an English country festival at which there was much drinking. ('At wakes and ales' — Ben Jonson.)

Ale: Beverage made by fermenting a cereal or mixture of cereals. By far the commonest cereal used is barley (q.v.). The subject of ale is best considered in conjunction with beer. See the combined entry on beer and ale under B. Here it is convenient to state a few bald facts. The name is derived from the OE. *alu* or *ealu*. It is a beverage with an authenticated history of more than 4,000 years and was well known to the Assyrians and other ancient peoples. The original difference between ale and beer was that the latter was flavoured with hops. In most English-speaking countries today the terms are used indiscriminately, but the name ale is not used for lager (q.v.) or for dark beer. In the United States a distinction is still drawn, the term ale being confined to the brewed beverage made by the top-fermentation process (q.v.). Some brewers distinguish between these names on the basis of strength, using ale for the beverage of higher alcohol content.

Ale, Audit: Special strong ale brewed in England at certain colleges of Oxford and Cambridge, intended to be drunk on the feast of Audit Day.

Ale, Brasenose: The distinctive drink brewed at that Oxford college.

Ale, Brown: Vague English term for mild ale. Usually abbreviated to 'a brown'.

Ale, Dr. Butler's: The recipe of the physician to James I, consisting of ale flavoured with various spices and medicaments. Wherever 'The Butler's Head' was seen as a tavern-sign, there the stuff, real or spurious, was sold.

Ale, Garland: Evergreens and flowers used on ale-stakes in taverns at festive times.

Ale, Mild: This is generally marked X or XX and is a dark beer brewed for immediate consumption. It usually has a slightly sweet taste from the addition of sugar.

Ale, Scotch: There are brews of various kinds made in Scotland but the characteristic ale thought of as Scotch is strong and of the Burton (q.v.) type.

Ale, Scurvy Grass: Water-cress infusion added to ale and supposed to be a preventive of scurvy.

Ale, Special: There were dozens, perhaps hundreds, of 'special' brews of ale and also of ordinary brews to which special names were attached. Some few of these were:

Bid-ale (served at benefit feasts at which guests were expected to make a gift).

Bride-ale (when the bride received the proceeds of all ale sold and the supposed origin of the word 'bridal').

Church-ale (sold at parish festivals).

Clerk's ale (for the benefit of the parish clerk).

College-ale (see Audit, Brasenose).

Cuckoo-ale (served on the spring day when that wily bird was first heard).

Give-ale (dispensed free, usually by the direction of a legacy).

Harvest-ale.

Lamb-ale (for lambing-time).

Leet-ale (for use at the annual courts of records).

Ale, Stock: Specially strong brew intended to be stored. The term is often used for beer of Burton (q.v.) type.

Ale, Stone: Staffordshire ale brewed originally by monks at Stone.

Ale, Taylor on: '. . . It is a seale of many a good Bargaine. The Physitian will commend it; the Lawyer will defend it, it neither hurts, nor kills, any but those that abuse it unmeasurably and beyond bearing; It doth good to as many as take it rightly. . . .'

John Taylor (1580–1653), *Drinke and Welcome*

Aleatico: Italian sweet red wine made over a wide region, including Tuscany, Umbria and Calabria. Also a grape sometimes wrongly called black muscat.

Aleberry: From ale and bre (broth). An old-fashioned drink (or soup) made by warming ale, sugar, spices and pieces of bread.

Alecost: Syn. for 'costmary' (q.v.), an aromatic perennial herb formerly used to flavour ale (q.v.).

Ale Draper: Old term for alehouse-keeper.

Alella: Spanish esteemed dry wine from Catalonia, red and white but chiefly the latter.

Alembic: A medieval still made of metal or glass, an essential part of the equipment of all alchemists and early chemists. The name comes from the Arabic *al-inbīq*, the still. The vast number of small rum and whisky stills used in Atlantic States of the U.S. in the 18th century were known as alembics. The term 'alembic' survives as the name of the cap of distilling equipment. See also Still.

Ale-Stake: A long pole with a bushy branch tied at the end of it, put out by the brewer to show he desired a visit from the ale-conner to approve legally the latest brew.

Alewife: Obsolete English term for woman who keeps an alehouse. Why this should have been adopted by Americans as the name of a fish of the herring family is a minor mystery of language; a medieval housewife was expected to be a competent brewer.

Alexander: Mixed drink of brandy, chocolate liqueur and cream.

Aleyard: A tall, slender glass formerly used as a measure and as a drinking vessel.

Aleyor: A dark-red wine of Majorca.

Alf-Bullay: German (Moselle) wine parish.

Alföld: Chief Hungarian district for ordinary wines.

Algaida: Spanish (Andalusian) table wines.

Algarinejo: Spanish (Granada) wine region. Reds, whites and brandy.

Algeria: This, the world's third- or fourth-largest wine-producer, has an output (nearly 400 million gallons) more than a third of that of France itself. Much of the wine quickly loses its identity, for it is commonly recognized that a vast gallonage goes north to France to be mixed not only with the wines of the Midi as *vin ordinaire* (q.v.) but also, much of it, to 'extend' the wines of Bordeaux and especially of Burgundy. It follows that much Algerian wine is of excellent quality. There is a little white wine made and, consonant with the climate, the red beverage wines are dark-tinted, big-bodied and of pronounced flavour, Burgundian in character.

Some of the better-known Algerian wines are from Médéa, Côte de l'Harrach, Mascara, Milliana and Mostaganem.

Algheri: Sardinian red table wine.

Algorobo Beer: Sacred beer made by Chaco Indian tribes and forbidden to women.

Alicante: A sweet red wine of East Spain.

Alicante Bouschet: Red grape-vine variety used for heavy yields of inexpensive, undistinguished wine in hot climates, especially Algeria, California and Southern France. It is responsible for most of the common red wine of the French Midi (*vin ordinaire*).

Aligote: Heavy-yielding white grape grown in Burgundy for mediocre wine. In France there are legal limitations on its use.

Alkermes: A curious liqueur made in France and Italy, intensely coloured red with cochineal.

Al Kohl: Arabic term ('the kohl') generally believed to be the derivation of the word alcohol. Kohl was an exceedingly fine powder used as a cosmetic, especially to paint the eyes. Supposedly because of the mobility or other property of alcohol the liquid was so named, though there is no good evidence that the Arabs so employed it. See also Alcohol.

Allasch: Liqueur — a variety of kümmel (q.v.).

Allella: Popular Spanish table wines from Catalonia. The better is the white, which is of the character of hock (q.v.).

All Saints: Large Australian (Victorian) vineyard at Wahgunyah on the Murray River border. There are 300 acres of carefully tended and selected vines producing excellent flor sherry and dessert wines. One of the few large unincorporated (despite the name) Australian wineries.

Allsopp: Noted name in English brewing. Founded in 1708 at the celebrated centre of Burton upon Trent, the brewery is now part of the large company Ind Coope Ltd.

Almadén: One of the best of the northern Californian wineries.

Almendralejo: Spanish table wines from Estremadura.

Almeria: Noted Spanish centre in Andalusia for table grapes and raisins exported to England. Some wine is also made.

Almibar: Syrup used to sweeten pale sherries.

Almijar: The open courtyard of a Spanish sherry establishment, where the grapes are received.

Almissa: Dalmatian dessert wine.

Almude: Portuguese wine measure varying from 3½ to 7 gallons, according to district.

Almus: German (Bavarian) dessert wine from Trieffeinstein.

Aloha: Cocktail of rum, lime and pineapple juice and mint.

Aloque: A white Spanish wine, also known in England as hollock.

Alosha: According to Howell (1634) this was a common Spanish drink 'which they drink between Meals and 'tis a hydromel', i.e. mead. In view of the ancient tradition of wine-drinking in Spain this sounds improbable.

Aloupka: Russian (Crimean) table wines, red and white.

Aloxe-Corton: Celebrated Burgundian wine-growing commune of the Côted'Or. Its red and white wines are equally renowned. Only pinot noir and chardonnay grapes are permitted. See also Corton.

Alphen: Red table wine from the old South African vineyard of same name.

Alqueire: Portuguese wine measure of half-*almude* (q.v.).

Alsace: French province between the Vosges mountains and the Rhine which produces pleasant rather than fine wines. They are ethereally pale green in colour, aromatic and can, indeed should be, drunk young. Most of the Alsatian wines have a varietal name of the principal grape used, combined with the village of origin. If a blend of grapes is used, the word 'edelzwicker' is usually shown on the label. The riesling is still the chief grape though many prefer the bouquet of gewurztraminer. The best wine villages are north of Colmar and include Riquewihr, Ammerschwihr, Mittelwihr, Bergheim and Kientzheim. Most of these were devastated during the Second World War but fortunately the vineyards have been replanted.

Alsatian: Cocktail of brandy, kirsch, black coffee.

Alsheim: German (Rheinhessen) wine region including Sommerhäuschen, Stratzenberg, Goldberg, Steinländ, Obere Hahl, Efmorgen, Rosenberg, Hammel, Fischerpfad, Pappen and Rüst.

Altar Wine: See Sacramental.

Alten: Austrian wine term. On a label it means the contents are at least two years old.

Altenahr: German (Ahr Valley) red wines, including Eckenberg and Uebig.

Altenbamberg: German (Palatinate) wine region, including Treuenfels, Rotenberg, Kehrenberg and Schlossberg.

Altenberg: German (Forst, q.v.) fine white wine. The same name is borne by vineyards of Avelsbach (q.v.), Wachenheim, Palatinate (q.v.) and Franconia.

Altenberg: German (Canzem) white wine.

Altenweg: German (Königsbach, q.v.) white wine.

Altesse de Frangy: White French wine from Savoy.

Altesses, Vin des: French (Bressan) white wine.

Alto: Esteemed South African red table wine from vineyard of same name.

Alto Douro: The legally defined region of northern Portugal where port wine is grown. It includes the Upper Douro Valley beyond Regoa. See also Douro and Port.

Altramura: Italian (Apulian) dessert wine.

Alzey: German (Rheinhessen) wine region, including Grün, Sybillenstein, Heissgasse and Liemenhohl.

Amabile: Italian (Piedmont) red table wine, slightly sweet and gassy.

Amarante: Portuguese white table wine.

Amarone: The term applied to a full-bodied Valpolicella (q.v.) wine of fine vintage.

Amazake: Sweet sake, non-alcoholic, used in Japan as a temperance drink. See also Sake.

Ambarès: French (Médoc) red wine area.

Amber: Anglo-Saxon liquid measure of about 7 gallons. In 694, Ini, King of the West Saxons, endeared himself to history by imposing the first English tax on ale of so many ambers according to the size of the farmer's holding.

Amber Bottles: The amber bottle is widely used today as a container for beer because it gives good protection against deterioration from ultra-violet light. The wine-makers of the Rhine Valley (who use amber and blue bottles so widely) must have made the same discovery empirically long ago.

Ambès, Bec d': French wine-growing area on the estuary of the Gironde. Moderate red wine.

Ambonnay: French (Marne) area for superior champagne grapes.

Ambrosia: The Greek mythical food of the immortals; hence, figuratively, anything that has a very special appeal to the palate.

Am Bruderweg: German (Niederingelheim, q.v.) white wine.

Amelioration: As applied to wine, the process of adding ordinary sugar to weak grape juice before fermentation. The resulting wine is always inferior and the process, although legal in some countries, is open to flagrant abuse. Also called 'chaptalization' (q.v.).

American Beauty: Cocktail of brandy, dry vermouth, port wine and grenadine.

Americano: Appetizer of sweet vermouth and bitters.

Americano: Italian popular name for a *cocktail* (q.v.) or mixed drink. Now obsolescent.

American Sauterne: The name applied in California with little or no discrimination to a dry white wine of no particular merit. It bears no resemblance to genuine sauternes (q.v.) except that it is alcoholic and colourless. Sometimes it is tagged with the still less justified name of 'haut sauterne'.

American Wine: Strictly, any wine made in the U.S. The term is used also in a more restricted way to indicate wine made from native American grapes (Concord, Delaware, Catawba, Norton, Scuppernong, Niagara, etc.) which have a characteristic spicy or foxy flavour. Since little wine is made from these *labrusca* grapes in California the term sometimes means U.S. non-Californian wine.

The great (indeed overwhelming) centre for American wine production is California, where 90% or more of the total of 130 million gallons is produced. The wines are made from European vines, usually grafted on native stocks to resist *Phylloxera* (q.v.). As in Australia, South Africa and some parts of South America, the misleading habit obtains of using European place-names for wines, but it is becoming common to use the grape variety and the location of the vineyard as a name, e.g. Smithfield Cabernet or Brownville Pinot. (Those are fictitious places.) Although this is a move in the proper direction, the use of the vine name can also be confusing.

The Californian wine industry is located principally in the north coast counties. Amongst the chief vineyard districts are San Bernadino, Riverside, Los Angeles, San Joaquin, Madera, Fresno, Merced, Kings, Tulare, Santa Cruz, Santa Clara, Alameda, San Francisco, Coutra Costa, Solano, Napa, Sonoma, Mendocino, Yuba, Sutter, Placer, Yolo, Sacramento, Kern, San Benito, Monterey and San Luis Obispo.

The wine industry of California is highly mechanized and scientifically controlled. Despite the vast gallonage of mediocre wine the interested searcher can find some unreservedly fine growths. There are some few Californian wineries now producing only beverage wines of top quality.

Outside California the chief wine-growing region is New York State, with smaller quantities produced in Michigan and Ohio. Actually there is some wine-growing in almost every state, but the volume is unimportant. Outside California the indigenous vines of the *labrusca* species of *Vitis* are used. *Labrusca* grapes yield wine of a peculiar spicy and so-called 'foxy' flavour. Although some experts steeped in the standards of Europe tend to disparage such wines, there are many experts and tourists, apart from U.S. citizens, who find them intriguing, novel and refreshing. A number of types are noted alphabetically.

In general the fortified and sweet wines are produced in the south and the dry table wines in the north.

Amer Piçon: Proprietary name of one of the many French fortified and flavoured apéritif wines.

Amertume: A disease of wine causing an unpleasant, bitter taste.

Am Höllenweg: German (Niederingelheim, q.v.) white wine.

Aminneum: Wine of classical times noted for longevity.

Am Klopp: German (Niederingelheim, q.v.) white wine.

Am Langenberg: German (Niederingelheim, q.v.) white wine.

Ammerschwihr: French (Alsatian) wine-growing commune. White and occasionally *vin de paille* (q.v.).

Amminian: Roman wine of antiquity, praised by Virgil.

Amoltern: German (Baden) white wine area at Kaiserstuhl.

Amon: A celebrated region, with Aton and Kantarah, of the Nile Delta (q.v.) from which some of the choicest wines of Egypt were grown in classical times.

Amontillado: The name of perhaps the most popular type of Spanish sherry. It should be restricted to such wine though it has been usurped by other sherry-producing countries. The word means 'from Montilla' though it is not made in that town near Cordoba. It is actually quite variable. It may be a *fino* (q.v.). It is usually sweetened a little.

Amoroso: Spanish medium sherry somewhat like an *oloroso* (q.v.) made to satisfy the demand for sweet wine. It is essentially amontillado (q.v.) plus extra colour and sweetening. It appears to be an English term and is not used in Spain.

Amoroso: Cocktail of mescal and lime juice.

Amoureuses, Les: Esteemed red burgundy of marked bouquet from vineyard in commune of Chambolle. As an example of the fanciful wordage applied to wine it is often stated that the wine of Les Amoureuses is more feminine in body than most burgundies!

Ampelography: The study of vines and in particular of the grape.

Ampelotherapy: The grape cure, but, alas, of the fresh fruit and thus to be mercilessly attacked as quackery!

Amphora: The cargo jar of the Greeks and Romans. The amphora was also a liquid measure, the Attic containing about nine British gallons and the Roman six. Amphoras were (as the name suggests) two-handled vessels.

The ornamental ones were richly decorated and had a foot but the everyday storage and transportation drudges were plain and had a pointed end which was pushed into the ground.

Ampuis: Town on River Rhône, a centre of the esteemed Côte Rôtie (q.v.) red wines.

Amrita: Hindu magical beverage of classical antiquity, the elixir of the gods. Possibly it was mead (q.v.).

Am Steinacker: German (Niederingelheim, q.v.) white wine.

Amstgarten: German (Kirrweiler, q.v.) wine estate.

Anacreon: Greek poet born about 560 B.C. whose fame rests chiefly upon his lyrics in praise of love and liquor. Actually what we possess of Anacreon's poetry is fragmentary and even these pieces are possibly spurious. His reported death by choking on a grape-stone is in character. But whatever be the truth, we are at least indebted to the poet for having inspired a vast output of lyrics (appropriately called Anacreontics) by many poets of many nationalities in praise of love and wine. Even the U.S. national anthem 'The Star-Spangled Banner' was originally an Anacreontic. This was 'To Anacreon in Heaven' written in 1800 by John Stafford Smith, a member of the Anacreontic Society, a London drinking-club.

The English antiquary William Oldys (1606–71) wrote what is called 'the perfect type of Anacreontic', which commences:

> Busy, curious, thirsty fly,
> Drink with me and drink as I.

However, this is not the genesis of the tag 'drinking with the flies'. As to this, see the entry Jimmy Woodser.

Añada: The Spanish term applied to young sherry wine, not more than a year old, which is being stored to ascertain whether the flor film will develop. See also Sherry.

Ananas, Crème d': Liqueur of pineapply flavour.

Anapa: Russian viticultural centre for production, especially, of sparkling wines.

Anbance: French (Loire Valley) white wines.

Anbruch: The German term for deterioration owing, especially, to ullage (q.v.).

Ancy: French white wine from Lorraine.

Andalus: Appetizer of dry sherry and orange juice.

Andalusia: To a wine-lover the most important thing concerning this piece of Spain is that it holds Jerez de la Frontera (q.v.) and hence the sherry industry.

Andreich: Czechoslovakian (Pressburg, q.v.) wines.

Andresses: Bordeaux wine estate, red and white.

Andron: French (Médoc) red wine estate.

Aney: French (Médoc) red wine estate.

Anfora: Italian liquid measure, about 114 gallons.

Angaston: Australian (S.A.) wine centre.

Angel Face: Cocktail of gin, calvados and apricot brandy.

Angelica: A name of many applications:
(*a*) A beverage (hardly to be classed as a wine) made by adding brandy to fresh grape juice so that no fermentation occurs.
(*b*) A genuine invention of the U.S. (California). A mixture of brandy and partly fermented white grape must (q.v.) from mission grapes. The name is supposed to be derived from Los Angeles. Also an alternative name for so-called Californian or 'white' port.
(*c*) A French (Basque) liqueur, sickly sweet and flavoured with, *inter alia*, the roots of the angelica plant.

Angélus: French (St. Émilion) claret estate.

Anglade: French (Gironde) wine estate, red and white.

Angles: French (Volnay, Côte-d'Or) wine estate.

Angludet: French (Médoc) wine estate, mainly highly esteemed red. Angludet is not 'classified' (see Médoc) but its good reputation affords still another example of the danger of giving rigid allegiance to an ancient table of wine precedence.

Angostura Bitters: The addition of bitter materials (quinine, hops, quassia, citrus pith, for example) to alcoholic beverages has long been practised in the pious hope of promoting appetite. In later times the convenient custom arose of employing alcoholic solutions (tinctures) so that it sufficed to add merely one or two drops to the glass. One of the earliest commercial applications was the work of the Capuchin monks of Angostura, a village of Venezuela. Later one of the concerns exploiting the mixture of the good monks (which is said to be based on sandalwood and a local angostura bark) moved the venture to Trinidad. Angostura bitters now sail to the four quarters of the earth.

Angoulême: Area of Cognac. See also Cognac.

Anguis: French (Basque) red wine.

Anice: French (Graves) white wine estate.

Anina: District of Jerez (q.v.) where fino sherry (q.v.) is grown.

Anisado: Peruvian drink of aniseed liqueur and milk.

Aniseed: Also anise (*Pimpinella anisum*), an annual which yields an essential oil widely used for flavouring, especially of liqueurs (q.v.). The most widely known aniseed-flavoured beverages are probably ouzo, anisette and absinthe substitutes.

Anisette: Liqueur of aniseed flavour.

Anjou: See Loire Basin.

Ankare: Old Scandinavian liquid measure (Swedish 39·26 l., Danish 37·5 l., and Norwegian 38·5 l.).

Anker: Small cask (German and Dutch) of about 8 gallons. Formerly a measure of wine and spirits of this volume.

Anniger Perle: Austrian white table wine.

Ansbach: German wine estate of Winkel, Rheingau.

Anseillan: French (Médoc) claret estate.

Antigua: Centre for rum production.

Antilles: Centre for rum production.

Antoniusbrunner: German white wine vineyard at Saarburg.

Antrim: Irish centre for whiskey manufacture.

Apagado: Spanish low-priced fortified wine.

Apaleador: Spanish name of the rod used to agitate wine during fining (q.v.).

Apéritif: An appetizer. A beverage drunk before meals in the pious hope of promoting appetite. Dry sherry is the Anglo-Saxon appetizer wine of choice, but France has a legion of proprietary beverages of the vermouth class.

Apezer: Hungarian white table wine.

Aphrodisiac: See Sex and Alcohol.

Apiculatus: The 'wild yeast', a variety of *Saccharomyces* with cells shaped like lemons. Part of the technique of good wine-making is to restrain the action of wild yeast and encourage that of the wine-yeast, *Saccharomyces ellipsoideus* (q.v.).

Apollinaris: German mineral water from Ahr Valley.

Apostles: The affectionate name given to the twelve large wine casks in the city cellar of Bremen.

Appelbrännvin: Scandinavian for apple brandy, applejack or calvados (q.v.).

Appellation d'Origine Contrôlée: The legal system, first used in France, to ensure that wine and brandy may only bear a certain name if the grapes are of a defined variety, grown within a defined area, harvested in a specified manner and in general made into wine under carefully stated rules. The result has been of enormous benefit to all concerned, by no means excluding the drinker. Other European countries have followed the lead of France but unfortunately none of the large wine-producers outside Europe have done so. It is manifestly unjust that while no Frenchman can use, for example, the name chablis or burgundy for a wine not conforming to rigid geographical limits, the wine trades of Australia, California, South Africa and elsewhere can place these hallowed French names on any white or red table wine respectively.

The system has been extended by France and other European countries to additional products beyond wine, such as sardines, oysters, poultry, truffles and more, all with good results. An A.O.C. is a guarantee of at least a respectable minimum of quality.

Apperley's Mixture: Celebrated Australian mixed drink around 1850 of ale, ginger beer, mint and sugar. Like many another mixed drink, it possibly tastes less foul than it sounds.

Applejack: American (U.S.) term for apple brandy distilled from hard cider, the counterpart of the French calvados (q.v.). The manufacture of applejack is, of course, limited to the apple-orchard areas and is mainly centred in the colder states of the Atlantic region. It is a venerable industry which has evolved from the old domestic (farm-house) scale. Originally the production was by 'congelation' (q.v.), the separation being effected by exposing barrels of apple cider to freezing weather. The still-liquid core contained most of the alcohol and was poured off, the frozen crystals, consisting mainly of water, being rejected. Perhaps this simple operation is still in limited use on farms but today the making of applejack is a large industry carried on in modern distilleries (q.v.).

Fine applejack is a superb spirit and the best American brands, especially if long aged in oak, can compare with those of Normandy and Brittany. It is puzzling that the prestige of U.S. applejack is not wider and higher but production is increasing, now approaching a million gallons of 50 degree proof.

Jersey Lightning is the colloquial and rather unkind name for applejack made on the small scale in the state of New Jersey. It is apparently a relic of the prohibition period.

It is surprising that England, whose hard cider is renowned, has no considerable apple brandy industry.

See also Calvados.

Apple Pie: Cocktail of rum, sweet vermouth, grenadine, apricot liqueur and lemon juice.

Apre: French wine term for harsh, rough, especially if due to excess tannin (q.v.).

Apremont: French (Savoy) white table wine.

Apulia: Italian wine province. The finest is stated to be white Bari.

Aqua: The whisky blender's term not for water but for whisky itself. It was an abbreviation of the old Latin name for alcohol (*aqua vitae*, or water of life) and continued in use well into the 20th century. See also Mosto de Yema.

Aquavit, Akvavit or **Akavit:** Scandinavian colourless spirit, often flavoured with caraway (cumin), thus technically a gin (q.v.). If unflavoured, it is identical with vodka (q.v.). The name, of course, is the equivalent of *eau de vie*, whisky and *uisquebeatha* or *usquebaugh* (q.v.).

Aqua Vitae: 'water of life'. The old term for alcohol and generally applied to any spirit (q.v.). It was especially used for brandy. The old name for whisky, *usquebaugh* (q.v.), is the Gaelic translation of the phrase. The Scandinavian aqvavit is the same.

Aragon: Spanish wine province, mainly reds for local use.

Aramon: Red grape with a prolific yield of common wine. Much grown in Algeria and southern France,

Ararat: The site of Noah's vineyard.

Arawatta: South Australian white table wine made in Barossa Valley.

Arbanats: French (Graves) wine estate, mainly red.

Arbin: French (Savoy) red table wine.

Arbois: A town and region in the Jura noted for its wide range of good wines — red, white, sparkling, *rosé* and yellow. It is also celebrated as the town in which Louis Pasteur spent his childhood and most of his vacations. In later life Arbois was also the centre of Pasteur's epoch-making experiments on the pasteurization (q.v.) of wine. Altogether a name that deserves to be known by every wine-lover.

Arcadia: Greek wine province. The name is more romantic than the wine.

Archbishop: English mixed drink. Hot, sweetened red wine in which rests an orange studded with cloves.

Archdeacon: The celebrated beer long brewed at Merton College, Oxford.

Arche: French (Sauternes) sweet white table wine.

Arche-Pugneau: French (Sauternes) sweet white table wine.

Arche-Vimeney: French (Sauternes) sweet white table wine.

Arcins: French (Médoc) wine-growing commune.

Ardenay: French (Loire) red wine.

Ardillats: French (Beaujolais) red wine.

Arenas: The sherry vineyards with sandy soil around Jerez (q.v.), suitable only for the lighter types and markedly different from the *albarizas* (q.v.).

Argentina: Under irrigation there is now a large and expanding wine industry. With a production of over 300 million gallons, Argentina is now one of the world's large wine-growers. The vineyards are mainly located close to the rivers that flow from the snowfields of the Andes. The best known are those of Mendoza, San Juan, San Rafael, Catamarca, La Rioja and Rio Negro. Quality is improving and there is a small but growing export trade. The best wine is reputed to be that of Nequén.

The art was introduced by the first missionaries. The influx of Italian vignerons has improved quality but the best wines of the Argentina cannot rival those of Chile.

There are large breweries operating on the most modern mass-production scale. All other beverage alcohol industries are established.

Argillières, Les: French wine of the Côte-d'Or.

Argol: The deposit of acid potassium tartrate which is found in the lees of wine and also which separates as a crust in racked or bottled wine on long storage. It is a valuable by-product used in foodstuffs (especially baking) and quite widely in industry (dyeing, tanning, etc.). Also known as winestone. See also Tartaric Acid.

Argos: Greek wine-growing district.

Arika: A Tartar spirit distilled from kefir (q.v.). The word is obviously a variant of arrack (q.v.).

Arinto: Portuguese white wine made from grape of same name. Used for Bucellas (q.v.).

Armagnac: French brandy made in certain parts of the department of Gers. The town of Condom is the centre. It is certainly one of the great brandies of France and that means of the world. Many say it is better than cognac. The French laws of naming apply as strongly to armagnac as to cognac. There are some significant differences. Armagnac is in lesser production, about a quarter as much being made as cognac. It is produced by a single distillation and therefore needs longer maturing. (Much armagnac is matured for over 20 years.) The finest vineyards are those of Bas-Armagnac whose centre is Grand Bas. The second important region is Ténarèze. The third is Haut-Armagnac. It is said that each district produces a recognizably distinct brandy.

Local gossip alleges that armagnac was the favourite drink of d'Artagnan. At any rate, it is a glorious spirit and very good value.

The three recognized grades in order of quality are grand, fin and petit armagnac.

Armanjan-des-Ormes: French (Sauternes) sweet table wine.

Armens: French (St. Émilion) claret estate.

Armsheim: German (Rheinhessen) white wine parish, including Horgen-grund, Hasensprung, Goldtal, Geiersberg and Hippel.

Arnaud-Blanc: French (Margaux) claret estate.

Arnaud Jouan: French (Bordeaux) white table wine.

Arnauld: French (Médoc) claret estate.

Arnaville: French (Lorraine) red wine.

Arôme: French wine term — aroma or bouquet (q.v.).

Arp: Ancient name for wine made from grapes in Egypt. See also Egypt.

Arrack: Asiatic spirit distilled from toddy (q.v.).

Arrière Goût: French wine term, literally 'after taste'; the final effect of wine in the mouth, often radically different from the first impression.

Arroba: Spanish measure of both weight and volume. An *arroba* of grapes is 21 lbs. and of sherry 3·66 imperial gallons.

Arrope: Spanish dark-brown, caramelized grape juice (must, q.v.), boiled down to about a fifth of the original volume. It is used in compounding sweet sherries and malagas (q.v.). The same material less concentrated is called sancocho. If arrope is added to fresh must and the mixture allowed to ferment, the result is *vino de color*, valued for blending purposes. It is stated that arrope is exported to tint and slightly sweeten whisky.

Arrosée, L': French (St. Émilion) red wine.

Arrumbador: Spanish wine-slang for cellarman, a rolling word for a rolling worker in a *bodega* (q.v.).

Arsac: French (Médoc) wine-growing commune, often sold as Margaux.

Arsenic: It is less astonishing than it may seem to mention arsenic herein. In 1900 there were a number of mysterious deaths of people in the English Midlands. Eventually the cause was found to be metallic poisoning. It was discovered that all had drunk a particular brand of beer which was heavily contaminated with arsenic. This had been introduced into the beer as contaminated glucose ('starch sugar') and that in turn had been made from starch converted to glucose by sulphuric acid prepared from iron pyrites (sulphide) naturally mixed with arsenic compounds. A Royal Commission showed that the cases of poisoning had been very numerous, 2,000 in Manchester alone, 800 in Salford and 500 in Lichfield. From evil cometh good. Ever since this time the raw material for brewing has been kept under stringent analytical supervision.

Artagnan, D': See Armagnac.

Artiminio: Italian (Tuscanian) red wine.

Artisan: See Bourgeois.

Artist: Cocktail of whisky, sherry, groseille and lemon.

Arvelets, Les: French (Côte-d'Or) red table wines.

Arvisio: Greek wine from island of Chios.

Arzente: The name proposed for special qualities of Italian brandy, as the name cognac is used in France. See also Jerignac.

Arzheim: German (Palatinate) table wines, including Spittert, Rosenberg, Kalmit and Kastanienheide.

Asali: An African native beverage said to be equivalent to mead (q.v.).

Ascham, Roger: British conservatism is probably just as overrated as most other allegedly national qualities. Surely there was no more thorough-going Englishman than Roger Ascham (1515–68). An extract from a letter he wrote to Edward Raven during a journey he was making up the Rhine: 'And surely this wine of Rhene is so good, so natural, so temperate, so ever like itself as can be wished for man's use. I was afraid when I came out of England to miss beer; but I am more afraid that when I shall come into England that I cannot lack this wine.' 16th- and 20th-century connoisseurs of wine seem to agree.

Asciutto: Italian wine term for dry (q.v.).

Asis: Biblical (Hebrew) word for wine, related to Hemer (q.v.). The word is a poetical synonym for 'that which is trodden out'. It is new wine, sweet wine, that which is supplied to Israel as a blessing (Jl. 3:18).

Aspergillus Oryzae: The mould used in Japan to convert the starter of rice to fermentable sugar in the preparation of sake (q.v.).

Aspisheim: German (Rheinhessen) wine-growing parish. Best wines include Sennchen, Muhl, Geig, Spangenberg and Sonnenberg.

Asselheim: German (Palatinate) wine parish, including Breitheck, Hohl and Hollenberg.

Assemblage: French term for blending various wines to produce a standard champagne.

Assmannhausen: German (Rheingau) wine district on right bank of Rhine, reputed to produce the finest red table wine of the country. It is made from the black pinot grape. A late-picked Assmannhauser (see Edel-fäule), which can only be made in exceptional years, is probably the most expensive table wine in the world. Amongst the best vineyards are Kützelborn, Breitheck, Hollenberg and Hohl.

Asti: A white wine from the town and district of that name in Piedmont, Italy. *Asti spumante*, or sparkling asti, is a well-known and greatly esteemed sparkling wine.

Asunik: The Scandinavian term for grain alcohol from the Baltic region.

Asztali bor: The Hungarian general term for table or beverage wine.

Aszu: One of the finest of the sweet, Hungarian tokay wines, regarded as being surpassed only by the rare and costly essenz (q.v.).

Atenberg: German white wine. See also Bergzabern.

Atholl Brose: Traditional Scotch mixed drink of honey, fine oatmeal and whisky, strongly agitated, bottled, corked and stored for some days. Cream may be included.

Athos, Mount: Greek monastery producing table wines.

Aton: See Amon and Nile Delta.

Attemperators: The spiral coils of metal (the most modern ones being of stainless steel) which are part of the equipment of fermentation (q.v.) vats. Either heated or chilled water can be passed through them to maintain a uniform temperature, usually between 75° and 85° F.

Attenuation: The action of yeast in 'thinning' or removing sugar from a fermenting mass of must (wine) or wort (beer) or other sugary liquid and partially replacing this lost sugar with alcohol.

Attica: Reputed the best Greek wine province.

Attorney: Australian drink of mixed equal parts of pineapple and passion fruit juices heavily laced with rum and then chilled.

Aubance: French (Loire) area for white wines.

Aube: French area. White wines grown for champagne-type.

Aubry: Established (1899) brand of armagnac (q.v.).

Auctioneer: The American barman's term for a garrulous drinker in a public bar.

Aude: French department responsible for the production of a vast volume of *vin ordinaire* (q.v.).

Audit Ale: See Ale, audit.

Auenstein: German (Württemberg) centre for Schillerwein (q.v.)

Auflangen: German (Nierstein, q.v.) white wine.

C

Augenscheimer: German (Moselle) white wine.

Auggen: German (Baden) white wines.

Augier: Old-established (1643) brand of cognac (q.v.).

Augster: Hungarian wine grape.

Auinquina: French apéritif, especially from the Dordogne, made from walnuts.

Auldana: South Australian vineyard near Adelaide, planted over a century ago and still producing a range of good red table wines.

Aum (also Aam, Awm, Ohm): A Dutch and German liquid measure, and a cask, varying from 30 to 35 British gallons.

Aunt Emily: Cocktail of applejack, gin, apricot brandy and orange juice.

Aupern: German (Hessloch, q.v.), white wine.

Auros: French (Gironde) red and white wines.

Aurum: Italian liqueur, aromatic in flavour and golden-yellow in colour.

Ausbau: German term for the maturing of wine.

Ausbruch: Fine variety of tokay (q.v.) wine.

Auslese: German term for specially selected, much applied to wine and particularly to grapes from which it is made. See also Beerenauslese and Trockenbeerenauslese, also Labels, German wine.

Ausone, Ch.: Ancient French vineyard of St. Émilion, supposed to be the site of the villa built by the poet Ausonius in the 4th century A.D. By general consent Ausone is the finest wine of the many fine wines of the district.

Ausoye: Also Aussay. Medieval English name for Alsace (wines).

Aussay: See Ausoye.

Aussy: French (Côte-d'Or) table wines.

Australia: As a producer of alcoholic beverages the position of Australia presents many anomalies. There is enough suitable soil, temperate climate and water to produce all the wine the world requires and in fact the Australian gallonage is slowly but steadily rising. Yet the local consumption of wine, especially beverage wine, is almost negligible, despite the fact that the general standard is almost certainly the highest in the world. The traditional drink is beer, with whisky in second place. The use of light wine is, however, increasing slowly, partly as the result of a large intake of European migrants since 1950. Australia makes every type of alcoholic beverage except a few spirits such as slivovitz and a few specialities such as perry. Wine of every description, beer, cider, brandy, whisky, gin, rum, liqueurs and so on, are all of excellent quality.

Australian wines are noteworthy. The finest bottlings are almost the equal of the celebrated wines of France, Germany and other European regions. There is, however, no type of wine made in Australia that some other country cannot make a little better. By this is meant that, e.g. the finest dry flor appetizer sherry of Spain, the finest port of Portugal, the finest light dry white beverage wine of the German Rhine, and so on, are all a little ahead of the best Australian equivalent production. However, as stated, the general average of quality leads the world. In Australia there is no vast bulk of *vin ordinaire* and this is to be regretted.

The principal barrier to the development of a world appreciation of Australian wine is the retention of misleading European place-names such as sauternes, chablis, burgundy, tokay and port, a foolish policy also shared by California and South Africa. However, the winds of change are blowing and some of the more enlightened vintners are commencing to use geographical names.

Beer is brewed in every state. Queensland is the chief centre for rum distillation. All the wine-growing states make brandy (in general not up to the standard of Australian wine). The principal whisky distillery is in Victoria, near Geelong.

A number of Australian wine centres are noted in their alphabetical positions.

Australian Wine Research Institute: Located at Adelaide, South Australia, this is clearly destined to become one of the great world centres in the field. By general consent the work of the Institute is largely responsible for the development of Australian flor (q.v.) sherries.

Austria: Now produces only about 30 million gallons of wine annually but the general quality is high, in that respect resembling Switzerland (q.v.). The finest Austrian wines, such as Gumpoldskirchner and Voslauer come from Burgenland, south of Vienna. Most of the wine comes from the region bordering Moravia. Wachen, Durrenstein, Krems, Retz, Poysdorf, Sievering, Nussdorf and Grinzing are all well known for vineyards. Austrian wines are, in general, light and delicate. Many are drunk young.

Austria produces, of course, superb brewed beverages.

Autolysis: The process of a natural living material such as yeast digesting itself, usually with liquefaction. It applies especially to protein and the action is due to the operation of enzymes. The autolysis of yeast may result in desirable flavour as in the case of the film of flor yeast in sherry.

Autumn Moonlight Party: The Japanese festival at which full moon is viewed and special white dumplings and sake (q.v.) are consumed.

Auvergne: This French province is said to possess but one fine wine, Les Chanturgues, but it has many devoted followers.

Auvernier: Swiss (Neuchâtel) white wine.

Aux Cras: French red wine of Beaune (q.v.).

Auxerre: French (Yonne) town, centre of red and white vineyards.

Auxey-Duresses: Notable red wine of Burgundy.

Auzeneau: Old-established (1830) brand of cognac (q.v.).

Avaux, Les: French red wine of Beaune (q.v.).

Avelsbach: German wine region at join of Ruwer and Moselle. The best estates are Hammerstein, Altenberg, Dom-Arolsbach, Herrenberg.

Avenas: French (Beaujolais) red wine.

Avenay: French (Marne) wine centre for champagne.

Avensan: French (Médoc) claret.

Aviation: Cocktail of gin, lemon and maraschino.

Avirey: French (Aube) red wine centre.

Avize: A section of the French Champagne district producing some of the best basic wine from white grapes.

Awamori: Okinawan 'wine', the name meaning 'heap of foam'.

Awn: The beard or termination grain-sheath of barley, oats, etc.

Ay: The most famous French (Marne) centre for champagne grapes.

Ayala: Old-established champagne of Reims.

Ayl: German white wine vineyard on Saar (q.v.).

Ayse: French (Annecy, Savoy) white wine.

Azores: Wines have been produced for centuries in these outposts of Portugal but they have never achieved either the volume or distinction of those of Madeira. Much wine, called Fayal, used to be made and exported. *Phylloxera* (q.v.) ended this.

Aztec Punch: Mixture of sweetened tequila, grape-fruit juice, lemon, cinnamon, and tea. Said to taste better than it sounds.

Azumbre: Spanish measure, about 3 pints.

Babelheim: French (Colmar, Alsace) white wine.

Baby: A quarter-bottle, containing about six fluid ounces.

Baby, Ch.: French (St. André) red and white wines.

Bacau: Romanian table wines.

Bacchanal: An alcoholic festivity. See also Bacchus.

Bacchante: A handmaiden of Bacchus (q.v.). A magic word.

Bacchus: Greek god of wine, hence Bacchanalia, Bacchante, etc. See also Dionysos.

Bacchus Wine: The pretentious name of an indifferent Greek wine from Santorin.

Bacharach: German Rhine town important as a commercial centre for white wines. The best local vineyards are Wolfshoele and Dell.

Bachel: White wine from Wachenheim, Palatinate (q.v.).

Bachingen: German (Palatinate) table wines.

Bachrag: Old name for Bacharach (q.v.).

Backhaus: German (Eibingen, q.v.) white wine.

Badacsony: Hungarian region for red and white table wines on Lake Balaton.

Bad Durkheim: Red and white wines from Palatinate (q.v.). The biggest wine-producing town of Germany.

Baden: German wine region, less important since *Phylloxera* (q.v.) devastated the vines.

Badiane: Home-made cordial of sugared brandy with spices and bitter almonds.

Bad Kreuznach: German (Nahe, q.v.) white wine.

Bagaceira: Also Bagaço. Portuguese term for sub-quality brandy made from the marc (q.v.) left after pressing. See also Grappa.

Bagasse: Residue of sugar cane after the sugar-containing juice has been expressed.

Bagatelle, Ch.: French (Médoc) red and white wines.

Bages: French (Médoc) red wine.

Bages Pauillac: French (Médoc) red wine.

Bagli: Italian storehouses for wine, especially in Sicily for marsala (q.v.).

Bagnols: French (Languedoc) red wine.

Bahlingen: German (Baden) white wine.

Baiken: German (Rauenthal, q.v.) white wine.

Baissards, Les: French (Hermitage, q.v.) red wine.

Baixo Corgo: The lower part of the district of the Douro Valley in Portugal that produces port wine (q.v.). See also Cima Corgo.

Bak: Ancient name for wine made from dates in Egypt (q.v.). See also Arp.

Baker's Hill: Australian (W.A.) wine centre.

Baking: The characteristic Californian process, but also used elsewhere (see Rancio), in the production of certain dessert wines, consisting in heating the bulk wine for some weeks or months to a temperature of about 130° F. to caramelize part of the sugar.

Balac, Ch.: French (Médoc) red wine.

Balance: The wine man's term for the combination of qualities which make a fine product. These include bouquet, taste, tannin, acidity and more.

Balaton: Hungarian wine-growing district. Moderate quality.

Balbaina: District of Jerez (q.v.) where *fino* sherry (q.v.) is grown.

Balderdash: It may come as a surprise to most to discover that the origin of this word is quite unknown and that although today it means nonsense, until about a century ago the word stood for a worthless mixture of liquors (e.g. wine and beer). Smollett, who was not as wise as some of his modern admirers would have us believe, wrote in 1764 of some alleged balderdash made by merchants of Nice, consisting of wine mixed 'with pigeon's dung and quick-lime'. There seems to be scope for a brochure on the idiotic terms of insult applied to alcoholic beverages. Cf. popskull, hooch, lunatic soup, plonk and a hundred more.

Balearic Isles: Wine has been grown here for 2,000 years or more. Quantity rather than quality.

Baleau: French (St. Émilion) red wine.

Balestard-la-Tonnelle: French (St. Émilion) red wine.

Balestrey: French (Graves) red and white wines.

Baliot: Swiss (Valais) white table wine.

Ballan: French (Touraine) red wine.

Ballantine: Old-established Scotch whisky distillers outside the D.C.L. combine.

Ballendean: Australian (Queensland) wine centre.

Ballet: Old-established brand of cognac (q.v.).

Balling: Trade name of one of the hydrometers or floating measures used to read the sugar-content sweetness of grape juice or other liquid. Such an instrument measures the strength in 'degrees Balling'. Other common hydrometers are the Brix and the Baumé, which give respectively about the same as, and half, the Balling reading.

Ballon: The French term ('balloon', of course) for the huge glasses used to hold a small amount of choice brandy so that, when warmed by the hands, the perfumed volatile constituents can be lovingly and slowly savoured. The English term is snifter (q.v.).

Balm Wine: American concoction reported to be composed of brandy with spices and prunes.

Balnot-sur-Laigne: French (Aube) red wine.

Balogues-Haut-Bages: French (Médoc) red wine.

Balsam: A word of many meanings, one of which is a substance which heals and restores. In this sense, balsam has often been used as a synonym for a prized alcoholic beverage. See, for example, Bounce-upon-Bess.

Balthasar: One of the numerous outsize bottles with Biblical names. A balthasar is supposed to hold about sixteen ordinary bottles, or nearly three gallons.

Balz: White wine from Wacheheim, Palatinate (q.v.).

Bamboo: Cocktail of sherry, sweet vermouth, lemon.

Banana Wine: Central African beverage, said to have an alcohol content approximating that of grape wine.

Banane, Crème de: French liqueur of banana flavour.

Bandol: French region near Toulon producing red, white and *rosé* wines, pleasant enough.

Banff: Scottish centre for the production of single (q.v.) malt whisky for blending purposes.

Bang: Mixed drink of spiced warm ale, cider, whisky.

Banque: According to James Howell (q.v.), writing in 1634, this was a drink 'rare and precious of the oriental countries as Cambaia and Calicut'. No further information is available.

Banyuls: Wine centre near Roussillon producing *vins doux naturels* (q.v.).

Baptize: As applied to wine, the archaic term for adding a little (perhaps one drop) of water. According to report, it was also the pious name for commercially adulterating wine with much more water than drops.

Bar: A public place for the sale of alcoholic liquor and also the actual counter where the sale is made. 'Private', 'Public', 'Saloon', 'Ladies', and similar bars explain themselves but the 'Jug-and-Bottle' bar was reserved for the sale of liquor to be taken away.

Barack Palinka: Hungarian apricot brandy.

Barateau: French (Médoc) red wine.

Barba-Carlo: Italian red table wine.

Barbados: West Indian island, celebrated for rum production and possibly the original commercial centre. Barbados rum is stated to be flavoured with a complex and lengthy mixture of ingredients other than those derived from sugar cane.

Barbados Buck: Cocktail of rum, lime and ginger beer.

Barbados Water: An archaic name for rum. Also a cordial of rum flavoured with peel of orange and lemon.

Barbaresco: A red wine of Piedmont, Italy.

Barbera: A red wine of Piedmont, Italy, from the grape of that name.

Barberton: Illicit South African liquor.

Barboussey: French (Rully, Burgundy) white wine.

Bar Cellarman: The important official responsible for the safe conduct of beer from cellar to bar.

Barde: French (St. Émilion) red wine. The name of six different estates of the Bordeaux region.

Bardolino: Italian (Veneto) good red wine.

Bärentrank: Lit. 'bear's drink': East Prussian beverage of potato or other spirit flavoured with honey.

Baret: French (Graves) wine, mainly red.

Barfly: American slang term for an over-enthusiastic drinker in a public establishment.

Bari: Italian (Apulian) wines, red and white.

Barin: French (Lorraine) mediocre red wines.

Barley: In the sense of this book, the grain of the cereal of the genus *Hordeum*. It is especially associated with the making of brewed beverages, but it is only one of several cereals used for the purpose. Similarly, in the lay mind malt (q.v.) means malted barley though all other grains can be malted and most are.

Barley Bree: Scots (obs.) for beer and for alcoholic liquor generally. The AS. word *bree* for the liquor in which anything has been boiled is obsolete elsewhere.

Barley Broth: Colloquial term for strong beer or ale.

Barley Island: Old term (obs.) for an alehouse.

Barley Wine: One of the world's great drinks: beer brewed at a much higher strength than usual.

Barm: Old name for yeast or leaven, still used in bread-making.

Barmaid: The female equivalent of barman (q.v.).

Barman: A male attendant at a bar (q.v.).

Barm Beer: Wort (q.v.) expressed from the yeast.

Barolino: Italian (Piedmont) red wine.

Barolo: Italian (Piedmont) red table wine considered by some judges to be the finest the country produces. The Barolo area is legally defined and includes the parishes of Grinzone, Serralunga, Castiglion Faletto, La Morra, Monforte, Verduno and Perno. The whole district is called Le Langhe. The grape used is the nebbiolo.

Barolo Chinanto: Italian medicated wine containing quinine.

Baron: Cocktail of gin, dry vermouth, curaçao and sweet vermouth.

Barossa: The beautiful South Australian wine-growing valley that gives its name, commendably, to a growing number of commercial wines, some proprietary, others varietal. There are still table wines, slightly effervescent and sweetish whites and dessert wines. Some of the best Australian brandies are from the Barossa region.

Bar Parlour: A small part of an inn, tavern or hotel usually reserved for constant and privileged customers.

Barr: French (Alsatian) white wine.

Barracos: Portuguese (Lisbon) red wine.

Barrail: French (Bordeaux) red wines. Four estates bear this name.

Barranquilla Green Jade: Colombian cocktail of gin, crème de menthe, cream and egg white.

Barre, La: French (Côte-d'Or) red wine.

Barrel: For general definition see Cask. The term 'barrel' is used as a conventional measure for certain solids as well as liquids but the capacity varies for different contents, according to custom. An English beer barrel contains 36 imperial gallons, and the U.S. liquid barrel 31·5 U.S. gallons.

Barricas: Spanish cask of about 48 gallons.

Barril: 'Barrel' in both Spanish and Portuguese.

Barril del Gasto: Spanish term for the barrel of cheap wine standing in the *bodega* (q.v.) for workers to drink.

Barriquant: French for keg or small cask.

Barrique: The French hogshead, varying according to the district: Anjou, Beaune and Sauternes about 50 gallons, Bordeaux 49¾, Champagne, Burgundy and Cognac about 45¼. An English barrique is a cask of about 50 gallons.

Barros: Spanish name for the heavy, dark soil around Jerez on which lesser sherries grow.

Barsac: French white wine-producing commune of the Gironde, adjoining Sauternes (q.v.). The wines resemble sauternes basically. Amongst the most celebrated of the barsacs are Coutet and Climens. Others are Suau, Cantegril, de Myrat, Doizy-Dubroca, Doizy-Daene, Védrines and Brouset-Nairac.

Bar-Spoon: A stirring spoon of special shape with a long handle.

Bartender: The equivalent American term for barman (q.v.).

Barthez: French (Graves) red wine.

Barthez-Pian-Médoc: French (Médoc) red wine.

Bartzch: Persian and north Asiatic beverage said to be made by fermenting hogweed.

Bas-Armagnac: District of Armagnac (q.v.).

Bas de Teurons: French (Côte-d'Or) red wine.

Basi: A Filipino beverage made from fermented sugar cane juice flavoured with herbs.

Basilicata: Southern Italian wine region.

Baskerville: Australian (W.A.) wine centre.

Bas Marconnets: French (Côte-d'Or) wines.

Basquaise: The flattish, round, long-necked bottle used as container for Armagnac brandy (q.v.). The name is derived from the nearby region where the bottle originated.

Basque, Le: French (Graves) red and white wines. Also a red wine estate of St. Émilion.

Bas-Rhin: Alsatian wine region including the areas of Marlenheim, Obernai, Goxwiller, Barr, Mittelbergheim, and Dambach.

Bassendean: Australian (W.A.) wine centre.

Basses-Vergelesses: French (Côte-d'Or) table wines.

Bastard or Brown Bastard: A wine, both red (or 'brown') and white, well known in Elizabethan times. Then the name (the illegitimacy is unexplained) died out. Apparently it was a Peninsular wine and resembled both muscatel and malmsey.

Vinner, writing about 1600, says, 'Bastard is in virtue somewhat like to muskadell, and may also instead thereof be used. . . .'

Shakespeare, in *Measure for Measure* (Act III, Sc. ii), writes, '. . . we shall have all the world drink brown and white bastard'.

There are many other references in Elizabethan literature.

Bastia: Principal wine-growing district of Corsica.

Basto: Spanish term for the coarse flavour of sherry resulting from extraction from stems and skins of grapes. Also used in Jerez for any sherry lacking quality.

Bastor-la-Montagne: French (Sauternes) sweet white wine.

Batailley, Ch.: French (Pauillac) red wine.

Bâtard: A white wine of Burgundy.

Bâtards-Montrachet, Les: Group of vineyards of the Côte-d'Or. White wines.

Bathtub Gin: Opprobrious American term for the bootleg (q.v.) gin made by the essence process (q.v.) during the prohibition period. This consisted in adding the flavouring (juniper, etc.) to the alcohol in the form of essential oils or essences. Provided the alcohol and other ingredients are wholesome there is no reason why the beverage prepared in this manner should not be pleasant, and acceptable, even if not of fine quality.

Another term is 'compound' gin and there is still a considerable manufacture of this. See also Gin.

Batzenberg: German (Baden) beverage wines.

Batzenwein: Old German term for cheap, bulk wine equivalent to *vin du pays* (q.v.).

Batzi: Swiss apple brandy of no special quality.

Baubens-Montagne: French (Médoc) red wine.

Baudes, Les: French (Côte-d'Or) red wine.

Bauge: French (Anjou) red and white wines.

Baumé, Antoine: French chemist (1728–1804), whose name is remembered as the inventor of useful specific gravity tables. See also Balling.

Bavarian Beer: See Munich Beer.

Bavaroise: Hot egg drink of rum, kirsch, hot tea.

Bayon: French (Gironde) red wines.

Bayonville: French (Lorraine) red wines.

Bayswater: Australian (W.A.) wine centre.

Bazadais: French (Gironde) red wine area.

Bazas: French (Gironde) red wines.

Bazir: Biblical term for the vintage. During the grape harvest, the people camped in booths in the vineyards.

B.B. Bitter and Burton: A synonym or nearly so for 'half-and-half' (q.v.).

Beaker: A drinking-vessel, more or less resembling a large mug without handle. The term is not a precise one. There was little resemblance to the modern beaker of the chemical laboratory.

Béarn: French (Pyrénées) region for Jurançon wine.

Beaucaire: French (Rhône) red wines.

Beaujeu, Hospices de: French (Beaune) red wine.

Beaujolais: A district at the south of Burgundy, France, noted for red wines.

Beaulieu: The name of a number of claret estates of the Bordeaux region.

Beaulieu-sur-Layon: French (Anjou) table wines.

Beaumont: French (Médoc) red wine.

Beaumont-Bertrand: French (Bordeaux) red wine.

Beaumont-en-Vernon: French (Touraine) red wine.

Beaux Monts: French (Côte-d'Or) red wine.

Beaune: Celebrated and venerable French city at the centre of the Côte-d'Or and the seat of the principal markets for these wines. The names of the vineyards around Beaune sound like a catalogue of many of the choicest wines of Burgundy. These include Blanche Fleur, Boucherottes, Les Grèves, Les Aigrots, Les Avaux, Bressandes, Les Cent Vignes, Champs Pimonts, Chaume Gaufriot, Le Clos des Mouches, Clos du Roi, Aux

Cras, Les Epenottes, Les Marconnets, La Mignotte, Les Perrières, Pertuisots, Saint Landry, Les Reversées, Les Seurey, Les Sizies, Les Theurons, Les Toussaints, Les Vignes Franches and Turilains.

Beaune, Côte de: See Côte de Beaune.

Beaune, Hospices de: A charitable institution in Burgundy, France, and the general name given to the fine wines that are sold for the benefit of the institution.

Beaunois, Le: The grape from which chablis (q.v.) is produced. Also known as pinot chardonnay.

Beauregard: French (Pomerol) red wine.

Beauséjour: French (St. Émilion) red wine. The name is borne by six separate estates of the Bordeaux, all producing claret.

Beau-Site: French (Médoc) red wine.

Beausite-Haut-Vignoble: French (Médoc) red wine. (*Vignoble* means vineyard.)

Beaux-Monts-Bas: French (Côte-d'Or) red wine.

Beaux Rogets: French (Côte-d'Or) good red wine.

Beberagem: Portuguese inferior red wine issued to the Oporto lodge labourers.

Bechtheim: German (Rheinhessen) white wine parish of Worms locality. Includes Dankental, Stein, Berg, Haferberg, Gotteshilfe and Geiersberg.

Beckstein: German (Baden) white wine.

Beenleigh: Queensland centre for rum production.

Beer: Beverage made by fermenting cereal, the process being called brewing. The history and nature of beer and ale are bound together.

Ale is an ancient word and came into English through the Anglo-Saxon *alu* or *ealu*. The etymology of the word 'beer' is dubious.

The art of making alcoholic beverages by fermenting cereals is extremely ancient and some believe it antedates wine-making. However, this is doubtful in view of the fact that wine can be obtained merely by allowing crushed grapes to ferment spontaneously, whereas the simplest possible process of brewing requires several steps. Be that as it may, brewing is as old as human records. Sumerian, Assyrian, Babylonian and Egyptian records dating back to 6,000 years testify to the fact that brewing was well established at the dawn of civilization. Beer and wine share the honours of being the principal alcoholic beverages of modern times and which is made in greater volume is still disputed.

The cereal used almost exclusively for making beer is barley, *Hordeum* spp. It is an ancient cultivated plant and was one of the regular corn crops of the common-field system of the middle ages.

The original distinction between ale and beer was that the latter was flavoured with hops. The introduction of hops for brewing into England was effected in the 16th century by Dutch settlers. The new beer trade met with fierce and sustained opposition from the English brewers of ale but the result was inevitable. Hops have a valuable preservative action but, more important, they impart a bitter and characteristically aromatic flavour that soon becomes appreciated. Not even gruit (q.v.), backed by all the authority of the Church in the middle ages, could compete with hops.

For some time, however, there has been no sharp demarcation and today the terms are almost synonymous, though even now the name ale is never applied to lager (q.v.), or to the dark-coloured stout, porter and similar. In the United States it is still largely customary to restrict the name 'beer' to the result of bottom fermentation (q.v.).

Modern brewing is a complex process perhaps more under scientific control than that of any other beverage industry. Nothing more can be attempted here than to give a bald outline of the principal steps. The first stage is malting. Barley grains are moistened and kept at an even temperature for some days until they sprout. The growing barley produces an enzyme called diastase which turns the non-fermentable starch into the fermentable sugar termed maltose. The germ of the grain is then killed by drying at high temperature in a kiln. For stout and porter the exposure to heat is prolonged until the malt is partly caramelized.

The next state, called mashing, consists in grinding the malt and treating it with warm water to dissolve out the sugar and other substances. Next comes hopping. The requisite amount of hop flowers is added to the wort (q.v.) and heated to high temperature. This destroys the diastase and also partly removes the bacteria, moulds and wild yeasts which are also present. Sugar may be added, if desired. This can be cane sugar, glucose, etc.

Now the mixture is cooled as rapidly as possible and pitched (q.v.) with selected yeast. This soon induces fermentation, the most important stage of all. After three to seven days the crude new beer is run off into huge storage tanks to undergo filtration, maturing at low temperature and eventual carbonation by running in carbon dioxide gas to produce the sparkling beer that modern taste demands.

The technical terms used in this outline are all the subjects of separate entries. It is emphasized that technological accuracy is not possible within the space of a few paragraphs.

If the beer is to be bottled, it is run through a complex automatic machine which fills the bottle, introduces the desired amount of carbon dioxide gas (q.v.) and seals the bottle with a metal top called a crown seal.

If the beer is to be sold in bulk or draught (q.v.) it is filled into suitable containers which are delivered to the retail establishments. The requisite carbon dioxide gas is then added as the beer is dispensed.

National taste in beer varies as to alcoholic strength, colour and flavour (amount of bitter hop extract). Americans in general prefer beer more heavily carbonated and served colder than British.

Lager beer is, in theory at any rate, given long storage (some months) in a lager or vat and kept chilled, until it matures. Many special types of beer and ale and technical and semi-technical terms relating to brewing will be found as separate entries. See also Ale.

Beer, British: The broad categories are mild ales, pale ales, stouts and lagers.

Beer, Chillproof: Beer treated with a protein-digesting enzyme (q.v.) and subsequently fined to render it capable of withstanding low temperatures without clouding. Also known as 'non-deposit beer'.

Beer, Kaffir: African native beer made usually from maize and kaffir corn. See also Mealie Beer.

Beer, Legal Alcoholic Limit of: In England there is no upper limit to strength of beer but a fermented malt product containing less than 2% proof spirit (about 1% alcohol) cannot legally be called beer.

Beer, Ship's: The common term until well into the 19th century for the strong beer supplied to ships.

Beer, Small: Beer of low alcoholic content, probably originally made from the washings of the mash (q.v.). Small beer has often been the cause of grumbling or worse in earlier English days. The origin of the term as one of contempt is obvious enough.

Beerage: The rather snobbish and derogatory allusion to the fact that many English brewers have been raised to the peerage. However, the ennobled whisky distillers probably out-number the brewers.

Beer and Skittles: Synonymous for good living — drink and play.

Beerenauslese: A German term for a choice wine made from allegedly individually selected grapes. See also Labels, German Wine.

Beer-Engine: The counter equipment for pumping up beer from cellar to bar.

Beer Fall: Refrigerator in brewery over whose pipes wort (q.v.) runs to be cooled.

Beer Garden: Open-air drinking place.

Beer-Grains: Brewer's grains, barley and barley malt.

Beerhouse: In England an establishment licensed to retail beer but not spirits.

Beer Money: Allowance made either in lieu of beer or for its purchase. Specifically, pay of a penny a day to British soldiers in lieu of issue of beer or spirits, established in 1800 and abolished in 1873.

Beerocracy: Derisive term for the politically-inclined wealthy English brewers. See also Beerage.

Beer-Pull: Handle of the beer-engine, the equipment for drawing draught beer from cellar to bar. Also the pump itself.

Beerstone: The scale (phosphate, carbonate, etc.) deposited in pipes and fermenting vessels in an old brewery.

Beerstreet: Hogarth's depiction of tranquillity and piety compared with the wickedness of Gin Lane.

Bee's Knees: Cocktail of gin, honey and lemon juice.

Bee's Wine: The queer name for a home-made alcoholic beverage in the north of England. It is definitely not mead nor is it made from honey. It is reported to be brewed from bread and sugar and may thus be a relative of kwas (q.v.) or lambic (q.v.).

Beeswine: Old name for mead (q.v.).

Beeswing: A filmy light crust of tartar, formed in ports and some other wines after long keeping in bottle. Hence: 'So old as to show beeswing.'

Beetroot Wine: See Country Wines.

Bégorge-Zédé, La: French (Médoc) red wine.

Behandlung: The German comprehensive term for all 'handling' or treatment of wine, broadly equivalent to the English cellar-treatment.

Beilstein: German (Burg, q.v.) white wine.

Bel-Air: This name is borne by at least 24 separate wine estates in the Bordeaux area, all producing claret and some white wine as well. Anyone knowing the Bordelais men of wine will be confident that not one of the 24 proprietors would accept a reasonable bribe to choose a new name. See also Bellegrave and Bellevue.

Belgrave: French (Médoc) red wine.

Bell: Old-established (1851) brewery of Stockport, England.

Bell: Old-established Scotch whisky distillers outside the D.C.L. combine.

Bell, The: English inn at Finedon said to date back to 1042.

Bellarmine: A large stoneware drinking jug with a big belly and a narrow neck, decorated with a bearded face, originally that of Cardinal Bellarmine, made in mockery by the Dutch Protestants. Also called 'greybeard' and 'longbeard'.

Bellegrave: The name borne by at least five wine estates of the Bordeaux all producing claret. See also Bel-Air.

Belle-Isle: French (Gironde) red wine.

Bellet: French wine-growing area near Nice reputed to produce the best wines of the Riviera.

Bellevue: The name of at least ten wine estates of the Bordeaux producing claret. See also Bel-Air and Bellegrave.

Belmont: French (Savoy) table wines.

Belmont: Australian (W.A.) wine centre.

Bel-Orme-Tronquoy-de-Lalande: French (Médoc) red wine.

Belvedere: Mixed hot drink of rum, milk and cinnamon.

Benais: French (Touraine) red wine.

Bender: German (Königsbach, q.v.) white wine. Slang (probably originally Australian) for drunken spree—'Go on a bender'.

Bending the Elbow: A rather censorious term for drinking, especially in public bars.

Ben Ean: Australian (Hunter River Valley) wine estate at Pokolbin. A typical example of the fine-wine country, where dry red and white and also sweet wines are all produced.

Benedictine: Liqueur, made to formula originated by Benedictine monks in France.

Bengal: Cocktail of brandy, maraschino, curaçao, pineapple juice, bitters.

Benicarlo: Spanish dark-red table wine from Castellon de la Plana.

Bensheim: German (Rheinhessen) white wine. Includes Kalkgasse, Geiersberg, Pfaffenstein and Kirchberg.

Bensse: French (Médoc) red wine.

Bentonite: American colloidal clay of peculiar absorbing properties, used in fining (q.v.).

Bercy: The industrial suburb of Paris where much cheap bulk wine is cut and blended. Really bad wine in France is often caustically called Château de Bercy.

Bere: Old name for four-rowed barley and still used in Scotland.

Beregszász-Nagyszöllös: Czechoslovakian (previously Hungarian) wine district near Tokay.

Berg: A name borne by many German white wines, of course of varying merit. Some of the more important are Dittelsheim, Oppenheim, Hessloch, Hochheim, Worms, Kiedrich, Nierstein, and Rauenthal.

Berger: Established (1852) brand of armagnac (q.v.).

Bergerac: French (Dordogne) red wine.

Bergheim: French (Alsatian) white wine.

Bergholtzell: French (Alsatian) white wine.

Bergkirch: German (Nierstein, q.v.) white wine.

Bergwein: German term for wines from hilly regions as distinct from the less esteemed wines from the plains.

Bergweine: German *rosé* wines from Baden.

Bergzabern: German (Palatinate) white wines, including Schank, Altenberg and Steinbühl.

Berliquet: French (St. Émilion) red wine.

Bermuda: It is curious that a description of the alcoholica of this enchanting and long-settled island would be largely a catalogue of negatives. Bermuda, unlike almost all other islands, especially of the Atlantic, appears to have no fame as a producer of rum, wine or brewed beverages. Perhaps sugar and the vine cannot compete economically with the onion and potato. Consider Madeira, Canaries, Jamaica, Cuba, Puerto Rico . . . !

Berncastel-Cues: Celebrated villages opposite each other on the Moselle. Berncastel, on the right bank, produces the finer wine of which the best is Doktor, from a former proprietor, Dr. Thanisch. The wines of the numerous vineyards of the two villages bear the general name Berncasteler.

Bernex: Swiss (Geneva) white table wine, slightly sparkling.

Bernonnes: French (Médoc) red and white wine.

Berri: Australian (S.A.) wine centre.

Bertinoro: Italian (Emilia) white wine, also known as Albana.

Bertins, Les: French (Pommard, Côte-d'Or) red wine.

Berweg: German vineyard of Bisserheim (q.v.).

Besigheim: German (Württemberg) wine district.

Bessarabia: Important wine-growing region of Russia, previously Romanian.

Bestes Fass: German term used by Rhenish vignerons, which ought to mean the 'best barrel' of the vintage and sometimes does. See also Bestes Fuder.

Bestes Fuder: German term used on the Moselle for 'best barrel'. See also Bestes Fass.

Bethlaba and Bethrima: Wine-growing regions of merit mentioned in Bible as suited for the service of the sanctuary.

Bettelmann: German (Hochheim, q.v.) white wine.

Bettenberg: German (Iphofen, q.v.) white wine.

Between the Sheets: Cocktail of brandy, rum, orange liqueur, lemon juice.

Beva Fresca: Italian wine beverage made by adding grape juice to mature wine.

Bevel: The outer surface of the head of a cask. See also Coper.

Bever: Obsolete university term for a drink, especially of beer.

Beverage Wine: The general meaning of this term is wine to accompany food but sometimes it denotes a popular, inexpensive line. Table wine means much the same. Beverage or table wine is a term usually restricted to dry, unfortified material but sauternes (q.v.) and sweet champagne may be covered. Dessert wines such as ports and appetizer wines such as sherries are definitely not beverage wines despite the fact that they are associated with a meal.

Bex: Swiss wine-producing area.

Beyaz: Turkish medium-dry white wine.

Beychevelle: French (Médoc) red wine. Although graded a Fourth Growth, this wine is popular and fetches a considerably higher price than some of the wines in higher categories.

Bèze, Clos de: A fine vineyard in Burgundy planted by the monks in 630.

Béziers: French town, one of the chief centres for the disposal of common red wines.

Bibber: One who drinks to excess. Derived presumably from Latin *bibere*, 'to drink', hence bibulous. A free drinker but hardly a drunkard. The term, now old-fashioned, was usually coupled with wine and a wine-bibber was one of the bottle-degrees used when port-drinkers were graded one-, two- or even four-bottle men.

Bible: There are many references to wine and viticulture in the Bible. A few disputed terms may refer to other alcoholic beverages (see Shekar). Some general observations are possible. The moderate use of wine and other intoxicating beverages was clearly approved by the ecclesiastical authorities. Over-indulgence was deplored and prohibited and there are occasional sharp references to wine but in general the attitude is genial. There is a matter-of-fact acceptance of wine and 'strong drink' in general as a valued servant of man.

There is considerable reference to the skilled craft of the vine-grower and the wine-maker. To a surprisingly large extent the operations and the techniques of more than 2,000 years ago are those still in force today. It is interesting to note that, in accord with the most enlightened modern practice, it was quite usual to refer to wines by their geographical areas. Thus the system of *appelation contrôlée* (q.v.) is ancient indeed!

About the use of wines for the communion and other ceremonial purposes there have been a number of strenuous attempts by non-conformist Protestant sects to interpret Biblical references in a manner designed to support total prohibition of alcohol. The comment of Macalister, late Professor of Anatomy at Cambridge and a noted Biblical scholar, taken from the article 'Food' in Hastings's *Dictionary of the Bible*, effectively illuminates the matter: 'An attempt has been made to obtain a textual support for total abstinence by differentiating intoxicating from unfermented wine in the Biblical terminology; but it is only special pleading without adequate foundation. The teaching of Scripture as to the pernicious effects of intemperance in any form is clear and explicit. . . .'

Further information upon Biblical references to wine and related matters will be found by consulting the following items:
Gephen, Sorek, Jezreel, Kerem, Sarigim, Enab, Eshkol, Boser, Bazir, Zimmick, Dibs, Gath, Tirosh, Shekar, Hemer, Asis, Sobe, Mesek, Homez, Oinos, Zumzammim, Mattaree, Hek, Arp, Bak, Nazir.

Biblical Bottles: A series of outsized wine bottles, mainly for show but occasionally put to ceremonial use or storage purposes, known by Biblical names. Their capacities are ill-defined and writers show little agreement. The following list is probably as near as is likely:

Magnum	Equal to 2 bottles
Jeroboam (double magnum)	Equal to 4 bottles
Rehoboam	Equal to 6 bottles
Methusaleh	Equal to 8 bottles
Salmanazar	Equal to 12 bottles
Balthazar	Equal to 16 bottles
Nebuchadnezzar	Equal to 20 bottles

'In my search for the origin of the custom of applying Biblical names to wine bottles of magnificent proportions', says Mr. M. Foster in the *London Tatler*, 'I have left behind me a trail of red-faced authorities confronted for once with an apparently insoluble problem.

'A magnum, holding two bottles, is easily understood, but we go on to a Jeroboam, four bottles, a Rehoboam, six bottles, a Methusaleh, eight bottles, a Salmanazar, ten bottles (and who was Salmanazar?), a Balthazar, sixteen bottles (and this is probably Belshazzar) and the mighty Nebuchadnezzar, twenty bottles. The names roll magnificently, kingly names to describe bottles of truly regal proportions, but why?

'Jeroboam was a mighty man of valor', the writer continues, 'who made "Israel to sin", but why should Rehoboam — who was an equally mighty man and just as wicked — be given the edge in having his name applied to a bigger bottle? There is an insulting distinction drawn between the aged Methusaleh, whose name is applied to an eight-bottle monster and the feasting Belshazzar, who is honoured by a sixteen-bottle giant. It is unfair to Methusaleh.'

Bibline: A sweet Grecian wine mentioned in classical writings.

Bichon-Bages: French (Médoc) red wine.

Bickensohl: German (Baden) white wine.

Bidwell: Ancient (1710) brewery of Norwich, now part of Bullard & Sons Ltd.

Bieleisee-Weine: Swiss light table wine from Berne.

Biella: Italian (Piedmont) red wine.

Biengarten: German (Gimmeldingen, q.v.) white wine.

Bienteveos: Literally 'see-thee-well' the raised platforms in the sherry (q.v.) vineyards of the Jerez district of Spain.

Bière: French for beer. *Bière de table* — table beer.

Bierhalle, Bierhaus: German for public house.

Bierschenke: German for pot-house.

Bierstube: Ger., lit. beer-room. It is a chamber for drink, savoury food, music and fun. In a private house outside Germany a *Bierstube* is a rumpus room.

Biffy: Cocktail of gin, Swedish punch and lemon juice.

Big: As applied to alcoholic beverages (chiefly wines and whiskies) this adjective has acquired a technical meaning. A big wine is one of strong flavour and probably higher alcohol content than usual. A big whisky has a particularly strong but agreeable aroma.

Bikaver: A Hungarian red wine of the Eger district. Also known as 'bull's blood'.

Bilge: The wide, bulging diameter of a cask. See also Cooperage.

Bin: A storage-place for bottled wine and other liquors. In a special sense, a bin of wine refers to one particular bottling.

Binder: The last drink of the session.

Bine: The stem of the hop vine (q.v.). The bine is trained to grow up a pole of height about 12 ft.

Bingen: German (Rheinhessen) wine-growing region at the mouth of the River Nahe. The wine of the district bears the general name Binger and includes Schwätzerchen, Schlossberg, Eisel, Rochusberg, Ohligberg, Mainzerweg, Rochusweg and Schlarlachberg.

Bingen Pencil: Colloquial term for corkscrew, from the German.

Binned: Bottles placed in a bin, i.e. in layers or tiers.

Birch Wine: A beverage (not a wine) made by fermenting sugar or other fermentable carbohydrate and flavouring with young birch twiglets. It has somewhat the same flavour as the Greek retsina (q.v.).

Birkenhead: Old-established English brewery of that city.

Birkweiler: German (Palatinate) white wines.

Birnenbranntwein: Pear brandy, especially from South Germany.

Birnenwein: German pear wine. See also Perry.

Birrell, Augustine: Another of the English writers of modern times who have helped to defend their countrymen from cranks. He wrote 'All good novels are full of inns. . . . The reason is obvious: the inn is the finest focal point for the observation of men and manners.'

Birthalmen: Transylvanian table wines.

Bisamberg: Good wine-growing district near Vienna.

Bischof: German drink of red wine flavoured with orange peel and spices.

Bischoffingen: German (Baden) table wines.

Bischofsberg: German (Rüdesheim, q.v.) fine white wine.

Bishop: Hot spiced wine drink. Usually port is the base. To this may be added, according to taste, cinnamon, allspice, ginger, mace, cloves, nutmeg, lemon and orange peel and whatnot. It may be laced with brandy or rum. See also Pope and Cardinal.

Bishop Barker: Old Australian term for a long beer, after an Anglican Primate. There seem to be juicy possibilities here!

Bismarck: German mixed drink, a blend of champagne and stout. In English-speaking countries this is called Black Velvet (q.v.). A barbarity in any language.

Bisquit: Old-established brand of cognac (q.v.).

Bisser: Bulgarian dessert wine.

Bisserheim: German (Palatinate) wine parish. Vineyards include Goldberg Orlenberg and Berweg.

Bissey-sous-Cruchaux: French (Burgundy) white wine.

Bisson: An officer of high rank and gastronomic interests in Napoleon's army whose name is noted here because he is said to have ordered French troops to pay military honours whenever they passed the Clos de Vougeot (q.v.) vineyard.

Biti: West African drink made by fermenting tubers of Osbeckia.

Bitsch: German (Mülheim, q.v.) white wine.

Bitter: Heavy draught beer characterized by heavy hopping and lack of sweetness.

Bitters: Generic term for plant extracts added to alcoholic (and a few other) beverages during manufacture or prepared in concentrated form for use in mixed drinks. The most celebrated is, of course, hops (q.v.), which quickly supplanted gentian, ground ivy, horehound, quassia, wormwood and others. However, some of these bitter principles, though no longer used in beer, still survive, with quinine and other alkaloids, in proprietary bitters such as angostura (q.v.) and in vermouths and other flavoured wines. Bitters are often added to gin and to sherries.

Bizay: French (Saumur) white wine.

Bizeaudun: French (Médoc) red wine.

Bizerta: Tunisian wine region, mainly from vineyards of Italian ownership.

Black and Tan: Mixture of stout or porter and beer, especially mild ale.

Blackberry: The flavouring of some pleasant liqueurs and 'wines'. See also Country Wines.

Blackcurrant: See Cassis.

Black Jack: An old-time leather beer-mug coated with tar. From the Roxburghe Ballads:

> Black Jacks to every man
> Were filled with wine and beere,
> No pewter Pot or Canne
> In those days did appear.

Black Pagoda: Cocktail of brandy, dry and sweet vermouths, curaçao.

Blackstone: Appetizer of sherry, gin and bitters.

Black Stripe: Buttered rum (q.v.) minus the butter.

Blackthorn: Cocktail of Irish whiskey, dry vermouth, pernod and bitters.

Black Velvet: A crackpot beverage, a mixture of equal parts of champagne and stout. The fact is that champagne, if good, is a complete beverage depreciated by *any* addition while if bad it has no merit over lemonade or other gassy diluent. Also known as a Bismarck.

Blagny: French (Côte-d'Or) white wine.

Blanc de Blancs: The French term, literally 'white from whites', to denote champagne produced wholly from white grapes, especially the chardonnay. Also used of some other white wines.

Blanc de Noirs: 'White from blacks', i.e. champagne made wholly from black grapes, especially the black pinot.

Blanc de Rouges: The French term for white wine made from black (i.e. dark red) grapes by removing the skins quickly after pressing.

Blanc Fumé: French esteemed white wine from Sancerrois.

Blanche: French slang for the colourless, rather raw spirit that is widely drunk in northern France, outside the wine-growing country.

Blanche Fleur: French red wine of Beaune (q.v.).

Blanchot: French (Chablis) white wine. See also Chablis Grand Cru.

Blandy: Old-established shippers of madeira (q.v.).

Blankenhornsberg: German (Baden) white wine.

Blanquefort: French (Médoc) wine commune. The wine is often sold as Ludon (q.v.).

Blanquette: French white grape grown in Hunter River Valley (q.v.) of N.S.W., Australia, for delicate white table wine.

Blanquette de Limoux: A white sparkling wine from the south of France.

Blatina: Yugoslavian red wine.

Blaxland: Gregory Blaxland has strong claim on the gratitude of Australian wine-lovers. Around 1820 he was already growing wine commercially. The quality was sufficiently high to warrant export and to gain prizes in Europe.

Blaye: French (Gironde) claret region.

Bleichert: German (Silesian) Schillerwein (q.v.). This is probably the wine praised by Samuel Pepys as 'Bleahard'.

Blended Whiskey: The American official term for a blend, not necessarily of several genuine whiskies, but of as little as a fifth real whisky and the balance neutral spirits (q.v.). All Scotch and Irish whiskies are blends of genuine spirits.

Blending: The practice of mixing together or 'marrying' different lots of wine or spirit to obtain uniform quality from year to year, or to produce a 'blend' that will be more appealing to the taste than any of the constituents taken individually.

The operation, like marriage or field sports, can neither be condemned nor praised in general terms. As of so much in life, it all depends. The 'extending' of expensive burgundy with cheap Algerian with the sole purpose of making more profit is mere adulteration, yet a judicious addition of robust material to a thin and disappointing vintage is reasonable enough. Almost all Scotch whisky is a blend of a number of types, and the result gives general satisfaction. Sherry is invariably blended. (See Solera.) Cognac (q.v.) and other fine brandies are usually blends, the laudable object being to make available a standard beverage from year to year. Almost all port is a blended product. The blender of spirits and wine is usually a highly skilled and conscientious person.

Blent: Archaic form of blended (*Twelfth Night*, Act I, sc. v).

Bleu, Le: 'The Blues', the defect or disease of white wines, especially those destined to become champagne (q.v.). The wine is bluish, opalescent and fails to become clear. Usually the fault can be corrected, or almost so, by adding citric acid and spirit, then tannin. Finally, gelatin is used as a clarifying agent.

Blimy: Cocktail of Scotch whisky and lime juice.

Blinder: Cocktail of whisky, grenadine and grapefruit juice.

Blockade Liquor: American term (archaic) for a type of moonshine (q.v.).

Blockesberg: Hungarian red table wine.

Blood: Wine has often been called 'the blood of the grape' following upon the Biblical use of this phrase (Deut. 32 : 14) but the metaphor hardly bears close inspection. The idea that red wine has especial value in nutrition as a producer of blood is fanciful. The origin of the belief is obviously the resemblance in colour between vertebrate blood and red wine but the pigments are highly dissimilar in composition and function.

Blood Alcohol: The analyst's term for the alcoholic content of the blood after consumption of appropriate beverages. Below 0·05% there is little noticeable effect; above 0·15% almost everybody is 'under the influence'.

Blood and Sand: Cocktail of whisky, cherry brandy, sweet vermouth and orange juice.

Bloody Mary: American mixed drink of vodka (q.v.) and tomato juice. The name is a typical straining for effect. See also Sangre.

Bloom: The rather pretty powdery deposit on the skin of ripe grapes consisting, *inter alia*, of a mass of yeast cells (q.v.).

Blow My Skull Off: Concoction supposed to be popular on the Australian gold diggings in the 50's, alleged to consist of rum, cayenne pepper, stout, lime juice, opium and a few other ingredients.

Blue Blazer: Sweetened whisky and lemon set ablaze and poured from vessel to vessel until the flame is extinct. The remainder is then drunk. The alcohol has, of course, been lost in the drama. An unconscionable waste of expensive spirit. 'Brandy Blazer' and 'Café Diable' are similar foolishness.

Blue Burgunder: Chief grape used for red table wines in Ahr Valley, Germany.

Blue Danube: Cocktail of apricot brandy and lemon juice.

Blue Fining: The use of potassium ferrocyanide to remove traces of heavy metals from white wine. The process is dangerous, as the exceedingly poisonous hydrocyanic (prussic) acid may be produced by careless usage. The process is only permitted in Germany.

Blue Jon (or Blew): The 18th-century term for one of the fractions of inferior quality obtained in distilling whisky. Charles I prohibited its sale, but apparently without success.

Blue Mildew: Serious disease of grapevines caused by the attack of the fungus *Pernospera viticola*. The remedy is to spray with Bordeaux mixture (q.v.).

Blues: Cocktail of whisky, curaçao and prune syrup.

Blum: German (Ellsheim, q.v.) white wine.

Blume des Weines: German for aroma of wine.

Boal: See Bual.

Boa Vista: Portuguese *quinta* (q.v.), long the ownership of one English family.

Bobbio: Italian (Pavian) table wines.

Bobby Burns: Cocktail of Scotch whisky, sweet vermouth and benedictine.

Boccale: Italian wine measure, variable but about $1-1\frac{1}{2}$ pints.

Boccetta: Italian for little bottle.

Bock: The French term for a large tankard of beer, usually of glass.

Bock Beer: Heavy, dark, strong beer brewed for consumption in early spring. It was first made, according to report, at Einbeck, in Germany. That name became confused with *ein Bock* (a goat). A drawing of a goat is usually associated with this beer, particularly in New York.

Bockelheim: German government wine estate on the Nahe. The wine is esteemed.

Bocksbeeren Likör: Baltic liqueur (q.v.), made from blackcurrants.

Bocksbeutel: Also Boxbeutel. The dumpy, flask-like bottles restricted in Germany to the *Steinwein* of Franconia (q.v.).

Bockstein: German (Ockfen, q.v.) white wine.

Bocoy: Spanish and Italian cask of about 600 litres.

Boddington: Successor to the ancient (1778) Strangeways brewery of Manchester.

Bodega: A sherry storage house (Spain). The word is sometimes applied in other countries to a wine shop or wine saloon.

Bodeguero: Owner of a *bodega* (q.v.).

Bodengeschmack: The German term for wine of earthy taste.

Bodenheim: German wine-growing parish of Rheinhessen.

Bodingrube: German (Lorch, q.v.) white wine.

Body: As applied to wine, a picturesque but imprecise term, referring vaguely to the density, flavour and alcohol content. However, even if the term is vague, there is no practical difficulty in distinguishing between a light red wine such as a typical claret and a heavy-bodied wine such as burgundy or Algerian.

Boeckelheimer, Schloss: The best wine of Kreuznach, Nahe, Germany.

Boer-Wyn: Vernacular name of cheap South African wine.

Bogazker: Turkish red wine whose name is stated to mean 'the strangler' because of extreme astringency.

Bohle: A German students' convivial bowl of flavoured wine resembling claret cup. See also Maybowl.

Bohlig: White wine from Wachenheim, Palatinate (q.v.).

Boilermaker: Drinking term of various meanings, especially:
    (a) Whisky followed by a long beer.
    (b) Salted beer designed to replace the sodium chloride lost in the perspiration of heavy physical labour, and whose lack results in muscular cramp.
A 'Scandinavian boilermaker' is a nobbler of akvavit (q.v.) followed by beer.

Boiling-copper: The vessel in which wort (q.v.) is boiled with hops.

Bois Communs: Area of Cognac. See also Cognac.

Boisé: Woody, a French term applied, usually censoriously, to wines and spirits which have absorbed a foreign flavour from a defective cask. It is also used for brandy doctored to give a false age by adding an extract of oak wood.

Boismartin: French (Graves) red wine.

Bois Ordinaire: Area of Cognac. See also Cognac.

Bol: Dalmatian red sweet wine.

Bolivia: Wine has been grown here for nearly 500 years. The main distinction of Bolivian wine seems to be that the vineyards are the highest in the world.

Bollinger: Old-established (1829) champagne of Ay.

Bolzano: See Bozen.

Bombard: A large leathern drinking-vessel or jug of Elizabethan days. (See also Gaspin.) Bombards came into use to replace pewter vessels of the same size, which proved too heavy.

Bommerlunder: German type of Akvavit (q.v.), lightly flavoured with anise.

Bommes: Important French communes of Sauternes (q.v.). Amongst the many fine sweet wines are Latour-Blanche, Rayne-Vigneau, Lafourie-Peyraguey, Rabaud-Promis and Sigalas Rabaud.

Bonarda: Italian (Piedmont) sweet dessert wine.

Bon Bois: Area of Cognac. See also Cognac.

Bonbonne: French glass or ceramic wine container of capacity 5 to 25 litres.

Bond: The store or cellar in which liquor is kept under Customs control until duty or excise is paid.

Bonded: The term applied to alcoholic beverages (and other dutiable goods) of placing them in a store controlled by the Customs, to whom the owner has given a bond until the duty has been paid. In the U.S. the term 'bottled in bond' has a value, since only spirits conforming to government regulation can be so handled.

Boniface: The name of the jolly landlord in Farquhar's *Beaux' Stratagem*, hence now an innkeeper in general.

Bonifacio: Corsican table wines, red and white.

Bonne Chauffe: French term for the heart or middle distillate of cognac brandy (q.v.). This is the finest fraction.

Bonnes Mares, Les: This name is borne by two fine vineyards, both in the Côte-d'Or (Burgundy). One is in Chambolle-Musigny, the other in Morey.

Bonnezeaux: French (Layon, q.v.) white wine.

Bonnigheim: German (Württemberg) red wines.

Bonnissol: Old-established (1864) brand of cognac (q.v.).

Bontemps, Compagnons de: A group or club of Bordeaux wine men whose object is to boost Médoc (q.v.). The name is derived from that of the small buckets used to hold finings.

Bonze: The swell or centre of a cork, where the circumference is greatest.

Boomerang: Cocktail of whisky, vermouth, Swedish punch and lemon.

Boorde, Andrew: This fascinating and many-sided character wrote much concerning drinks and drinking. In 1542 he says, in his *Dyetary of Helth*, 'Ale is made of malte and water: and they the which do put any other thynge to ale than is reheersed except yest, balme or godesgood do sophisticat theyr ale. Ale for an Englysshe man is a natural drynke.' ('Balme' and 'godesgood' are synonyms for yeast.) Many modern people of sound judgement would agree with Dr. Boorde, but making an exception of hops.

Boot: Trick beer glass. (See also Yard.) A pewter or other vessel in which mulled ale used to be carried out to the coachdriver. Also a leather bucket used in the old days for holding a bottle for hand corking (before the era of corking machines).

Booth: Old-established (1740) brand of gin, now part of D.C.L. (q.v.). The Booth family had been associated with wine and brewing in London since the 16th century. The firm is reported to be London's oldest gin distiller.

Bootlegger: Illegal seller of liquor on which excise has not been paid, especially in U.S. See also Sly Grog.

Boozah: An acid beer made in Egypt from time immemorial. See also Shekar.

Booze: An opprobrious term for liquor but actually a word with a long and not undistinguished ancestry. It is a variant of the ME. *bousen*, to carouse or drink heartily. However, it is probably much older again and is obviously connected with the Egyptian word *boozah*, the name for a type of beer which is said to have been known for 3,000 years, and which some believe to be the mother of all brewed beverages. However, Clifford Hornby (*Rural Amateur*) states that the word is really a corruption of *bowze*, the ancient term in falconry for a hawk drinking.

Bordeaux: This ancient, sprawling, still expanding city, the metropolis of the Gironde, has long been the centre of a vast industry for growing, treating and selling wine. Around Bordeaux every year about 80 million gallons of wine are made, rather more red than white and most of it good. The red wine is called claret, a name known and respected wherever wine is drunk. Claret is an English word not used in France. It ought to be restricted to red bordeaux but it has been unfairly adopted by almost every country outside Europe that makes dry red table wine.

There are over 10,000 separate vineyards in the Bordeaux region, some of whose names are respected for quality throughout the world, others producing a barely drinkable liquid. Many of the better wines are separately listed.

The viticulture and wines of Bordeaux have probably been more extensively studied than those of any other region within or without France. On the whole this has been to the advantage of grower and consumer, not of course excepting the hundreds of winebrokers who act as intermediaries at the reasonable rate of 2% commission. One exception is the unduly rigid order of precedence which keeps one wine in lofty eminence and another in good-humoured subjection long after the positions should have been reversed. However, on the whole the Bordeaux wine industry is honest, competent, romantic and reasonable.

The principal districts of Bordeaux are the Médoc, Graves, St. Émilion, Pomerol, Sauternes and Barsac. Areas of lesser importance are the Palus and Entre-Deux-Mers (the district lying between the Garonne and Dordogne).

All these Bordeaux regions are separately noted. The Médoc classification is especially important. See also Médoc.

Bordeaux is not, of course, a homogeneous area. Sauternes and Barsac produce sweet white wines having little in common (except high price) with the red wines of the finest Médoc châteaux.

Bordeaux Mixture: Basic copper hydroxide and carbonate. Originally, a Bordeaux wine-grower sprayed his vines adjoining the road with copper sulphate to prevent pilferage. He found that vines so treated were not attacked by the dread downy mildew. Since then it has become a widespread fungicide. Despite modern chemical discoveries of fungicides it is still the grower's mainstay.

Bordeaux Wines, Classification of: In 1855 a group of recognized expert judges of the wines of Bordeaux set down a classification of the finest wines of the Médoc region. This has been treated ever since as a document of veneration. It is generally stated that so accurate and valid was the classification that, subject to a few minor variations, the listing is still applicable more than a century later. However, the tendency to accept this or any similar list as a sacred cow is to be deplored. Undoubtedly, it may lead to gross injustice, both initially and by creating groups of *élite*, semi-*élite* and untouchables. For example, Château Mouton-Rothschild is universally accepted as one of the great wines (and the fact that dealers pay the highest price is sufficient proof), yet this is not included in the very top drawer. Moreover, the fact must be recognized that vineyards wax and wane. It is a sad fact that many wines of France and Germany are now living on their reputation while up-and-coming vignerons may find almost insuperable barriers to entrance to the magic circle.

Nevertheless, the 1855 classification still has a formidable prestige which cannot be argued away. It consists in the classification of 62 of the best vineyards into five *crus* or growths. See also Médoc.

Borderies: Area of Cognac. See also Cognac.

Borges: Old-established shippers of madeira (q.v.).

Borgogna Nero: Italian name for the pinot noir (q.v.) grape.

Borie Manoux: French (Bordeaux) red wine.

Bornlay: German (Moselle) white wine.

Borrow, George: Beer never had a more staunch and sturdy friend. Who has ever put the matter better? 'Good ale, the true and proper drink of Englishmen. He is not deserving of the name of Englishman who speaketh against ale, that is good ale.' (*Lavengro*.)

Bosco, Le: French (Médoc) red wine.

Boser: The sour, ripening grapes of the Bible.

Bösing: See Pezinok.

Bosom Caresser: Cocktail of brandy, curaçao, grenadine and egg yolk.

Bota: Spanish butt or cask, especially for sherry. A sherry *bota* holds the equivalent of about 60 *arrobas* or 1,500 lb. of grapes and is used for both fermentation and ageing.
Also a Spanish leather wine bottle used by peasantry. See also Porrón.

Bota Chica: Spanish name of a shipping butt of about 110 gallons.

Bota Gorda: Spanish name of a storage or *bodega* butt containing about 140 gallons.

Botanicals: The name for the leaves, flowers, berries or other parts of plants added to alcohol before distillation to produce gin, liqueurs and other beverages.

Botas de Jerez: The special boots worn by the men who tread out the juice in making sherry (q.v.). The phrase means, of course, Jerez boots.

Botelha: Bottle in Portuguese. In Spanish it is *botella*.

Botjka: Russian liquid measure of about 490 litres.

Botrus: Latin for bunch of grapes.

Botrytis cinerea: The whitish mould which is encouraged to attack the ripe grape in the production of sweet table wines, especially sauternes. This attack is termed 'noble rot' (*pourriture noble*, q.v.).

Botte: Italian wine cask of capacity 600 litres in Naples and 416 litres in Palermo.

Bottle Age: The beneficent change that occurs in wine after bottling whereby it acquires bouquet and softness. Some wines, especially whites, mature quickly in bottle and are at their best after a year or two. Others may improve over decades.

Bottle Ale: Shakespeare uses this term in *Henry IV* and *Twelfth Night*, but the meaning is obscure. In *Henry IV, Pt. II*, Act II, Sc. iv, Doll Tearsheet attacks Pistol with the expression: 'You bottle-ale rascal.' In *Twelfth Night*, II. iii. 29: 'The Myrmidons are no bottle ale-houses.' Bottles for ale were just coming into use in Shakespeare's day. They must have been very expensive. A mystery indeed.

Bottle Fever: The absurd term applied to wine if it seems temporarily to deteriorate after bottling.

Bottles: For the purpose of this book, bottle means a container for alcoholic beverages. In modern times bottles are almost invariably of glass, the few exceptions being the earthenware or porcelain vessels used traditionally or for decoration. However, no doubt the ubiquitous modern plastics will find their use for bottles. The word does not here include the large stoneware or earthenware amphorae and jars used for bulk storage.

The original containers of stoneware and untanned skin or leather had small utility except as dispensing agents for immediate use. The cheapening of the manufacture of commercial glass in the 17th century in conjunction with the development of the other essential — a tight practical stopper or closure, cork (q.v.) — led to a prompt and enormous expansion in the use of bottles for the storage and transport of wine, spirits, beer and other alcoholic beverages.

It would be impossible outside the covers of a book specially devoted to the subject to make even a skeleton catalogue of the various shapes and sizes of bottles used by the beverage industries. In wine alone, there are many shapes traditionally used for regional types. To name but a few examples, almost any reader will have seen and handled the bottles used in Bordeaux, Burgundy, Champagne, Chianti and the Rhine and other parts of Germany.

Although bottles are of endless variety in shape and size, custom has established a particular size as the standard container for alcoholic beverages. In England this is the curiously named 'reputed quart' which is not a quart (quarter) but a *sixth* of an imperial gallon, i.e. $26\frac{2}{3}$ fl. oz. The half and quarter bottles are about 13 and 6 fl. oz. respectively.

The standard wine bottle is about the same capacity throughout the world. In the United States the wine bottle is generally $\frac{4}{5}$ quart or 1 pint 9·6 fl. oz., the half bottle $\frac{2}{5}$ pint or 12·8 fl. oz., allowance being made for the difference between the imperial and U.S. gallons. For spirits $\frac{1}{5}$ gallon is common.

In France the capacities of regional wine bottles are defined by law. (A litre is about 0·22 gallon. There are 100 centilitres to the litre.) The champagne bottle contains 80 centilitres, Burgundy 80, Bordeaux 75, Anjou 75, Alsace 72.

Claret (Bordeaux red) is usually bottled in dark green glass containers with a short neck. Graves and sauternes (Bordeaux white) use the same shape but clear glass. The bottles of Burgundy are wider. Champagne bottles are rather like those of burgundy but are much heavier and are pushed in at the bottom (punt) to withstand pressure and aid sedimentation. German and Alsatian bottles have long, slender, gradually tapering necks. The Moselles are of green glass and the Rhines usually brown. The Franconian wines use the *Bocksbeutel*, a squat green flagon. There are hundreds more shapes.

Outsize bottles are mainly for decoration. The 'imperial' used in Bordeaux contains 6 to 8 ordinary bottles.

Bottles, Biblical Names of: See Biblical.

Bottlescrew: Obsolete (18th-century) name for corkscrew (q.v.).

Bottle sickness: This is supposed to be a temporary unpleasant flavour in freshly-bottled wine. It is probably mythical.

Bottle-stink: The inelegant term for the unpleasant aroma of some red wines apparent immediately after opening the bottle. Such wines should have the cork drawn some hours before serving or better, decanted. Occurs sometimes in old bottled sherries.

Bottoms: The trade term for the lees of wine (q.v.) in casks.

Bötzingen: German (Kaiserstuhl, q.v.) wine centre.

Bouché: French wine term for bottled.

Boucheau: French (Gironde) red wine.

Bouchères: French (Côte-d'Or) white burgundy.

Boucherottes: French (Côte-d'Or) red burgundy.

Bouchet: Established (1877) brand of armagnac (q.v.).

Bouchon: French for cork.

Bouchonné: Corky, corked. Applied to wine tainted by the cork.

Bouchots, Les: French (Côte-d'Or) red burgundy.

Boudots, Les: French (Nuits-Saint-Georges, q.v.) red burgundy.

Boudriotte: French (Côte-d'Or) white burgundy.

Bougros: See Chablis Grand Cru.

Bouillage: French for fermentation (q.v.), lit. 'boiling'.

Bouilleurs de cru: The French wine-producers who are legally permitted to produce about five gallons of brandy annually for their own domestic drinking. There is a fierce triangular economic war between the home distillers, the prohibitionists and the commercial brandy-selling firms whose constantly changing alliances and allegiances are beyond the scope of this book.

Bouirueil: French red wine from Touraine.

Boukha: North African (Tunisian) spirit made from fermented figs. Sounds nice!

Boulestin: Old-established brand of cognac (q.v.).

Bounce: Drink made from fruit juice and spirit.

Bounce-upon-Bess: An old Irish term for strong whiskey. There is a very old Irish song called 'The Priest and his Boots' (quoted by Crokes in his *Popular Songs of Ireland*) which says:

> Drink deep of that liquor which Irishmen bless,
> For you'll find no such cordial as Bounce-upon-Bess.
> Compared with this balsam, all drink is small beer;
> What raises the spirits can never be dear.

Bouquet: The French wine term that has been adopted throughout the world (even with a creditable attempt at Gallic pronunciation) to denote the aroma of fine wine. After the eye has taken in the colour, the nose is the next sense to appreciate wine. The delicate perfume that slowly develops in a fine wine is due to the formation of esters (q.v.) by action between some of the alcohol and the tartaric and other fixed acids present in sound wine. Probably for this reason the wines higher in acidity from the cooler climates (e.g. the Rhine) are those which develop the most pronounced and pleasing bouquet (q.v.).

Some of these perfumes may be evident immediately fermentation is complete but mainly the development is on storage, both in bulk and, in the case of wine but not of spirits, in bottle. German white wines acquire bouquet with speed but French reds may need ageing in bottles for years before attaining the desired fragrance.

Wines are sometimes said to have the fragrance of raspberries, truffles, vanilla, violet and much more. Why wine should be especially valued for resembling something else is one of the mysteries of oenology.

Bouqueyran: French (Médoc) red wine.

Bourbon-Haut-Brion: French (Graves) red wine.

Bourbon Whiskey: American spirit (also known as corn whiskey) legally required to be made from not less than 51% maize and aged in charred white-oak barrels. The name is derived from Bourbon County in Kentucky, where corn whiskey was supposed to have been first made. Choice, matured bourbon whiskey has a superb bouquet (q.v.) and is one of the great spirits of the world.

Bourg: French (Gironde) canton which, with Baye, produces much wine, red and white.

Bourgeois: As applied to wine, this French term means a good but unclassified growth of the Bordeaux region, especially Médoc (q.v.). *Artisan* is somewhat similar, perhaps a little lower in esteem. Any wine lover reasonably free from snobbery and prejudice can usually obtain high value for his money by ignoring the classified growths and seeking out sound *bourgeois* wines.

Bourgogne: French for Burgundy (q.v.).

Bourgueil: French (Touraine) red wine.

Bourketown Mosquito Net: Drink one bottle O.P. rum with swamp water. This 'recipe' is Australian!

Bousa: Babylonian brewed beverage stated to be mentioned in writings at least as old as 2200 B.C. The connection with the opprobrious term 'boozed' is obvious. See also Booze.

Bouscaut: French (Graves) red and white wines.

Bousse d'Or: French (Côte-d'Or) red burgundy wine.

Bouteille: French for bottle.

Boutylka: Russian liquid measure, 0·76 litre.

Boutza: Cretan red table wine.

Bouvraie: French (Anjou) white wine, non-sparkling.

Bouzeron: French (Burgundy) white wine.

Bouzy: A district of Champagne which produces pleasant red wines. The name is only amusing to speakers of English.

Bowen: Queensland centre for rum production.

Bowl: A vessel for holding alcoholic beverages, hence convivial drinking, e.g. 'the flowing bowl'.

Bowle: German drink made from sparkling wine (or still wine and mineral water) to which is added fruit in season. Maibowle uses fragrant woodruff instead of fruit.

Boxbeutel: See Bocksbeutel.

Boyanup: Australian (W.A.) wine centre.

Boyd-Cantenac: French (Médoc) red wine.

Bozen: Original Austrian name of the Italian wine village now called Bolzano.

Brachetto: Italian (Piedmont) red wine.

Brackenheim: German (Württemberg) red and white wines.

Braga: Romanian millet beer, a common beverage of the country.

Brage Beaker: Apparently identical with bragging cup. The communal drinking vessel of the Norsemen over which boastful vows were made.

Bragget: Also Bracket and Braggon. Old beverage known in time of Chaucer. It was made by spicing ale and sweetening it with honey. James Howell (q.v.) wrote in 1634 'the natural drink of this part of the Isle may be said to be Braggot'. Modern bragget is beer flavoured with cinnamon and cloves and sweetened with honey. Bragget Sunday was so-called from the English custom of drinking the stuff in mid-Lent.

Bragot: Ancient Welsh drink made from beer, honey, cinnamon and galingale (a type of rush). Known as the 'heroes' drink'.

Brainstorm: Cocktail of whisky, vermouth and benedictine.

Brakspear: Old-established (1840) brewery of Henley-on-Thames.

Bramble Tip 'Wine': Country wine (q.v.) made by fermenting sugar and bramble tips.

Bramfen: Yiddish for whisky, obviously derived from Branntwein (q.v.).

Branaire-Ducru: French (Médoc) red wine.

Branch: American term for water used to dilute spirits. 'Bourbon and branch' is Bourbon whiskey and water.

Brandewijn: The old Dutch name for brandy, meaning burnt (or distilled) wine. See also Brandy.

Brandy: The potable spirit distilled from wine. It takes about five gallons of wine to yield a gallon of brandy of 50% alcohol. This is a very rough figure, for apart from the strength of the wine (which may vary from 8 to 15% alcohol), the method of distillation affects the yield. The name brandy is also applied to spirit distilled from the fermented juice of other fruits but always with the name of the source fruit preceding, e.g. apple, plum, pear, raspberry, and indeed any ripe, sweet fruit. Many of these fruit brandies have special names. See Applejack, Calvados, Slivovitz, Kirsch, etc. However, the simple name brandy is always taken to mean the spirit derived from the grape.

The exact origin of the name brandy is arguable. In England it first came into use in the 17th century as *brandwine* and originally meant potable spirit from any source. An Act passed in 1690 stated: 'Whereas good and wholesome brandies, aquae-vitae and spirits may be drawn and made from malted corn . . .' This clearly means that what we today call whisky could then be termed brandy. There is general agreement that the word is derived from the Old Teutonic root *brand*, meaning 'burnt', but whether the immediate origin is the Dutch name *brandewijn*, 'burnt or distilled wine', is doubtful.

France is usually accepted as the mother of modern brandy and still produces the undoubtedly finest, but actually it seems that the honour should go to Italy. It is stated that it was brought to France in 1533 to help celebrate the royal marriage of Catherine of Medici. The finest brandy, as stated, is made in France and the best of all comes from Cognac and Armagnac. Both are legally required to be wholly pot-stilled and are also rigorously controlled in other respects. For details see the respective alphabetical entries. See also Distillation, Pot-Still and Patent Still.

There is no geographical significance or legal right attached to the term 'brandy' and the spirit is now made in every part of the world where the grape is grown. Every epicure would agree that fine brandy is the world's finest spirit. It is a case of brandy first and the rest simply nowhere. However, even the connoisseur of brandy will cheerfully agree that whisky, rum, gin and the rest have their valued place.

All brandy is made by distilling the alcohol from fermented grape juice but the process may take many forms. In some regions, especially the French ones of Cognac and Armagnac, the grapes are grown for the specific purpose of becoming brandy. These grapes make a thin, acid wine valueless as a beverage but whose very deficiencies enhance their virtue as the raw material for exquisite brandy. In other places brandy may be made from surplus or slightly defective wine. Residues such as the mass of skins and other debris or the lees from racked wine may also be distilled. Such brandy is known in France as *eau-de-vie-de-marc*, in Italy as *grappa*, in Germany as *Hefebranntwein*, in South Africa as *dop* and so forth. Though the resulting spirit is often of low quality, this does not necessarily follow. For example, the brandy made from residues in Burgundy (*Marc de Bourgogne*) is esteemed. Brandy made in France from lees (q.v.) is named *eau-de-vie-de-lie*.

Like whisky, brandy may be made by distillation either in a pot-still or a patent or continuous still, or it may be a blend of both types.

More brandy is made in California alone than in the whole of France. The general quality is ordinary but improving. This also applies to Australian brandy, most of which is used to fortify sweet wines. There is, however, a moderate but expanding production of fine pot-stilled American and Australian brandy. There are some choice, fragrant brandies made in Italy, Spain and Greece.

The characteristic fragrance of a fine brandy develops upon long storage (ageing or maturation) in suitable containers. These are oak casks of moderate capacity (around 60 gallons in most countries), and there is a slow but fairly steady loss of alcohol in the process. This fragrance is due to a complex mixture of organic compounds of which the principal is ethyl pelargonate. It is interesting that a somewhat similar bouquet develops in some few of the fine bourbon (q.v.) whiskies of the U.S. Once the maximum fragrance of brandy has developed in cask, the spirit should be bottled to avoid further loss of alcohol. The enormous age claimed for certain brandies and the suggestion that they have been maturing since the time of Napoleon is mere trade puff and a snare for the gullible. Moreover, brandy, like all other spirits and unlike wine, does not improve in the bottle. It follows that the high price paid for old bottles of brandy (as distinct from bottles of old brandy) is mere liquor snobbery.

The adulteration of brandy (in the sense of adding foreign matter in order to simulate age) is rather common. Vanilla and honey are added for this purpose. Sugar is commonly added merely because the general taste is not for entirely dry beverages. Adulteration is an ugly word and these additions are not harmful except to the pocket.

The colour of brandy is acquired. All spirit is colourless as it comes from the still. A certain amount of colouring matter is extracted from the cask during storage but it is caramel (q.v.) which accounts for the familiar tint.

There is a widespread popular belief that brandy has medicinal properties absent from other types of spirits. There is no warrant for this. The values of fully matured whiskies and brandies, for example, are identical. The description 'hospital' attached to much commercial brandy has no valid meaning. Fine brandy is a superb and wholesome element of good living and in this lies sufficient justification for its existence.

The number of mixed drinks of which brandy is a constituent is legion and some of these are separately noted.

See also Spiritus Tenuior, Sp. Vini Gallici, Sp. Vini Vitis and Rakia.

Brandy, Age of: French brandy-makers and merchants have adopted a series of stars and letters to indicate age. However, these are at best only roughly approximate and their honesty and validity vary with the firm concerned. The use of these symbols in other countries is still less reliable. For what it is worth, the series is shown below:

Brandy of 1 star is roughly 4 years old.

2 stars is roughly 6 years old.

3 stars is roughly 7 to 10 years old.

Brandy marked V.O. (Very Old) is roughly 12 to 15 years old.

V.S.O. (Very Superior Old) is roughly 15 to 20 years old.

V.S.O.P. (Very Superior Old Pale) is roughly 25 to 30 years old.

Some distillers or blenders of fine brandies refuse to use stars or letters on their labels.

Brandy, British: Spurious liquid made by artificially flavouring 'silent' spirit. Similar to Hamburg brandy (q.v.). It is also an obsolete term of great historical interest. At one time the words brandy and brandywine had a wide significance. An Act passed in 1690 contains in the preamble the statement 'Whereas good and wholesome brandies . . . may be made from malted corn. . . .' In 1860 the Spirits Act (repealed 1880) stated that 'all spirits which shall have had any flavour communicated thereto . . . shall be deemed a British compound called "British brandy".' See also Brandy.

Brandy, High-Proof: See High-Proof Brandy.

Brandy Blazer: See Blue Blazer.

Brandywine: An obsolete word that has had varied meanings, but has always signified some from of distilled liquor. (Brand = burn.)

Brane-Cantenac: French (Médoc) red wine.

Branntwein: Lit. 'burnt (i.e. distilled) wine', the original German name for brandy.

Brännvin: Scandinavian equivalent of *Branntwein* (q.v.) and especially applied to Norwegian aquavit (q.v.).

Brasenose ale: Sweetened and warmed ale containing roasted apples, supposed to have originated at Brasenose College, Oxford. Also known as lambswool.

Brasses: French (Beaujolais) red wine.

Bratislava: See Pressburg.

Brauneberg: German (Moselle) white wine district. It includes the vineyards of Spitze, Juffer, Falkenberg, Bürgerslay, Hasenlaufer and Schloss.

Braune Kupp: German vineyard of Wiltingen (q.v.), Saar.

Brauenfels: German vineyard of Wiltingen (q.v.), Saar.

Braye, St. Jean de: Red wine from Orleans.

Brazil: Makes nearly 40 million gallons of wine annually and is also a large importer. As might be expected, Portugal is the main supplier. The climate of Brazil is not conducive to high-grade wine production. Almost all the wine is grown in the Rio Grande do Sul.

Brazza: Red wine from Dalmatian island.

Break down: To add water to reduce alcoholic strength, especially of spirits.

Breed: A vague term applied to wine denoting distinction.

Breisgau: German wine-growing district. Main town Freiburg.

Breitheck: See Assmannhausen. Also German (Palatinate) white wine from Asselheim.

Brescia: Italian (Lombardian) centre for good wines.

Bressandes: French (Côte-d'Or) red burgundy wine.

Bretzenheim: German (Nahe) white wine.

Breuil: French (Médoc) red wine. Also a white wine of Anjou.

Brewage: Old-fashioned term for a mixed drink. Macaulay writes of the sugar refiners of Bristol treating their visitors to 'a rich brewage made of the best Spanish wine and celebrated over the whole kingdom as Bristol milk'.

Brewer: One writer's definition: 'An artist who, by his choice of barleys and other ingredients and his sensitive control of the entire brewing process produces ale and beer for National delight.'

Brewers, The Worshipful Company of: The Brewers' Company was formally constituted by Royal Ordinance in 1406 as the 'Mistery of Free Brewers'. In 1437 it was granted a charter by Henry VI to control 'the brewing of any kind of malt liquor in the City and its suburbs for ever'. Membership of its Court is limited to London Brewery directors. The Brewers' Hall was totally destroyed in the Luftwaffe raid on the City on the night of 29 December 1940. The third hall recently erected in Aldermanbury Square, London, stands on land most of which has been the freehold of the Brewers' Company for over 550 years. The Guild of Brewers owns records, first kept in Norman French, from the 14th century.

Brewer's Grains: The malt grains which are retained in the mash tun (q.v.) after the maximum economic extraction of liquid malt or wort (q.v.) has been drawn off. These grains are later sold to contractors for use as fresh cattle food or for drying and manufacture of cattle cake.

Brewers' Guild: The Incorporated Brewers' Guild was founded in 1906 in England in the interests of the trade generally. Its *Journal* is a recognized trade periodical and its Benevolent Fund has done much to relieve distress among brewers and their dependants.

Brewers' Society, The: In 1904 the Country Brewers' Society, London Brewers' Association and Burton Brewers' Association amalgamated into The Brewers' Society. It is now the national organization of the brewing industry.

Brewery: Establishment used for brewing (q.v.).

Brewhouse: Another word for brewery, little used today.

Brewhouse hand: A craftsman in the brewery responsible for the boiling and flavouring of the wort (q.v.), prior to the fermentation (q.v.).

Brewing, Institute of: The world's leading scientific brewing organization concerned with research of interest to the trade. The Brewing Industry Research Foundation at Lyttel Hall, Nutfield, Surrey was opened in 1951.

Brewster Sessions: Special sessions of local Justices of the Peace to consider applications for new licences and renewals of existing licences in England.

Brèze: French (Anjou) white wine.

Brick Iron: The block used by coopers when rivetting cask hoops.

Bride-Ale: The beverage provided freely at the nuptial festivity, from which the adjective 'bridal' is said to be derived.

Bridgetown: Australian (W.A.) wine centre.

Briedel: German (Middle Moselle) white wine. Vineyards include Weisserberg, Schäferlay and Mergerei-Ketterhausberg.

Bright: Clear, transparent.

Bright: Large Canadian winemaker. See also Canada. T. G. Bright & Co. Ltd. has a capacity exceeding 6 million gallons.

Brigne: French (Anjou) white wine.

Brillette: French (Médoc) red wine.

Brisach: German (Baden) wine village.

Brisgau: German (Baden) white wine.

Bristol: This romantic old English city, now just on a thousand years old, had its earliest origin in trade and has kept its mercantile importance ever since. It has always been a great town of wine. Even by the time of about 1100, Bristol had developed a wine trade with the south of France. Ever since this, there has existed a great bond of affection and, of course, common monetary interest between Bristol and Bordeaux.

This bond has transcended wars and politics and as between cities may be unique. In the course of time, the wine trade of Bristol extended to Spain and Portugal and most of the rum from the West Indies also entered England through this port. Some of the English wine and spirit merchants have been established in Bristol for literally hundreds of years. Though Liverpool has attracted some of the commerce, Bristol remains a city of prime importance in the wine and spirit trade. It is said that Bristol bottles more sherry than Spain and more port than Portugal.

Many travellers have written engagingly of Bristol, not the least of them Samuel Pepys. See also Bristol Milk.

Bristol Milk: Although this name has been adopted as a trade-mark for sherry (q.v.) by a firm of merchants, it is actually centuries older without specific commercial associations. Pepys writes in his diary under the date 13 June 1688, 'did give us a good entertainment of strawberries, a whole venison pasty, cold, and plenty of brave wine and above all Bristol Milk'. This was probably not sherry but a species of rum punch (q.v.). However around that same time the term already meant either sherry in general or a particular sort of it. Thomas Fuller (1608–91) writes in his *Worthies of England,* 'This metaphorical milk, whereby Xeres or Sherry Sack is intended'. Defoe (1660–1731) writes, 'Bristol Milk, which is Spanish sherry, nowhere as good as here' (i.e. in Bristol's taverns). Macaulay (*History of England,* v. i, p. 335) states of the feastings of the Bristol sugar-refiners; 'the repast . . . was accompanied by a rich brewage made of the best Spanish wine and celebrated over the whole kingdom as Bristol Milk'.

British Compounds: The draggletail excise term applied to flavoured spirit.

British Soldier's Delight: Popular name of the 1860's for a mixed drink of gin and soda with a slice of lemon.

British Wine: A somewhat vague term. It can mean, e.g., an alcoholic beverage made by fermenting a mixture of syrup made from cane sugar or from glucose, mixed with the juices of any available berry, vegetable or herb. Such a product is becoming more commonly known as country wine. It may vary from awful to excellent according to raw material and skill. A more general use of the term is for true wine made from the grape. However, the grapes are grown perhaps thousands of miles from the U.K. and are transported in the form of concentrated juice, usually preserved with sulphur dioxide (q.v.). Although these wines are of mediocre quality or worse there is no reason why they should not be very much better if unpreservatized juice of higher concentration were used and all processes fully controlled.

British wine may also be made from raisins and other dried vine fruits. Again it is difficult to understand why quality is not higher. After all, a Hungarian wine such as tokay and a German sweet white labelled trockenbeerenauslese are made from grapes which are almost raisins, while true port (q.v.) is usually topped with concentrated grape juice.

Brix: See Balling.

Broadsheet, Captain Dudley: An alleged worthy of 18th-century London who set up as a seller of gin. He used a wooden carving of a tom cat as his sign. Customers placed money in the cat's mouth and the equivalent quantity of gin ran out of a pipe in its leg. This is supposed to be the origin of the name 'old tom gin'.

Broadwater: Australian (Queensland) wine centre.

Brochofsberg: German white Rhine wine from Rüdesheim, Rheingau.

Brochon: French (Côte-d'Or) red wine.

Broken Spur: Cocktail of gin, sweet vermouth, port, anisette and egg yolk.

Brolio: Italian (Tuscany) red wine. True chianti.

Brombeer-Likör: German blackberry liqueur (q.v.).

Broni: Italian (Lombardian) red wine.

Bronnen: German (Rüdesheim, q.v.) fine white wine.

Bronte: A Sicilian wine district from which Nelson took his title. The Sicilian wine beloved of British sailors was, however, marsala (q.v.) and wine sold in England as bronte was apparently really this. The name bronte is more romantic than the wine.

Bronx: Cocktail of gin, dry and sweet vermouths and orange juice.

Brooklyn: Cocktail of whisky and vermouth.

Broom 'Wine': Country 'wine' (q.v.) flavoured with broom.

Brouillards, Les: French (Volnay) red burgundy.

Brouillis: French term for the main fractions in distilling brandy, especially cognac. Alcohol content about 25%.

Brouilly: French (Beaujolais) red burgundy.

Broustet-Nairac: French (Sauternes) sweet white wine. See also Barsac.

Brouzac: French (Médoc) red wine.

Brown: Old (1830) Preston brewery.

Brown: French (Graves) red and white wines. One of the numerous Bordeaux properties with English names.

Brown Ale: Vague English term usually meaning mild ale but also applied to Burton beer (q.v.). 'A brown' is colloquial for beer.

Brown Bastard: See Bastard.

Brown Betty: Mixed hot spiced drink of brandy and ale with toast.

Brown-Cantenac: See Cantenac-Brown.

Brown Jack: Cocktail of gin, brown sherry and passion-fruit juice.

Brown Sherry: Dark, sweet wine made by blending oloroso (q.v.) with P.X. (q.v.) and color (q.v.).

Brown Velvet: Stout and port mixture, a waste of both.

Brown Water: Australian slang term for beer. The English simple 'brown' is better.

Brudersberg: German (Nierstein, q.v.) white wine.

Brühl: German (Gau-Bischofsheim, q.v.) white wine.

Brühl: German (Erbach, q.v.) white wine vineyard.

Brulay: French (Lorraine) table wines.

Brulées, Aux: French (Côte-d'Or) red burgundy.

Brum: Balinese sweet pink or white rice wine.

Brunet: Old-established brand of cognac (q.v.).

Brunswick Sour: Mixed drink of sweetened rye whiskey with claret floating on top, and decorated with lemon and fruit.

Brussonnes, Les: French (Côte-d'Or) white burgundy.

Brut: The term for dry or not-sweet, applied especially to champagne. Immediately after disgorgement (see Dégorgeur), all champagne is *brut* and some so prefer it. For most markets, however, it needs to be sweetened. It is given a dose (dosage) of syrup. See also Champagne.

Bruttig: German (Lower Moselle) wine centre.

Brutton, Mitchell Toms Ltd.: Old-established (1771) brewery of Yeovil, Somerset.

Bual: A type of madeira wine (q.v.). It is the English spelling of *boal.* The bual grape is now scarce and madeira is mainly made from other fruit. Experts say the quality of the wine has declined accordingly. Bual is about half-way between the dryish sercial and the syrupy malmsey. See Madeira.

Bubastus or Bubastis: A wine of antiquity praised by Herod. It was probably Egyptian but appears to have been popular in Rome.

Bucellas: Portuguese (Lisbon) yellow wine that was popular in royal circles in England a century ago. *Sic transit . . . !*

Buchanan: Old-established Scotch whisky blending firm (part of D.C.L. q.v.), whose brand-name 'Black and White' was actually coined by the public because it was sold in a black bottle with white label.

Bucherburger: Swiss (Rheineck) red wine.

Bucholz: German (Breisgau) white wine.

Buckwood: Ancient (1705) brewery of Portsmouth in which descendants of the Buckwood family still function.

Budafoc: Wine-growing district near Budapest.

Büdesheim: German (Nahe) white wines. Chief vineyards Langestein, Scharlachberg, Steinkautweg, Ackere, Karsborn, Schnackenerg, Heussling, Sketzling and Bubenstück.

Budget: In one of its original but now obsolete uses, this word meant a skin or a leather bottle. Hence, e.g. 'a budget of wine'.

Buergerspital: Steinwein (q.v.) (Franconian) vineyard, a charitable foundation.

Buffet Bar: Occasionally used to describe a snack bar or saloon lounge.

Buhlertal: German (Baden) red wine.

Buhslay: German (Erden, q.v.) white wine.

Bukett: German term for aroma of wine.

Bukhara or Bokhara: Asiatic ancient city of U.S.S.R. and now a rapidly developing centre of viticulture for both raisins and wine.

Bulgaria: Amongst the esteemed wine centres are Varna, Plevna, Rustschik, Sistowa and Sulindol. The general quality of Bulgarian wines is reported to be rising.

Bulgarische Sonne: Lit. 'Bulgarian sun'. White wine made from the furmint (q.v.) grape.

Bulimba: Old-established Brisbane (Queensland) brewery.

Bullay: German (Moselle) white wine centre. Vineyards include Herrenberg, Bornlay and Kronenberg.

Bulmer: The largest cider-making firm in the U.K. It had its origin in the cider made in the rectory orchard by the Rev. C. H. Bulmer, Rector of Credenhill, a village near Hereford. His younger son took up the operation in 1887 and the present large factory in Hereford is the result.

Bumbo: An 18th-century cold drink made of sweetened rum or gin flavoured with nutmeg. Sounds worth revival.

Bumper: Drinking-vessel filled to the brim and commencing to run over.

Bundaberg: Queensland centre for rum production.

Bundarra: Winery in the Glenrowan district of Victoria producing dry reds.

Bung: Slang for brewer, also for publican.

Bung ho!: A popular toast of obvious derivation.

Bung hole: Aperture through which the beer enters the cask at its broadest part and which is finally closed by the shive (q.v.).

Burck, Le: French (Bordeaux) red wine.

Burckheim: German (Baden) red wine.

Burg: German (Zell, Moselle) wines. Vineyards include Beilstein, Werdelstück, Graubach, Fahr, Kirche and Katschel.

Burg: German (Laubenheim, q.v.) white wine.

Burgberg: German (Klotten, q.v.) white wine estate.

Bürgele: German (Kirchhofen, q.v.) white wine estate.

Burgenland: South of Vienna, the principal area in Austria for fine wines.

Burger: White wine grape widely grown in California for cheap wines.

Burgerberg: Hungarian (Adlersberg) red wine.

Bürgerslay: German (Brauneberg, Moselle) white wine.

Burggrafen: German (Rauenthal, q.v.) white wine.

Burgsponheim: German (Nahe, q.v.) white wine.

Burgundian Appetizer: Two parts white burgundy wine, one part Dijon cassis.

Burgundy: The English name of the former French province of Bourgogne and applied to the wines grown within a region strictly defined under French law. Any wine (red, white or sparkling) made within this geographical area can legally be called burgundy. In English-speaking countries the name is used generically for a dry red wine high in colour, tannin and alcohol and thus precludes a genuine burgundy such as the esteemed dry white wine chablis. Unfortunately other countries have also unfairly adopted the name burgundy for their heavy red table wines.

The finest burgundy, both red and white, is grown on the Côte-d'Or, a narrow line of hills a few miles south of the city of Dijon of gastronomic fame. The northern portion is called the Côte de Nuits and the southern Côte de Beaune.

One of the finest white burgundies is chablis, grown around the town of that name. Red and white sparkling burgundy are made on the Côted'Or but cannot compete for esteem with champagne.

There are said to be around 20,000 separate vineyards in Burgundy, many of them quite small, 2 or 3 acres. Almost all the proprietors have their own ideas of wine-making. Thus, compared with Bordeaux, a greater proportion of burgundy is sold in bulk for bottling elsewhere, outside the stringent French laws of origin and type. Nevertheless a considerable number of the finer estates bottle their own wine.

It is generally conceded that the practices of Burgundy are much more 'flexible' than those of Bordeaux. Cane or beet sugar may be added to the must to increase the alcohol content and blending with Algerian and other suitable 'big' wines is fairly common, though not, of course, in the fine establishments.

Many of the fine wine districts and estates of Burgundy are separately noted.

Burgundy, Classification of Wines of: There has been no official classification comparable with that of the Médoc (q.v.). Perhaps this is really a matter for thanks. However, there have been many unofficial lists. They do little harm provided one remembers steadily (*a*) that they represent merely opinion and (*b*) the validity of any list can alter radically with the passage of time. One such list, quoted by Samuel Chamberlain (*Bouquet de France*, 1952) is shown below:

Red Wines
La Romanée-Conti
Le Chambertin
Le Musigny

Le Richebourg	Le Clos de Vougeot
	La Tâche
	Le Corton
Les Romanées	Les Mazoyères-Chambertin
Le Clos de Tart	Le Clos des Lambrays
Le Clos Saint-Jacques	Pommard-Rugiens
Les Echézeaux	Beaune
Les Bonnes Mares	Le Clos de la Vigne au Saint
Gevrey-Chambertin	Pernand-Vergelesses
Chambolle-Musigny	Savigny-les-Beaune
Vougeot	Pommard
Vosne-Romanée	Volnay
Nuits-Saint-Georges	Monthélie
Aloxe-Corton	Auxey-Duresses

Santenay

White Wines
Le Montrachet

Les Meursault	Les Puligny-Montrachet
Le Corton Charlemagne	Le Pouilly-Fuissé
Les Chablis	Aligotés des Hautes-Côtes
Les Chassagne-Montrachet	de Nuits et de Beaune

Pinot Rosé de Marsannay

Burgweg: German white Rhine from Rüdesheim, Rheingau.

Burgy: French (Burgundy) white wines.

Burignon: Swiss (Chardonnes) white wine from vineyard owned by city of Lausanne.

Burkard: German (Rheingau) wines.

Burkheim: German (Baden) white wine.

Burmester, J. W. & Co.: Old-established (1750) shippers of port (q.v.). It is stated to be still of German ownership.

Burnet 'Wine': Country 'wine' (q.v.) made by fermenting sugar and burnet flowers.

Burns, Robert (1759–96): At 30 Rabbie became an excise officer but before this he had written 'Freedom and whisky gang thegither'. Was ever a poet so beloved? Was ever a poet a total abstainer? As he observed, 'A man may drink and no be drunk'.

Burnt Ale: The alternative term for pot ale, the residue of the wash (q.v.) after the extraction by distillation of the low wines (q.v.) in the making of whisky.

Burra: Stated to be Hindustani for large. Thus a burra-peg is a big drink.

Burrenstein: Austrian wine-producing area.

Burrweiler: German (Palatinate) white wines.

Burton: A strong ale, dark in colour, made with a proportion of highly dried or roasted malts. It is not necessarily brewed in Burton upon Trent, and the term is in general use for all varieties of 'strong' or 'old' ales.

Burtonizing: The process in brewing of artificially increasing the permanent hardness of the water to make it resemble the water of Burton upon Trent, whose ales have long been renowned.

Burton upon Trent: English town noted for its heavy ale, from which the name of 'Burton ale' is derived. Some of the virtue of the ale has been attributed to the hard water of the town, hence the term 'burtonizing' for the treatment of soft water by suitable chemical additions.

Burton Union System: The distinctive process of brewing evolved at Burton upon Trent, but little used elsewhere, which involves the use of a large number of small vessels, and is therefore commercially expensive.

Busby, James: An Australian (New South Wales) colonist who migrated from England with the specific object of extending wine-making in the new land. In 1824 he introduced a large collection of vine cuttings from Europe and these are the foundation of the present-day Australian vineyards. In the process of time confusion has resulted from the placing of new names on some of these European varieties. Busby wrote books and pamphlets on the technology of wine-making and did much to advance the infant art. His name should be revered not only by all wine-loving Australians but by all those who appreciate the lofty character of a great forward-looking pioneer.

Bush: The traditional symbol for an inn, usually mounted on a pole. Some suppose the custom to be derived from the Roman use of a clump of ivy and vine leaves as a symbol of Bacchus (q.v.). The exact meaning of the proverb 'Good wine needs no bush' is still hotly debated though it probably always signified that something of true merit does not need advertisement.

Bush: A small metal ring screwed into the bouge (q.v.) of the cask in which is later inserted a wooden bung. A similar but smaller bush is used for the tap hole in the head of the cask.

Bussard or Busse: French (Anjou) wine measure of about 56 gallons.

Bute: The Bute family deserves mention here because of the valiant effort to establish wine-growing in Wales (Cardiff) in the 70's and 80's. See also Castle Coch.

Butler, Nephew & Co.: Old-established (1730) shippers of port (q.v.).

Butlerage: Former name for a duty payable to the king's butler, on wine imported into England. See also Prisage.

Butt: A large cask of varying capacity; a butt of ale is 108 gallons, and of wine usually 105 or 126 gallons. The cask so named is virtually the same as a pipe (q.v.).

Butta-Fuoco: Italian (Lombardian) sweet red wine.

Buttered Beer: A popular 16th-century drink consisting of spiced and sugared strong beer supplemented with yolk of egg and butter.

Buttered Rum: Mixed hot drink of rum, molasses and lemon plus butter.

Buttery: Originally a place for storing wine (from Latin *butta*, a cask). Later, by confusion with butter, a buttery came to be known as a place where both food and liquor are stored and served.

Butto or Puttonyo: A measure of specially dried furmint grapes used in producing tokay wine. The number of butten of about 30 lb. added to a cask of ordinary grapes, ranging from one to five, determines the grade of the wine. See also Tokay.

Buxy: French (Burgundy) white wine.

Buzau: Romanian red wine district.

Buzz: The college name for a short glass of port from the bottom of the decanter. Also a small plane used by coopers.

Byford: Australian (W.A.) wine centre.

Byrrh: One of the myriad French proprietary appetizers made by flavouring fortified sweetish wines. All these trade products are basically similar in type (though not necessarily in flavour) to vermouth (q.v.). Another popular line is Dubonnet.

Bzenec: Czechoslovakian wine district.

Cabaceo: Spanish term for a blend of wine.

Cabanne: French (Médoc) red wine.

Cabannieux: French (Graves) red wine.

Cabernet or Carbenet: Celebrated and widely grown grape for production of fine red table wines. It is the foundation of the blend that produces the best growths of the Médoc (q.v.). It is also grown in other parts of the world where quality is valued above quantity. Outside France the wine so made is often called by the name of this vine. Cabernet Sauvignon is the same. An alternative but corrupt spelling is Carbenet.

Cabernet Franc: Red grape responsible for some of the good wine of Médoc, France. It is also called Bouchet.

Cabinet: A term applied, particularly in Germany, to a specially selected and rare wine, fit for the maker's 'cabinet' (*Kabinett*).

Cabrières-les-Lilex: One of the Châteauneuf (q.v.) wines.

Cacao, Crème de: A liqueur of chocolate flavour.

Cach: French (Médoc) red wine.

Cachasa or Cachaca: Crude rum distilled from sugar-cane in the Amazon region of Peru. Also made in Brazil.

Cacho: Portuguese for bunch of grapes.

Cadaujac: The name of several French (Graves) vineyards of red and white wines.

Cadet: French (St. Émilion) red wine.

Cadet-Bon, Le: French (St. Émilion) red wine.

Cadet-Piola: French (St. Émilion) red wine.

Cadillac: French (Entre-deux-Mers) red and white wines.

Cadiz: Spanish seaport. Here sherry sails abroad.

Cadus: Old Roman measure of about 1½ amphorae or 40 litres.

Caecuban Wine: A Roman wine of antiquity frequently praised by Horace.

Café Diable: Hot drink of sweet black coffee, spices and brandy, set afire. Also known as Blue Blazer.

Cagliari: Italian (Sardinian) red wine.

Cagnes: French (Provence) ordinary wines.

Cahors: French (Gascony) red wine district.

Cailleret: French (Montrachet) red wine. The name Cailleret is also borne by three other vineyards of Burgundy, two in Volnay (red) and Chassagne (white).

Cailles, Les: French (Côte-d'Or) red wine.

Caillou: French (Barsac) sweet white wine. Also a red wine (claret) of Pomerol.

Calabria: A somewhat grim region of southern Italy where the vine and the olive yield only as the result of vast toil by the sturdy and obstinately patriotic natives. It is said, however, that the earnest searcher can find excellent bargains, e.g. Ciro (q.v.).

Calcavella: Alternative name for Carcavellos (q.v.).

Calebre: Syn. for *vino maestro*.

Caledon: South African (Cape Province) wine district.

Calene: Roman wine of classical times grown in Campania.

California: The principal wine-growing state of the United States. The area planted to vines is nearly 200,000 acres, mainly in small vineyards whose grapes are sold to large district wineries, either co-operative or proprietary. The wine industry of California is quite old and was established by the Spanish missionaries long before the region was annexed by the U.S. Today California produces more than 90% of the wine of the U.S. of which about two-thirds is sweet, fortified types (so-called ports, sherries and muscats). Most of this is poor stuff. Since prohibition was repealed, and especially since the end of the Second World War, there has been a determined and creditable effort to raise the percentage and the quality of the light table wines. Some of these are now superb but the proportion is still small. Apart from the lack of general appreciation of fine wine in the U.S. and the snob-appeal of importations, a large part of the Californian vine acreage is planted with inferior, high-yielding types which are being replaced too slowly.

　　There is a growing tendency to substitute varietal names of wines for false European place names. Most of the Californian wine-growing areas are separately noted.

　　The whole of the Californian grape vintage is obtained from European vines, mostly grafted on native stocks as a protection against *Phylloxera* (q.v.). It should be carefully noted that the wine industries of California and of the other states, especially New York and Ohio, are quite distinct. The wine of the Eastern States is almost entirely made from indigenous grapes.

California Coffee: Another idiotic waste of good liquor. A mixture of brandy and coffee, heavily spiced. The alcohol is then burnt away. See also Blue Blazer.

Californian Sherry: A distinctive blended wine, but bearing little resemblance to genuine sherry. It is not made by the flor, and is baked. An unfortunate name.

Californian Tokay: The absurd or worse name given to a compounded drink whose basis is angelica (q.v.). It is utterly distinct from true tokay (q.v.).

California White Port: A travesty on a distinguished name. Some of it is an indifferent sweet wine decolourized with activated carbon.

Calisaya: Spanish bitter (q.v.).

Calliste: Greek (Santorian) dark red wine.

Calon Ségur, Château: Fine red wine from St. Estèphe, Bordeaux.

Caloric Punch: Scandinavian mixed drink of sweetened rum and flavourings. Often sold bottled.

Calouère: French (Côte-d'Or) red wine.

Caluso: Italian (Torino) fortified white wine.

Calvados: Apple brandy, usually of fine quality, distilled in the district of that name in Normandy, France. It is one of the world's great spirits.

Calvé-Croizet-Bages: French (Médoc) red wine.

Calverley, Charles Stuart (1831–1884): Surely many an aspiring modernist could study Calverley's comic poetical technique with advantage. Who else could have written these lines?
> O Beer! O Hodgson, Guinness, Allsopp, Bass,
> Names that should be on every infant's tongue!

Calvi: The principal Corsican table-wine district.

Calvimont: French (Graves) red wine.

Camara: The Spanish candle and holder used to observe the brightness of wine.

Camara de Lobos: The Madeira village which is the centre of the wine-growing district.

Cambon-la-Pelouse: French (Médoc) red wine.

Camden Tablets: Trade-name for *alkali* (*potassium*) *bisulphite*, a convenient (perhaps too convenient) method of adding sulphur dioxide to wine or food.

Camensac: French (Médoc) red wine.

Camino-Salva: French (Médoc) red wine.

Campania: Celebrated Italian wine province. Here are grown Lachryma Christi and Falernum.

Campari: Like the French the Italians have a large number of proprietary appetizers of the vermouth (q.v.) type, of which this is one.

Campbell & Menzies: Established (1874) shippers of port (q.v.).

Campbeltown: Scottish centre in Kintyre which gives its name to the single (q.v.) or pot-stilled malt whisky used for blending.

Camperos: French (Barsac) sweet white wine.

Campidano: Sardinian white wine of Caligari.

Campiglione: Italian (Piedmont) red wine.

Camponac: French (Graves) red wine.

Camus: Old-established brand of cognac (q.v.).

Can: Colloquial expression for tankard. Hence canful.

Cana: Spanish wine glass of cylindrical shape, resembling, as the name suggests, a length of sugar cane or bamboo.

Canada: Despite the French-speaking segment of the Canadian population, this country is not a large wine-consumer. The amount drunk per head is 0·5 gallon per annum (1964), though it is slowly rising. The local production of wine is about eight million gallons a year and in addition two and a half million gallons are imported. In view of the climate it comes as a surprise to most that the local production is so high. More than 90% is grown in the Niagara Peninsula of Ontario. The vines are *labrusca* (q.v.) hybrids. The climate is such that, despite the high latitude, it is said that the probability of harvesting a grape crop is more secure in Niagara than almost anywhere else in N. America. Every type of wine is produced and there is strict legal control, including a prohibition against blending foreign with local wine. There are more than a dozen wineries, nine located in Niagara. Two of these (Jordan and Bright) have capacity in excess of six million gallons. The Canadian wine industry is expanding.

Canada has an extensive whisky-distilling industry. Some of the material has a distinctive and esteemed character. Much rye whisky is exported.

There is a large and well-equipped brewing industry.

Cañada: Spanish wine measure of about 8½ gallons.

Canadian: Cocktail of Canadian whisky, bitters and sugar.

Canadian Whisky: See Whisky.

Canarese: Italian (Piedmont) red wine.

Canary Wine: The Canary Islands, Spanish Atlantic outposts, were once important as wine-producers. Canary sack was a celebrated and highly esteemed wine from Elizabethan times until well into the 19th century. Then the dreaded fungus disease *oïdium* more than decimated the vineyards and wine-growing has never recovered its old importance. A pity: with modern methods the vines could grow again and from all accounts canary was a superb dessert wine. As Shakespeare said, '. . . you have drunk too much canaries; and that's a marvellous searching wine . . .' (*King Henry IV, Pt. 2*, Act II, Sc. iv).

It is interesting to note the high value placed upon the wine of Canary in the 17th century, and especially in England. The following quotation is from one of the *Familiar Letters* of James Howell, writing in 1634:

'Good wine carrieth a Man to Heaven. If this be true, surely more English go to Heaven this way, than any other; for I think there's more

Canary brought into England, than to all the World besides: I think also there is a hundred times more drunk under the Name of Canary-Wine, than there is brought in; for Sherries and Malagas well mingled, pass for Canaries in most Taverns, most often than Canary itself; else I do not see, how it were possible for the Vintner to save by it, or to live by his Calling; unless he were permitted sometimes to be a Brewer. When Sacks and Canaries were brought in first amongst us, they were us'd to be drunk in Aqua vita measures; and 'twas held fit only for those to drink, who were us'd to carry their Legs in their Hands, their Eyes upon their Noses, and an Almanack in their Bones. But now they go down every one's Throat, both Young and Old, like Milk.'

There is, of course, still some wine, mainly sweet, grown in the Canaries.

Canasta: Spanish cane basket used in vineyard.

Canelli: Italian (Piedmont) chianti wine. Also Italian grape sometimes wrongly called golden muscat. Italian wine-making town noted for muscatel.

Canette: Old English jug (diminutive of 'can'), holding about a quart. In France and Belgium also a retail measure for wines and beer, about 1½ pints but variable.

Canetto Pavese: Italian (Lombardian) red wine, usually slightly sweet.

Canned Beer: Beer filled into lined tins (cans).

Canoa: Spanish wedge-shaped wine funnel.

Cañocazo: One of the lesser grapes used in Spain for sherry.

Canon: French (St. Émilion) red wine.

Canon, Château: Red wine of St. Émilion district of Bordeaux.

Canonao: Italian (Sardinian) red wine.

Canon-Lange: French (Gironde) red wine.

Cant: The piece of timber in the head of a cask in which the cork hole is bored.

Cantebau: French (Graves) white wine.

Canteen: (Fr.: *cantine*, It.: *cantina*, a bottle-case), a liquor and general shop attached to a military post. The term is also still applied to a receptacle to hold liquids, especially part of a soldier's kit. See also Sutler.

Cantegril: French (Barsac) sweet white wine. Also a dry white of Graves.

Cantegrive: French (Médoc) red wine.

Canteiro: The term applied to the finest Madeira wines matured only in the sun (i.e., without artificial heat). Many old Portuguese families have all their capital in canteiro wines, recalling some of the farmers of Cognac.

Canteloup: Seven separate wine estates of various districts of Bordeaux bear this name, mainly red wines (clarets).

Cantemerle: French (Médoc) red wine. Also white of Graves and red of Cubzadais.

F

Cantenac: An important wine-growing commune of the Médoc (q.v.). It contains many classed and celebrated growths, including Kircoan, Cantenac-Brown, Palmer, Brane-Cantenac, and many more. The commoner wines have acquired the legal right to the use of the name Margaux.

Cantenac, Ch.: French (St. Émilion) red wine.

Cantenac-Brown: French (Médoc) red wine.

Canteperdrix: French red wine of Beaucaire (q.v.).

Canzem (Kanzem): German (Saar Valley) white wine centre. The principal vineyards are Unterberg, Kelterberg, Altenberg, Höreker and Berg.

Cap: The expressive term for the mass of skins, pips, stalks and debris that collects on top of a fermenting vat, buoyed up by the carbon dioxide gas (q.v.).

Capataz: Spanish term for overseer, often used as equivalent of cellarmaster.

Capbern: French (Médoc) red wine.

Cap Breton: French (Biscayan) ordinary red wine.

Cap Corse: Vineyard area of Corsica.

Cap-de-haut-Bergeron: French (Médoc) red wine.

Cap de Mourlin: French (St. Émilion) red wines.

Cap-de-Ramon: French (Médoc) red wine.

Cape Smoke: South African vernacular term for an inexpensive and rather crude brandy made from dregs. However, see Grappa.

Cape Wines: Generic term in the English wine trade for the wines of South Africa.

Capillaire: A term of no particular precision, applied to the flavoured syrup used for sweetening alcoholic beverages during manufacture. See also Gomme.

Capri: Red and white wines from the island off the Naples Riviera. In 1904 H. M. Vaughan wrote: 'The casual traveller rarely tastes a good sample for it is usually doctored and "improved" for purposes of keeping by the wine merchants of Naples. Thus the rasping red liquid that appears on the table of a London restaurant and the scented, strong-tasting white stuff that is sold in the hotels of the island itself or of Naples under the name Capri, have little in common with the pure, unadulterated product of these sunny, breezy vineyards.' But things seem to have improved since 1904.

Caprike: A wine of Elizabethan times, mentioned by Holinshed (*Chronicles*), variously supposed to originate from Capri and Cyprus.

Capsule: In relation to beverages, the cap or sheath of metal foil, usually bearing a distinctive trade-mark, that covers the top of a bottle and must be broken before the cork is removed. The use is now decorative but the original purpose was to protect the cork from weevil.

Carafe: Glass water-bottle for table use but the term is also applied to a similar holder for wine.

Carafe Wine: The pleasant but inexpensive wine served in flasks on the table of French restaurants. Perhaps the chief source of French carafe wine is Beaujolais (q.v.). All carafe wines are drunk young.

Caraffa: Italian liquid measure, about a pint.

Carafon: A small carafe (q.v.).

Caramel: An amorphous, brittle mass made by heating cane or other sugar to about 180° C. Its composition is obscure. It is the wholesome colouring matter used so widely in the liquor industries. Beers and stouts owe their colour mainly to caramel produced in the process of roasting the malt grains but more may be added in the brewing process, if fancy dictates. Almost all the characteristic yellow, brown or reddish-brown tints of whisky, brandy and rum are due to the addition of caramel. Although it has a distinctly bitter taste, the amount required to give an agreeable tint is so minute that no foreign flavour is introduced. A certain amount of colour of matured whisky, brandy, rum and sherry may be derived from the wooden vessels used for storage but these are frequently deliberately charred and the pigment so produced is itself closely related chemically to sugar caramel.

Caratello: Italian barrel.

Caraway: To many this is one of the most nauseating of all flavours. It has, however, always had a wide circle of lovers. Seed-cake (which means a spongy sweet cake studded with caraway seeds) is still popular and was the accepted accompaniment to Madeira wine ('madeiry'). It is also the flavouring of choice of Scandinavia in the form of akvavit (q.v.). For long it had esteem as an aphrodisiac and caraway wine or caraway brandy was often served by wives to husbands and presumably vice versa. Kümmel is the liqueur of this flavour.

Carbohydrate: A class of chemical compounds of carbon, hydrogen, and oxygen. The starches and sugars are carbohydrates, and beverage alcohol is derived from these by the action of enzymes (q.v.).

Carbonated: Beverage to which carbon dioxide gas has been artificially added. See also Sparkling.

Carbonated Wine: Sparkling wine of indifferent quality made by charging still wine with carbon dioxide gas. Such wine soon loses its sparkle and goes flat because the gas is not combined chemically but is merely dissolved. See also Champagne.

Carbonation: The infusion of CO_2 gas at low temperature in bottling beer immediately on arrival from the brewery.

Carbon Dioxide: The gas of chemical formula CO_2. It is produced in about equal weight with alcohol when sugar is fermented by the action of yeast. Normally the gas is allowed to escape, but is retained in bottled beer, and in sparkling wine and cider.

Carbonnieux: French (Graves) white and red wines. There is a tradition (or a fable) that the ecclesiastical proprietors of this estate once had a thriving trade shipping the wines to Turkish Moslem faithfuls who bought it as French mineral water. See also Aga Khan.

Carboy: Large glass or earthenware bottle protected by wicker or wooden frame. See also Demijohn.

Carcavellos: Portuguese (Tagus) wine, red and white.

Cardinal: A variant of Bishop (q.v.). See also Pope.

Cardinal de Sourdis: French (Bordeaux) red wine.

Cardinal-Villemaurine: French (St. Émilion) red wine.

Cardow: Scotch distillery at Strathspey which has long been producing a celebrated malt whisky prized by blenders.

Carelle-sous-la-Chapelle: French (Côte-d'Or) red wine.

Carema: Italian (Piedmont) red wine.

Carigliano: Italian (Sicilian) wines.

Carignane: Southern French sweet dessert wine. Also the name of a rather coarse red grape widely planted in southern France and California for cheap wine.

Cariñena: Spanish golden dessert wine from Aragon.

Carles: French (Barsac) sweet white wine.

Carlowitz: Yugoslavian and Austrian red wine.

Carlsberg: The celebrated brewery of Copenhagen, founded by J. C. Jacobsen in 1845. Here he made the first bottom-fermented (q.v.) beer in Denmark. Lager (q.v.) beer from Copenhagen was being exported to Scotland by 1869 and was possibly the first bottom-fermented beer to appear in the U.K.

Carmeilh: French (Bordeaux) red wine. There are a number of estates of this name.

Carmes-haut-Brion: French (Graves) red wine.

Carmignano: Italian (Tuscany) red wine (Chianti).

Caronne-Sainte-Jème: French (Médoc) red wine.

Carouse: To drink deeply.

Carpano: Another of the Italian proprietary appetizer wines. See also Campari.

Carquelin: French (Beaujolais) red wine.

Carrascal: District north-west of Jerez (q.v.), Spain, noted for production of *oloroso*-type sherry (q.v.).

Carrasset: French (Médoc) red wine.

Carrot wine: See Country Wines.

Carruades: The wine from Lafite (q.v.) which is considered not quite up to the very high standard of that celebrated château. There are numerous other Médoc wines which bear the name Carruades.

Carthaginia: Celebrated wine region of classical times. It is interesting to remember that the large wine-growing areas planted by the French in modern times in North Africa are often actually on the same sites as these ancient Carthaginian vineyards.

Cartillon: French (Médoc) red wine.

Caruso: Cocktail of gin, dry vermouth and mint liqueur.

Casa de la Gares: The Spanish crushing house where the sherry grapes are treated.

Casa do Douro: The regional Portuguese body which annually decides how much port wine will be made and its price.

Casa Ferreirinha: Old-established (1751) shippers of port, long directed by the remarkable Doña Antonia Adelaide Ferreira (b. 1810) until her death in her eighties. The estates are of legendary wealth and operated in magnificent style.

Casale d'Elsa: Italian (Chianti) red wine.

Casal Garcia: Portuguese dry white wine.

Cascade: Principal brewery of Tasmania since 1883.

Cascarilla: South American bitters (q.v.), made from an alcoholic extract of the bark of that name.

Casciano: Italian (Chianti) red wine.

Casco: Spanish for cask.

Casel or **Kasel:** A German (Ruwer) white wine district. Amongst the vineyards are Walterberg, Nieschen, Taubenberg, Hitzlay, Herrenberg, Kehrnagel and Dominikaner.

Cashew: According to report, a spirit has long been made at Goa from the nut of the cashew (*Anacardium occidentale*). The chemistry seems obscure.

Cask: A vessel of characteristic, bulging, cylindrical shape, formed of curved wooden staves supported by flat circular ends or heads, and bound together by hoops. Used mainly for liquids, especially alcoholic beverages. The design of the cask provides a graceful combination of strength, tightness, and durability, with ease of handling, dismantling and repair. Although 'cask' and 'barrel' have largely the same meaning, the term 'barrel' is generally used in a special sense and as a measure of capacity, whereas 'cask' is the generic term for all such vessels of similar construction, irrespective of size or purpose.

Names of some of the more generally used vessels, with their capacities expressed in litres (1 litre = about 1·76 U.K. pints or 1·057 U.S. quarts):

ARROBA	Spain	varies from	12 to 18 litres
BARIL	Lisbon		16·74 ,,
,,	Malaga		30 ,,
BARILE	Rome		58·34 ,,
BARREL	U.S.A.		119·24 ,,
BARRIL	Madeira		15·44 ,,

BARRIQUE	Bordeaux	225	litres
,,	Algeria	220	,,
,,	Beaujolais	216	,,
,,	Champagne	200	,,
,,	Cognac	205	,,
,,	Côte-d'Or	228	,,
,,	Côtes du Rhône	225	,,
,,	Mâcon	215	,,
,,	Yonne	248	,,
BOTTE	Sardinia (large)	500	,,
,,	,, (small)	44·54	,,
BRENTE	Switzerland	50	,,
DREILING	Vienna	1358	,,
EIMER	Switzerland	37·5	,,
,,	Vienna	56·58	,,
,,	Württemberg	293·92	,,
FUDER	Prussia	824·42	,,
,,	Württemberg	1763·57	,,
,,	Austria	1810·85	,,
OHM	Baden	150	,,
,,	Bavaria	128	,,
,,	Saar	144	,,
,,	Alsace	50	,,
,,	Switzerland	40	,,
OKA or OKKA	Balkans	1·28	,,
OXHOFT	Hamburg	226	,,
PIÈCE	Burgundy	228	,,
,,	Champagne	200	,,
,,	Cognac	250	,,
,,	Saumur	220	,,
,,	Vouvray	250	,,
PIPE	England	477	,,
,,	Lisbon	502	,,
,,	Madeira	416	,,
,,	Oporto	535	,,
,,	Tarragona	510	,,
,,	Valencia	75·39	,,
STUCK	Rhineland	1200	,,
VEDRO	Russia	12·39	,,

(From *A Dictionary of Wine* (London, Cassell, 1935), by André Simon, that master of the gastronomic arts.)

For beer the common British vessels are the kilderkin (18 gallons), the firkin (9 gallons) and the pin (4½ gallons). Formerly made of oak, they are now largely fabricated from stainless steel.

Cas Rougeot: French (Côte-d'Or) red wine.

Casse: The general French term for certain disorders or defects that develop in wines.

Cassis: The syrup made from blackcurrants, widely used in France. A little added to vermouth (q.v.) or *vin blanc* is the almost universal apéritif. It is the basis of the beloved liqueur crème de cassis, a Burgundian specialty. Also the name of a wine-growing region near Marseilles.

Castel Bracciano: Italian (Latium) white wine.

Castel del Bosch: Spanish (Catalonian) red and white wine.

Castel del Remy: Spanish (Catalonian) white wine.

Castel Gondolfo: Italian white wine from Latium (Castelli Romani, q.v.) Here the Pope has a country house.

Castellen Schlossberg: German Steinwein vineyard near Würzburg (q.v.).

Castelli di Canelli: Italian (Piedmont) white table wine.

Castelli di Jesi: Italian white table wine.

Castelli di Sommariva: Italian (Piedmont) white table wine.

Castelli Romani: The sweet golden wines from the Roman area in the Apennines foothills, made by the sauternes process (see pourriture noble). The most noted are Frascati and Marino. Lesser wines are Albina, Castel Gondolfo and Genzano.

Castell Toblino: Tyrolean dessert wine.

Castelnaud: French (Sauternes) red wine. Interesting as one of the very few reds of the area.

Castelnau-Rivière-Basse: French Basque table wine.

Castera: French (Médoc) red and white table wines.

Castiglione-Faletto: Italian (Piedmont) red wine.

Castiglion Faletto: See Barolo.

Castillon: Old-established (1814) brand of cognac (q.v.).

Castle Coch: The name of the long-vanished red wine grown near Cardiff by the Bute family. See also Bute. Alas, climate won. The wine could only be made by liberal sugaring.

Casual: An occasional visitor to the pub. See also Regular.

Catalan: Wine from Catalonia, Spain.

Catalonia: Important Spanish wine province, mainly red table.

Catamarca: Argentine wine district.

Catavino: Spanish name for a wine-glass holding about 6 fl. ozs., of stemmed tulip shape and widely used for drinking sherry.

Catawba: Longfellow may not be a major poet but he was a sound oenophile, free from wine-snobbery. He wrote:

> Very good in its way
> Is the Verzenay
> Or the Sillery soft and creamy;
> But Catawba wine
> Has a taste more divine,
> More dulcet, delicious and creamy.

Catawba flourishes to perfection on the banks of the Ohio and of its tributary the Sciota. See also Applejack.

Catherine Hayes: Australian mixed drink of claret, sugar and orange named after a character of goldrush days.

Catullus: He died in 54 B.C. in his early thirties but his poetry still lives and abounds in praise of wine and, of course, women.

Caub: Ancient wine market of Germany on the Rhine. There are still vineyards around the town but of lesser importance.

Caucasus: Wine-growing region of Russia between the Caspian and Black Seas.

Caudle: A hot beverage made by mixing gruel with wine or spirits. Also 'caudle cup', to hold the same.

Cave: Fr. for underground cellar. A storehouse for bottled as opposed to bulk wine.

Cavé: Established (1883) brand of armagnac (q.v.).

Caversham: Australian (W.A.) wine centre.

Caviste: French for cellarman, a person of consequence.

Cazanove: Old-established (1811) champagne of Reims.

Cecil Plains: Australian (Queensland) wine centre.

Celery 'Wine': Country 'wine' made by fermenting sugar and celery. See also Country Wines.

Cellar: In the sense of this book, a storage place for alcoholic beverages, bulk or bottled. It may be situated above or below the ground. 'Cellaring' is the term applied to the many forms of treatment applied to wines, spirits and brewed beverages during storage and includes blending, filtration and much else. Upon the proper temperature (55–65° F.) and hygiene of the hotel cellar depends the condition of the draught beer served in the bar.

Cellarage: The general term covering all the operations of producing ('educating') wine after the fermentation is over. This includes storage at the correct temperature, fining, racking, filtration, polishing, transfer from one vessel to another, making up ullage, bottling, corking, binning and more. These terms are explained in their places. Wine cellars are not necessarily below ground level. The lodges of Oporto, the *chais* of some parts of France and the *bodegas* of Spain are all at ground level. Lager beer (q.v.) and whisky and other spirits are also subject to cellarage.

Cella Vinaria: The room, not necessarily underground, of a Roman house used for wine-making.

Cellier: French name of an above-ground cellar. In the Bordeaux this is called a *chai*.

Centrifuge: A mechanical filter consisting of a rapidly rotating bowl on which the sediment is deposited.

Cent Vignes: French (Burgundy) good red table wine.

Cépage: The French term whose nearest English equivalent is 'vine sort' (variety of grape). The French maxim *Le cépage fait le vin* only partly tells the story. Soil, climate and cellar-treatment are equally important, or almost so.

Cephalonia: A Greek island long known for its red wine.

Cercié: French (Burgundy) wine centre.

Cerdon Rosé: French pink table wine (Bresse).

Ceres: South African (Cape Province) red and white wines.

Ceret: The Roman name for Jerez (q.v.).

Cerigo: One of the many Greek islands producing wine.

Cérons: White Bordeaux sweetish table wine of sauternes character.

Cérons: French (Graves) white and red wines.

Certan: French (Pomerol) red wine.

Certosa: Italian ecclesiastical liqueur said to be named after a Carthusian monastery near Pavia.

Cervione: French (Corsican) table wines.

Cestas: French (Graves) red wine.

Chabanneau: Old-established brand of cognac (q.v.).

Chabiots: French (Côte-d'Or) wine.

Chablais, Le: Swiss wine-producing area.

Chablis: Celebrated French (Burgundian) white wine which takes its name from the small town of the Yonne Département around which the vineyards cluster. The wine is so highly esteemed that the name is widely misused outside France. It is ironical that although the name is rigidly controlled by law within France, so that only wine made in a defined place in a defined way from defined grapes may be called chablis, in the U.S., Australia and elsewhere any dry white wine, good, bad or indifferent, may bear the title at the whim of the maker or merchant.

Under the French law of 1938 only the wine from seven vineyards is allowed to be labelled 'Chablis Grand Cru' (q.v.). 'Chablis Premier Cru' followed by the name of the vineyard may be applied to the wine of Mont-de-Milieu, Montée de Tonnerre, Chapelot, Vaulorent, Côte-de-Fontenay, Fourchaume, Vaillon, Chatain, Sèchet, Montmain, Les Forêts, Butteaux, Mélinots, Beugnon, Les Lys, Côte de Léchet, Beauroy, Troëme, Vosgros, La Chapelle-Vaupelteigne, Villy, Lignorelles, Maligny, Ligny-le-Chatel, Fléys, Béru, Viviers, Chemilly-sur-Serein and Rameau.

All wine entitled to the name chablis must be made from pinot chardonnay grapes. (See Chardonnay.) Wine not from the above-mentioned vineyards may only bear the simple name chablis, followed if desired by the name of the vineyard.

As the total area of land occupied by the vineyards legally entitled to the name chablis is less than 3,000 acres there is obviously only a comparatively small output of wine. One may suspect that even in France and despite the law, much more wine bears the label than comes from the hallowed region.

True chablis has a faint greenish glint and a so-called flinty taste, very characteristic. It is the gourmet's wine of choice to accompany oysters and delicate fish but actually it is good with all food.

Chablis Grand Cru: This is the highest appellation applicable to chablis wine and by French law (1938) can be used, followed by the name of the vineyard, only by seven growths: Blanchots, Les Clos, Les Preuses, Valmur, Vaudésir, Bougros and Grenouilles. The wine must be made exclusively from the pinot chardonnay grape.

Chabrol: French residue of soup. The reported custom in the Dordogne is to pour a little red wine into the last few mouthfuls and drink the mixture from the plate. Rational!

Chacé: French (Anjou) pink wine.

Chacoli: Spanish white wine widely made for production of the best brandy. The wine is poor, thin acid stuff, the brandy excellent. The same applies to cognac (q.v.).

Chaffots: French burgundy red table wine.

Chagny: French (Côte-d'Or) white table wines.

Chai: French term for a building used for storing bulk wine. Hardly to be classed as a cellar.

Chainette: French (Auxerre) red wine.

Chaintré: French (Burgundy) white wine. Also the name of a wine of Saumur.

Chalambar: Australian (Victorian) red table wine from Great Western.

Chalice: Eucharistic wine-cup.

Chalkis: Greek white wine district.

Challonais, Côte: French (Burgundian) district producing celebrated red and lesser white wines. The finest red is Mercurey (q.v.).

Chalon: See Château Chalon.

Châlon-sur-Saône: Important French wine market in the Lower Burgundy region.

Châlons-sur-Marne: Important centre for champagne in France (Marne).

Chalon Yeast: Celebrated film-forming yeast developed at Chalon, in the Arbois district near Dijon, similar in action to the flor yeast of Spain. See also Flor.

Chalumeaux: French (Burgundy) white wine.

Chalybon: Syrian wines, red and white.

Chalybonium: The highly esteemed wine of ancient Persia mentioned by Athenaeus and said to be made at Damascus. See also Helbon.

Chambertin: A notable French red wine of Burgundy. There is a legend that in the 7th century a peasant owner named Bertin planted the same vines as his neighbours the monks. Thus the Champs de Bertin became Chambertin. This was the favourite wine of Napoleon, who carried along plenty of it on his campaigns, including the disastrous ones. For decades the credulous bought 'Emperor's Chambertin back from Russia'.

Chambéry: French (Savoy) wine centre noted for vermouth but also producing table wines.

Chambolle-Musigny: See Musigny.

Chambourg: French (Touraine) red wine.

Chambray: French (Touraine) red wine.

Chambrer: To place a wine in a room, or *chambre*, where it will reach room temperature, as is usually done with red wines.

Chamery: French (Reims) champagne vineyard.

Champagne: A sparkling wine whose carbon dioxide gas is the natural product of fermentation. The name is derived from a former province of France of the same name, north east of Paris, where the wine was first produced regularly and in quantity. It was supposedly invented about 1670 by Dom Pérignon, the cellarmaster of the Abbey at Hautvillers, but according to Marrison, sparkling wines (cloudy and not very popular) were sold in Italy as Refosco and Nosco Spumante some centuries before the advent of champagne.

Champagne under French law is limited to the wine made from named grapes grown in a defined area of which the principal focus is the city of Reims. There are many other sparkling wines (*vins mousseux*) made in France but all bear their own geographical or other approved names.

Outside France the name champagne has been usurped by every country that makes sparkling wine though some of it, e.g. sparkling burgundy and moselle, is differently though equally incorrectly named: Champagne should mean French champagne. A recent legal decision in London has confirmed this.

In France, clustered around Reims and Épernay, there are 35,000 acres closely planted to the black and white pinot vines (the latter being also called the chardonnay, q.v.). The wine may be made from black or white grapes alone or from a blend of the two, but only wine made from these may be called champagne. Wine made from pinot noir grapes is termed *blanc de noirs* ('white from blacks') and from the pinot chardonnay, *blanc de blancs* ('white from whites'). The black pinots are grown principally north of the Marne and the whites on the chalk south of the Marne around Épernay. The most celebrated wine-growing communes are Verzenay, Mailly, Bouzy, Ay and Ambonnay for blacks and Cramant and Avize for whites.

There are some thousands of vignerons and almost all of these sell their grapes to one or more of about 200 firms in the towns. These firms are called shippers or merchants but they are actually genuine winemakers, not mere middlemen. These shippers actually make the champagne, up to 50 million bottles a year, in their town cellars.

There is little vintage champagne made. Most is a blend of the product of the various districts and like sherry (q.v.) probably the better for it. The process of blending grapes from different vineyards is called *coupage*. It also applies to blending wine.

The grapes must be first-class. If even a small percentage of the fruits are mildewed, the incurable disease, 'the yellows', will appear in the wine. There must be no delay in pressing. This particularly applies to the black grapes, for delay would result in the extraction of the unwanted red colour. The part of the load of grapes first pressed is called the *vin de cuvée* and yields the best champagne. It amounts to about half the possible yield of juice. After this come the second and third pressings, termed *tailles*. These go to make second-quality sparkling wines. The final pressing, called the *rebèche*, is used to make *vin ordinaire* (q.v.).

For details concerning the actual manufacture of champagne see also Sparkling Wines.

Except for *brut* champagne, all is sweetened or dosed. For the rather dry champagne appreciated by the English buyer about 1% of pure cane sugar is added. About five times this or more is used for the Russian and other Slavic tastes. A little fine brandy may also be added. Grand Mousseux champagne has a pressure of 67 to 75 p.s.i., Mousseux 60 to 67 and Crémant under 60.

There is still made, perhaps more as a novelty, a little very dry still wine from champagne grapes, called *champagne nature*.

The following grades and terms of sweetness are recognized:

Nature	No added sweetening
Brut	Up to 1%
Extra dry	Up to 3%
Sec or Dry	Up to 5%
Demi-Sec	Up to 8%
Demi-doux	Up to 10%
Doux	Up to 12%

It is possible to buy in England small flattened sticks to enable idiotic buyers to beat the gas out of champagne. As the sole reason for the high cost of sparkling wine is the great effort and expense involved in imprisoning the gas, human folly could hardly extend further.

Champagne, Fine: A grade of cognac brandy. The name 'fine champagne' is applied to the best cognac, and is restricted by French law to the product of particular vineyards in the Charente. The brandy is called *grande* or *petite* champagne according to the location of the vineyards. The name has no connexion with Champagne wine or region. See also Cognac.

Champagne Cocktail: The recipes are legion but have one phase in common. They all include, and therefore waste, this delicate and expensive wine. The champagne cocktail is the acme of vulgarity, the crude wish to impress by wealth. To the champagne may be added liqueurs, bitters, spirits and fruits. The ultimate degradation is Black Velvet, a blend of champagne and stout. Both are honest beverages in their own right but to mix them — one might as well spread sliced onions on ice-cream.

Champagne Cup: Mixed drink of champagne laced with brandy, diluted with iced water or soda water, with addition of orange and lemon slices, cucumber and whatnot. A wastage of an expensive and luxurious wine.

Champagne de Cru: The general term applied to *blanc de blancs* (q.v.).

Champans: French (Côte-d'Or) red wine.

Champenoise Method: The process of making sparkling wines by fermentation in the bottle. See also Champagne.

Champigny: French (Touraine) red wine.

Champs Canet: French (Côte-d'Or) white wine.

Champs-de-Cour: French (Burgundy) red wine.

Champs Fulliot: French (Côte-d'Or) red wine.

Champs Pimonts: French (Côte-d'Or) red wine.

Champs Traversins: French (Côte-d'Or) red wine.

Chancellor Ale: Strong brew made at Oxford (Queen's) for special occasions.

Channelle: A liqueur of cinnamon flavour.

Chante-Alouette: French (Hermitage, q.v.) white wine.

Chantelle: French (Auvergne) red wine.

Chantpieure: French suction tube for sampling wine. Synonymous with pipette or vellinch (q.v.).

Chanturgues, Les: French red wine from Auvergne (q.v.).

Chapeau: French term for the desirable froth on a beverage, especially beer.

Chapelle, La: French (Hermitage, q.v.) red wine.

Chapelle-Chambertin: French (Côte-d'Or) fine red wine.

Chapelle-de-Guinchay: French (Burgundy) red wine.

Chapître: French (Côte-d'Or) red wine.

Chaponières: French (Côte-d'Or) red wine.

Chapoulié: Established (1884) brand of armagnac (q.v.).

Chaptalization: The process of adding sugar to grape juice (must) at vintage time to 'assist' or 'ameliorate' the resulting wine, i.e. to increase the alcohol content. In many countries the practice is prohibited as adulteration. It is by no means uncommon in Germany and is also permitted, but only under strict conditions, in France. The process takes its name from the French chemist J. A. Chaptal (1756–1832). It is known in Germany as Chaptalisieren and also as Mostzuckerung (q.v.).

At first sight the process seems indefensible and it always produces a sub-standard wine but it is useless to sidestep the fact that in years of wet, cold vintage it may be impossible in Burgundy and the Rhineland to make an acceptable wine without sugaring.

Countries such as California, South Africa and Australia never need to add sugar to musts but this is a matter of warm climate and no ground for boasting.

Chardonnay: A fine grape also known as white pinot, pinot chardonnay and, in the Chablis district, as beaunois. It is used for the production of champagne (q.v.), for white burgundies and for some of the white wines of Alsace.

Charentay: French (Burgundy) red table wines.

Charente: A descriptive term for French brandy less known than, but identical with, cognac and subject to the same legal limitation.

Charlemagne: French (Côte-d'Or) red wine.

Charles: Cocktail of brandy, sweet vermouth, bitters.

Charmat, Chaussepied or Tank Method: Also known as bulk process. The method of making sparkling wine by carrying out the final fermentation in a closed vessel. The process was invented by the French chemist Maumené over a century ago. It is largely used in the U.S. and Australia for inexpensive sparkling wines.

Charmes, Aux: French (Côte-d'Or) red wine.

Charmes, Les: French fine red wine from Chambolle-Musigny (q.v.).

Charmes Dessous: French (Côte-d'Or) white wine.

Charmots: French (Côte-d'Or) red wine.

Charneco: A wine, apparently sweet, well known in Elizabethan times. The name is said to be derived from the village of Charneca, near Lisbon. It is mentioned in Shakespeare.

Charnières: French (Côte-d'Or) red wine.

Charnu: Another of those peculiar and not very useful French terms applied to wine. It means fleshy or pulpy. How this applies to wine is difficult to see, but perhaps it means something precise to a French tasting committee.

Charpignat: French (Savoy) white wine.

Charring: Application of flame to the interior of a spirit cask to produce a charred surface. This is an integral and legally obligatory part of the ageing of certain types of American whiskey but the origin was accidental. Middle-west farmers used to distil their own spirit from their own grain. The only oak casks available were those in which they had received salt fish from the East Coast. They charred the interiors to remove the fishy odour. The whiskey thus stored dissolved out colour and acquired a characteristic flavour now accepted as normal for American whiskey other than corn.

Charrington: The Anchor Brewery, estab. 1757 and still operating, is part of the large English company, Charrington & Co. Ltd.

Chartreuse: Celebrated, widely imitated and expensive liqueur first made by the Carthusian monks at their monastery in France at Voiron near Grenoble. On their expulsion in 1793 they carefully took away their formula. They resumed production when they returned in 1816 but were again expelled in 1903 and then set up production in Spain at Tarragona, making, of course, the genuine liqueur from the original recipe. The trade-mark had been confiscated and the French government sold this and the remaining stocks of liqueur to a firm which then commenced to exploit an imitation under the original trade-mark. In 1938 the monks returned to Grenoble and resumed manufacture of their liqueur under the original formula at their original distillery. Production is still carried on also at Tarragona.

There are two types of genuine 'Liqueur des Pères Chartreux', green and yellow, the former being stronger in alcohol. It is said that they should properly be drunk mixed. Both types are said to be made from over 100 herbs, flowers and other ingredients. Be the facts what they may, it remains true that no satisfactory imitation for chartreuse has ever been made.

Chartron, Quai des: The place in Bordeaux where the great merchants have their cellars.

Chartrons: French (Médoc) red wine.

Charveyron: French (Bressan) red wine.

Chaser: A long drink (beer) drunk after a short (whisky or rum). The habit is more prevalent in America, Scotland and Ireland than in England. See also Sean O'Farrell and Boilermaker.

Chassagne: French (Côte-d'Or) white wine.

Chassagne-Montrachet: French (Côte-d'Or) commune which produces the best white wine of Burgundy. Amongst the noted vineyards are Grandes Ruchottes, Montrachet, Batards-Montrachet, Boudriotte, Brussonnes, Chassagne, St. Jean, Maltroie, Morgeots. There are also some good red wines.

Chasselas: Useful wine grape, the best known variety being the golden chasselas, in Germany called the Butedel. It is grown in Burgundy and Australia for dry white wines of moderate quality.

Chasse-Spleen: French (Médoc) red wine.

Chassors, Château de: White and red wines from Poitou.

Château: A French word meaning castle, mansion, or estate. Applied to the names of French wines, and used mainly in the Bordeaux region. On the Rhône, it means, simply, estate or vineyard so-and-so. Many châteaux are mere modest villas. See also La Tour.

Château Bottling: The process of bottling French wine on the actual estate where it was made. The term on the label is usually *Mis en bouteille au château*. See also the entry German Wine Labels for equivalent terminology. The custom was supposed to have originated in the Bordeaux at Lafite (q.v.) about 1840 and has always been especially characteristic of the best wine of that region.

The term *mise du Château* is of similar meaning. It must be admitted that although the term is usually a guarantee of origin it is by no means necessarily so of quality. Only a wine snob will deny that many blended wines put up by skilled shippers and merchants are superior to some of the veritable château bottlings. Much 'straight' estate wine is bottled in England to take advantage of the much lower rate of duty. This wine, if bottled abroad, would bear the proud insignia. Once again it is a case of the wine drinker needing to know his way around and to keep an unprejudiced mind.

Château Chalon: This is actually not a château but a small town in the Jura (France) near Arbois. There are a number of vineyards, including L'Étoile, Voiteur and Ménétrue. They make a small quantity of a pale yellow wine, long aged and packed in squat bottles (*clavelins*). The wine is made similarly to flor sherry (q.v.) which it closely resembles. Many of the finest sherry-type wines in Australia, the U.S. and South Africa are produced with flor yeasts originally obtained from Chalon.

Château Chalon is one of the most discussed of French wines. There is so little of it that it is nearly all consumed locally. Some say the grape (savagnin) from which Chalon is made is a tokay (q.v.) brought to the Jura from the Crusades. The wine has extraordinary longevity. There are even pious stories. One, according to S. Chamberlain, is that to drink a bottle of Chalon is like parting with a cherished heirloom.

Château de Bercy: French derisive name for cheap, poor wine, blended in Bercy, suburb of Paris.

Château d'Yquem: See Yquem.

Châteaumeillant: French (Berry) red wine.

Châteauneuf: Many French wine estates bear this name, including Avignon (red and white), Petite Champagne (cognac), Graves (red), Médoc (red) and Gironde (white).

Châteauneuf-de-Chabre: French (Savoy) red wine.

Châteauneuf-de-Gadogne: French (Avignon) red wine.

Châteauneuf-du-Pape: Celebrated French red wine of the Rhône Valley. The vineyards include La Fortia, St. Patrice, Nallys and Nerthe.

Châteauneuf-du-Rhône: French (Rhône) red wines.

Château-Renard: French (Provence) red wines.

Château Wine: One that is produced regularly, year after year, from the same vineyard or estate, and named accordingly. A 'château-bottled wine' is one that has been bottled on the estate by those who produced it.

Chatelet: French (St. Émilion) red wine.

Chatelet-la-Carte: French (St. Émilion) red wine.

Chato: Spanish wine-glass. The name means stubby, hence the short stem.

Chatolle: French (Médoc) red wine.

Chaucer: It is not surprising that the English poet Geoffrey Chaucer (1340–1400) should write so often and so accurately about the wines of his period for most of the Chaucers were vintners or civil servants of the excise. The poet had a wide knowledge of both the wine technology of his day and of the many types and qualities of beverage, spiced, medicated and other wines. However, when he wrote:

> Wel loved he garleek, oynons and eek lekes,
> And for to drinken strong wyn, reed as blood

he fell into the common error, still widespread, that red wine is necessarily 'stronger' than white and dark red more so than light.

Chauché Gris: White grape grown for ordinary wines in southern France. In California it is quite wrongly called grey riesling.

Chauffe-vin: Heat-exchanger used in a cognac pot-still (q.v.).

Chaumées, Les: French (Côte-d'Or) white wines.

Chaume Gaufriot: French red wine of Beaune (q.v.).

Chaumes: French (Côte-d'Or) red wine.

Chavignol: French (Cher) white wine.

Chavignol: French (Sancerre) white and *rosé* wines which Chamberlain grades as two of the outstanding local wines of France.

Cheers or Cheerio: A toast.

Cheese: The heavy wooden ball used in the game of skittles.

Chef de Cave: that important French functionary, the chief of the wine cellar, whose decisions make or mar.

Cheille: French (Touraine) red wine.

Chénas: French (Beaujolais) red wine.

Chenevery: French (Côte-d'Or) red wine.

Chénin Blanc: French white grape especially grown in Anjou. In California wrongly called white pinot.

Chenôve: French (Côte-d'Or) red wine.

Cherry Bounce: An old-fashioned drink that used to be made in Kent by fermenting morello cherries with added sugar. See also Country Wines.

Cherry Brandy: There are two widely dissimilar products bearing this name. One is a true fruit brandy made by distilling fermented cherry juice, with or without some crushed kernels, which contain a glucoside which introduces a minute amount of hydrocyanic or prussic acid into the distillate and provides a characteristic almondy flavour. On the European continent it is known as kirsch (q.v.). The other is often and more correctly known as cherry liqueur and is made partly by distillation and partly by steeping ripe black cherries in sugared brandy.

Cherry Whisky: Liqueur made by steeping cherries in sweetened whisky.

Chesterton: Gilbert Keith Chesterton (1874–1936) would surely have given a vast chuckle and reached for his pen if anybody had been foolish enough in his presence to express doubt of the value of wine, ale and spirits. The jollity of sane drinking never had a doughtier singer. Consider:

> Before the Roman came to Rye or out to Severn strode,
> The rolling English drunkard made the rolling English road.
>
> *The Rolling English Road*

G

> The righteous minds of innkeepers
> Induce them now and then
> To crack a bottle with a friend
> Or treat unmoneyed men,
>
> But who hath seen the Grocer
> Treat housemaids to his teas
> Or crack a bottle of fish-sauce
> Or stand a man a cheese?
>
> *Song Against Grocers*

And Noah he often said to his wife when he sat down to dine,
'I don't care where the water goes if it doesn't get into the wine'.

Wine and Water

Cheval Blanc, Château: One of the best growths in the St. Émilion district, about 25 miles due east of Bordeaux.

Chevalier: French (Graves) white and red wines.

Chevalier-Montrachet: French (Côte-d'Or) fine white wine.

Chevelu: French (Savoy) white wine.

Chevret, En: French (Côte-d'Or) red wines.

Chi: Millet beer made by the Lepchas of NE. India.

Chian: Greek wine from the island of Chios. This has been famed for literally thousands of years but, like most Greek table wine, is at best mediocre. The chief vineyards of the island are Arvisio, Merta and Mista.

Chianti: Perhaps the Italian wine best known outside Italy. Undoubtedly one of the chief reasons for its popularity is the quaint woven-straw covered bottle (flask or *fiasco*) in which the wine is packed.

The name *chianti* is not legally controlled and as a result the wine is extremely variable but it is beyond doubt that a fine chianti is fine indeed. Contrary to general knowledge there is some white chianti made but this is little known beyond the country.

A group of the landowners making the best chianti formed an association in 1924 and any wine bottled under their registered trade-mark, a black rooster on a golden ground, is likely to be good. This wine is mainly grown on an area of under 200,000 acres between Florence and Siena on the slopes of the Chianti Hills. (Chianti Ferrese.)

In deference to export taste, chianti today is being made less astringent. It may also be slightly *pétillant* (q.v.).

One thing is sure. Chianti remains a romantic wine and both natives and foreigners will continue to regard it as one of the jewels of Tuscany.

Chiaretto or Chiarello: Italian diminutive for *chiaro*. Both words are applied lovingly to pale-tinted wines such as the *vino rosato* of Verona and Lake Garda.

Chica: South American beverage term of numerous meanings. In Argentina it means the ordinary red wine (consumo, q.v.) of the Mendoza district. In Peru and Bolivia it is applied to a native beer of mealie (q.v.) type made from maize to which molasses may be added. A characteristic feature of Peruvian chica is that the boiled maize is 'converted' (q.v.) by adding a little moco or masticated corn, thus resembling the Polynesian kava (q.v.). Chica in Central America refers to a wide variety of alcoholic beverages. The name is also stated to be used in Chile for fermented pineapple juice.

Chichée: French (Yonne) white wine of chablis type.

Chiclana: Spanish wine of Manzanilla (q.v.) type.

Chig-ge: Inner-Mongolian spirit made by the village distillation of fermented milk (see Koumiss) of cow, ewe or mare. Inner-Mongolian hospitality requires chig-ge to be served at the start and close of a visit.

Chignin: French (Savoy) white wine.

Chigny: French (Marne) wine commune.

Chilar: Sherry-type grape of Lake Sevan (q.v.) said to be indigenous.

Chile: Chile produces 80 million gallons of wine annually, almost as much as Greece, and ranks fourteenth in the wine world. Despite natural handicaps much of the wine is of excellent quality and there is a valuable export market. The chief wine-growing areas are near Valparaiso, Santiago and Talcahuano. Some of the better-known estates are Undurraga, Linderos, Concha y Toro and Santa Rita. By common consent Chile produces the finest wine of all the South American countries.

Chilènes: French (Côte-d'Or) red wine.

Chill Haze: The cloud produced in certain beers on cooling, due to the precipitation of proteins and other colloids. See also Chill-Proof and Non-Deposit Beer.

Chilling: The process of reducing the temperature of beverages to nearly zero (0° C. or 32° F.). The Americans are largely responsible for the present craze of drinks 'on the rocks', i.e. mixed with ice, but the habit is more than 2,000 years old. An Athenian banquet included vases of wine packed with ice. Many drinks, especially the delicate white beverage wines, are chilled too drastically, so that the taste is masked. Common wine, red or white, diluted half with iced water, makes an excellent quencher. To drop ice into beer is unjustly thought barbaric.

Chilling Rooms: Where beer is stored and chilled at the bottling depot prior to filtration, carbonation and filling.

Chiltern: Australian (Victorian) wine centre.

Chime: Also Chimb and Chine. The circular rim at the head of a cask, formed by the ends of the staves where they join the head, also the bevel itself.

Chin-Chin: An English drinking salutation of Edwardian times that has now almost disappeared from the London scene but is still heard from ageing imbibers in the provinces and outposts. The substitution of 'mud in your eye' is hardly an advance. Curiously enough, 'chin-chin' has crossed the Channel and apparently become acclimatized in France. See also Drinking Salutations.

Chinese Drinking: 'The Chinese does not drink to get drunk. He drinks so that the other man will get drunk.' (Milton Barnett, *The Chinese in New York*.)

Chinon: A townlet in France near Tours, noted as the birthplace of that mighty drinker Rabelais, who was said to be particularly fond of its wine, a light, fragrant dry red still made and esteemed.

Chios: Another of the many Greek islands where wine has been made and known for thousands of years. Sales are made on sentiment rather than merit.

Chiroubles: French (Beaujolais) wine commune.

Chitting: The appearance of the first rootlets while the barley is growing during the initial stage of the malting process.

Chivas: Old-established Scotch whisky distillers outside the D.C.L. combine.

Chive: A tool used by the cooper (q.v.) to plane a level bed in the ends of the cask staves into which a groove is cut for the head.

Choicheux, Les: French (Côte-d'Or) red wine.

Choker: Cocktail of whisky, absinthe and bitters.

Chopin: A liquid measure, usually of pewter. Authorities disagree on its exact capacity, but it was apparently between a pint and a quart.

Chorey: French (Côte-d'Or) red wine.

Chota Peg: Anglo-Indian for small drink, usually a half-sized glass of whisky and soda. See also Peg.

Chouchen: Celtic term for mead (q.v.).

Chouilly: French (Marne) white wine for champagne (q.v.).

Christian Brothers: An esteemed Californian wine.

Christmas Tree: Cocktail apparently identical with Old Fashioned (q.v.).

Chung: Tibetan beer made from grim, a species of barley that ripens at high altitudes.

Church Ales: The excellent old English custom of congregational feasting, often with the object of raising funds for building. See also Clerk Ale and Sygate. The Whitsun feasts of some churches survive without, alas, the ale.

Chusclan: French (Tavel) *rosé* wine.

Ciborium: Drinking-vessel, used in lieu of a pyx (q.v.) in Catholic churches.

Cider: Also Cyder. Beverage made from the juice of apples. If fermented and therefore alcoholic, the term hard cider is frequently used. Soft cider means plain apple juice.

The sugar content of apples is far below that of ripe grapes suitable for wine-making and the natural alcoholic content of cider never reaches that of normal wine. It may contain as little as 3% by volume of alcohol and unless fortified with sugar before fermentation the upper limit of alcohol is rarely above 8%. In England and Europe a certain amount of sparkling cider is made, some of it by the true champagne process. This may be a beverage of high quality, indeed a humble competitor of champagne itself. However, the bulk of cider is 'still'. Much of it is unfortunately sold preserved by the addition of germicidal chemicals but if manufacture is efficient this preservation is not necessary in bottled cider. Bulk cider (draught) is available in some English and northern French inns. Some of it is delectable.

Cider is obviously a venerable beverage. It is particularly valuable in cold climates for the apple will flourish under far more rigorous conditions than the vine. The antiquity of cider is shown by the derivation of the name. In English it comes from the ME. and OF. *sidre* and the modern French form is *cidre*. This comes in turn from the Latin *sicera* (strong drink) through the Greek *sikera* which itself was a loan word from the Hebrew *shēkār*. The term 'cider' has actually been used in earlier times in English as a synonym for strong drink, despite the low alcoholic content. England produces some of the best cider in the world, both still and sparkling. There is also fine cider in Normandy and Brittany (N. France). Cider is also a popular drink in northern Spain. It has been made for four centuries in the U.S.A., spreading from the east coast to the State of Washington. Much American cider is of excellent quality but for some obscure reason it has never become an esteemed commercial product.

Apple brandy is the spirit distilled from hard cider. Little, if any, is made in the U.K. but it is a prized product of Normandy under the general name calvados (q.v.). In the U.S. the corresponding spirit is termed applejack (q.v.).

Any ripe apples can yield cider of a sort but to produce a beverage of high quality a blending of apples is essential to give the requisite sugar, acid, tannin and other constituents.

Cider is a beverage of unique character. With the assistance of modern technology the consumption will doubtless increase.

For French legal requirements of cider, see Cidre, also Perry.

Cider, Crab: See Crab Cider.

Cider, English Makers: Although there are 30 concerns listed as commercial cider manufacturers in the U.K., most of these are small localized establishments. The bulk of the commercial cider trade is in the hands of five firms — Bulmer, Whiteways, Coates, Gaymer and Taunton, the first-named actually producing more than half the total. There are, in addition, a large number of farmers who make cider as a side-line. Some of these farm products are excellent and have high local reputations.

Ciderand: Obsolete and rather arch name of a drink containing 'cider and other ingredients'. Fielding mentions this and perhaps invented the word.

Ciderjack: Syn. for 'applejack' (q.v.).

Ciderkin: Weak and inferior cider made by steeping pomace from cider-making.

Cider Royal: Strong cider sweetened with honey.

Cidre: French name for cider, and legally applicable in France only to a beverage containing, *inter alia*, a minimum of 3·5% alcohol by volume. A weaker beverage must be termed *petit cidre*. Though cidre may legally be made by the addition of water, the term *cidre pur jus* is reserved for cider made without dilution.

Cillabub: See Syllabub.

Cilli: Yugoslavian red wine.

Cima Corgo: The upper part of the district of the Douro Valley in Portugal that produces port wine (q.v.). See also Baixo Corgo. The Cima is stated to produce less but better wine.

Cinq-Mars: French (Touraine) red wine.

Cinque Terre: Lit. 'five estates', the name of the celebrated Italian white table and dessert wines made on the Italian Riviera between Spezzia and Levanto.

Cinsaut: Dark grape used for sweet dessert wine.

Cirò: Wine from Calabria (q.v.). Some 2,000 years ago it was praised by Pliny.

Cissac: French (Médoc) red wine.

Citizens of the Fork: The Australian (Melbourne) group of gastronomes and wine-lovers whose tongues are not too deeply in their cheeks at their dinners.

Citran: French (Médoc) red wine.

Citrongenever: Dutch lemon gin (q.v.).

Città di S. Angelo: Italian (Abruzzi) wine region.

Civita Lavinia: Italian (Latium) white wine.

Clairac: French (Garonne) sweet white wine.

Clairboise: French liqueur of raspberry flavour.

Clairet: Light and pale red wine from the Bordeaux, practically a *rosé* (q.v.).

Clairette: A white sparkling wine of the south of France.

Clairette de Die: French (Vaucluse) *pétillant* (q.v.) red wine.

Clairette de Gaillac: French (Albi) *rosé* sparkling wine.

Clarac: Established (1875) brand of armagnac (q.v.).

Clare: Australian (S.A.) wine centre.

Clarence, Duke of: He cannot escape mention here for was he not reputed to have been drowned in a butt (q.v.) of malmsey (q.v.)?

Claret: A light, clear, red wine. (Derived from OF. The modern French is *clairet*, with similar meaning.) The word 'claret' has no actual geographical significance, and is not used in France for the wines of any district in particular. In England, however, for many centuries, the word has been applied specifically to the red wines of Bordeaux, and therefore should be qualified when used to designate similar wines from any other part of the world. See also Bordeaux.

Claret Cup: Mixed drink of limitless variability. The basic recipe is red wine, lemonade, mint leaves, lemon slices, all well chilled.

Clarette: Spanish mongrelization of the name claret to describe some of their red wines.

Clarke: French (Médoc) red wine.

Clarke-Merle-Blanc: French (Médoc) white wine.

Claro de Lias: Spanish term for the cheap wine decanted from lees (q.v.).

Clarre, Clarree or Claré: A wine well known in Chaucer's time and frequently mentioned. It has been suggested that clarree, etc., was a Gascon wine shipped from Clairette and that its popularity eventually led to the whole of the red wine of Bordeaux region becoming known as claret (q.v.). The name was also applied to a wine flavoured with honey and spices and strained until clear. Piment (q.v.) seems to have been identical.

Clary: French (Tavel) *vin rosé* (q.v.).

Classic: Cocktail of brandy, curaçao, almond liqueur and lemon juice.

Claudel, Paul: The author of the wise remark 'A cocktail is to a glass of wine as rape is to love'. Cocktails are usually drunk to excess because they are taken on an empty stomach and are too large and strong. It has been observed correctly by the Italian-American research physician, Giorgio Lolli, that a modern dry martini is only an exotic name for iced straight gin. Indeed, a single large dry martini on an empty stomach can make drunk a man or woman of average weight. The moral is clear: supply the guests of the cocktail hour with plenty of appetizing food. See also Cocktail.

Clavelin: The squat bottle of about four-fifths ordinary size used for Château-Chalon (q.v.).

Clavoillon: French (Côte-d'Or) red wine.

Clément: Old-established brand of cognac (q.v.).

Clerc-Milon-Mondon: French (Médoc) red wine.

Clerk Ale: The old Anglican feasts, with copious ale, for the benefit of the parson. See also Church Ales and Sygate.

Clessé: French (Burgundy) white wine.

Clevner: Alternative name for the Traminer grape, used in Baden.

Clicquot (Veuve Clicquot-Ponsardin): Old-established (1777) champagne.

Climat: The term applied to a vineyard in Burgundy. It indicates the importance of soil, altitude, position, drainage and reflection of the sun's rays. The term *cru* is used elsewhere in France with about the same meaning.

Climens, Ch.: Celebrated French (Barsac) sauternes wine (q.v.).

Clinet: French (Pomerol) red wine.

Clinton: An American wine, from the grape of that name.

Clocher: French (Médoc) red wine.

Clos: One of the notable wines of Chablis, France. The word *clos* otherwise means an enclosed, cultivated area, especially a vineyard, and is used before the names of many of the fine wines of Burgundy, e.g. Clos de Tart, Clos de Vougeot.

Clos Arlots: French (Côte-d'Or) red wine.

Clos Blanc: French (Côte-d'Or) red wine.

Clos de Bèze: Fine French (Burgundy) red wine.

Clos de Tart: Fine French (Côte-d'Or) red wine.

Clos de Vougeot: Fine French (Côte-d'Or) red wine.

Clos de la Mousse: French (Côte-d'Or) red wine.

Clos de la Roche: French (Côte-d'Or) red wine.

Clos des Fourches: French (Côte-d'Or) red wine.

Clos des Lambreys: French (Côte-d'Or) red wine.

Clos-des-Mouches: French (Burgundy) red wine.

Clos des Ormes: French (Côte-d'Or) red wine.

Clos des Papes: One of the Châteauneuf (q.v.) wines.

Clos du Moulin: French (Alsatian) white wine.

Clos du Roi: French (Aloxe-Corton, Côte-d'Or) red wine.

Clos du Roi: French fine red wine of Beaune (q.v.).

Closerie, La: French (Médoc) red wine.

Clos Fourtet: French (St. Émilion) red wine.

Clos Gauthey: French (Côte-d'Or) red wine.

Clos, Le: French (Chablis) white wine.

Closing Time: A sad occasion.

Closiot: French (Barsac) sweet white wine (sauternes).

Clos Micot: French (Côte-d'Or) red wine.

Clos Saint-Denis: French (Côte-d'Or) red wine.

Clos Saint-Jean: French (Côte-d'Or) red wine.

Clos Saint Odile: French (Alsatian) white wine.

Closed fermentation: See Fermentation, Closed.

Clot Fallet: Algerian table-wine of good repute.

Clover Club: Cocktail of gin, grenadine, lime and egg white.

Club: Old term for one's share of the cost of a drinking party. Pepys writes in his diary (20 June 1665), 'Our club comes to 34s. a man, nine of us'. In *The Delights of the Bottle or the Compleat Vintner* (1721), appears:

> Next these a sort of sots there are,
> Who crave more wine than they can bear,
> Yet hate, when drunk, to pay or spend
> Their equal Club or Dividend.

Club Soda: American term for mineral water, soda water.

Clüsserath: German (Moselle) wine parish.

Coaching Glass: An 18th-century drinking-vessel which had no feet and could not stand. Drinks in these glasses were brought out to coach travellers and consumed at a draught.

Coaster: A small circular holder or tray for bottles and decanters, originally fitted with small wheels for easier movement ('coasting') on the table.

Cobbler: American long, iced, mixed drink with wine or spirit base, and added fruit.

Cobbold: Old-established (over 200 years) brewery of Ipswich, England.

Coblenz: Centre of the German Moselle wine trade at junction of Rhine and Moselle.

Cochem: German (Lower Moselle) wine parish.

Cochineal: Scarlet colouring matter extracted from a cactus-feeding insect, sometimes used by unscrupulous wine-makers to tint pale wines. Many a *rosé* (q.v.) depends upon this sacrificial insect.

Cochylis: A vicious pest of the vineyard. The grubs of the cochylis moth soon ruin the ripening fruit.

Cock: Old term for spigot (q.v.) and a sign for the availability of beer. Such an inn-sign as Cock and Bottle had nothing to do with poultry.

Cock-a-Doodle Broth: Arch term for brandy and egg.

Cock Ale: A famous 17th-century beverage. There were many recipes but here is one from Smith's *Compleat Housewife* (1736): 'To make Cock Ale, take ten gallons of ale and a large cock, the larger the better. Parboil the cock, flea him and stamp him in a stone mortar until his bones are broken. You must craw and gut him when you flea him. Put him into two quarts of sack and put to it three pounds of raisins of the sun stoned, some blades of mace and a few cloves.

'Put all of these into a canvas bag and a little while before you find the ale has done working, put the ale and bag together into a vessel. In a week or nine days time bottle it up, fill the bottles but just above the necks and leave the same to ripen as other ale.'

Cockburn Smithes & Co.: Old-established (1814) shippers of port (q.v.) and one of the historic firms of the Oporto wine industry. There are still members of both families in the business.

Cocked Hat: Trick beer glass. See also Yard.

Cocktail: Mixed drink of American origin, of spirit (q.v.) base and of widely varying composition.

The drinking of cocktails is usually a function of the late afternoon and is a comparatively modern development. Despite this, the origin of the word is still perplexing. There are many theories, most of them obviously fantastic, and their examination is a pretty exercise in semantics. One of the less preposterous accounts places the invention of the term in New Orleans, where one Pechaud, a pharmacist, was accustomed to entertain parties of Freemasons after their meetings with a drink composed of brandy, bitters and sugar. He served his drinks in double-ended eggcups, called in French *coquetiers*. This word the Americans pronounced 'cocktay', hence 'cocktail'.

Amongst the crazier theories, one is the solemn yarn that a Mexican Indian maiden named Xochtil served a mixed drink to an American general.

However, on the sound principle that the simplest explanation is the most likely, one may prefer to believe that such a drink is intended to 'cock the tail' (cf. 'buck up', 'horsey keep your tail up', 'high-tail', etc.). It should be remembered that most cocktails are strong in alcohol, taken on an empty stomach and in gay surroundings, the ideal combination for speedy action.

As to the drinks themselves, one book of recipes lists over sixteen hundred absolutely separate, distinct and named ones while another is content with a modest seven hundred. What is certain is that the vast majority of these recipes are mere curiosities which no bartender would know how to mix or perhaps even recognize by name. An official of the New York Bartenders' Union states that there are less than fifty cocktails served with regularity in the U.S. and probably less than half that number are common in the British Commonwealth.

Any cocktail is composed basically of a shot of spirits to which is added one or more highly-flavoured ingredients (alcoholic or otherwise), the whole being thoroughly chilled. The flavourings may consist of vermouths, wines, liqueurs, fruits, vegetables (onions, cucumber, etc.), herbs, spices, egg, milk and indeed almost anything that strikes the fancy.

Throughout this book are listed alphabetically some of the commoner cocktails served in the English-speaking communities, together with an outline of their recipes. As to these compositions, a warning is necessary. There is *no* authentic cocktail recipe. From a dozen books one may gather a dozen different, or at least differing, recipes for the same named drink. Let these recipes generate no wrath. Somebody mixes them as indicated!

Even if it were desirable or useful, it would be impossible to make a complete printed list of mixed drinks. It is safe to say that there are fresh inventions every day. The problem is not simplified by the fact that not infrequently the same name is used for widely-differing concoctions and the same mixture may appear under several names. For example, a mixture of gin, dry vermouth and sweet vermouth appears to have more names than a prince.

As this is a book of bald fact rather than of advocacy, the writer says no more on the subject of mixed drinks than his belief that the aesthetics of mixing would not suffer from the loss of 99% of these pompous 'formulae'. See also Claudel, Paul.

Cocktail Hour: The American invention of pre-dinner drinking, usually from about 5.30 to 6.30. See also Claudel, Paul.

Coenen: German (Saar) wine parish.

Coffee: Cocktail of brandy, orange liqueur, black coffee.

Coffee Liqueur: A type whose flavour is made by extracting coffee beans.

Coffey, Aeneas: The Irish distiller who invented the patent still (q.v.) in 1830, which still bears his name.

Coffey Still: See Patent Still.

Cognac: The small French city in the middle of Charente and Charente Maritime which is the centre of the celebrated brandy-distilling industry. The spirit called cognac is pure grape brandy of superlative quality. With the possible exception of armagnac (q.v.), cognac is believed to be without equal in the world. It is curious that although geographical names such as chablis, burgundy, port and tokay are allowed to be used indiscriminately, no brandy-producing country permits misuse of the hallowed name cognac, which justly remains a place-name exclusively the property of France. In France itself the use of the name is severely controlled by law. The wine must be made from the *folle blanche* grape or seven other specified varieties. The fermentation must be in accord with defined custom and the wine must be made into brandy in a pot-still, operated in a carefully-defined manner.

The brandy is aged for long periods in casks made from oak from the adjoining forest of Limousin.

Only grapes grown in a defined geographical area of the Cognac district are entitled to be made into cognac but this area is itself divided by law into sub-districts. These are conventionally (and perhaps often too rigidly) linked with quality. Seven grades are distinguished. Champagne (which has nothing to do with Reims or sparkling wine) is itself divided into Grande Champagne and Petite Champagne. Next is the Borderies, then Fins Bois, Bons Bois and Bois Ordinaires. A blend of Grande and Petite Champagne is the top rung of cognac and is sold as Fine Champagne.

The cognac industry is a complex one of selecting, maturing and blending. Some of the firms are centuries old. As the names testify, there has been English and Irish blood in the industry even before the Napoleonic era. Of course a cognac bearing that simple, unadorned name may have a more delectable bouquet than a top-rung 'fine champagne'.

Considering its technology, cognac is not expensive. It may be held for twenty years or more for maturation and the loss of alcohol in the process may exceed 24%. Cognac (with armagnac) is an essence of French art and civilization, the ultimate in the alcoholic pleasure of the palate (i.e. nose). See also Brandy.

Cogno: Italian (Florence) wine measure of about 100 gallons.

Cointreau: A proprietary liqueur of orange flavour.

Coirm: The early Irish (Gaelic) name for beer.

Collage: French for fining (q.v.).

Collar: The frothing-head on a glass of draught beer between the top of the beer and the rim of the glass. Also called suds.

Collares: Portuguese beverage-wine, mostly red.

Colle d'Elsa: Italian (Tuscany) chianti (q.v.) district.

Colline: Italian (Apulian) white wine.

Collins: Generic name for an American mixed, cold, long drink of a sweetened spirit, with lemon juice and much cracked ice. Tom or John Collins uses gin. A rum, whisky, bourbon or other Collins is of obvious composition. A John Collins closely resembles a gin sling. The origin of the name is said to be that of John Collins, a waiter at Limmer's Hotel in N.Y. who was celebrated for his gin slings. A Tom Collins may have been made with old tom gin (q.v.).

Colmar: French (Alsatian) wine market.

Cologny: Swiss (Geneva) white wine.

Colombard: French (Cognac) white grape. In California grown for mediocre and so-called 'chablis'.

Colombier-Monpelou: French (Médoc) red wine.

Colonel: American vernacular for a whiskey salesman. The word suggests an association with impoverished Southerners.

Colonie: French (Margaux) red wine.

Color: Name of the Spanish evaporated, treacly must (q.v.) used in compounding Malaga wine (q.v.) and tinting brown sherry (q.v.). See also Arrope.

Color de Macetilla: Sweetening used for sherry consisting of one-third fresh must (q.v.) and two-thirds concentrated must.

Columbia: Cocktail of rum, raspberry syrup and lemon juice.

Columbia Spirit: American syn. for 'methyl alcohol' (q.v.).

Columella: Roman writer of 1st century who gives information on the current viticultural and wine-making practices.

Comb: The American barman's term for the instrument used to remove excess foam or head from a glass of beer.

Combes: French (Côte-d'Or) red wine.

Combettes, Les: French (Côte-d'Or) white wine.

Comblanchien: French (Côte-d'Or) red wine.

Come: French (Médoc) red wine.

Comète, Vin de la: French for 'comet wine', especially that made in the year of Halley's Comet. Such wine was supposed to be of special excellence but there is no real basis for the belief.

Comète-Labarde: French (Médoc) red wine.

Comet Wine: See Comète.

Comings: See Culms.

Commanderia: Dessert wine from the island of Cyprus.

Commanderie: French (Médoc) red wine.

Commissar: Mixture of vodka and orange liqueur.

Commissatio: Roman drinking bout, borrowed from the Greek *symposium* (q.v.).

Common Clear Rum: Old term for rum, especially Jamaican, of mild flavour.

Commugny: Swiss wine-producing area.

Commune: The French name for a small parish dominated by a village or town. Sometimes the name of the commune is changed by adopting the title of one of its celebrated vineyards. Thus the Burgundian communes of Vosne-Romanée and Aloxe-Corton were originally merely Vosne and Aloxe. Similarly with Gevrey-Chambertin and Puligny-Montrachet.

Como: Greek (Syra) red dessert wine.

Comporte: The tub containing about 150 lb. used in France to transport the ripe grapes from the vineyard.

Concha y Toro: Chilean wine estate of quality.

Concia: The name for the spirit used to fortify marsala (q.v.).

Concongella: Wine hamlet in western Victoria.

Concord: A famous American grape, used both for table purposes and wine-making.

Condom: The town in Gers (France) which is the centre for the production of the celebrated armagnac (q.v.) brandy.

Condrieu: White table wine from the Rhône Valley.

Cone: See Hops.

Conegliano: Italian wine region north of Venice. Verdiso and Prosecco are amongst the principal red wines. Also the name of a grape.

Congelation: The process of concentrating the alcoholic content of a beverage by freezing. Without entering into the intricacies of physical chemistry, it was long ago discovered that comparatively pure water could be obtained from a solution by freezing and collecting the first crop of crystals. These are ice and by removing and melting, nearly pure water results. This has saved many a life in arctic regions and affords a means of preparing fairly pure water from the sea. Obviously the reverse process is possible.

    If, for example, wine or cider is chilled until ice crystals appear and these are removed, the remaining liquid is correspondingly richer in alcohol. Applejack (q.v.) was previously prepared in this fashion from hard cider. It is somewhat surprising that the process has not been investigated more fully in modern times for the production of variants of brandy and whisky. Congelation, as distinct from distillation, retains all the constituents of the original liquor except the water.

Congenerics: The technical term applied to the substances produced in small amount in addition to ethyl alcohol (q.v.) during the process of

fermentation, distillation or maturation. These congenerics are of highly
varied chemical nature and include glycerol and other polyhydric
alcohols, homologues of ethyl alcohol, ketones, aldehydes, esters, acids
and, indeed, representatives of many organic groups. Some congenerics
are probably harmful, some undesirable at least in flavour. But others,
again, are highly important for they give to a particular beverage its
special and desirable character.

Congius: Roman liquid measure, about ¾ gallon.

Conoid: A cask for the containment of liquids is known to mathematicians as
a double conoid, derived of course from the shape of a beheaded cone at
each end. The cask is one of the most remarkable vessels the ingenuity of
man has ever evolved. See also Cask.

Conseillante, La: Fine red wine from Pomerol, Bordeaux.

Constance, Lake: Seat of the Swiss wines called Seeweine.

Constant-Bages-Monpelou: French (Médoc) red wine.

Constantia: The wine generally recognized by this name is a sweet, red,
fortified growth produced in a vineyard near Cape Town, the property of
the government and first planted in the 16th century by the Dutch
settler Simon van der Stel. About a hundred and fifty years later the
wine gained quite a marked popularity in England and Europe. There
are other wines made at Constantia by lessees of vineyards from the
government. The general quality of the Constantia wines has been well
maintained and has markedly contributed to the good repute of South
African wines in general.

Constantia Berg: South African muscatel wine grown at Groot Constantia.

Consumo: The Portuguese name for the ordinary wine copiously drunk with
food by the masses. It is the equivalent of the French *vin ordinaire*, undistinguished but wholesome and very cheap. Undoubtedly one reason
which prevents countries such as the U.S. and Australia from becoming
wine-drinkers is the lack of *vin ordinaire*.

Conthey: Swiss (Valais) white wine.

Contracting Cup: An Elizabethan drinking-vessel from which drank
couples unable to make a long journey to a church to marry. The ceremony was considered binding by the contracting parties.

Convert: The term used in brewing to denote the transformation of starch
into sugar, usually by the agency of an enzyme (q.v.). Also called
saccharification (q.v.).

Cooler: As the name implies, a mixed drink served in a large glass with
much cracked ice and soda.

Coombes: See Culms.

Coonawarra: Australian red table wine of merit produced on the estate of
that name, far distant from other wine regions, in the south-east of South
Australia. This is an admirable example of legitimate nomenclature and
fine winemanship.

Cooper: Old-established Adelaide brewery still producing beer of high alcoholic strength by final fermentation in the bottle.

Cooper: A craftsman who makes and repairs casks; also, in England, a merchant who is engaged in the sampling, bottling, and retailing of wine. The drink known as a 'cooper' is a mixture of stout and porter. The word is also used as a verb, meaning to repair, fill, or in other ways attend to casks. See also Cask.

Cooperage: The art of making and repairing casks (coopering), of which there are three main branches — 'wet' or 'tight' cooperage for the highly skilled work of making casks for liquids, 'dry' cooperage for inferior vessels to hold dry goods, and 'white' cooperage for the making of straight-sided pails and tubs. The word 'cooperage', or 'coopery', is applied also to the place where the work is carried out, and the fee charged for the services of a cooper is also known as 'cooperage'. See also Cask.

Co-operative Wineries: Wine-making establishments owned jointly by grape-growers of the same district. Usually these establishments are the subject of more-or-less amiable contempt by the connoisseur and in many cases this is fair enough. However, in Australia, South Africa, Algiers and, of course, the communist countries, some of the cooperatives are making really excellent wines.

Coper or Cooper: A small ship that acts as a floating grog shop for the supply of liquor and a few other dutiable commodities to fishing vessels in the North Sea. The traffic, unfortunately known as 'cooperage' (although usually pronounced 'coperage'), has caused great concern to the governments of Britain and other nations interested in the North Sea fisheries.

Copper: Brewing-vessel in which the wort (q.v.) is boiled with the hops (q.v.). Such vessels were previously almost invariably of copper or lined with that metal but there is a tendency to replace with stainless-steel or other non-corroding material, though the name 'copper' is retained.

Copper-sidesman: The brewery hand who operates the copper.

Cop's Bottle: U.S. slang term for the worst whiskey in the saloon — offered to policeman gratuitously or demanded as of right.

Copus: Old beverage made of hot beer, wine and spice.

Corbières: French (Aude) red and white table wines.

Corbin-et-Jean-Faure: French (Graves) red wine.

Corbin-Michotte: French (Graves) red wine.

Cordial: Syn. for 'liqueur' (q.v.) in the field of alcoholic beverages.

Cordial Médoc: French liqueur of mild chocolate flavour made at Bordeaux but with no connection with the celebrated wine district of Médoc.

Corgo: Portuguese wine-growing valley of Alto Douro, important region for port wine (q.v.).

Corinth: Name widely applied to Greek wines, not necessarily grown in that area.

Corio: Chief centre of Australian whisky industry, near Geelong, Victoria. Before *Phylloxera* (q.v.) a noted wine region.

Cork: Noted Irish (Cork) whiskey, founded *c.* 1850.

Cork: Indispensable companion of the bottle. A stopper so named because of the material from which it is made, the outer layer of the bark of an evergreen oak (*Quercus suber*), a tree which may have a yielding life of 150 years. It was originally limited to Portugal and Spain but cultivation has now extended to Italy, Algiers and elsewhere. The first stripping of the cork is made when the trees are 15 to 20 years old, this first yield being useless for bottle stoppers. Thereafter the trees are stripped at intervals of about 8 years. In northern Russia cork is obtained from the birch tree.

Corks are cut by machinery, tapered for fortified wines, spirits and the like, and straight (cylindrical) for light wines.

Until cork came into use, probably in the late 15th or early 16th century, the storage of wine in small volume was virtually impossible, as the only method of sealing was by means of a plug of oiled rag or the like. Sparkling wine (q.v.) was only possible in the 17th century, when good-quality cork had become available.

The resiliency, lightness, tightness to air and water and freedom from attack by wine long made cork virtually irreplaceable. The expensive corks for champagne and other sparkling wines are made not from a solid piece but from a number of pieces welded together. Recently hollow stoppers of inert plastic have commenced to take the place of cork for sparkling wines and their use will presumably extend to still wines as well.

'Corked' or 'corky' wine is a taint caused by the use of defective bark containing excess tannin and other extractives. A cork withdrawn from a bottle of wine or other liquid should have no smell other than that of the contents of the bottle.

Corkage: Originally, a fee charged for opening and serving a customer's own bottle; now, an additional charge sometimes made on any bottle that is opened and consumed on the premises.

Corkscrew: Known originally as a bottlescrew, the inventor is unknown but the beloved article appears to have been introduced during the latter half of the 18th century. There are myriads of stories poking sly fun at those who of habit carry one of these tools. Mrs. Beeton counselled that three should be carried to a picnic.

Probably the first printed reference to a corkscrew in English was the 'bottle-scrue' mentioned by Nicholas Amherst in 1720 in his *Poems on Several Occasions*.

No earnest drinker should lack an engine-turned instrument for removal of corks, a sharp, substantial piece of craftsmanship that will last a lifetime and put to scorn the modern flimsy twisted wire. Like a fine pocket-knife, it cannot be bought for a few pence.

Corma: A type of mead, weaker than zythus (q.v.), alleged to have been drunk by the Norse in Gaul.

Corn: *Zea mays*, Maize or Indian corn, is the most important grain crop of the United States, though it reaches the market chiefly as milk, eggs and meat. It is also the origin of corn whiskey, more generally known as bourbon (q.v.). Corn whiskey is one of the very few truly native alcoholic beverages of the United States and is rightly not without honour in its own country.

Maize is a prolific and hardy crop and is now grown in most agricultural sections of the world. It is widely used for the production of potable spirit, including the so-called grain whisky of Scotland and Ireland and the schnapps of Europe. These, however, bear no resemblance to bourbon whiskey in bouquet.

Cornas: French (Rhône) red wine. It is reputed to resemble Hermitage and the vineyard is said to have been in continuous production for over a thousand years.

Coronata: Golden-white table wine from Genoa, Italy.

Corps: The French wine term for the body or alcoholic strength and vigour of a beverage. Perhaps the nearest English equivalent is the disappearing term 'essential guts'.

Corsé: The French wine term for full-bodied, rather rich.

Corsica: An unimportant wine-producer due to the scarcity of arable land. Cap Corse, Calvi, Sari, Ajaccio, Bastia and Bonifacio are the principal vineyard areas. Reports of quality are conflicting.

Cortados: The second-best class of new Spanish sherry wine, stronger and darker than the *palmas* (q.v.) and intended to be turned into *oloroso*. A *palo cortado*, intermediate between palma and cortado, may develop into a *fino*. See also Sherry.

Cortaillod: The best Swiss red table wine of Neuchâtel. Pinot grape.

Cortese: Italian (Piedmont) white table wine.

Corton: Wine estate in Burgundy (commune of Aloxe-Corton) noted for fine red. There are many other excellent wines from adjacent vineyards, including Ch. Charlemagne, Grancey and Bressandes.

Corton-Bressandes: See Corton.

Corton-Charlemagne: See Corton.

Corton-Grancey: See Corton.

Corvées, Les: French (Nuits-Saint-Georges, q.v.) red burgundy.

Corvina: Valued Italian grape vine from which Bardolino (q.v.) amongst others is made.

Corvo: Good red and white Sicilian table wines.

Corvo di Casteldaccia: Italian (Sicilian) white wine.

Cos d'Estournel, Château: Fine red wine from St. Estèphe, Bordeaux.

Cos-Labory: French (Médoc) red wine.

Cossart-Gordon: Old-established shippers of madeira (q.v.).

Costmary: Also known as alecost. A shrub of the *Chrysanthemum* genus,

H   M.D.D.

native to E. Mediterranean, formerly used as a flavouring agent for ale. It is curious how the hop (q.v.) quickly conquered all other flavourings.

Costrel: Flat drinking-vessel (also called a 'pilgrim's flask'), with handles for attaching a belt or shoulder-strap.

Côte: The French word which means (as well as many other things) a slope or gentle hillside. If a slope happens to have the right direction to catch the sun and the right soil to produce the grapes, you may then have a place of superlative value for growing fine wine. Hence the word is found associated with many of the finest French wines.

Côte, La: Swiss wine-producing area.

Côte de Beaune: The Burgundian Côte-d'Or (q.v.) consists of two main ridges of which the more southerly bears this name and the more northerly the Côte de Nuits (q.v.). Both ridges hold many celebrated vineyards. For named vineyards see Côte-d'Or.

Côte de Nuits: See Côte de Beaune.

Côte-d'Or: The Golden Slope. Whether the adjective is more aptly applied to the quality or the cash value of the wine or to the sunlight that the ridges trap is arguable. The name is that of a French département where the finest red and white burgundy wines are produced. The centre is the city of Dijon, that place of wine and food. The Côte de Nuits (q.v.) is reputed to produce the finest red and the Côte de Beaune the best white burgundy. Some of the celebrated communes (starting from the north) are Gevrey-Chambertin, Morey-St. Denis, Chambolle-Musigny, Vougeot, Flagey-Echézeaux, Vosne-Romanée, Nuits-St. Georges, and Prémeaux. They belong to what is known as the Côte de Nuits. Further south, the Côte de Beaune comprises the following Communes: Aloxe-Corton, Pernand-Vergelesses, Savigny, Beaune, Pommard, Volnay, Monthélie, Meursault, Chassagne-Montrachet, Puligny-Montrachet, and Santenay. Less important wine-producing Communes of the Côte-d'Or are: Marsannay-la-Côte, Fixin, Brochon, Corgoloin, Comblanchien, Ladoix-Serrigny, Auxey-Duresses, and St. Aubin.

Côte Rôtie: Celebrated French wine region, a ribbon of vineyards a few miles long, bordered by the Rhône and close to the ancient city of Vienne. The name means Roasted Slope and refers, of course, to the superbly warm ripening sun. The red wine is sold under the same name. It is made with a proportion of white grapes, matures very slowly and is said by some to have a flavour of truffles. It is reliably stated that wine has been grown here for over 2,500 years. The name is also given to a good red wine of the Côte-d'Or (q.v.) as well as to the finest red wine of the Côtes du Rhône (q.v.).

Côtes de Blancs: A valley in the Champagne district of France which, with the Montagne de Reims and Marne Valley, produces the finest white grapes from which champagne is made.

Côtes de Bordeaux: A common English label for unspecified but by no means necessarily inferior red or white Bordeaux.

Côtes du Rhône: The general name for the wines grown along the Rhône between Vienne and Avignon. The name means the Rhône Slopes. It is a region of celebrated wines including Côte Rôtie, Hermitage and Châteauneuf-du-Pape (q.v.).

Couet: Notable sweet white wine of Bordeaux.

Couffran: French (Médoc) red wine.

Couhins: French (Graves) red wine.

Coulée de Sarrant: French (Anjou) white wine.

Country Wines: Misleading name for British alcoholic beverages (mainly English) made by fermenting sugar mixed with fruits, vegetables, flowers or herbs. The alcohol is formed from the sugar. The rest is merely flavouring. They are not wines and the error is heightened by coupling the name of the flavouring agent. They can be quite pleasant and wholesome beverages, hence the mis-labelling is additionally regrettable. Amongst the commoner 'wines' are cowslip, dandelion, elderberry, carrot, parsnip, rhubarb, parsley, rose-hip, beetroot and ginger. There are many others. These beverages are also known as 'home' wines.

Coupage: French term for mixing wines to obtain an acceptable blend. Especially applied to the addition of a wine high in alcohol to one deficient. Much *vin ordinaire* is so prepared.

Coupe: A glass especially designed for champagne by English glass-blowers about 1830, consisting of an expansive, hemispherical bowl supported on a tall, slender stem, much decorated. With less 'gingerbread', the coupe is still in general use. Also French for cup.

Coupé: French term of numerous meanings. In the matter of wine it can mean blended and also watered or cut.

Couperie: French (St. Émilion) red wine.

Courage, Barclay & Simonds Ltd.: Large English brewing company incorporating many old-established concerns.

Courni: The ancient Irish name for ale. Dioscorides wrote in the 1st century that the Hiberni (Irish) loved this beverage.

Couronne: French (Médoc) red wine.

Courtier: A broker, a very important functionary in the world of wine in France. This especially applies to the wines of Bordeaux.

Courvoisier: Old-established brand of cognac (q.v.).

Coutelin-Merville: French (Médoc) red wine.

Coutet: The name of two wine estates of Bordeaux. One at Barsac produces sauternes (q.v.) and the other at St. Émilion red wine (claret). Both have merit.

Couvent: French (St. Émilion) red wine.

Cowslip Wine: One of the large number of English 'wines', all of which consist of alcohol from fermented sugar flavoured with cowslip flower, rhubarb, elderberry or what you will. Wines they certainly are not. See also Country Wines.

Crab Cider: Old name for sharp-flavoured cider, made from the tart English apples of that name.

Crackling: Term syn. with pearl (q.v.) employed by some Canadian and U.S. wineries to denote a slightly sparkling wine. *Rechiotto, perlant, crémant* and *frizzante* are broadly equivalent.

Cradle: A kind of basket, in which wine is carried and served, when it is desired to avoid disturbance of crust or sediment.

Cramant: French wine-growing district of the Champagne producing very fine *blanc de blancs* (q.v.).

Crambambull: An old English beverage made from warmed, sweetened beer, fortified with rum and containing eggs.

Crank: A strong alcoholic beverage alleged by Benjamin Rush, in his *Moral and Physical Thermometer*, to be the 'cause of quarrelling and bloatedness'. See also Hysteric Water and Jailers.

Cras: French (Côte-d'Or) red wine. Also a vineyard of Meursault producing white burgundy.

Crate: The receptacle in which bottles are transported. Normally made with wooden slats and partitions to hold one or two dozen bottles. Modern crates are of stout steel wire.

Crater: The great mixing bowl placed in the middle of a Roman dining table for the mingling of wine and water at the orders of the *Arbiter bibendi* (q.v.).

Crawler: One who visits the pubs in a district, drinking a glass of beer in each. A pub-crawl is the actual operation.

Craytur: See Creature.

Cream of Tartar: See Tartar.

Creature: Usually preceded by 'the'. Syn. for spirits, especially whisky. In Irish dialect often spelt 'craytur'.

Crémant: The French wine term for 'lightly sparkling', as distinct from *mousseux* (q.v.).

Crème: French term ('cream') widely applied to liqueurs, but not only in France, when it is desired to suggest special 'richness', i.e. sweetness. The term has no more significance than the stars on a brandy label. Examples are crème de banane, crème de cacao, crème de moka, which are all more than usually sweet.

Crème de Menthe: Liqueur of peppermint flavour, and usually emerald-green in colour.

Crème de Tête: A French wine term to suggest super-superlative, what the 1920 Englishman used to call the utterly-utter. The best wine of Château d'Yquem (q.v.) used to be so labelled but now all but the finest is sold merely as sauternes.

Creole: Cocktail of whisky, vermouth, benedictine.

Crepy: White French wine from Savoy.

Creysse: French (Bergerac) red wine.

Criaderas: The 'nurseries' of the sherry wines. See also Sherry.

Crimea: This region of southern Russia has been known for over 3,000 years as a centre of wine-growing. The Greek colonists who entered the Black Sea at least as early as this period, are believed to have been the first to carry vinestocks to this region. Here is grown both the most and the best of the wines of the U.S.S.R. The best vineyards and wineries are near Yalta.

Crinze: An earthenware drinking-vessel, a cross between a tankard and a small bowl.

Crock: French (Médoc) red wine.

Croft & Co.: Old-established (1678) shippers of port, one of the historic great firms of the Oporto wine industry.

Croix: The name of two wine estates of Bordeaux, the first at Pomerol and the second at Lormont, both producing red wine.

Croix-Blanche: French (Médoc) red wine.

Croix-de-Gay: French (Pomerol) red wine.

Croix-de-Merlet: French (Blayais) red wine.

Croix-Maron: The French nobleman of the 17th century who is supposed to have been the first to distil brandy commercially to use up the over-production of wine. To him is also ascribed the report: 'In cooking my wines I have discovered their soul.'

Croix Noires: French (Côte-d'Or) red wine.

Croix-Rouge: French (Médoc) red wine.

Croizet: Old-established (1805) brand of cognac (q.v.).

Croque-Michotte: French (Graves) red wine.

Cross-grain: White wine mentioned by Brillat-Savarin as a speciality of Genin's dining-rooms.

Crossing the Yuba: Mid-19th-century Californian drinking-toast.

Crown Cork: A cork-lined metal cap mechanically applied. See also Crown Seal.

Crown Seal: The metal closure crimped on the top of beer and temperance drinks. It consists of a metallic seal containing a wad of compound cork, the latter forming an airtight seal which retains the gas. The crown seal is a very cheap and efficient closure but is not used for fine beverages.

Croze: A cooper's tool used for cutting the groove into which is fitted the cask head.

Crozes-Hermitage: The hillside vineyards just south of the Hermitage slope of the Rhône. Good red and white wines.

Cru: A French word meaning (among other things) a growth, and widely used in wine parlance. It is applied either to one vineyard or to a group making wines of the same sort. *Vin du cru* is wine of the region. *Boire du vin de son cru* is to drink wine that one has actually grown, a delightful phrase for a delightful act.

Cru de Bercy: Alternate name for Château de Bercy (q.v.).

Cru de la Vigne du Diable: The expressive name for the finest vineyard of Cortaillod (q.v.).

Cruots: French (Côte-d'Or) red wine.

Cruscaut: French (Bordeaux) red wine.

Crussal: French (Côtes du Rhône) white wine.

Crust: A hallowed word to Englishmen of an earlier age. It is the crust of acid potassium tartrate (cream of tartar) deposited by some wines, especially ports, as the wine matures. Bottles of port used to bear a dab of whitewash to show how to hold the bottle when decanting, to avoid disturbing the crust and producing muddy wine. Ruby and vintage ports used to be put into bottles whose insides had been roughened with metal wire to give a surface on which the crust could grip.

Crusta: Mixed spirit drink with a crust of powdered sugar around the rim of the glass.

Crusted Port: Wine similar in character to vintage port (q.v.) but of no declared year. See also Crust.

Cruzeau: French (St. Émilion) red wine.

Csopaki Furmint: Hungarian esteemed white table wine.

Cuarto: Spanish for quarter-cask.

Cuba: Noted as producer of rum. The spirit is characteristic, differing from most other rums in the addition of a complex mixture of flavourings. See also Daiquiri.

Cuban: Cocktail of rum, apricot liqueur and lime juice.

Cuckoo Ale: That dispensed in spring in rural England when the first bird song is heard.

Cues: German wine region of Moselle.

Cujac: French (Médoc) red wine.

Cullet: The glass-trade term for broken glass, always in demand for adding to a new 'melt'. The amount of cullet that accumulates in a bottling cellar is astonishing.

Culms, Coombes or Comings: The rootlets of barley sieved from the grain at the end of the malting process and used for poultry and cattle food

Culture: In the sense of this book, a pure growth of a selected yeast.

Cumières: French wine-growing centre of the Marne (champagne).

Cup: A lightly alcoholic beverage for summer consumption, usually made in large jugs. The composition is very variable but is often wine broken down with mineral water and plenty of ice. There is usually an addition of cut citrus or other fruit, decoration of mint, cucumber, etc. Spirits may be added. There is plenty of room for artistry and individuality here. Indeed, the gastronomic skill of a host or hostess might be gauged from the quality of the cup served.

Cupa: Latin for vat, butt or large cask and the origin of cooper (q.v.).

Curaçao: Liqueur of rum base originally made on the Dutch island of that name in the West Indies. The main flavour is derived from the peel of the local green-skinned citrus fruit (orange).

Curate: The Irish term for an assistant barman. And pfwy not, indade?

Curé-Bon-la-Madeleine: French (St. Émilion) red wine.

Cussac: French (Médoc) red wine commune, usually sold under the better known name of the adjoining commune of St. Julien.

Cut: As applied to beverages, adulterated with water.

Cuvage: French for the art of handling vats of wine.

Cuve: French term for a fermenting vat of any size. The construction of such vats varies. Timber such as oak or jarrah (an Australian hardwood), cement, stone and glass-enamel are all used. Undoubtedly, the modern plastic industry will not neglect this field.

Cuvée: French for contents of a vat; hence, a blend or vatting. The term is used mainly with reference to the bulk blend or vatting of still, dry, wines prepared for conversion to champagne.

Cyathus: Roman dipper holding one twelfth of a pint, used for filling the poculum (q.v.) with wine from the crater (q.v.).

Cygne, Cru du: A group of Bordeaux vineyards producing similar white wine. See also Cru. The vineyards include Laurenzane and Gradignan.

Cynar: Italian apéritif. An acquired taste.

Cyprus: Wine from the Mediterranean island of that name. In England the term has been mainly applied to sweet, fortified wine. See also Commanderie, Olympus, Othello, Duc de Nicosie.

Cytase: The enzyme in malt which converts insoluble to soluble starch.

Czechoslovakia: This is essentially a beer-drinking country. That of Pilsen (Pilsener) is world-famous and is much exported. But there are also vineyards producing a considerable volume of wine, pleasant enough but undistinguished. The chief wine regions are Ruthenia and Slovakia.

Dabhaus: White wine from Oppenheim, Rheinhessen.

Dachsberg: German wine estate of Winkel, Rheingau.

Dackenheim: German (Palatinate) white wine of moderate quality.

Dad and Mum: Australian mixed drink consisting of hot meat extract laced with rum.

Dadloms: A game of table skittles played with miniature 'cheeses' (q.v.).

Dagger Ale: An obsolete term for a type of ale supposed to have originated at the Dagger Inn, Holborn, London.

Dagobert: King of the Franks, whose daughter owned a vineyard at Uerzig, on the Moselle, in the year 690.

Dago Red: Opprobrious American term for inexpensive dry red table wine of the type drunk regularly and copiously with food by the Mediterranean peoples. It is thus sharply differentiated from the sickly sweet fortified 'port' or 'tokay' so beloved by millions of uncultivated palates. See also Marchiafava's Disease.

Daiquiri: American long mixed drink of Cuban rum of that name, lime juice, syrup, served very cold. There are variants using orange juice, grenadine, etc. The name, according to H. L. Mencken, is supposed to have been invented by American army engineers stationed at Daiquiri, near Santiago de Cuba, in 1898. When they ran out of gin and whisky they found it possible to drink the pale Cuban rum by mixing it with lime juice.

Daisy: A general and vague American term for a long, chilled drink of spirit base with citrus juices.

Dalmatia: Grows a considerable amount of wine but is best noted for the maraschino (almond-flavoured) liqueur from Zara.

Dalsheim: German wine-growing parish of Rheinhessen.

Dalwood: Good red table wine from the Hunter River Valley (New South Wales, Australia) estate of that name. Now nearly 150 years old, Dalwood Hermitage is justly esteemed.

Daly: Noted Irish (Tullamore) whiskey, founded 1829.

Dama de Lobos: Finest wine district of Madeira.

Damascus: Variety of wine-grape supposed to have been derived from Damascus.

Dambach: Bas-Rhin (q.v.) wine area.

Dame-Jeanne: See Demijohn. This is the French equivalent.

Damery: French commune of the Marne Valley producing white wine for champagne.

Damiana: Mexican liqueur flavoured with this botanical, more a drug than a beverage.

Dammsberg: German (Laubenheim, q.v.) white wine.

Dampierre: French (Anjou) pink wine.

Damson Wine: Another of the so-called wines of England which are really fermented sugar flavoured with fruit juices. See also Country Wines.

Dandelion Wine: See Country Wines.

Dankental: German (Worms) wine estate. See also Bechtheim.

Danziger Goldwasser: Liqueur from Danzig in which float particles of genuine gold leaf. Caraway flavour.

Dao: Wine from the high country of Central Portugal, both red (*Dao tinto*) and white (*Dao branco*).

D'Arche: French (Médoc) red wine. Also a sweet white wine (sauternes).

Dardanup: Australian (W.A.) wine centre.

Darts: A game, the origin of which is lost in antiquity, but is said to descend from knife throwing. Although much in vogue at court during the reign of Henry II, the game was not universally popular until the end of the 19th century when it was revived as a pastime in public houses. It consists of throwing a dart at a board which is divided into scoring segments. Many variations from the standard board are in use both in local and league tournaments, and the game has now acquired national status.

Dart widow: One who waits at home. See also Darts.

Daru: A potent northern India (Rajasthan) spirit derived, it is stated, from flowers of the Mahwa tree (*Bassia latifundia*).

Dash: Small quantity, a few drops.

Date wine: Common Indian alcoholic beverage. A spirit (date brandy) is also made.

Daubhaus: German (Hochheim, q.v.) white wine. Also a red wine estate of Ahr.

Daugay: French (St. Émilion) red wine.

Dautenpflanzer: German (Münster, q.v.) white wine.

Dauzac: French (Médoc) red wine, also sparkling white.

David: If he wrote the Psalms he also wrote (in the 104th) 'Wine maketh glad the heart of man'. If he did not, he should have.

D.C.L.: See Distillers Company Ltd.

Dead House: Obsolete Australian term of goldrush days for the room in the pub where 'dead-drunks' could 'sleep it off'.

Deal Wine: The name given to Rhine wines in Elizabethan times owing to the port of Deal being their chief entry into England.

Deauville: Cocktail of applejack, cognac and orange juice.

Debourrage: French term for the practice of making white wine by holding the pressed juice (must) until the debris settles, fermentation being postponed by heavy 'sulphuring' (q.v.).

Debrö: Perhaps the finest white wines of Hungary.

Decant: To pour a liquid from one vessel to another, usually with the object of leaving a sediment or precipitate behind.

Decanter: A glass receptacle into which the contents of a bottle of wine or spirits is poured for service at the table.

Decilitre: French equivalent of 0·176 British pint.

Decoction Process: A type of mashing (q.v.) in which part of the mash is heated in a cooker, then returned to the bulk and the process repeated. See also infusion.

Deep-sinker: Old Australian term for a long beer.

Dégorgeur: The skilled and important champagne craftsman, the disgorger, whose job it is to carry on after the *remueur* (q.v.). He deftly removes the cork, allows the sediment to fly out and within a split second inserts a new cork.

    During recent years the freezing method has come into use. The top layer of the neck of the bottle is frozen and the little plate of ice holding the sediment is ejected. See also Champagne.

De Hilde: French (Graves) red wine.

Deidesheim: Important German (Palatinate) group of vineyards producing basically similar wine and thus constituting the equivalent of a French *cru* or growth. Some of the principal vineyards are Weinbach, Strasse, Schafsbohl, Peterhohle, Nonnenstuck, Grain, Hohenmorgen, Kränzler, Langenmorgen, Hergottsacker, Gehen, Vogelgesang, and Mühle.

Deitelsberg: German (Hallgarten, q.v.) white wine.

Dekeleia: Greek red and white beverage wines from the Marathon district.

Delaforce & Co.: Old-established (1868) shippers of port (q.v.).

Delamain: Old-established (1824) brand of cognac (q.v.).

Delaware: Native American pink grape which many consider the best indigenous example. Widely used for making white sparkling wine (champagne) in Ohio and New York.

Delbeck: Champagne of Reims.

Del Garso: Italian red table wine from Trieste region.

Delimitation: The highly commendable legal system now operating in most European wine-growing countries which limits the use of a name possessing goodwill to the vineyards within a defined area. The process is strictly geographical and tends to increase the value of place names. Countries such as the United States, Australia and South Africa still have to learn the value that accrues ultimately to a place name linked with a wine or other beverage or for that matter any other commodity of merit.

Dell: See Bacharach.

Delmonico: Squat American glass used for sours (q.v.) and similar spirit drinks.

Demerara: District in British Guiana near Georgetown, noted for production of rum. Demerara rum is especially highly flavoured and is therefore valued for blending purposes.

Demestica: Greek red wines.

Demi: In France this means, in the wine trade, a half-litre or 0.88 British pint.

Demi-Firkin: Small beer barrel of four and a half gallons capacity. (See also Firkin.) Also known as pin (q.v.).

Demijohn: A glass or stoneware jar with narrow neck of capacity 1 to 10 gallons, usually cased in wicker with single or double handle. The word is interesting. It does not mean a 'half John' but is variously derived in the standard dictionaries. Some trace it from the French 'Dame Jeanne' ('Lady Jane'), others from the old Persian town Damagan, which had a famous glass industry. Possibly 'Dame Jeanne' and 'demi-john' are both corruptions of Damagan. The terminology of beverages and containers provides many involved examples of the curious evolutions of words.

Demi-Queue: French measure of capacity for wine in cask, varying with location. Expressed in British gallons, the approximate volumes are: Burgundy 44, Champagne 39, and Paris 44 (or 46 if sold with the lees).

Demi-sec: Lit. 'half-dry', but, as applied to champagne, indicates that the wine is relatively sweet.

Demoiselle: The delightful French name for a small nip of spirits. The term is mostly used in Normandy for calvados (q.v.). It is also the West of England name for a tot of spirits. Perhaps this was introduced by the French prisoners of Napoleonic times. See also Trou.

De Myrat: French sweet white wine. See also Barsac.

Denaturant: A substance added to alcohol to make it nauseous and unfit for drinking, without destroying its value for certain commercial purposes. The object is to avoid legally the heavy excise duty on potable alcohol. The different denaturants approved by the authorities are all substances that cannot be removed from the alcohol, except by a costly and difficult process. At one time crude wood (methyl) alcohol was used, hence methylated spirit.

Denis-Mounié: Old-established (1838) brand of cognac (q.v.).

Deoch an Doruis: Also corrupted to Doch and Doris. A Scotch name for a parting drink, and also for a stirrup-cup for which no charge could be made under the Scottish hospitality customs.

Depth Bomb: Mixed drink made by adding a jigger of whisky to a large glass of beer. Also a cocktail of applejack, brandy, grenadine and lemon juice.

Derby: Cocktail of gin, peach bitters and mint.

De Rigueur: Cocktail of whisky, grapefruit juice and honey.

Dernau: German (Ahr) red wine.

Désert: French (Graves) red wine.

Desmirail: French (Médoc) red wine.

Desplats: French (Médoc) red wine.

Dessert Wine: The somewhat imprecise English term for wine drunk with the last course (the 'dessert' or 'sweets') of a meal. Dessert wine is sweet, heavy and fortified (q.v.). Examples are port, madeira, oloroso or other sweet sherry, roussillon, malaga, marsala and mavrodaphne. Sauternes and *doux* champagne are quite sweet but they are not usually accounted dessert wines; and they are drunk earlier in the meal.

There is sound gastronomy and physiology in relegating dessert wines to the close of the meal, for sugar is the great destroyer of appetite. Some dessert wines are actually strong syrups.

The French term *vin de liqueur* and the German *Likörwein* have much the same meaning as dessert, and this also applies to the Portuguese *vinho generoso* and the Italian *vino di lusso*. See also the curious French term Vins Doux Naturels.

Detzem: German (Moselle) white wines, including the vineyards of Maximiner-Klosterlay, Stolzenberg, Würzgarten.

Deutelsberg: German (Rheingau) vineyard. Fine hock.

Deutz et Geldermann: Old-established champagne of Ay.

Devenish: Ancient Weymouth brewery operating at same address since 1742.

Devil's Blood: Mixed drink made from tequila, orange juice and chillies.

Devil's Chapel: Old name for an alehouse, arising from the fact that originally there were alehouses actually physically attached to churches.

Dew: Australian slang term for illicit spirit. See also Moonshine.

Dextrins: Less-readily fermentable bodies which are a natural result of the conversion of starch into sugar. The presence of these dextrins in the wort in correct proportions has a direct relationship to its character and the final quality of the beer.

Dezaley: Fine Swiss (Canton de Vaud) white wine.

Dezize-les-Maranges: French (Burgundy) wine commune.

Dhron: German (Moselle) white wines, including the vineyards of Hofberg, Roterd, Sängarei, and Stengelberg.

Diamond: Cocktail of applejack and grenadine.

Diana: A native American grape from which table wine of strong flavour is made. Also a mixed drink of brandy and crème de menthe.

Diastase: The enzyme, formed especially in sprouting grain, which converts starch to sugar. It is thus of primary importance in brewing (q.v.).

Dibs: The 'artificial honey' of Palestine which was made by boiling down ripe grape juice to a thick syrup. It has been an important article of commerce and export for over 2,000 years and until recently was the main source of sweetening for cakes and pastry. Under the Hebrew name *debash* it is mentioned in the Bible as an export from Palestine to Tyre (Ezek. 27 : 17).

Dickens: It is at least curious that this great master of observation of all phases of English life writes so little about alcoholic beverages. Still, Dick Swiveller did say: 'Did you ever taste beer?' 'I had a sip of it once', said the small servant. 'Here's a state of things!' cried Mr. Swiveller. . . . 'She *never* tasted it — it can't be tasted in a sip!' However, see also Spontaneous Combustion.

Didiers: French (Côte-d'Or) red wine.

Dié, Clairette de: French white wine of Dié.

Diedel: White wine from Palatinate (q.v.).

Diedesfeld: German (Palatinate) white wine.

Dienheim: German (Oppenheim, Rheinhessen) wine district. It includes the vineyards of Falkenberg, Rosswiese, Saar, Gumben, Goldberg, Krötenbrunnen, Langweg, Neuweg, Ebenbreit, Guldenmorgen, Tafelstein, Geierscheid, Sohlbrunnen and Silzbrunnen.

Dieterkapp: German (Nackenheim, q.v.) white wine.

Dietlingen: German (Karlstuhe) red and white wines.

Diez Hermanos: Established shippers of port (q.v.).

Digny: White French wine from Savoy.

Dillmetz: German (Hattenheim, q.v.) white wine.

Dillon: French (Médoc) red and white wines.

Dimiat: Bulgarian wine of pale green hue from grape of same name of the Black Sea coast.

Dinstlgut: Austrian cooperative winery near Loibner making good wine.

Dionysos: In classical Greek mythology, the god and giver of wine. He later became known as Bacchus (q.v.), especially among the Romans. Dionysos was first the god of the hills and rivers before eventually becoming the deity of vine and wine.

Diplomatic Punch: Mixture of iced gin and madeira to which is added fresh strawberries and cucumber.

Dip Rod: Stick graduated to show content of a vessel. Also dipstick.

Dirmstein: German (Franconian) red and white wines.

Disgorgement: The process of removing sediment, by extracting and replacing the cork, during the manufacture of true sparkling wines. See also Dégorgeur.

Disraeli: 'I rather like bad wine,' said Mr. Mountchesney, 'one gets so bored with good wine' (*Sybil*). Even if this is whimsy, de Castella has wisely said, 'What Australia needs is *vin ordinaire*'.

Distillation: The process of converting a liquid into gas or vapour which is then condensed back to the liquid form. It was of immense importance to the alchemists, those precursors of modern scientists, and it is certain that the process of distilling an alcoholic beverage such as wine or beer to isolate the 'spirit' or essential heart must be of great antiquity. Distillation was certainly practised widely by the 10th century.

Distillation has for its object the separation of a liquid from another liquid or a liquid from solids. Thus it is by distillation that motor 'spirit' is separated from crude liquid petroleum and pure water is made from sea-water, leaving behind a residue of salt.

The beverage alcohol distilling industry is of enormous dimensions. All such products are grouped as spirits and include whisky, brandy, calvados, rum, gin, arrack, vodka, and other specialities, all of which are noted in their places.

The equipment for effecting distillation is termed a still. Every still consists of three essential parts, the still itself in which the liquid is heated, the condenser to cool the vapour and the receiver in which the desired product or distillate is collected. It follows that all spirituous beverages are distillates.

There is a large literature on the technology of distillation which should be consulted for detailed information. Only a few facts can be mentioned here. The simplest form of still is the pot-still (q.v.). This remains the best equipment for making the finest brandies (see Cognac), whiskies (see Single), rum, calvados, etc. See also Still.

A commercial improvement is the continuous or Coffey still (q.v.) which enables a spirit of any desired purity to be produced without stopping the operation. See also Congelation and Patent Still.

The production of spirits (q.v.) by distillation is a vast and world-wide industry and is everywhere subject to strict government supervision. A licence must be obtained and almost all countries rely upon a heavy impost upon spirits to make up a material part of the national revenue. Illicit distilling is therefore common and, contrary to popular belief, the product is not necessarily inferior. See also Moonshine.

Distillers Company Ltd.: The powerful Scottish combination of malt and patent whisky and gin distillers formed in 1877. Within the next fifty years it acquired a major share of the Scotch whisky trade and also moved into the bread-yeast, chemical, drug and other industries. Under the direction of William Ross, D.C.L. became essentially what it is today. The policy has been to allow considerable autonomy to the firms which it absorbed and competition between the constituent companies has been fierce. Many of the celebrated Scotch whisky firms are part of D.C.L. These include John Walker, Dawson, Dewar, Haig, Buchanan, White Horse and Sanderson. D.C.L. is also a major distiller of gin and includes the firms of Gordon and Booth.

Distiller's Safe: The device which allows the distiller of Scotch whisky to observe and test the spirit during the process without having actual access to it.

Dittelsheim: German (Rheinhessen) white wines, including the vineyards of Hayerweg, Leckerberg, Berg, Kloppberg and Gaiersberg.

Dive: Originally the name of any 18th-century inexpensive London basement restaurant serving a simple 'ordinary' (q.v.) of boiled beef, tripe, cowheel and sausages with, of course, beer included. Now a syn. for an establishment of ill-repute, especially where liquor is sold illegally.

Dividend: Old term for a share of the cost of a drinking party. See also Club.

Dizy-Magenta: French (Marne) wine-growing commune for champagne (q.v.).

Dock Glass: A goblet holding exactly a quarter of a pint, used originally by Excise Officers for wine-tasting at the docks.

Doctor Bonum Magnum: The nickname (because of his taste in claret) of the Rev. Alexander Webster, the 1755 Moderator of the General Assembly of the Church of Scotland.

Dog's Nose: Yorkshire drink of pale ale, spiked with gin. Also a hot mixed drink of sweetened porter and gin with nutmeg. See also Purl.

Dohr: German vineyard of Wiltingen (q.v.), Saar.

Doisy, Ch.: Celebrated French wine estate adjoining Ch. Climens of Haut Barsac (see Barsac), making sweet white wine (sauternes). Ch. Doisy is now divided into three distinct estates. Châteaux Doisy-Dubraca, Doisy-Daëne and Védrines.

Doktor: Celebrated German (Moselle) vineyard of Berncastel. Though only of 13 acres, the vineyard is divided amongst a number of owners. One of these is the group of heirs of Dr. Thanisch, the original owner. However, there is a story that the actual origin of the name was the boost given to the wine by an Elector of Trier in the 14th century, who said it was a certain cure for fever. At any rate by common accord Berncasteer Doktor is one of the great German wines and therefore one of the world's choicest. See also Berncastel-Cues.

Dolceacqua: Red table wine, the best Rossesse (q.v.) from Liguria, Italy.

Dolcetto: A red beverage-wine of Piedmont, Italy, from the grape of that name.

Dôle de Sion: Swiss red wine, considered by many the finest of the country.

Dolium: Antique large earthenware jar of Roman times, used for storage of wine, oil. See also Amphora.

Dolly O'Hare: Cocktail of gin, dry vermouth and apricot liqueur.

Domaine: French for estate.

Domaine de Nalis: One of the Châteauneuf (q.v.) wines.

Dom-Avelsbach: German wine estate in Avelsbach (q.v.).

Domdechaney: German fine white wine (hock); the most noted vineyard of Hochheim, Rheingau.

Domecq, Pedro, S.A.: Old-established (1824) distillers of brandy and shippers of sherry (q.v.).

Dominikaner: German white wine estate of Casel (q.v.).

Dominikanerberg: German (Ruwer, q.v.) white wine.

Dominique, La: French (Graves) red wine.

Domlay: German (Ahr) red wine estate.

Domprobst: German (Graach, q.v.) white wine.

Domtal: German (Nierstein, q.v.) white wine.

Domthal: German (Rheinhessen) white wine.

Donauperle: Lit. 'pearl of the Danube'. Bulgarian white wine from the Feteasca grape.

Doornkaat: East Friesian village which gives its name to a brand of gin.

Doosberg: German (Östrich, q.v.) white wine.

Dop Brandy: South African term for a second-grade brandy equivalent to grappa and marc (q.v.). Cape Smoke is reputedly a bit worse again.

Doppelkorn: German spirit (lit. 'double corn'). This contains a minimum of 38% alcohol. There is also a korn of 32% alcohol.

Doradillo: Grape from Jaen, near Granada in southern Spain, a coarse, heavy-yielding variety much grown in Australia for distillation of fortifying spirit (q.v.).

Dorado: Cocktail of tequila, honey and lemon.

Dordogne: It is necessary for oenophiles to know that though the valley of this river produces great volumes of red table wine, none is legally allowed to be called bordeaux except that produced on both banks during the course of the river through the Gironde département.

Dorsheim: German (Nahe) white wine.

Dosage: French, not English, term for the process of adding syrup to *brut* (q.v.) champagne, with or without brandy, to meet the market demand. The heaviest dosage was for the pre-Tsarist Russian taste. See also Champagne.

Dosierung: German for Dosage, addition of syrup to wine in process of making sparkling wine.

Double: Applied to ale and stout to designate a stronger brew than 'single'.

Doum: Egyptian palm wine made from the *doum* palm.

Doumens: French (Médoc) red wine.

Douro: A river in Portugal, famed for the port wine produced in its vicinity. The town of Oporto, from which the name port is derived, is at the mouth of the river. See also Alto Douro.

Doux: A French word which, when applied to a wine, usually means 'sweet'.

Dowel: A wooden peg used to join together the pieces of timber of a cask head.

Dowling Brace: A tool used by a cooper (q.v.) to bore holes in the pieces of timber into which the dowel (q.v.) is inserted.

Down: Irish centre for whiskey manufacture.

Downright: A cooper's tool used to shave the outside of a cask stave.

Down the Hatch: A toast; usually for the first drink.

Drachenblut: German (Drachenfels) white wine.

Draff: The residue of husks remaining after the extraction of wort from malt (q.v.). It is used as cattle food.

Dragon's Milk: Old name for strong ale.

Drakenstein: South African white table wine.

Dram: A tot (q.v.) or small draught (q.v.) of spirits. Derivation obscure but not connected with drachm of apothecary's measure.

Drambuie: A Scotch proprietary liqueur, said to have a whisky base.

Dram Shop: The 18th-century term for the London establishments that sold only spirits, especially gin.

Drasnodar: Russian region for production of sparkling wine (q.v.).

Draught: A word of varied meaning. It is bulk liquor as opposed to bottled, especially beer drawn from a cask. It is also used for the amount of liquor drunk at a single act. Other meanings are the actual operation of drawing from a large container, and the act of drinking or inhaling. It is also an old word (also draft) for a substantial portion. Pepys, for example, often writes of having drunk a 'draft of wine' and of his 'morning draft'.

Drawback: Refund of duty or excise on proof of re-export or of loss.

Dreiling: Austrian measure of about 38 gallons.

Dreimännerwein: Lit. 'three-man wine', one of abnormal strength, but also used for inferior stuff — one man to drink it and two to hold him down!

Dreimorgen: German (Ellsheim, q.v.) white wine.

Dresden: There are a few vineyards here in the German Democratic Republic and also near Freiburg but the climate makes the production of fine wine a seeming impossibility.

Drink: A violently abused word reflecting the prejudice and often the ignorance of the prohibitionist. It is impossible to say with conviction why so innocent, general and simple a word should have acquired a specialized and often sinister meaning. Consider the sentence: *Drink this drink of ginger beer* and thus avoid *getting drunk by drinking drink*. The fact that this has meaning is a sad reflection upon the influence of a certain type of citizen upon the fate of words. See also Temperance.

Drinking Fallacies: See Fallacies, Drinking.

Drinking Salutations: For many years the custom has existed of speaking a word or phrase in company when lifting the glass for the first sip or swallow. The origin is obscure but the object is to invoke the god, saint or spirit of jollity. Every national group has its favourite and fashionable collection and the items rise and fall. See also Chin-Chin. Some typical

British items are 'down the hatch', 'mud in your eye', 'cheers', 'here's how', 'all the best' and 'bottoms up'. The Germanic *prosit*, the Scandinavian *skaal* and the French *à la vôtre* (*santé*) are widely known.

Driver: A wedge-shaped tool used by coopers (q.v.) to drive down the hoops of a cask.

Dromersheim: German (Rheinhessen) white wine district, including vineyards of Kolben, Hütte, Laberstall, Hasenlauf and Honigberg.

Dropping System: The process of brewing whereby, after partial fermentation in an open vessel, the whole mixture of wort (q.v.) and yeast is dropped to another vessel on a lower floor.

Drunk: Everybody knows the meaning of this word as applied to those who have over-indulged in alcoholic beverages, but there is no satisfactory scientific definition, although there are over 1,400 synonyms in English alone for the term. Incidentally, the next candidate for the honour is Finland with over 600 synonyms. In English, and apparently also in many other languages, there are few censorious synonyms for drunk. The overwhelming majority of the terms are good-natured, tolerant, amusing. The moral should be clear.

Many countries have now adopted a legal or quasi-legal definition of drunkenness, though the figures are quite arbitrary. If the alcohol content of the blood is not above 0·05% sobriety is assumed. Between 0·05% and 0·15% of blood alcohol, evidence may be brought to prove sobriety or the reverse. A person whose blood contains more than 0·15% of alcohol is classed as drunk or 'under the influence' of alcohol and no rebutting evidence of conduct may be called. Admittedly there may be occasional injustices but on the whole the system works well and should eventually have the effect of teaching drivers of motor cars caution and control of themselves.

The mental and physical state of being drunk is an astonishingly complicated one and cannot of course be pursued here, though the subject is of intense interest. It is, however, permissible to mention that there is a growing body of opinion that the act of getting drunk may often have beneficial results. For example, it is now clear to modern sociologists that to get drunk occasionally may keep a family together by making it possible for the imbibing spouse to continue facing life. See also Alcohol, Physiological action of.

Drunkery: An opprobrious 18th-century term, especially American, for a rum-shop.

Dry: The curious term applied to liquor and which may be taken as the opposite of sweet. Though often applied to gin and other spirits (which are invariably entirely 'dry' as first distilled) a little sugar, glycerin or other sweetening agent is sometimes added.

As applied to wine, the term is variable. Dry champagne is distinctly sweet. White beverage wines such as graves are certainly dry wines but slightly less so than most red table wines. Ports, madeiras and similar dessert wines are by their nature quite sweet but the term dry is sometimes used to denote less sweet than usual.

As used for sherry the word dry is highly involved and is much bound up with snobbery and hypocrisy. Put bluntly, many think that social refinement requires dry sherry to be demanded though they much prefer it to taste distinctly sweet. The wine trade caters to this group by labelling some sweet sherry dry.

Sauternes is lusciously sweet and so are some of the comparable white Rhine wines. Many 'dry wine' faddists seem to have no objection to drinking these unfortified (q.v.) sweet wines earlier in the meal than dessert.

Dry Hopping: The process of adding a small amount of finest hops at racking (q.v.) to draught pale ales and strong Burton-type (q.v.) beers whereby a flavour prized by beer fanciers is produced.

Dry Inches: The exciseman's picturesque term for the ullaged volume of a cask. See also Inches.

Dry Martini: Cocktail of four parts dry gin and one part dry vermouth. Add cracked ice and serve with green olive and twist of lemon peel. This is probably the most popular of all cocktails. There are dozens of variants. If an onion is used instead of olive, the drink is called a Gibson. In the U.S. there is increasing idiotic whimsy concerning the most approved proportion of gin to vermouth. Some recipes appear to be essentially straight gin.

Dublin: Not the least of 'Dear, Dirty Dublin's' claims on affection is as the mother of that excellent beverage stout (q.v.).

Dubonnet: One of the numerous proprietary apéritif (q.v.) flavoured wines which give the lie to the myth that the French despise the British sweet tooth.

Duc de Nicosie: Sparkling wine from Cyprus.

Duc d'Epernon: French (Graves) white wine.

Duchesse: Cocktail of dry and sweet vermouths with absinthe.

Ducru-Beaucaillou: French (Médoc) red wine.

Ducru-Ravez: French (Médoc) red wine.

Dudgeon: Old-established (1719) brewery of East Lothian.

Duff, Gordon & Co. Ltd.: Old-established (1772) shippers of sherry. See also Osborne.

Duhart-Milon: French (Médoc) red wine.

Dulamon: French (Médoc) red wine.

Dulce Apogado: Hardly a sherry or indeed a true wine, this is a liquor made by adding brandy to unfermented white must and used for blending purposes. It is similar to angelica (q.v.).

Dumas, Alexandre: He was, of course, a great one for food and drink. It suits the man and the wine to believe that he really did say, 'Le Montrachet! It is on your knees with head bared that it should be drunk.'

Dunder: Residue of a previous fermentation added to a new brew in some types of rum-making, for the purpose of producing additional flavour.

Duppa, James and Jeffrey: English brewers whose names appear in the Second Charter of the Virginia Company of 23 May 1609. Their names survive as the subjects of numerous complaints of foisting on the settlers 'stinking beer which . . . hath been the death of 200'.

Dupuis: Old-established (1850) brand of cognac (q.v.).

Dupuy: Old-established brand of cognac (q.v.).

Dur: French wine term for harsh, especially of young wines.

Durbach: German (Baden) white wines.

Durfort-Vivens: French (Médoc) red wine.

Dürkheim: German (Palatinate) fine white wines, including the vineyards of Proppenstein, Schenkenböhl, Spielberg, Michelsberg, Fronhof, Hochbenn, Hochmess, Heidfeld, Nonnengarten, Feuerberg, Schlossgarten, Forst, Halsberg and Gaiersbühl.

Dürnsteiner: Austrian table wine from Danube.

Dust: The very light, harmless sediment in wine which is not removed by decanting.

Dutch: 'To go Dutch' means that each member of a party pays his own way.

Dutch Razor Blade: Cocktail of gin, lemon juice and cayenne pepper.

Dutruch-Grand-Poujeaux: French (Médoc) red wine.

Dutton: Old-established (1799) brewery of Blackburn, England.

Duttweiler: German (Palatinate) white wines, including the vineyards of Siederich, Hohweg, and Kalkberg.

Duvet: Swedish wine term meaning flax.

Earthquake: Cocktail of gin, whisky and absinthe.

East India: An old term for wines which had been sent on a journey to Asia, particularly from Madeira and Spain, to mature them.

East Indian Sherry: The name applied to a full-bodied sweet sherry of the oloroso type (q.v.). Such sherry used to be sent on a journey in sailing ships to the East Indies to mature it. Perhaps there was some benefit.

Eau-de-Vie: General French term for potable alcohol; lit. 'water of life'. See also Aqua Vitae.

Eau de Vie de Cidre: French for alcohol distilled from cider (q.v.).

Eau de Vie de Fruits: French term for alcohol distilled from fruits.

Eau de Vie de Grain: French term for alcohol distilled from cereal or grain.

Eau de Vie de Lie: French term for the sub-quality brandy (lower than *eau de vie de marc*) made from wine lees left in casks after racking.

Eau de Vie de Marc: Brandy made from grape residues. Some of it is excellent. See also Grappa.

Eau de Vie de Vin: Grape (wine) brandy.

Eau Nuptiale: Old French concoction, presumably supposed to be a stimulant but see also William Shakespeare and the entry Sex and Alcohol. It was directed to be made from sweetened *eau de vie de vin* (alcohol), rose-water and various herbs. See also Caraway.

Eauze: The village in the middle of the Armagnac (q.v.) brandy district where the growers and buyers meet each year to make their deals.

Ebenbreit: German white wine. See also Dienheim.

Eberbach, Kloster: German abbey (Cistercian) near Hattenheim, Rheingau, and the centre of the celebrated Steinberg wines. Now secularized and the property of the government.

Ebernburg: German (Palatinate) white wines.

Ebernigen: German (Freiburg) red and white wines.

Ebro Valley: The important northern Spanish district which includes the Rioja (q.v.).

Ebulliometer or Ebullioscope: Instrument for testing the approximate alcoholic strength of a beverage by observing the boiling point.

Ebulum: Also Ebulam. An old mixed drink made from ale flavoured with elder, juniper, ginger and spices.

Ecclesiasticus 9:10: 'A new friend is as new wine: when it is old thou shalt drink it with pleasure.' How early in man's civilized history he learnt of the improvement of most alcoholic beverages by ageing!

Echézeaux, Grands: Fine red burgundy from the Côte-d'Or. Several vineyards bear the name, without the 'Grands'.

Echt: German wine term for non-sugared. See also Chaptalization.

Eckenberg: German (Ahr Valley) red table wine.

Écu, A l': French (Côte-d'Or) red wine.

Edel: The German term restricted to high-class, pure or fine quality of wine, brandy, etc.

Edelfäule: German equivalent for *pourriture noble* (q.v.) or noble rot. Some of the finest lusciously sweet Rhine wines are made by the *Edelfäule*.

Edelgewächs: German wine-making term for an especially fine growth or vintage.

Edelmann: German (Laubenheim, q.v.) white wine.

Edelweiss: Italian liqueur containing rock-candy on twigs.

Edenkoben: German (Palatinate) ordinary white wine.

Edesheim: German (Palatinate) white wines.

Ediger: German (Moselle) white wines, including the vineyards of Osterlaemmchen, Feuerberg, Hasensprung and Pfaffenberg.

Efmorgen: German (Rheinhessen) wine estate.

Eger: Hungarian town surrounded by extensive vineyards growing some of the finest wines of the country. See, for example, Egri Bikaver.

Egg Nog: Mixed, sweetened, warmed spirit drink containing beaten egg.

Egg Sour: American mixed drink of egg yolk, anisette and brandy.

Eggy-Hot: An old Cornish beverage made from hot beer, rum, eggs and sugar, poured from jug to jug until foaming. See also White Ale.

Église, Clos l': French (Pomerol) white wine. There are a number of other Pomerol vineyards with similar name.

Égrappoir: French name for the pierced cylinder used to extract the stalks from the grapes in wine-making.

Egri Bikaver: See Bikaver.

Egri Kadarka: Hungarian red table wine from Eger.

Eguisheim: French (Alsatian) white wine.

Egypt, Ancient: Alcoholic beverages were widely used in ancient Egypt. The commonest beverage was *hek*, a beer made from barley. Wine from grapes was common and was called *arp*. Wine was also made from dates under the name bak. See also Bousa.

Ehrenberg: German (Ruwer, q.v.) white wine.

Ehrentrunk: German term for ceremonial drink offered as special honour.

Ehrwein: Term applied in Germany to a particularly fine wine.

Eibelstadt: German (Franconian, q.v.) white wine.

Eibingen: German (Rheingau) white wine district, including the vineyards of Flecht, Wüst, Lay, Kirchenpfad and Backhaus.

Eichstetten: German (Kaiserstuhl, q.v.) wine centre.

Eigengewächs: Followed by the name of the vigneron, this German term means that it is his own growth, a guarantee of authenticity if not of actual quality.

Eimer: Central European wine measure varying from 12 to 15 gallons with locality.

Eisel: German (Bingen, q.v.) white wine.

Eiserberg: Dry white wine from Östrich (q.v.).

Eiserpfad: German (Östrich, q.v.) white wine.

Eiserweg: German (Östrich, q.v.) white wine.

Eiskummel: Very strong kümmel (q.v.).

Eistrich Beer: Eastern Beer. A product imported from Europe in the 14th century.

Eiswein: Lit. 'ice wine', the German name for wine made from very ripe grapes damaged by frost. These grapes are gathered while the ice still remains on them. The freezing concentrates the must.

Eitelsbach: German town in Ruwer Valley, near Trier, the centre of a group of vineyards producing excellent white wine classed as moselles. The finest of these vineyards are Eitelsbacherhofberg, Sonnenberg and Karthäuserhofberg.

Eitelsbacherhofberg: German (Ruwer, q.v.) white wine.

Elazig: Turkish district reputed to produce the best wine, which includes the celebrated okuzgozu, supposed to be the world's most highly pigmented wine.

Elba: This small island off the Italian coast produces red and white table wines but is better known for other reasons.

Elbow Bending: Colloq. for drinking.

Elderberry: The black berries of the elder shrub (*Sambucus nigra*) were for centuries the sheetanchor of the wine-faker. The purple juice was employed to give colour to wine that was considered deficient. The scent of the flowers bears some resemblance to that of muscatel grapes and an infusion has been used (and perhaps still is) to make a poor imitation. Until the Portuguese government took a hand, much port was coloured up with elderberry juice. On the domestic front so-called elderberry wine is still made. A cane sugar syrup is fermented and flavoured with elderberry flowers and berries.

Elderberry Wine: See Country Wines.

Elderflower Wine: Country wine (q.v.) flavoured with elderflowers.

Eleanor of Guienne: A woman who should be remembered with appreciation by all wine-drinkers of British association. She it was who brought to the English crown on her marriage all the superb Bordeaux region and other wine-growing areas. For three hundred years England was thus the principal wine-growing country of the world. Perhaps the loss of these lush regions is the chief reason why England has never tried to maintain any significant wine-producing section.

Elephantine: Island in the Nile near Assuan, where Roman legions of this most southerly outpost were said to have grown quite good wine.

Elevenses: Vernacular English term for the regular mid-morning drink, usually of ale.

Elijah's Cup: Wine put on the table at the Jewish Seder celebration and intended for the prophet Elijah in case he joins the feast.

Elisenberg: German (Mülheim, q.v.) white wine.

Elixir: Originally a preparation designed to change base metal into gold or to prolong youth indefinitely; the word has also been applied to sovereign remedies and to the best qualities of liqueurs (q.v.) and spirits (q.v.).

Eller: German (Moselle Valley) white wines of quality. The best vineyards are Kapley, Kalmont and Hölle.

Ellerstadt: German (Palatinate) red and white table wines.

Ellisland: A village in Scotland producing whisky and remembered as the place of employment of Robert Burns as an exciseman in 1789.

Ellmendingen: German (Baden) red and white table wines.

Ellsheim: German (Rheinhessen) white wine district, including the vineyards of Spielberg, Nenenberg, Marchans, Rosengarten, Dreimorgen and Blum.

Elsesser: The name under which Elizabeth I drank Alsatian wine. See also Ausoye.

Elster: German (Forst, q.v.) fine white wine.

Eltville: Important German wine-growing centre in the Rheingau, known as the city of wine and roses. Sparkling wines are a feature.

Elvira: A green grape, sometimes wrongly termed Missouri riesling, which originated in a Missouri nursery about 1865. It is said to be the basis of the best New York State wine.

Embarcador: Spanish for shipper (q.v.).

Embotellado en Origen: Spanish for original bottling, the equivalent of *mise du Château* (q.v.).

Emilia: Italian wine-growing province. The best wines are Sangiovese and Trabbiano.

Empire Wines: The term refers to what was the British Empire and meant in particular the wines of Australia and South Africa. Canada produces no wine for export nor does New Zealand and the growth in Mediter-

ranean and other outposts is negligible. Now that South Africa has
become a foreign power the term has lost meaning.

Enab: Biblical term for the grape.

Enclos-Pomerol, L': French (Pomerol) red wine.

Endingen: German (Kaiserstuhl, q.v.) wine centre.

Enfant-Jésus: French (Côte-d'Or) red wine.

Engaddi: Also En-Gedi and Engeddi. This means 'fountain of the kid' and
is the name of a spring of warm water which gushes from the cliffs
overlooking the centre of the western shore of the Dead Sea, on the road
to Bethlehem. It is also the name of the small adjacent village. Palms and
vines once flourished but for many centuries it was a wild and desolate
place. It is reported that vines again grow there.

Engaddi is of special interest from the Biblical reference to it. The
Vulgate translation from the Song of Songs (Canticles 1: 14) is 'A
cluster of Cyprus my love is to me in the vineyards of Engaddi'. However, the translation in the Revised Version is 'A cluster of henna flowers
my love is to me in the vineyards of En-gedi'. Scholars consider the
Revised Version the more reliable.

The belief that the *Malvasia* (q.v.) grape (the vine of Cyprus) had
been introduced into Palestine even before the time of King Solomon
appears to have no sound foundation. 'Cyprus' in the Vulgate version
apparently refers to a cypress tree, not to a vine.

André Simon writes: 'A small town in the valley of the Jordan. The
vine still grows there as it did about 1000 B.C. when Solomon wrote the
"Song of Songs": "A cluster of Cyprus my love is to me, in the vineyards of Engaddi". This shows that even in the days of Solomon the
vine of Cyprus, the Malvasia grape, was highly prized.'

However, it seems certain at least that the grape has been grown at
Engaddi for at least three thousand years.

Engelberg: German (Kröv-Kövenig, q.v.) white wine estate.

Engelgrube: German (Neumagen, q.v.) white wine.

Engelmannsberg: German (Hattenheim, q.v.) white wine.

Engelsberg: German (Nackenheim, q.v.) white wine.

Engerweg: German (Rüdesheim, q.v.) fine white wine.

English Wines: The climate (lack of sun rather than of warmth) precludes
the commercial cultivation of the vine in England. The only true English
wine is cider (q.v.). The hundred or so 'wines' bearing such names as
elderberry, cowslip, ginger, damson, parsnip, sage, horehound and
gooseberry are in no sense wines. They are fermented cane-sugar syrups
flavoured with the herb or fruit. Yet parts of southern England could
ripen vines and produce material amounts of wine. However, see the
entry Eleanor of Guienne, also Country Wines.

Enkirch: German (Moselle Valley, Zell district) fine white wine. The vineyards include Steffensberg, Hinterberg and Monteneubel.

Enology: See Oenology.

Entire: (Or Entire Butt.) The original name for Porter (q.v.). A special brew, first produced in 1722, equivalent to a mixture of ale, beer and two-penny (q.v.). The term entire is also a British trade description indicating that the licensee sells only one brewer's beer.

Entre-Deux-Mers: The area of the Gironde département lying between the two rivers Dordogne and Garonne where a vast volume of red and white wine of moderate quality is grown.

Entre Deux Vins: French for half-seas over, drunk.

Enzien: Swiss flavoured spirit made from alpine plant of that name.

Enzyme: An organic catalyst, a substance which can bring about chemical change in a large amount of another substance, without being used up in the process. Important enzymes are the zymase (q.v.) of yeast and the diastase (q.v.) of malt.

Épenots: French (Côte-d'Or) red wine.

Epenottes, Les: French red wine of Beaune (q.v.).

Epernay: Next to Reims, the most important centre of the champagne trade.

Épesses: Swiss (Vaud) wine centre for table whites.

Épineuil: French (Yonne) centre for red and white wines.

Epinotte: French (Chablis) white burgundy.

Epluchage: French for plucking. The process of picking individual grapes for production of wine of special quality. This applies in France to certain sauternes, champagnes and other expensive wines, in Germany on the Rhine to the finest hocks and in Hungary to the choicest tokay (*essenz*).

Eppan: Wine district of South Tyrol.

Equatorial Akvavit: Scandinavian akvavit (q.v.) which has been aged for at least two years in a sherry cask aboard a sailing vessel. The label shows the itinerary of the ship, which must have crossed the equator at least twice. A pretty conceit — but after all, akvavit is only alcohol and flavouring.

Equinox: There is a curious and widely-held myth (for myth it is) that port goes out of condition for a short time at the end of March and September. Many merchants refuse to fine or bottle port at that time.

Erasmus: It is apparently not generally known that he said (or is reputed to have said) that Burgundy 'may well be called the mother of men, having such noble milk within her breasts to suckle her sons'.

Erbach: German (Rheingau) centre for white wines, including the vineyards of Markobrunn, Steinmorgen, Brühl, Rheinhell, Sichelsberg, Michelmark, Hohenrain, Honigsberg, Kissling, Pellen, Langenwingert, Steinwegen and, nearby, Reinhartshausen.

Erbach-Eltville: Wine parish of the Rheingau (q.v.).

Erdbeerlikor: German strawberry liqueur.

Erden: German (Moselle) white wine centre, including vineyards of

Treppchen, Buhslay, Rotkirch, Herrenberg, Herzlay, Kranklay, Kammer and Prälat.

Erlach: Swiss (Berne) red wine.

Erlau: One of the chief Hungarian red wine districts.

Erlenbach: German (Württemberg) red and white wine centre.

Erloch: Red table wine from Berne, Switzerland.

Ermitage: Alternative French form of hermitage. Also the name of several red wine estates of Graves and Médoc.

Ernoldsheim: French (Alsatian) white wine.

Erntebringer: German wine estate of Winkel, Rheingau.

Erpolzheim: German (Palatinate) table wines, red and white.

Escala: Spanish term for the tiers of casks of a *solera* (q.v.).

Escherndorf: German (Franconian) white wines, including vineyards of Berg, Lump, Kirchberg, Eulengrube, Hengstberg, Fürstenberg and Escherndorfer.

Eshkol: Biblical term for grape cluster. See also Enab.

Eshkol Rishon: Israeli dry red wine.

Espumosa: Spanish wine-term for sparkling.

Essence Process: See Essential Oil, also Liqueurs.

Essenheim: German wine-growing parish of Rheinhessen.

Essential Oil: The odoriferous constituents of leaves, berries, etc. which are usually of an oily nature (though not true 'fixed' oils). They can be added direct to alcohol to produce gin, liqueurs, etc., of secondary quality, though wholesome enough. This is the 'essence process'. See also Liqueur.

Essenz: The finest and richest of Hungarian tokay wines (q.v.). See under Aszu p. 23.

Essingen: German (Palatinate) white wines.

Esslingen: German (Württemberg) red, white and sparkling wines.

Estatuto del Vino: The fundamental law of Spain of 1932 which regulated making and naming of wine.

Esters: A class of organic chemical compounds which result from the union of an alcohol and an acid. Many of the esters are of pleasing aroma, and are largely responsible for the characteristic flavours of alcoholic beverages.

Est! Est!! Est!!!: The name of an Italian golden sweet wine grown on the slopes of Montefiascone, north of Rome. The name is said (and it sounds credible) to be derived from the travels of Cardinal Fugger, who made a tour through Italy at the end of the 16th century and sent his valet ahead to test the wine of the inns. When the wine was satisfactory he chalked *Est!* on the door, and *Est! Est!!* if it was exceptional. At Montefiascone he was so enraptured that he scrawled *Est! Est!! Est!!!* and the name has stuck. It is irritating to see the name on wine other than Italian.

Estournel, Cos d': French (Médoc) red wine.

Estremadura: An area north of Jerez (q.v.) where grapes are grown for producing sherry. It is also the name of a Spanish dessert wine of muscatel character.

Estufas: The heated rooms in which madeira wines are stored as part of the maturing process. The result is the curious and characteristic 'cooked' flavour of caramel. This baking process is also used in California, where it is termed 'rancio'.

Étampé: The French term for branded or stamped, covering both labelling and the printing of the name and date on the cork. This latter is an almost complete guarantee of authenticity.

Ethyl Pyrocarbonate: See Sparkling.

Etiquettes: The necklets or small labels on wine bottles.

Etna: Sicilian table wine grown, of course, on the slopes of the active volcano. An Italian would start a vineyard in purgatory or the Antarctica, if possible.

Étoile-de-Cantenac: French (Médoc) red wine.

Étoile-Pourret: French (St. Émilion) red wine.

Ettaler Klosterlikör: Bavarian monastery liqueur.

Ettenheim: German (Offenburg) wine district.

Eulengrube: German (Escherndorf, q.v.) white wine.

Euphoria: A sense of well-being and buoyancy. A lovely word about a lovely condition. The euphoric effect of alcohol is probably attained when enough has been drunk to give a blood-alcohol content of about 0·07%, which means an elated sobriety.

Évangile, L': French (Pomerol) red wine.

Everybody's Irish: Cocktail of Irish whiskey, green chartreuse and crème de menthe.

Ewell: South Australian vineyard, now 120 years old, especially noted for light white wine of Moselle type.

Excise: The government tax or duty levied on alcohol which is contained in beverages, or has not been treated with a denaturant (q.v.) to render it unfit for drinking purposes.

Expences (Expenses): Elizabethan for drink money, tip (*Twelfth Night*, Act 3, Sc. 1).

Export: A fanciful word applied in most countries to most liquors and intended to convey the idea of special quality (i.e. fit for export).

Exshaw: Old-established brand of cognac (q.v.).

Extension: Official permission to remain open beyond the usual licensed hours. Extensions may be granted for special functions and national holidays.

Exterminator: Mixture of vodka and *fino* sherry.

Extract: The term means malt extract, the result of agitating malt with water and consisting of a solution of maltose (malt sugar), protein and mineral matter. It is the true raw material or progenitor of beer.

Eye-Opener: Obsolete Australian term for a mixed drink in goldrush days that was drunk in the morning.

Ezerjó: Hungarian white (golden) dry wine from Mor.

Fabricant: French wine term, lit. 'maker' but especially applied to the person who tastes and decides how champagne will be blended.

Factory House: The prosaic name for the magnificent and venerable port wine exchange and social club of the port shippers (q.v.) at Oporto.

Fahr: German (Burg, q.v.) white wine.

Fahrberg: German (Kobern, q.v.) white wine estate.

Faible: French wine term for weak, poor body.

Fair and Warmer: Cocktail of rum, sweet vermouth and curaçao.

Falerno: The general name for the red and white wines of the Campanian vineyards of Naples, near Vesuvius. The ancient wine known as Falernum was extravagantly praised by the Roman classical writers. It is generally agreed that the modern Falerno wines are of no consequence. Falernum was praised by Horace but by the time of Diocletian it had declined in esteem and presumably in quality.

Falkenberg: German white wine. See also Dienheim.

Falkenstein: German (Oberemmel, q.v.) white wine.

Falkensteiner: Austrian red table wine.

Falklay: German (Reil, q.v.) white wine.

Fallacies, Drinking: In the light of the physiological action of alcohol, it is not surprising that the subject of drinking is shot through with false beliefs. Here one can merely make bold mention of a few of the commoner. Alcohol is not a stimulant but the pharmacological opposite, a depressant. It is a volatile anaesthetic and it has a specific action upon the brain, removing the inhibitions or brakes upon conduct that play so large a part in civilized life.

'Mixing drinks' does not, in itself, increase the intoxicating power of alcoholic beverages. The action depends on the quantity of alcohol taken and most people are close to drunk when they start to mix drinks.

Alcohol does not enhance sexual power. It actually has the opposite effect though it may act as an aphrodisiac by removing inhibition.

Brandy is not more 'medicinal' than whisky or other wholesome, matured spirit. Alcoholic strength is the criterion.

Drinking does not necessarily make people jolly. The truth seems to be that alcohol enhances the mood in which it is taken.

Champagne is not a preventive or cure for sea-sickness nor, for that matter, is any other alcoholic beverage.

A hearty drink before going into a bitterly cold atmosphere is not a good plan but a very bad one, since alcohol is a vaso-dilator (blood-vessel expander) and thus causes rapid loss of body heat.

Stout is not more 'nutritious' than beer (or the reverse). There are no 'fumes' of drink to 'go to the head' or anywhere else.

Alcoholic beverages do not necessarily improve on long storage. The subject is complex and many factors must be considered. Some beverages such as white wines, beer and gin may have a comparatively short life of peak quality. Spirits never improve in bottle.

Bottled port or other wine does not go regularly 'out of condition' at the start of autumn and spring.

Red wine is no more a 'blood-maker' than white. The pigments of wine and blood are chemically quite dissimilar.

The foregoing examples far from exhaust the list.

Fallen Bright: The wine-makers' term for the process of clarifying by natural sedimentation. The German term is *Helleich* or *Hellmass*.

Falschungen: German for falsification, adulteration, sophistication or inferior imitation.

Fanning-Lafontaine: French (Graves) red wine.

Fargues: Commune (q.v.) of the Sauternes (q.v.) district, and the name of the excellent sweet wine made there.

Faro: See Lambic.

Fass: German for cask, vat, barrel. A *Fassbinder* is a cooper. In Austria a *Fass* is a liquid measure of about 125 British gallons.

Fasschen: German name for a keg or small cask.

Fassweise: German term for 'on draught'. *Fasswein* is the German term for wine sold and dispensed from the barrel, i.e. draught.

Fatin: French (Médoc) red wine.

Fatvin: Swedish term for bulk wine, lit. 'barrel wine', i.e. wine before bottling.

Fautenböhl: German (Meckenheim, q.v.) white wine.

Faversham: One of the oldest breweries in the U.K. (Kent), established 1698.

Favraud: Old-established brand of cognac (q.v.).

Fayal: The town in the Azores which is the wine centre and port of shipping. Also the name given to wine from the Azores.

Faye: French (Layon, q.v.) white wine.

Faye-sur-Layon: French (Anjou) white wines.

Federweisser: Cloudy new wine directly after fermentation. This is sold widely in Germany. See also Heuriger.

Feex: The approximate pronunciation of the modern Greek word in common usage for beer in general. For many years it was the name of a particular beer brewed in Athens by a German called Fuchs, who was given a monopoly by the reigning king in the nineties. Feex is, of course, Greek for Fuchs.

Feigenbranntwein: German for fig brandy.

Feinter: German vineyard of the Wehlen district (q.v.) of the Moselle Valley.

Feints: The fraction collected after the whisky has been distilled over. It is usually added to the 'low wines' (q.v.) for re-distillation.

Fellbach: German (Stuttgart) centre for red and white wines.

Fels: German (Könen, q.v.) white wine.

Felsenberg: German (Herxheim, q.v.) wine estate.

Felsenkeller: German natural rock cellars used for maturing wine.

Fenchelberg: German (Nackenheim, q.v.) white wine.

Fendant: Swiss name for a white grape said to be identical with the better known golden chasselas.

Fendant de Sion: Swiss (Valais) table wines, reputed to be the finest of the country.

Fendant Vert: Swiss white grape used for the best Vaud (q.v.) wines.

Ferintosh: The first recorded whisky distillery in Scotland. The reference is in an Act of the Scottish Parliament of 1699.

Fermentation: In the sense of this book, the conversion of sugar into ethyl alcohol by the action of yeast. The name is derived from the Latin *fervere*, to boil, and refers to the bubbling that occurs. Yeast is a microscopic unicellular plant that is widely distributed throughout the world. One species, the wine yeast, *Saccharomyces ellipsoideus*, is found naturally on the skin of ripe grapes, largely making up the pretty bloom.

The 'splitting' of the molecule of sugar into ethyl alcohol and carbon dioxide gas in about equal weights is effected by the enzyme (q.v.) zymase. It is possible to extract this from yeast and thus it is not essential to employ the living yeast plant though in practice this is invariable as the only economic method.

There is an optimum temperature for each strain of yeast, for wine yeast between 75° F. and 85° F. The rate of fermentation can be regulated to some extent by control of temperature. Some wines and other beverages are best made by rapid fermentation. In other cases a slow, sustained action is desired.

Beer and whisky yeasts are closely related to bakers' yeast, *Saccharomyces cerevisiae*. Rum, pulque, mead, cider and other beverages are made with specialized strains.

Wine can be made readily enough by relying upon the yeast naturally present on the skin but since there are invariably 'wild', undesirable yeasts present, it is becoming increasingly common to employ a culture of pure yeast carefully bred for special virtues, first adding sulphur dioxide to the 'must'. This acts as a preservative. It restrains the 'wild' yeasts but not appreciably the added pure culture.

The carbon dioxide gas is allowed to bubble away to waste in most wine-making, the exception being sparkling wine (champagne and similar). In brewing beer it is modern practice to collect the carbon dioxide and compress it into cylinders. The 'still' beer is aerated while being dispensed.

The subject of alcoholic fermentation is a vast and technical one and a specialized text must be consulted for detailed information.

Fermentation, Closed: The system, first developed in Germany and especially applicable to wine, of fermenting in closed stainless-steel tanks under pressure. Now widely used for the production of both still and lightly-sparkling wines and other beverages. The types known as crackling and pearl wines (Perlweine) are usually made in this manner.

Fermented Out: Means that fermentation has been completed and the resulting liquor is 'dry' (not sweet).

Fermenting Squares: Copper-lined wooden vessels in the brewery in which the yeast is pitched into the wort (q.v.) to commence the initial part of the conversion of the wort to beer.

Fermenting Tanks: Slate or stone vessels in which the conversion of wort to beer is completed in the brewery. In these vessels the yeast head is skimmed off in the form of barm beer (q.v.). The process is now nearly obsolete.

Fermenting Vat: See Cuve.

Ferran: French (Graves) red wine.

Ferrand: French (St. Émilion) red wine.

Ferrande: French (Graves) red wine.

Ferric Casse: Wine defect caused by contamination with traces of iron. One remedy is blue fining (q.v.) but it is better to avoid the trouble by using plastic and other innocuous pipes and vessels.

Ferrière: French (Margaux) red wine.

Fessenbach: German (Baden) table wines.

Feuer: German (Hambach, q.v.) white wine.

Feuerberg: German (Dürkheim, q.v.) red wine.

Feuerberg: German (Friedelsheim, q.v.) white wine.

Feuerheerd Bros.: Old-established (1815) shippers of port (q.v.).

Feuillette: Half a French *barrique* (q.v.). It is also the characteristic barrel of the Chablis (q.v.) region, half the size of a *pièce* (q.v.).

Fèves: French (Côte-d'Or) red wine.

Fiasco: The name of an Italian wine bottle of flask-like shape, of capacity about 2 to 4 pints. Especially applied to the straw-covered container for chianti wine (q.v.).

K   M.D.D.

Fichots: French (Côte-d'Or) red wine.

Fiesta de la Vendimia, La: The Spanish vintage festival, especially in the sherry country, Andalusia. It is a time of high revelry.

Fiètres: French (Côte-d'Or) red wine.

Fieuzal: French (Graves) red and white wines.

Fig: As with all sugary fruits, wine and hence brandy can be made from the fig.

Figeac: French (St. Émilion) red wine.

Fighting Cocks, The: English inn at St. Albans, said to be the oldest in the U.K. The building is supposed to date back to 795.

Filhot: French (Sauternes) sweet white wine.

Filler: A long-stemmed glass vessel with a bulb end, pierced by a small hole. It held about a quarter of a pint and was used as an alternative to a ladle for serving punch.

Fillette: The attractive French name 'little girl' for a half-bottle of wine, especially in Touraine.

Film Yeast: Syn. for 'flor' (q.v.), the surface yeast growth that is an essential stage in the production of true sherry.

Filtration: The process of clarifying or 'polishing' wine to make it brilliantly clear, by passing it through a suitable medium, such as paper or cloth, either mechanically or by gravity. The same result is secured by fining (q.v.).

Filzen: German white wine vineyard on Saar (q.v.).

Findling: German (Nierstein, q.v.) white wine.

Fine: The common French term for any after-dinner brandy, by no means necessarily of fine quality. Fine Bourgogne is made from wine lees but may be excellent.

Fine Champagne: French term which has nothing to do with sparkling wine but refers to the best cognac (q.v.) which must be made from grapes produced within a defined area. Usually made by blending Grande and Petite Champagne. See also Cognac.

Fine Fourchette: 'Fine fork' — a knowing one in food and drink.

Fine Maison: French term for the regular brandy of the hotel or restaurant, usually nothing remarkable. In fact this 'house brandy' can be anything, according to the skill and morality of the proprietor. See also Fine.

Fines-Roches, Château des: One of the Châteauneuf (q.v.) wines.

Finger Lakes: A district in New York State which is an important centre of wine production despite the severe winter climate. Here grow all the best native American vines — Catawba, Niagara, Delaware, Diana, Elvira, Dutchess, Moore's Diamond and others. Some authorities consider the Finger Lakes wines the flower of American production, despite California!

Fining: The process of clarifying liquors, especially wine. The object is to remove the microscopically small particles which cause a cloudy appearance. This is effected by introducing a substance which will cause the particles to coagulate, coalesce or aggregate. The action is probably the result of positively-charged fining particles discharging the negatively-charged clouding particles. Fining agents have been used empirically for centuries, amongst them ox-blood, egg-white, milk, casein, agar, tannin, fish or animal glue, Spanish clay, bentonite clay, isinglass, and a hundred and one patent preparations. Ultra-efficient mechanical filtration is superseding the older fining methods.

Finings: Material added to clarify beer or wine. May consist of isinglass or other coagulant.

Finish: Vague wine term for the impression left in the mouth just as one swallows. It may be sharp, soft, tannic, mellow, sweet, dry and much, much more.

Fino: Pale dry sherry (q.v.), one of the two basic styles of sherry. Should be delicate and free from bitter flavour.

Fins Bois: Area of Cognac. See also Cognac.

Fiori Alpini: Italian liqueur of flavour recalling eau de Cologne, containing sugar candy crystals on twigs.

Firewater: Spirits (q.v.). The word is a literal translation from the Algonquin Indian term *scoutiouabou*. It is, however, used derisively today for any distilled product of alleged crudity.

Firing Glass: So called because Freemasons knocked them simultaneously on the table, in acknowledging a toast, and produced a noise said to resemble the firing of a gun. The foot of the glass was made especially thick to withstand such treatment.

Firkin: Beer cask of 9 gallons. Two firkins are equal to a kilderkin (q.v.).

Firn: German term for bouquet of wine derived from age.

Fischerpfad: German (Rheinhessen) wine estate.

Fish House Punch: Mixed drink named for an old American dining club. A mixture of rum, brandy, peach liqueur and lemon juice.

Fix: Mixed cold spirit beverage containing sugar and lemon juice, similar to or identical with a 'sour' (q.v.) and a 'sling'.

Fixin: French (Côte-d'Or) wine *commune*, including the vineyards of Chapître, Arvelets, Hervelets, Meix-Bas and Perrière; all red wines.

Fizz: American effervescent mixed drink of varying composition, often similar to a Rickey (q.v.).

Fjolne, King: If the name of Clarence (q.v.) is preserved in his butt of Malmsey, why not this Norse king who is said to have been drowned in a vessel of mead?

Flächenhahl: German (Nierstein, q.v.) white wine.

Flagey-Echézeaux: French (Côte-d'Or) wine commune comprising many celebrated vineyards. By general consent the finest is Les Grands Echézeaux. Others are Beaux Monts Bas, Beaux Monts Hauts, Champs

Traversins, Echézeaux du Dessus, En Orveaux, Les Poulaillières, Les Quartiers des Nuits, Les Rouges du Bas and Les Treux.

Flagon: Glass or pewter vessel formerly fitted with a lid and handle for the storage of wine or beer. Today it describes the glass two-quart bottles in which beer and wine are sold.

Flap: A brandy and soda.

Flapdragon: An old beverage, or rather concoction, consisting of raisins and other tid-bits floating in blazing spirits. These were supposed to be eaten aflame.

Flasche: The German long-necked green wine-bottle.

Flaschenreife: German for bottle-maturing of wine.

Flaschenwein: The local term for good and mature wine of the Palatinate (q.v.).

Flask: Formerly a bulbous bottle with a long, narrow neck, but now, more commonly, a small, flat glass or metal container to fit the pocket.

Flecht: German (Eibingen, q.v.) white wine.

Fleckinger: White wine from Forst, Palatinate (q.v.).

Flembingen: German (Palatinate) white wine.

Fleur, La: French (Pomerol) red wine. The same name is also borne by red wine vineyards in Entre-deux-Mers and the Médoc.

Fleurennes: French (Médoc) red wine.

Fleurie: A light, red wine from the Beaujolais district, France.

Fleur-Milon, La: French (Pauillac) red wine.

Fleur Pétrus, La: French (Pomerol) red wine.

Fliers: Wine-term for haze caused by cooling. No permanent deterioration is involved.

Flip: An 18th-century mixed drink consisting of a quart of bitter beer spiked (q.v.) with a gill of rum and heated with a flip-iron or loggerhead (q.v.). The term is now applied to any alcoholic beverage containing beaten egg (both white and yolk), usually spiced and heated. There seems no basic difference between a 'flip' and a 'nog' (or 'nogg').

Flogger: Hammer for corking. See also Boot.

Flor: Lit. 'flower', the name applied to the film of yeast which forms on the surface during the process of making *fino* sherry. It is a variety of wine yeast (*Saccharomyces ellipsoideus*, var. *beticus*). See also Sherry and Château Chalon.

Florida: Cocktail of rum, sweet vermouth and grapefruit juice.

Flower Wine: See Country Wines.

Fluid Ounce: The British unit is the volume of one standard ounce weight of pure water, measured at a temperature of 62° F. and atmospheric pressure of 30 inches. The U.S. fluid ounce is the one-sixteenth part of a U.S. pint, and is about 4% greater in volume than the British fluid ounce.

Flûte: French tall, slender wine glass (and also, of course, a musical instrument). A *flûteur* is both a piper and a tippler.

F-Measure: A liquid measure used in 14th-century London for a farthing's worth of beer.

Fob: The word used in a brewery to describe beer froth.

Fockenberg: German (Nierstein, q.v.) white wine.

Folle Blanche: One of the principal vines of the Cognac region. It makes good brandy but poor white wine for drinking.

Fonbadet: French (Médoc) red wine.

Fondue: Swiss alcoholic soup, drunk from communal bowl as prelude to meal.

Fongravet: French (Médoc) red wine.

Fonpetite: French (Médoc) red wine.

Fonplégade: French (St. Émilion) red wine.

Fonréaud: French (Listrac) red wine.

Fonroque: French (St. Émilion) red wine.

Fonta, La: French (Gironde) red and white wines.

Fontanelle: French (Médoc) red wine.

Fontanet: French (Médoc) red wine.

Fontbonne-Agassac: French (Médoc) red wine.

Fontesteau: French (Médoc) red wine.

Forditas: A type of tokay wine (q.v.).

Foreshots: The term used in whisky manufacture for the first fraction obtained in distillation. This contains alcohol and various other constituents. The foreshots are added to the 'low wines' (q.v.) for redistillation.

Forêts, Les: French (Chablis) white wine.

Formidable: Wonderful French term for a large beer glass.

Forst: German (Palatinate) renowned white wine district, including the vineyards of Freundstück, Kirchenstück, Jesuitengarten, Ungeheuer, Fleckinger, Granich, Elster, Ziegler, Langenmorgen, Pechstein, Musenhang, Altenberg, Halmenboehl and Schnepfenflug.

Fortia, La: See Châteauneuf-du-Pape.

Fortification: The addition of alcohol, usually in the form of brandy, to partially or fully fermented wine.

Fortified Wine: Wine treated by the addition of alcohol, usually in the form of brandy. Fortified wines include port, marsala, roussillon, malaga, sweet sherry, oloroso and many other sweet dessert wines. Dry wines such as *fino* sherry are also fortified. The alcohol percentage of the resulting beverage is usually 18% to 20%. This is sufficient to render the wine free from spoilage on opening, as yeast and most bacteria cannot develop in alcoholic beverages of this strength.

Contrary to popular belief fortified wines such as port and sherry are comparatively modern, certainly no older than the early part of last century. Fortification was probably first used for preservation, affording a method of shipping wines from countries of warm climates to northern Europe and the U.S. Most appetizer wines such as vermouth and the many variants are flavoured fortified wines.

Foucauld: Old-established (1847) brand of cognac (q.v.).

Foudre: The name of the largest French wine-storage casks. See also Fuder.

Fouettage: French term for the whisking of wine with egg white, gelatin or other clarifying agent.

Fouloir: French term for the mechanical grape-crusher used in wine-making. If combined with an *égrappoir* (q.v.) it is termed a *foulo-grappe*.

Founder's Port: The term applied to fine or allegedly fine wine such as might have been laid down by the founder of a college or similar body.

Fountaingrove: North Californian winery at Santa Ross, Sonoma County.

Four-Ale: Old term for mild beer. Origin obscure.

Four-Ale Bar: Old term still surviving as a rather quaint synonym for public bar. See also Four-Ale.

Fourcas-Dupré: French (Médoc) red wine.

Fourcas-Hostein: French (Médoc) red wine.

Fourchaume: French (Chablis) white wine.

Foureaud: French (Médoc) red wine.

Fouroque: French (St. Émilion) red wine.

Fourtet, Clos: Vineyard of St. Émilion, Bordeaux, producing good red wine.

Foxy: The term applied to the flavour of wine made from some varieties of native American grapes. It is a name of opprobrium and intended to suggest the objectionable and penetrating odour of the fox but actually many people find the flavour by no means unpleasant.

Fraction: In distillation, a portion of the distillate that comes over within a specified range of temperature. In the production of potable spirits, certain fractions are rejected as being unpalatable or containing undesirable substances.

Fraise: Brandy distilled from strawberries, an Alsatian speciality. Only the wealthy can afford the genuine stuff.

Fraisia: French liqueur of strawberry flavour.

Framboise: Spirit of raspberry flavour distilled from fermented raspberry juice usually fortified with sugar. It is a true spirit or fruit brandy not to be confused with raspberry liqueur (sirop de framboise or crême de framboise). Both brandy and liqueur are specialities of Lorraine and Alsace and are quite costly.

Frame Saw: A specially constructed saw used by coopers (q.v.) to cut the circular shape of the head of the cask.

Franc-de-Goût: French wine-term meaning fruity.

Franciscan Fathers: California has special cause for gratitude. In the first half of the 19th century they brought European vines from Spain via Mexico and planted vineyards from San Diego to San Francisco and Sonoma.

Franconia: The centre for Frankenwein, also known as Steinwein. Franconia is one of the important German wine districts of which Würzburg is the market city. Some of the principal Franconian wine parishes are Iphofen, Horstein, Thüngersheim, Randersacker, Nordheim-A.M., Frickenhausen, Sommerach, Eibelstadt, Hammelburg, Rödelsee and Eschendorf. The wine is put up in characteristic dumpy bottles called *Bocksbeutels*. The brittle white wine is highly esteemed.

Frankenwein: The German name of the wine of Franconia. The word is a synonym for Steinwein (q.v.).

Franklin, Benjamin: A great advocate of temperance; he regularly drank beer and wine. He thus used the term temperance (q.v.) in its only true sense.

Frappato di Vittoria: Italian (Sicilian) dry red wine.

Frappé: French word meaning iced or chilled, especially in relation to liquor.

Frascati: Pleasant Italian white table wine from Latium. See also Castelli Romani.

Frasco: Portuguese and Spanish for flask.

Frecciarossa: Italian dry wine, red and white, from Pavia.

Free House: In the sense of this book, an establishment licensed for the sale of alcoholic beverages which is not the property of a brewery, distillery or winery and is free to sell all brands. Some people naïvely believe that free houses should be encouraged.

Free-Run Wine: The wine which runs freely from the pomace after the fermentation. In good wines other than burgundies, it is always kept separate from the further yield of wine obtained by pressing the pomace, as this latter is of poorer quality.

Freiburg: German (Upper Baden) wine centre.

Freinsheim: German (Palatinate) white wine district, including the vineyards of Goldberg, Schwarzes Kreuz, Oschelskopf, Hahnen, Hochgewann and Rosenbuckel.

Freisa: Italian esteemed red table wine from Piedmont. Also a good red Italian (Piedmont) grape. Grown in California as Fresia.

Freitas Martins Caldeira & Co.: Old-established shippers of madeira (q.v.).

Fremières, Les: French (Côte-d'Or) red wine of Morey.

Fremiers, Les: French (Côte-d'Or) red wine of Pommard.

Fremiet: French (Côte-d'Or) red wine of Volnay.

French Cream: Brandy in tea. Australian term in goldrush days, but perhaps of wider application.

French Hoek: South African wine centre.

Freundstück: German (Forst, q.v.) fine white wine.

Friary: Old-established English brewery of Guildford.

Frickenhausen: German (Franconian, q.v.) white wine.

Friedelsheim: German (Palatinate) white wine district, including the vine-yards of Letten, Schlossgarten, Feuerberg and Tiergarten.

Friesenheim: German (Baden) white wine.

Fritzehöll: German (Nackenheim, q.v.) white wine.

Friularo: Italian (Veneto) red wine, also the grape used.

Frizzante: Italian term for a slightly sparkling wine.

Frog Mug: Originally made at the Sunderland potteries as a form of practical joke. On draining the mug the unsuspecting drinker found a large imitation frog inside.

Frohngewann: German (Gau-Bickelheim, q.v.) white wine.

Froichots, Les: French (Côte-d'Or) red wine.

Fromy: Old-established (1815) brand of cognac (q.v.).

Fronhof: German (Dürkheim, q.v.) white wine.

Fronsac: A Bordeaux district producing a large amount of moderate wine marketed under the simple name Bordeaux Rouge.

Frontignac: Small-berried wine-making red muscat (q.v.) grape much used in Australia. The name is a corruption of Frontignan, a village in the South of France near Marseilles.

Frontignan: The popular French dessert wine of the Languedoc. Despite the description V.D.N. or *vins doux naturels* (q.v.) the wine is fortified (q.v.). It is made from the muscat grape and the same type of wine is produced in warm climates throughout the world. The name or something like it is also imitated.

Fronton: A pink French table wine from Gascony.

Frostgeschmack: German term for the defective taste of wine, resulting from frost harming unripe grapes.

Froth: The layman's word for 'fob'. It is also commonly used to describe the 'head' on a glass of beer.

Froth-Blower: (Colloquial) beer drinker or member of the Ancient Order of Froth-blowers.

Fruhschoppen: German term for a drink before lunch.

Fruity: Term applied to wine to indicate a pronounced flavour of the grape. Not a desirable term, since grapes vary so widely in flavour.

Füchsel: Czechoslovakian (Pressburg, q.v.) wines. Also Austrian *rosé* wine.

Fuchsloch: German (Gau-Odernheim, q.v.) white wine district.

Fuddling-Cup: An intricate drinking vessel of Elizabethan days, made of a number of pots interconnected by holes, which could not be drunk by a 'fuddler' without spilling the contents.

Fuder: The huge German cask, usually of about 6 *Aums* (q.v.) but variable. It can range in capacity from 180 to nearly 400 gallons, according to locality. It is, of course, more essentially a vessel for storage than for transport. The French counterpart is the *Foudre*.

Fudling: An archaic and opprobrious name for spirits.

Fuées, Les: French (Côte-d'Or) red wine.

Fuençaral: Spanish (Madrid) dessert wine.

Fuggle: The most widely grown of English hops. Often blended with Golding (q.v.).

Fuissé: French wine commune adjoining Pouilly (q.v.).

Fu Kwat Tsau: Chinese (Cantonese) medicinal wine in which tiger bone has been dissolved. See also Kop Kaai and Yeuk Ts Oi Po Yeung.

Fullwein: German term for sound wine used to make up ullage (q.v.).

Fumadelle: French (Médoc) red wine.

Fumarium: Roman chamber in which wine was mellowed by means of smoke. Perhaps not so fantastic as might appear. Smoke is bactericidal and the resulting flavour probably not inferior to some wines.

Funchal: The wine market and shipping port of Madeira.

Fünfkirchen: Wine district of Hungary.

Funkenberg: German (Müden, q.v.) white wine.

Furiani: French (Corsican) dessert wine.

Furmint: A distinctive white grape from which is made the celebrated Hungarian wine tokay (q.v.). The Californian 'Flame Tokay' is quite distinct.

Furmint Edes: Hungarian white wine from Kecskemét.

Fürstenberg: German (Escherndorf, q.v.) white wine.

Fusel-Oil: The term (rather unscientific) applied to a certain fraction of newly distilled spirit, present to the extent of from 0·1% to 0·7% by volume of the whole. It consists of a mixture of higher alcohols (amyl, isobutyl, propyl, etc.), and traces of other bodies. These are harsh and unpleasant in taste. They are slowly converted to fragrant esters (q.v.) during the ageing process in wood vessels, hence the importance of such maturing.

Fuzerta: Portuguese *rosé* (q.v.) wine.

Gaiersberg: German white wine. See also Dittelsheim.

Gaiersbühl: German (Dürkheim, q.v.) white wine.

Gaillac: French (Languedoc) red and white wines.

Gaillard: French (Côte-d'Or) red wine.

Gaiole: Italian (Tuscan) red wines.

Gairnfarn: South Austrian red wine district.

Gaisbach: German (Baden) red and white wines.

Gaisböhl: German (Ruppertsberg, q.v.) white wine.

Galamus: French (Roussillon) sweet dessert wine.

Gale: Old-established English brewery of Portsmouth.

Galgenberg: German (Nierstein, q.v.) white wine. See also Kreuznach.

Galgenpfad: German (Lorchhausen, q.v.) white wine estate.

Gallisieren: The German term for amelioration or chaptalization (q.v.). Most countries rightly prohibit this practice of adding cane-sugar to weak musts (q.v.) in wine-making.

Gallizing: The high-falutin' synonym for the adulteration of acid wine by adding water and sugar. It is applied only to cheap and inferior wine. It 'immortalizes' the French inventor, one Gall.

Gallon: A liquid measure used in English-speaking countries. The word is derived from the ONF. or ME. *galon*. It is connected with the modern French word for bowl, *jale*. It is a romantic measure and illustrates the quirks and conservatism of man. The British imperial and the American gallons were once identical but are now markedly different. The imperial gallon contains 277·274 cubic inches and the American gallon only 231. The U.S. gallon is actually the original English wine gallon. Up to 1826 both the U.K. and American gallons were the same, 231 cubic inches (the 'ale gallon' being 282). In the U.K. the act of 1826 very sensibly replaced both the 'wine' and the 'ale' gallons with a new measure, the imperial gallon. Hence the present confusion, not diminished by the fact that both imperial and U.S. gallons are divisible into 4 quarts or 8 pints. Perhaps this foolish and unnecessary confusion will not be resolved until both pig-headed nations adopt the metric system of liquid measure.

The British imperial gallon is the volume of ten standard pounds' weight of distilled water, weighed in air, with water and air at the temperature of 62° F. and the barometer at 30 inches.

Galway Pipe: South Australian dessert wine of quality.

Gamay: Black grape producing fine wines, especially Burgundy.

Gambrinus: A mythical Flemish King who is wrongly supposed to have invented beer.

Gamza: Bulgarian red table wine.

Gan: French (Jura) white wine.

Ganymede: In classical mythology a boy who became cup-bearer to the gods. Now applied to a youth who serves liquor. See also Hebe.

Garandmak: Russian wine grape of Lake Sevan (q.v.) said to be indigenous.

Garde, Vin de: French term for a wine of high quality, fit for keeping or 'laying down'.

Garenne, La: French (Côte-d'Or) white wine.

Gargle: Irish slang for alcoholic beverage.

Gargoyle: Cocktail of gin, vodka and passion fruit juice.

Garrafa: Portuguese for bottle. There are several other common words for 'bottle', including *botelha* and *frasca*, the latter also meaning 'flask'.

Garten: German (Oppenheim, q.v.) white wine.

Garvey: Old-established (1780) shippers of sherry (q.v.). It is still a family concern.

Gascony: The chief port was Bordeaux, and for 300 years this town was legally as much part of England as the three great wine-importing centres, London, Bristol and Hull. See also Bristol and Eleanor.

Gaspin: A drinking-vessel of leather, half-way between a black-jack (q.v.) and a bombard (q.v.).

Gastebois: French (Médoc) red wine.

Gatas: Portuguese *vinho verde* (q.v.) wine.

Gath: Biblical term (Hebrew) for wine press. Also known as *yekeb*. The first flow of the juice was offered to God.

Gattinara: Italian (Piedmont) dark red table wine.

Gau-Algesheim: German (Rheinhessen) white wines, including vineyards of Stolzenberg, Heppel, Steinert and Goldberg.

Gau-Bickelheim: German (Rheinhessen) white wine district, including vineyards of Innerst, Fels, Neuberg, Goldberg, Steinweg, Kapelle and Frohngewann.

Gau-Bischofsheim: German (Rheinhessen) white wine district, including vineyards of Sahler, Wehling, Vikarei, Rosteisen, Herrnberg, Brühl and Kellerberg.

Gaude, La: French (Provence) red wine.

Gaudichots, Les: French (Côte-d'Or) red wine.

Gauge: To ascertain the capacity or contents of a cask or other vessel, by measurement and calculation; an operation that calls for considerable experience, if accuracy is required. The customs and excise officer who performs this work is known as a 'gauger'. In the case of spirits, the operation is often accompanied by the testing of contents and calculation of proof strength.

Gaultier: Old-established brand of cognac (q.v.).

Gau-Odernheim: German (Rheinhessen) white wine district, including vineyards of Fuchsloch, Tiefental, Petersberg and Schallenberg.

Gautret: Old-established (1847) brand of cognac (q.v.).

Gavi: Italian (Piedmont) white wine.

Gay, Ch. le: French (Pomerol) white wine.

Gay, Domaine du: French (Graves) red wine.

Gaza: Wine-growing region mentioned in the Bible.

Gazin: French (Graves) red and white wines, also Pomerol and Gironde red wines.

Gean Whisky: An old-fashioned liqueur made from whisky and black cherries.

Gehaneweg: German (Ockenheim, q.v.) white wine.

Gehen: German (Deidesheim, q.v.) white wine.

Gehren: German (Rauenthal, q.v.) white wine.

Geiersberg: German (Worms) wine estate. See also Bechtheim.

Geierscheid: German white wine. See also Dienheim.

Geierslag: German (Moselle) white wine estate.

Geierslay: German wine estate of Wintrich, Moselle.

Geig: German (Rheinhessen) white wine from Aspisheim.

Geisberg: German vineyard (dry white) of Ockfen (q.v.).

Geisenheim: Celebrated German (Rheingau) white wine district, including the Rhine Viticultural Experimental Bureau and the vineyards of Schorchen, Steinacker, Rothenberg, Kosakenberg, Morschberg, Mänerchen, Katzenloch, Decker, Lickerstein, Kläuserweg, Altbaum, Kirchgrub, Becht, Gebstein and Muckenberg. Some esteemed sparkling wine is also made in this area.

Gelendshik: Russian winery near Crimea for sparkling wines.

Gelos: French (Jura) white wine region.

Gemarkgasse: German (Nierstein, q.v.) white wine.

Geneste: French (Graves) red and white wines.

Genet, En: French (Côte-d'Or) red wine.

Geneva: Syn. for 'gin'. Corruption of Dutch *jenever* (juniper, q.v.). There is no connection with Switzerland!

Geneva: Centre in Switzerland for light, aromatic table wines (Bernex, Lully, Satigny, Jussy, Meinier).

Genevrières, Les: French (Meursault) white wine.

Genevrières Dessus: French (Côte-d'Or) white wine.

Genièvre: French for juniper. See also Jenever and Gin.

Gennes: The Burgundian name for the solid mass of debris (stalks, skins and seeds) resulting from wine pressing and from which brandy (*marc de Bourgogne*, q.v.) is distilled after the harvest.

Gensingen: German (Rheinhessen) white wines, including the vineyards of Kisselberg, Im Kirschberg, Im Schemel and Hinter dem Mühlenberg.

Gentil: A term applied to Alsatian wines to indicate a superior blend. See also Zwicker.

Genzano: Italian dry wine from Latium (Castelli Romani, q.v.).

Georges: Old (1788) brewery of Bristol, now Bristol Brewery Georges & Co. Ltd.

Gephen Hayyayin: The Biblical name for the wine-vine (*Vitis vinifera*) widely cultivated in Palestine in ancient times.

Gephen Nokri: 'The degenerate plant of a strange vine', the wild vine bearing worthless grapes mentioned in the Bible (Jer. 2 : 21).

Gerace: Italian (Calabrian) white wine.

Gerichtspfad: White wine from Wachenheim, Palatinate (q.v.).

Gerlick: German (Hambach, q.v.) white wine.

German Wine Labels: See Labels, German Wine.

Germany: Celebrated alike for beer and wine, nothing more need be said here beyond the fact that some contend that the white wines of the Rhine and the beers of Bavaria are the standards for the judging of all others. Every type of alcoholic beverage is made in some part or other of Germany. Quality varies almost unbelievably.

Geropiga: A syrupy, spirituous, grape juice used for sweetening wines, especially port.

Gersbohl: White wine from Palatinate (q.v.).

Gerumpel: German white wine from Wachenheim (q.v.).

Gesindewein and Haustrunk: German wine terms signifying that the contents are for consumption by the staff of the owner of the estate.

Gevrey-Chambertin: Noted French (Côte-d'Or) wine district, including the vineyards of Chambertin (q.v.), Clos de Bèze, Clos de la Roche, Mazy, Saint-Jacques, Charmes, Ruchottes and Latricières.

Gewächs: See Wachstum.

Gewürztraminer: A famous variety of Traminer. The grapes have a curiously spicy and earthy flavour which is not universally popular.

Gewürztraube: German white grape, one of the finest varieties of riesling (q.v.).

Gezuckerte Weine: German for sugared wine. See also Chaptalization.

Ghemme: Italian (Piedmont) red wine.

Gibson: Cocktail identical with dry martini (q.v.) except that a pearl onion is substituted for the olive.

Giesler: Old-established (1838) champagne of Avize.

Gilbey: Large distillers of whisky and gin, outside the D.C.L. combine.

Gill: Liquid measure, one-quarter of a pint. In some regions, a gill (e.g. of ale) is half a pint.

Gill: Beer flavoured with ground ivy (as alleged) instead of hops. Unlikely!

Gimlet: Mixed drink of gin and lime juice, diluted and iced. One of the best quenchers in hot weather.

Gimmeldingen: German (Palatinate) white wine district, including vineyards of Neuberg, Kieselberg, Schild, Biengarten, and Meerspinne.

Gin: Technically a gin is any unsweetened or only slightly sweetened, flavoured spirituous beverage, for example lemon gin, orange gin, mastika, akvavit. Sloe gin used to be an English speciality made from the berry of the blackthorn (*Prunus spinosa*) but the name is now given to a liqueur (q.v.) of the same flavour.

However, the unqualified name 'gin' is today universally applied to a spirit flavoured predominantly with the essential oil of juniper.

The junipers are evergreens of the pine family (*Pinaceae*). The common juniper (*J. communis*) is widely distributed. The best berries, which are the source of the flavouring, come from trees grown at high altitudes and the chief sources are Italy, Austria, Switzerland and the Balkans. They contain an essential oil of highly aromatic and characteristic odour and of pronounced medicinal properties. To this gin owes its diuretic character and possibly the widespread consumption of gin has generated the belief that alcohol itself has the same action.

Gin is probably the most widely consumed of all spirits. Today most gin is used as a major constituent of mixed and fancy drinks, as a cursory inspection of the recipes for cocktails and similar beverages will confirm. However, it has had to live down a long, rather opprobrious history.

Gin was probably first made in Holland. When William III (Dutch William) came to the English throne, the excise duty on French wines and brandy was raised and gin took their place. In London gin was sold cheaply in all quarters and a large part of the population was debauched. Yet it was the social system that was to blame, not the beverage itself. (See Rum in similar regard.) Gin Lane was a synonym for depravity.

Today gin is a highly-esteemed and widely-used spirit, mainly as an ingredient of mixed drinks. The flavour of good (i.e. discreet) gin seems to blend well with almost all other beverages.

The name 'gin' is derived from the French *genièvre* or the Dutch *jenever*, both meaning juniper. By a curious corruption, a common English synonym for gin is geneva, though there is no connection with that Swiss town nor indeed is gin an especially favoured drink in Switzerland.

The manufacture of the best gin is by distillation (q.v.) but there are variations in method. In Britain the mash (q.v.) is usually a mixture of maize, malt and rye. After distillation the botanicals (q.v.) are added and the mixture distilled again. This may be repeated several times. In the U.S. the chief difference is that the alcohol alone may be more rigorously distilled. In Holland the process differs in so far as the mash is mainly of malted barley, the flavouring agents are added to the mash and the distillation may be performed several times. However, some Dutch gin makers start with spirit known as *moutwyn* or malt wine bought from specialist makers at Schiedam and this is distilled again with the added flavouring agents or botanicals. The same process is also used by many British, Australian and other makers of gin.

The essential character of gin is derived wholly from the added botanicals or flavourings. In addition to juniper there may be used coriander, lemon, ginger, angelica, orange peel, cassia, licorice, cinnamon, cardamon, caraway and more. Every maker ferociously guards his secret blend.

It is possible to make acceptable but not fine gin by the essence or compound process, consisting of merely adding flavouring to alcohol. See also Bathtub Gin.

London dry gin is a type. The 'London' merely means unsweetened and it may be made anywhere. Old Tom (q.v.) is the common name for gin sweetened with sugar or glycerine. (For alleged origin of the name Old Tom see entry Broadsheet.) Another characteristic gin is Plymouth, said to be made by adding a little mineral acid (sulphuric) before distillation, resulting in the production of a trace of ether and other aromatic substances. The name Plymouth has also ceased to be geographical.

Gin is ready to drink almost immediately after it is made. It may actually deteriorate on long storage.

Gin, Compound: See Bathtub Gin.

Gin and It: Abbreviation of gin and Italian vermouth. See also Sweet Martini.

Gin and Tonic: Mixed drink. Gin, lime and quinine water. Piously supposed to have recuperative properties but a pleasant mixture, irrespective.

Gin and Two: Mixed drink consisting of more or less equal parts of gin, French vermouth, and Italian vermouth. Sometimes fruit or olive is added.

Ginebra: Spanish for gin (juniper).

Gin Fizz: Gin, lemon and iced soda.

Ginger: Long used for spicing wine. Until comparatively recent times it was the custom of innkeepers to put on the bar counter a large dredger or vessel with a perforated top filled with ground ginger. Customers sprinkled ginger on top of their porter and stirred the drink with a red-hot poker.

Ginger Ale: Carbonated, sweetened, non-alcoholic beverage flavoured with ginger extract. Pleasant with gin.

Ginger Beer: Beverage made by fermenting a mixture of syrup and ginger-root. Although considered a temperance drink, ginger beer may sometimes have an appreciable alcohol content.

Ginger Wine: A beverage made in basically the same fashion as ginger beer, but after fermentation sugar and spirit are added. It is, of course, in no sense a wine. See also Cowslip.

Gin Pahit: Identical with pink gin (q.v.). Pahit is Malay for bitter.

Gin Palace: Although this sounds an opprobrious term to the modern ear, it was not actually so. It was the name given to the bright, clean and gay London establishments which, following the liberalizing Beerhouse Act of 1830, replaced the sordid drinking establishments.

Gin Pennant: Nautical slang for the green and white flag run up as an invitation to a neighbouring ship. H.M.S. *Agincourt* was known as 'The Gin Palace' (q.v.) as a tribute to its reputation and also as a play upon its name.

Gin Sling: Mixed drink of gin with lime or lemon and soda, to which may be added a dash of grenadine, cherry brandy or other liqueur. Straits, Raffles, Penang, Java and other slings differ only according to the dash of liqueur.

Gin Spinner: Early 19th-century term for a London gin-distiller.

Gin Twist: The mid-19th-century name of the popular drink of the period, composed of gin, hot water, sugar and lemon.

Gipfel: German (Nittel, q.v.) white wine.

Giro: Italian (Sardinian) sweet red and table wines.

Girondas: French (Côtes du Rhône) red wine.

Gironde: French *département* which produces a large amount of superb wine. The chief city is Bordeaux (q.v.).

Gironville: French (Médoc) red wine.

Giscours: French (Médoc) red wine.

Givry: French (Chalonnais, q.v.) red wine.

Glan: German (Nahe) white wine district, including vineyards of Meissenheim and Offenbach.

Glana: French (Médoc) red wine.

Glasgow Hot Pint: Sweetened whisky and ale to which is added a beaten egg.

Glass: The common term for the container from which the beverage is finally drunk. In polite circles wines and spirits are always drunk from a glass but beer may be dispensed in a pewter or other metal or a ceramic mug and liqueurs may be poured into small silver cups. Glasses cover an enormous range in size and design and have always been the special object of the finest craftsmen in glass. Glasses are of comparatively recent origin, and until medieval times or later were used only by the aristocracy.

There are many conventional shapes and sizes for the different types of wines, e.g. sherry, dry table wines, sparkling wines and desserts. These frequently change fashion and many of the accepted shapes are based upon snobbery. Commonsense should operate. Size is, of course, related to alcoholic strength and fortified wine glasses are naturally smaller than those for table wines.

Glasses should be colourless so that the eye can enjoy the beauty of the reds, greens, goldens and browns of the wine-makers' delicate art. The tulip-shaped glass is ideal for all beverage wines.

Glenlivet: A famous pot-stilled whisky from the district in Scotland of that name. It is prized as an addition to other whiskies for enhancing flavour. (See also Whisky.) The Scots even have a song:

Phairson had a son who married Noah's daughter
And nearly spoilt ta flood by drinking up ta water,
Which he would have done — I at least believe it —
Had ta mixture been only half Glenlivet!

Glenloth: Large vineyard near Adelaide, noted for table reds.

Glenrowan: Australian (Victorian) wine centre.

Gletscher: Swiss (Sion) fine white wine.

Gleukos: Biblical term for 'new sweet wine'.

Glöck: German (Nierstein, q.v.) white wine.

Glögg: Also Glügg. Swedish punch-like hot drink of sweetened brandy, sherry, red wine, bitters and whatnot, with the addition of blanched almonds. Traditional at Christmas.

Gloria: A French term for coffee laced with brandy or calvados (q.v.).

Glühwein: The German equivalent of Glögg (q.v.).

Glukus: Generic name mentioned in classical writings for sweet wines.

Glycerine or Glycerol: The sweet polyhydric alcohol which is usually found in small but varying proportion as a by-product of alcoholic fermentation. Sweet wines made by the 'noble rot' (*pourriture noble*, q.v.) process may contain much more glycerol than usual (up to 2%) and this may contribute to their luscious taste.

Goblet: A drinking-cup with foot and stem. Also a drinking-vessel shaped with a wide bowl and smaller rim, without a handle. The name came originally from the Latin *cupa*, a cask, and the shape is similar to a cask which has been cut in half.

Göcklingen: German (Palatinate) white wine.

Goddisgood: The general name for brewer's yeast (q.v.), barm or leaven in medieval England. Around 1450 brewers were compelled by law to 'graunte and delyver to any person axying berme called goddisgood, taking for as much goddisgood as shall be sufficient for the brewe of a quarter malte a ferthing at the moost'.

Godet: Old-established brand of cognac (q.v.).

God-Forgive-Me: A tall two-handled stone mug for heating cider or beer by standing direct in the ashes (Wessex).

Godown: A swallow of liquor.

Goldbachel: White wine from Wachenheim, Palatinate (q.v.).

Goldberg: A common German white-wine estate name. There are Goldbergs at Gau-Bickelheim, Algesheim, Herxheim, Freinsheim, Bisserheim, Niedersaulheim, Oppenheim, Ostofen and Dienheim.

Golden Fleece: Mixed drink of yellow chartreuse and Danziger Goldwasser.

Golden Lady: Cocktail of gin, brandy, grapefruit juice and orange.

Goldfuss: Czechoslovakian (Pressburg, q.v.) wines.

Golding: A delicately flavoured English hop used for pale ales and bitter beers, usually blended with Fuggle (q.v.).

Goldlay: German (Reil, q.v.) white wine.

Goldschmidt: German (Ruppertsberg, q.v.) white wine.

Goldtal: German (Rheinhessen) white table wine.

Goldtroepchen: One of the Austrian Gumpoldskirchner (q.v.) white wines. Also a fine white wine from Piesport, Moselle.

Goldwasser, Danziger: Liqueur of caraway flavour in which float particles of gold leaf.

Goldwingert: German (Graach, q.v.) white wine.

Gols: Austrian wine centre in Burgenland.

Gombaude-Guillot: French (Pomerol) red wine.

Gomes, Luis: Old-established shippers of madeira (q.v.).

Gomme (Syrup): French name of the heavy simple syrup of cane sugar dissolved in water that is used at the bar for preparing mixed drinks.

Gonnheim: German (Palatinate) white and red wines.

Gonzalez, Byass & Co. Ltd.: Old-established (1835) shippers of port from Oporto and sherry from Jerez.

Goods: The curious term in brewing applied to the contents of the mash-tun (q.v.) after the mashing process has been completed. See also Liquor.

Gooseberry Champagne: The reprehensible term applied to an English beverage made by fermenting gooseberries with added sugar. See also Country Wines.

Gooseberry 'Wine': Country wine (q.v.) made from sugar and gooseberries.

Gordo Blanco: Spanish white grape widely grown in Australia both as a table grape and for distillation.

Gordon: Old-established (1769) brand of gin, now part of D.C.L. (q.v.).

Gorse 'Wine': Country wine (q.v.) flavoured with gorse or whin flowers.

Gossip: See jailer.

Gottesfuss: German vineyard at Wiltingen, Saar. Surely an indelicate name.

Gotteshilfe: German (Worms) wine estate. See also Bechtheim.

Gottesthal: German (Östreich, q.v.) white wine.

Goulet: Old-established champagne of Reims.

Goût américain: 'American taste' in champagne. For South America it is usually made sickly sweet.

Goût anglais: French term ('English taste') for dry champagne. See Goût français.

Goût de Bouchon: French for unpleasant corky taste in wine resulting from the use of defective cork stopper.

Goût de Terroir: The characteristic earthy taste of certain wines, supposed to be derived from the particular soil where the vine grows. In some cases this taste is regarded as meritorious, viz.: *Gewürtztraminer* (q.v.).

Goût français: 'French taste'. Term for very sweet champagne. See Goût anglais.

Goutte d'Or, La: French (Meursault) white wine.

Governo: The must made from late-gathered grapes in Tuscany and added to chianti (q.v.) to give a slight sparkle.

Goxwiller: Bas-Rhin (q.v.) wine area.

Graach: German (Moselle) celebrated white wine district, including vineyards of Münzlay, Kirchlay, Hochlay, Domprobst, Himmelreich, Abstberg, Goldwingert, Petrus and Stablay.

Grace Cup: Medieval monkish drinking vessel.

Gradignan: French (Graves) red and white wine commune including the vineyards of Haut-Bailly, Lafon, Monlerens and Laurenzane.

Graf Eltz: German (Kiedrich, q.v.) white wine.

Gräfenberg: German white wine grape of riesling (q.v.) type. Also an important vineyard at Kiedrich, Rheingau, and a white wine of Piesport (Moselle).

Gragnano: Southern Italian dark red wine from Sorrento and elsewhere.

Graham, W. & J., & Co.: One of the historic names in the Oporto wine trade. Founded in 1820, the family direction continues. Two of the storage vats, Gog and Magog, each hold 160 pipes (q.v.) of port.

Grain: White wine from Deidesheim, Palatinate (q.v.).

Grain d'Orge: French term ('barley grain') for the characteristic tint of some wines, especially the Swiss ones of Cortaillod.

Grains of Paradise: The seeds of a reed-like plant, a member of the ginger family, mentioned here because they were the essential flavouring of the spiced wine Hippocras (q.v.).

Grain Spirit: Alcohol produced from cereals.

Grain Whisky: The common term for whisky made in a patent still (q.v.), mainly from unmalted grain. The term is hardly logical, for all whisky is made from grain.

Grand Bas: See Armagnac.

Grand Clos: French (Touraine) red wine.

Grand Corbin: French (Graves) red wine.

Grand-Corbin-David: French (Graves) red wine.

Grand-Corbin-Despagne: French (Graves) red wine.

Grand-Duroc-Milon: French (Pauillac) red wine.

Grande Champagne: Area of Cognac and source of the best grade of cognac brandy (q.v.).

Grande-Côte: French (St. Émilion) red wine.

Grande Rue: French (Côte-d'Or) red wine.

Grandes Murailles: French (St. Émilion) red wine.

Grandes-Vignes: French (Pomerol) red wine.

Grand-Faurie: French (St. Émilion) red wine.

Grandjo: Portuguese sweet table wine of sauternes type made by the same method. See also pourriture noble.

Grand-la-Lagune: French (Médoc) red wine.

Grandmaison: French (Graves) red and white wines.

Grand Marnier: A proprietary liqueur of orange flavour.

Grand-Mayne: French (St. Émilion) red wine.

Grand Pontet: French (St. Émilion) red wine.

Grand-Puy-Ducasse: French (Médoc) red wine.

Grand-Puy-Lacoste: French (Médoc) red wine.

Grand-Saint-Julien: French (Médoc) red wine.

Grand-Saint-Lambert: French (Médoc) red wine.

Grands Echézeaux, Les: Fine French (Côte-d'Or) red wine.

Grand Slam: Cocktail of Swedish punch and two vermouths.

Grand-Soussans: French (Médoc) red wine.

Grands Vins, Les: French for wine from the famous vineyards.

Grand Vin: Vague French term for the best wine (as alleged) of a type. *Caveat emptor?*

Granich: German (Forst, q.v.) fine white wine.

Granny: Colloquial English term for old-and-mild (ale).

Grant: Old-established Scotch whisky distillers, outside the D.C.L. combine.

Grape Juice: The unfermented juice of ripe grapes, a beverage of increasing popularity. Even in France the production and presumably the consumption has increased fiftyfold since before the 1939 war. Fortunately for oenophiles the breeds of grapes which generate fine wine usually do not yield agreeable grape juice. There would be little dispute that unfermented grape juice is inferior as a beverage to that of citrus and some other fruits.

Grape Spirit: Syn. for both alcohol and brandy, *eau de vie de vin* (q.v.).

Grappa: Italian spirit distilled from the fermented remains of grapes after pressing. Can be good. See also Marc de Bourgogne and Eau de Vie de Marc.

Grappe: French for bunch of grapes.

Grappolo: Italian for bunch of grapes.

Grasshopper: Mixed drink of peppermint and chocolate liqueurs, with cream.

Graubach: German (Burg, q.v.) white wine.

Grauberg: German (Minheim, q.v.) white wine.

Grauves, Les: French (Champagne) wine commune.

Gravains, Aux: French (Côte-d'Or) red wine.

Graves: Important French wine-growing district of the Gironde, beginning almost at the city of Bordeaux. The name refers to the gravelly soil. Red and white wines are made, the latter being more widely known though many judges consider the reds superior. Some of the most celebrated wine estates of the world are in the Graves district. These are separately noted.

Graves de Saint-Émilion: French wine-growing district of the Bordeaux, a part of the St. Émilion area which is more gravelly than the rest. It contains many fine vineyards, the most celebrated being Château Cheval Blanc.

Graves Supérieure: French law limits the use of this name to graves wine containing 12% or more alcohol. It is not necessarily otherwise superior to plain graves.

Gravières, Les: French (Côte-d'Or) red wine.

Great Western: Australian (Victorian) wine centre, especially for sparkling wines. It is ironical that here (under different proprietorship, of course) are produced both fine Australian sparkling wine by the most meticulous champagne process and also carbonated wines. Also the name of an American wine centre.

Great Wines: The term applied by convention to twenty or so wines of France and Germany which are reputed to be of superlative quality. These more or less rigid lists of vinous nobility are neither wholly praiseworthy nor reliable. There are indubitably many other wines of equal merit, and perhaps greater. Moreover, quality varies from year to year. See also Médoc.

Great Year: A superlative or vintage year. See also Vintage.

Greco di Gerace: Noted Italian white wine from Calabria.

Greco di Todi: Italian table wine from Umbria.

Greece: Despite the small size and the restricted area of arable land, Greece, with an annual production of nearly 90 million gallons, is about 13th on the world's list of wine-producers. Grapes have been grown in Greece for perhaps 3,000 years and though some of her wines have been celebrated, the general quality in modern times is not high. Perhaps more of the grapes of Greece are dried and sold as currants and raisins than are made into wine. Much Greek wine is flavoured with sandarac resin. This retsina wine is very much an acquired taste but apparently one can learn to like it. The best-known Greek wine is probably the sweet dessert mavrodaphne. There is some excellent Greek brandy made, much better than the general run of wines. There are also some distinctive specialities such as the flavoured spirits ouzo (aniseed) and mastika (resin).

It should be remembered steadily that as far back as 600 B.C. the Greeks established flourishing cities such as Nice and Marseilles on the Mediterranean and also are believed to have introduced the grape vine. Perhaps this is a good example of the pupil outdistancing the master.

Greek Civilization: Not the least important aspect is that the Greeks planted the vine and established wine-making wherever they journeyed. Spain, southern France, Sicily, southern Italy, Crimea and other areas all owe their first vines to the Greeks.

Greenall: Old-established English brewery of St. Helens, Lancs.

Greenbushes: Australian (W.A.) wine centre.

Green Dragon: Cocktail of gin, crème de menthe, peach bitters, kümmel and lemon juice.

Green Hungarian: Local name for a white grape widely grown for ordinary wine in N. California.

Green Malt: Malt which has germinated for the full eleven days, but has not yet been dried in the kilns.

Grenache: Grape for red wines, much of fine quality. It is said to be the source of the famed Spanish rioja (q.v.). Grenache is widely grown for dessert wines in Australia, South Africa and Southern France. It is also the name of a sweet, yellow French (Roussillon) dessert wine.

Grenadine: A pomegranate syrup used as a flavouring.

Grenouilles, Les: French (Chablis, q.v.) white wine. Highly prized.

Grèves, Les: French (Côte-d'Or) red wine. The name is borne by several vineyards of Burgundy.

Grévin: Old-established champagne of Epernay.

Greybeard: See Bellarmine.

Griffith: Australian (N.S.W.) irrigated wine area. Some of the wines are excellent.

Grigioni: Italian red table wine from Sondrio, Lombardy.

Grignolino: Italian (Piedmont) red grape and wine.

Grillet, Château: Noted white wine of Rhône Valley (Condrieu).

Gringnolet: Brandy made from black cherries. Also a liqueur.

Grinzinger: Austrian red and white wine grown near Vienna, including the vineyards of Schenkenberg and Steinberg. Usually drunk new. See also Heurigen.

Grinzone: See Barolo.

Griotte: The French for black-heart cherry and for the delicious liqueur (q.v.) made from it.

Gris de Toulois: French (Lorraine) faintly pink table wine.

Gris-Meunier: Pink wine from Orleans.

Grist: Malt grains which have been cleaned and cracked, whence they are conveyed to the grist cases, preparatory to mashing (q.v.). After extraction of the malt in the mash tun, the spent grains are sold as cattle food. See also Brewer's Grains.

Groaning Beer: The brew provided for visitors or attendants at a childbirth.

Grog: Diluted spirit, usually rum, after Grog, nickname for Admiral Vernon, who first ordered Navy rum in tropics to be diluted. The term is also used derisively of spirits in general.

Grog-Blossom: Slang term, now archaic, for the red nose supposed to be due to intemperance.

Grog Boss: The gentleman at a Canadian logging celebration elected to control the drinking. For a more genteel but broadly similar appointment see Arbiter Bibendi and Rex Convivii.

Grogging: The illicit practice of steeping a freshly emptied spirit cask with hot water, to extract the spirit that has soaked into the wood.

Groseille: The French for gooseberry and for the delicate and attractive liqueur (q.v.) made from this fruit. The name is also that of a French liqueur made from redcurrants.

Grossbockenheim: German (Franconian) white wine.

Grossbottwar: German (Württemberg) red wine.

Grossheppach: German (Württemberg) Schillerwein (q.v.).

Ground Ivy: A flower of the genus *Nepeta* of the family *Labiatae*. It was supposed to be used for flavouring beer before the use of hops (q.v.).

Growler: American slang term for a covered can of beer. Origin obscure.

Gruaud-Larose: Celebrated French (St. Julien) wine-growing estate.

Gruit: A mixture of herbs for flavouring ale which originated in medieval Germany. It was at that time a Roman Catholic monopoly and in 1381 Archbishop Frederick issued a decree emphasizing that all must buy their gruit from the episcopal warehouses. Gruit consisted of a mixture of bog myrtle, rosemary, yarrow and other minor ingredients.
    The introduction of hops met with fierce resistance by the sellers of gruit. See also Beer. However, hops easily won the battle.

Grumello: Italian (Lombardian) red wine.

Grün: German (Rheinhessen) wine estate.

Grünberg: The most easterly (Silesian) wine-growing district of Germany. The wines are adjudged moderate.

Grünhauser: Fine moselle wine from a vineyard over a thousand years old. This is the Maximin-Grünhauser Herrenberger winery associated with the abbey in Trier.

Gruzilly: French (Rhône) wine-growing commune.

Guadeloupe: Centre for rum production.

Guarapo: Colombian and Central American sugarcane brew, the home-brew of the region.

Guaro: Central American spirit, a variant of aguardiente (q.v.).

Guasti: Californian wine estate.

Guebwiller: French (Alsatian) white wines.

Guienne: Duchy of this area of southern France between Gascony and Poitou, including the famous Bordeaux district, was acquired by England in 1152. This union led to a relatively enormous development of the wine trade and to an interchange of commodities; within two years the importation of Bordeaux wine to England and English woollen goods to France had commenced. By 1199, in the first year of John's reign, it had become necessary to enact maximum prices for the sale of wines of Anjou and Poitou. See also Eleanor.

Guinness: One of the great names of brewing. The Dublin brewery commenced operations in 1759 at St. James's Gate. There are many ramifications.

Guipuzcoa: Noted Spanish cider from the region of that name.

Guiraud: Fine sauternes (q.v.) wine from vineyard near village of the same name.

Guldenmorgen: German white wine. See also Dienheim.

Gumben: German white wine. See also Dienheim.

Gumpoldskirchner: Noted Austrian red wine. Some white is also made.

Guncina: Italian red table wine of the Bolzano area (q.v.).

Gundersheim: German (Württemberg) Schillerwein (q.v.).

Gundersheim: German (Worms, Rheinhessen) white wine district, including vineyards of Hackgraben, Bruchert, Hansrück and Höllenbrand.

Gunnawarra: Australian (Queensland) wine centre.

Guntersblum: German (Rheinhessen) white wines including vineyards of Steig, Vögelsgärten, Rost, Kehl, Autental, Himmeltal, Muhl, Herrngarten and Eiserne Hand.

Gunterslay: Moselle (Piesport) vineyard.

Gutedel: German name for the chasselas grape (q.v.).

Gyle: A brewing term of varied meanings:
    (1) A batch of beer produced at a single brewing.
    (2) Wort (q.v.) during fermentation which is added to an already finished stout or ale.
    (3) A fermenting vat.

Gyle Number: The stencil on a cask to denote the brew or gyle.

Gyngleboy: A leather bottle or black jack ornamented with silver bells.

Gyöngyös: Hungarian beverage wines, red, white and sparkling.

Haanepoot: South African name for a muscatel-type grape.

Haardt: German (Palatinate) white wine.

Haardtberg: The best vineyard of Dernau (q.v.).

Hackgraben: German (Gundersheim, q.v.) white wine.

Haferberg: German (Worms) wine estate. See also Bechtheim.

Hagnau: German (Baden) white wine.

Hahnen: German (Freinsheim, q.v.) white wine.

Hahnheim: German (Rheinhessen) white wines, including vineyards of Pfaffenrötter, Knopf, Mönchberg and Moosberg.

Haig: A name celebrated in whisky as well as arms. The firm is now part of D.C.L. (q.v.). Robert Haig possibly commenced distillation at Bemersyde about 1627 and was certainly actively distilling in 1655. Field-Marshal Earl Haig was chairman of the company for some years before his death in 1928. The Haig dimple bottle is known almost everywhere. See also Stein.

Hainfeld: German (Palatinate) white wine.

Haircloth: Blankets of horsehair placed over the slatted floor of the kiln on which hops are spread and dried.

Hair Sieve: See Haircloth.

Haiti: Centre for production of rum of no special merit.

Halbrot: Swiss light red table wine made from mixed white and red grapes, the counterpart of the German Schillerwein.

Half-and-Half: Or 'arf and 'arf. Mixture of ale and porter.

Half-Bottle: Twelve to the gallon. Bottle of half the capacity of an ordinary wine or beer container.

Halfpiece of Wood: Ale measure used in the 15th century.

Hallau: Swiss red table wines from the Schaffhausen district.

Hallgarten: German (Rheingau) fine white wine district, including vineyards of Jungfer, Schönhell, Hindelberg, Mehrhölzchen, Deitelsberg and Hinterzaune.

Hall of Counterfeits: The room at Fécamp which houses specimens of the vast number of imitations of benedictine (q.v.).

Halmenboehl: German (Forst, q.v.) fine white wine.

Halmheim: German (Rheinhessen) white wine centre.

Halsberg: German (Dürkheim, q.v.) white wine.

Hambach: German (Palatinate) white wine district including vineyards of Feuer, Hörst, Gerlick, Kirchenberg, Sommerhalde and Kaiserstule.

Hamburg Brandy: Imitation concoction made by flavouring potato spirit. An insult to the name of a great city and a great spirit.

Hameau de Blagny: French (Côte-d'Or) white wine.

Hammel: German (Rheinhessen) wine estate.

Hammelburg: German (Franconian, q.v.) white wine.

Hammerstein: German government vineyard in Avelsbach (q.v.).

Hammerton: Old-established (1730) English brewery of Stockwell.

Hammond: Combination of many English breweries stemming from the original one established at Bradford in 1840.

Hanap: Tall drinking-vessel of goblet shape, richly made of pewter or silver, and used only on ceremonial occasions. Each was kept in a 'hanaper', from which the word 'hamper' is said to be derived.

Hangover: Once slang but now respectable medical term for the condition of malaise resulting next morning from over-indulgence in alcohol the night before.

Hansen, Emil Christian: The Danish biochemist and microbiologist to whom modern brewing owes so great a debt. Hansen originated in 1883 the pure-culture process of growing commercial yeast (literally billions of cells) from a single cell of selected quality. Hansen's techniques are equally important in modern wine-making and distilling.

Hard: (liquor, stuff, etc.). A synonym, especially in the U.S., for any form of spirits (q.v.). Logically, soft liquor should be applied to beer and light wine but the term 'soft drink' is used exclusively for 'temperance' or non-alcoholic beverages, including some of those modern gastronomic atrocities composed of carbonated solutions of synthetic flavours, with or without saccharin and benzoic, salicylic, sulphurous and other preservative acids. Hard cider is fermented apple juice.

Harden and Young Ester: The phosphorus-containing compound named after its discoverers, which forms one link in the chain of the breakdown of sugar to alcohol during fermentation.

Hardy: Old-established (1863) brand of cognac (q.v.).

Harfe: German Steinwein vineyard near Würzburg (q.v.).

Harlen: German (Königsbach, q.v.) white wine.

Haro: Spanish town of the Rioja (q.v.) surrounded by good vineyards.

Harpignies, Henri: This pupil of the painter Corot spent his vacations in Burgundy and was a lifelong abstainer — from mineral water.

Hartenberg: German (Harxheim, q.v.) white wine.

Harxheim: German (Rheinhessen) white wine district, including vineyards of Lieth, Heuer, Osterberg, Hartenberg and Neumorgen.

Hasenbiss: German (Ostofen, q.v.) white wine.

Hasenlauf: German (Dromersheim, q.v.) white wine.

Hasenlaufer: German (Brauneberg, Moselle) white wine.

Hasensprung: German wine estate of Winkel, Rheingau.

Hatch, Down the: British drinking salutation.

Hati Koi: Greek wine region also known as Côte de Parnasse.

Hattenheim: Celebrated German (Rheingau) white wine district, including the vineyards of Schutzenhausen, Pfaffenberg, Hinterhaus, Engelmannsberg, Nussbrunnen, Willborn, Mannberg, Wisselbrunnen Dillmetz, Rheinhartshausen, Burgweg, Marcobrunnen, Steinberg, Hallgarten, Jungfer, Schonhele, Wurzgarten and Deutelsberg. In particular here is situated Kloster-Eberbach, the home of the prized Steinberg wines (q.v.).

Hauben: German (Niedersaulheim, q.v.) white wine.

Häuschen: German (Laubenheim, q.v.) white wine.

Häuserweg: German (Rüdesheim, q.v.) fine white wine.

Hausmarke: German for proprietorial name or trade mark.

Haustrunk: German term for an inexpensive wine-like beverage made from sweetened pressings. See also Gesindewein.

Haut-Armagnac: District of Armagnac (q.v.).

Haut-Bages: French (Médoc) red wine.

Haut-Bailly, Ch.: Red wine of Graves district of Bordeaux.

Haut-Barsac: Alternative name for Barsac (q.v.). Haut-Barsac is the portion of the Barsac commune which makes the best of the celebrated sweet table wines of sauternes type.

Haut-Bergey: French (Graves) red wine.

Haut-Bommes: French (Sauternes) sweet white wine.

Haut-Brion, Ch.: Celebrated French vineyard of 125 acres generally accepted as amongst the finest wine-growing estates of the whole country. The wine of this ancient estate has always had a lofty reputation, as much in England as elsewhere. On 10 April 1663, Samuel Pepys writes in his diary '. . . to the Royall Oak Tavern . . . and here drank a sort of French wine, called Ho Bryan, that hath a good and most particular taste that I never met with'. Dryden, Swift and Defoe also praise it. Some chauvinistic or mock-chauvinistic Irishmen have contended or suggested that the name is a version of O'Brien and that it must have had a Hibernian founder but there is no ground for this. The vineyard has been famous since the 14th century and the spellings of the name have been various — de Haubrion, d'Aubrion, Daubrion, Obrian, Hobrien and Ho Bryan.

The vineyard is now right in the settled area of the city of Bordeaux and a tramway runs through the estate. How long it can withstand the pressure of the city remains to be seen.

Although Haut Brion is not in the Médoc, when the wines of that celebrated red wine region were classified in 1855, this wine was placed equal with the three finest — Châteaux Lafite, Latour and Margaux.

Until 1900 the wine was not labelled by the estate but the corks were branded with name and year. The label was that of the merchant who sold the wine.

There is a small amount of highly esteemed white Haut-Brion made.

Haut-Brion la Mission: French (Graves) red wine. Not to be confused with Ch. Haut-Brion.

Haut-Camensac: French (Bordeaux) white wine.

Haute-Barde: French (Graves) red wine.

Hauterive: French (Médoc) red and white wines.

Haut-Gardère: French (Graves) white wine.

Haut-Madère: French (Graves) white wine.

Haut-Médoc: The section of the Médoc (q.v.) which produces the finest red wine (claret).

Haut-Peyraguey: French (Bommes, Sauternes) fine sweet white wine.

Haut-Pourret: French (St. Émilion) red wine.

Haut Sauterne: See American Sauterne.

Haut-Sauternes: A fancy name of no legal or geographical significance which is applied by some French bottlers to their particular wine to suggest high quality.

Hauts Doix: French (Côte-d'Or) red wine.

Haut-Simard: French (St. Émilion) red wine.

Hautvillers: The Benedictine abbey near Reims whose cellar-master, Dom Perignon (1668–1715), is generally believed to have invented the process of making champagne and other sparkling wines fermented in the bottle. See also Champagne.

Havelock: Mixed drink of brandy and ginger 'wine'.

Hawaiian: Cocktail of gin, orange juice, pineapple juice and curaçao.

Hayerweg: German white wine. See also Dittelsheim.

Head: (1) The flat end of a cask. (2) The froth on the top of freshly poured beer or similar effervescing drink. See also Chapeau.

Heart Spirit: The middle or principal part or fraction of the distillate from a pot-still (q.v.), the heads and tails being drawn off for re-distillation. The heart spirit may itself be subjected to a second distillation. This is the process used in the production of cognac and armagnac brandies and of the finest Highland malt whiskies.

Heavy Wet: Old term for particularly strong ale.

Hebe: The Greek goddess of youth, and cupbearer of Olympus, hence a barmaid or waitress. See also Ganymede.

Hectolitre: 100-litre measure, equivalent to about 22 imperial or 26·4 U.S. gallons.

Heddesheim: German (Nahe, q.v.) white wine.

Heeltap: Liquor left at bottom of glass. 'No heeltaps.'

Hefe: German for yeast (q.v.).

Hefebranntwein: German and Austrian term for sub-standard brandy made from wine lees left in casks after racking. Lower in quality than Trester-branntwein (q.v.). See also Grappa and Eau de Vie de Marc.

Hega: Egyptian brewed beverage of some 3,000 or more years ago.

Heggebeer: Norwegian red liqueur made from the bird-cherry.

Heidelbeerwein: A German fruit wine made from a type of redcurrant.

Heidfeld: German (Dürkheim, q.v.) white wine.

Heidsieck: Old-established champagne of Reims, not to be confused with Piper-Heidsieck.

Heilbronn: German (Württemberg) ordinary wines.

Heiligenbaum: German (Nierstein, q.v.) white wine.

Heiligenstadt: Wine district near Vienna. Beethoven loved to spend holidays here. It triggered much of his music and also his tragic will written at the approach of deafness.

Heimersheim: German (Ahr) red wine.

Heisenstein: German (Reil, q.v.) white wine.

Heissgasse: German (Rheinhessen) wine estate.

Hek: Ancient name for beer made from barley in Egypt. See also Egypt.

Helbig: German (Ruppertsberg, q.v.) white wine.

Helbon: District near Damascus noted for wine. Ezekiel (27: 18) mentions this.

Helleich: The German term for new wine which has become clear.

Hemer: This frequent Biblical word (Hebrew) apparently means new red wine still sparkling, foaming and fermenting. See also Asis.

Hengelberg: German (Dhron) white wine.

Hengstberg: German (Escherndorf, q.v.) white wine.

Henley: Cocktail of whisky, syrup and mint-leaves. See also Julep.

Hennessy: Old-established (1740) brand of cognac (q.v.).

Heppel: German (Gau Algesheim, q.v.) white wine.

Heppensten: German vineyard (dry white) of Ockfen (q.v.).

Hepsema: The beverage of classical Greek times made by boiling down must (q.v.) to a syrup. Also known as *siraion*. A similar beverage was made by the Romans and called *sapa*, *carenum* or *defrutum*. The syrup is still made as a sweetening agent. In France it is called *moût cuit* and in Italy *mosto cotto*. *Mosto agustin* is a still thicker Italian product.

Hequ or Hequp: Ancient Egyptian name for beer. Very early records of brewing (*c.* 2000 B.C.) have been found in Egypt.

Hérault: See Pinard.

Herb Beer: Light alcoholic beverage made by fermenting decoction of herbs with sugar. Also called herb wine. See also Country Wines.

Herbert, A. P.: Not least of the many Englishmen of letters of robust commonsense who have upheld sane and hearty drinking.

Hergottsacker: German (Deidesheim, q.v.) white wine.

Hermannshölle: German (Niederhausen-Schlossböckelheim A.D. Nahe, q.v.) white wine.

Hermitage: French red wines from the Rhône Valley at Tain, including the vineyards of La Sizer, La Chapelle and Les Baissards. There is some white wine grown in the vineyards of Les Recoulles, Les Murets and Chante-Alouette.

Hermitage: Also known as Syrah and Sirrah. Black grape, basis of good wine, largely grown in hotter climates.

Herne Hill: Australian (W.A.) wine centre.

Herrenberg: 'Lord's Hill', the name of many German white wine vineyards on the Rhine. Some of the vineyards are situated in Filzen, Mertesdorf-Grünhaus, Saar, Erden, Moselle, Oppenheim, Casel, Ockfen and Avelsbach.

Herrnbaumgarten: Wine district of Lower Austria.

Hervelets: French (Côte-d'Or) red wine.

Herxheim: German (Palatinate) red and white wines including vineyards of Goldberg, Steinberg, Felsenberg, Himmelreich and Sommerseite.

Herzlay: German (Erden, q.v.) white wine.

Hesitation: Cocktail of Swedish punch, whisky, lemon.

Hessia or Rheinhessen: German wine-growing region including the cities of Worms, Mainz and Bingen, all on the Rhine.

Hessigheim: German (Württemberg) red wines.

Hessloch: German (Rheinhessen) white wine district including vineyards of Aupern, Berg and Lende.

Heuer: German (Harxheim, q.v.) white wine.

Heurigen: New wine of Austria and also by extension the wine cafés themselves, especially of Vienna at Grinzing.

Drinking the Heurigen (literally 'this-year's' wine though it is last year's which is drunk) is a time-honoured Austrian custom. The Heurigen usually have a quartet for musical accompaniment and serve the wine in a traditional glass mug. The wine varies a good deal in quality from place to place but to drink the Heurigen is an act of jollity rather than gastronomy.

Heyl: German (Laubenheim, q.v.) white wine.

Highball: American long iced spirit drink, unflavoured as opposed to a julep.

Highland: General name for the single (q.v.) Scottish pot-stilled whiskies produced for blending purposes in nearly a hundred distilleries.

High-Proof Brandy: The U.S. term for the brandy which can be distilled legally at a strength up to 190° proof (95% alcohol), provided it is not used as a beverage. Such h.p. alcohol is used mainly for fortifying dessert wines. Beverage brandy may not be distilled in the U.S. at a higher strength than 170° proof (85% alcohol).

Higiu: Chinese (Pekinese) name for wedding wine.

Hilde: French (Graves) red wine.

Hills: The protective mounds which cover the roots of hop plants. Once a field of hops has been planted, the hills are not disturbed until the plant has lost its virility. This may be up to thirty or more years. When new fields of hops are required the hops are planted in hills either by cuttings from old plants or by perennial roots which are plants grown in the nursery for one year.

Hilo: Defect (oiliness) of sherry.

Himbeer: German raspberry liqueur.

Himmelreich: One of the Austrian Gumpoldskirchner (q.v.) white wines.

Himmelreich: Another of the German wine names borne by many estates, including those situated at Herxheim, Moselle and Graach. See the comments under Schlossberg.

Himmelsleiter: German (Mülheim, q.v.) white wine.

Hindelberg: German (Hallgarten, q.v.) white wine.

Hine: Old-established brand of cognac (q.v.).

Hinkelstein: German (Kreuznach, q.v.) white wine estate.

Hinkelstein: German (Nierstein, q.v.) white wine.

Hinterberg: German (Enkirch, q.v.) fine white wine.

Hinter der Kirche: German (Hochheim, q.v.) white wine.

Hinterfels: German (Norheim, q.v.) white wine.

Hinterhaardt: White wine from Palatinate (q.v.).

Hinterhaus: German (Rüdesheim, q.v.) fine white wine. Also wine from Hattenheim.

Hintersaal: German (Nierstein, q.v.) white wine.

Hinterslay: German (Niederemmel, q.v.) white wine.

Hinterzaune: German (Hallgarten, q.v.) white wine.

Hippel: German (Rheinhessen) white table wine.

Hipping: German (Nierstein, q.v.) white wine.

Hippocras: An old-time English beverage of wine flavoured with spices, and apparently similar to the modern vermouth. What is less usually known, however, is that the straining cloths used in the making were called Hippocrates' Sleeves; hence the name.

Hitz: German (Laubenheim, q.v.) white wine.

Hitzlay: German white wine estate of Casel (q.v.).

Hiya: Cold sake (q.v.).

Hoan Tsie'u: Chinese 'yellow rice wine', a type of sake (q.v.).

Hobnob: Originally to drink together with familiarity.

Hochbenn: German (Dürkheim, q.v.) white wine.

Hochgewachs: German term for the finest growth of a wine.

Hochgewann: German (Freinsheim, q.v.) white wine.

Hochheim: German white wine district at the southern end of the Rheingau, and including the vineyards of Sommerheil, Domdechaney, Rauchloch, Hinter der Kirche, Kirchenstück, Weid, Stein, Berg, Falkenberg, Bettelmann, Daubhaus, Hoelle, Neuberg and Pfandloch. One theory (there are others) of the origin of hock, the general English term for Rhenish wines, is that the name is derived from the village Hochheim.

Hochheimer Domdechaney: Fine hock from the River Main area.

Hochlay: German (Graach, q.v.) white wine.

Hochmess: German (Dürkheim, q.v.) white wine.

Hock: See also Rhine Wines. Hock is the English name for the white wines of the German Rhine and is believed to be derived from the village Hochheim on the River Main. It replaced the more general term Rhenish. Unfortunately, the name has been adopted by the U.S., South Africa, Australia and other countries for almost any local dry white wine, good or bad. In England the name hock includes the wine of the Rheingau, Rheinhessen, Palatinate, Nahe and Franconia. Hocks are put up in brownish-red bottles.

Many hock parishes and individual wines will be found listed herein. It is merely necessary to say here that many believe a fine hock to be the pinnacle of the wine-maker's art.

Hockbrueck: German (Oppenheim, q.v.) white wine.

Hockenmühle: German (Ockenheim, q.v.) white wine.

Hod: Small Hungarian vessel, perforated at bottom, used in production of the richest and rarest of tokay (q.v.), the Essenz or Essence. The overripe grapes are placed in the hod and the juice drips away merely by the pressure of the mass itself. The resulting wine is one of the vinous wonders of the world but according to reports it is no longer exported, being all reserved for those of the right political colour. According to the number of hods added, the wine is designated Aszu 2 Hods, 3, 4, 5 or 6 Hods.

Hoelle: German (Hochheim, q.v.) white wine.

Hofberg: German (Dhron) white wine. Also white wine from Osann.

Hofstück: German (Ruppertsberg, q.v.) white wine.

Hogarth Glass: Short, wide-based vessel, so called because it so frequently appeared in that artist's pictures.

Hogen or Hogan: The obsolete English name of a strong ale, possibly spiced. Walpole, a bountiful host, was famous for his home-brewed hogen. In 1653 J. Taylor wrote: 'There is a high and mighty drink called hogen-mogen-rug.' (See Rug.) In 1663 Dryden (*Wild Gallant*) wrote: 'I was drunk, damnably drunk with ale, great hogan-mogan bloody ale.' The Hogen-Mogen was one of the high-mightinesses of the Netherlands States-General.

Hogshead: A large cask of varying capacity, normally from 50 to 60 gallons, and the vessel most commonly used for the shipment of bulk wines and spirits. As a measure, the English beer hogshead is 54 gallons, and the wine hogshead $52\frac{1}{2}$ gallons; but the capacity of the cask called a 'hogshead' varies considerably, and may exceed 70 gallons.

Hohe: White wine from Wachenheim, Palatinate (q.v.).

Hoheberg: German (Ruppertsberg, q.v.) white wine.

Hohenmorgen: German (Deidesheim, q.v.) white wine.

Hohenrain: German (Erbach, q.v.) white wine vineyard.

Hohenwarther Weltiner: Austrian table wines.

Hohl: German (Palatinate) white wine from Asselheim.

Hohlweid: German (Niederemmel, q.v.) white wine.

Hohweg: German (Duttweiler, q.v.) white wine.

Holinshed: Shakespeare was under so great an obligation to Holinshed's *Chronicles* for some of his plots, and was so keen an observer of alcoholica (see also Shakespeare) that it is surprising he did not pass on some of the alleged virtues of whisky, printed in 1577:
'Being moderalle taken it sloweth age, it strengtheneth youth, it helpeth digestion, it cutteth flegme, it lighteneth the mind, it quickeneth the spirits, it cureth hydropsie . . . it keepeth the weason from stifling, the stomach from wambling, the heart from swelling, the bellie from wirtching, the guts from numbling, the hands from shivering and the sinewes from shrinking, the veines from crumpling, the bones from aking and the marrow from soaking.'

Hollander: Cocktail of gin, apricot brandy and grape juice.

Hollands: General term in England for Dutch gin. See also Schiedam and Schnapps.

Hollbacken: German (Kirchhofen, q.v.) white wine estate.

Holle: German for hell and the appearance of the word in many wine-regional names refers to the collection of the sun's rays. Hot as hell in German wine country means moderate enough temperature elsewhere. There are good white wines of this name from Eller and Ockenheim.

Hollenberg: German (Palatinate) white wine from Asselheim.

Hollerheck: German (Baden) white wine.

Homburg Kallmuth: German Steinwein vineyard near Würzburg (q.v.).

M   M.D.D.

Home Wines: Syn. for 'country wines' (q.v.).

Homez: Biblical (Hebrew) word for sour wine or vinegar, rather drily described in Hastings' *Dictionary of the Bible* as 'the common refreshing drink for labourers' and 'used in the harvest field' (Ru. 2 : 14). Perhaps it was no worse than *piquette* or even small beer (q.v.).

Honehei: Czechoslovakian (Pressburg, q.v.) wines.

Honey: Formerly an extremely important source of fermentable carbohydrate, honey today plays but a minor part. There is still some mead (q.v.) produced here and there and honey is the distinctive flavoured sweetening agent for some Polish and other liqueurs. Centuries ago honey was widely used to sweeten wines which were all too frequently sour.

Honey Brandy: Spirit made by distilling mead (q.v.). Alas, a modern rarity.

Honeymoon: In ancient Norse times, when mead (q.v.) made from honey was the universal alcoholic beverage, a marriage was followed by a month of feasting. The word is also a tribute to the old idea that eating honey induces virility. See also Mead.

Honeysuckle: Cocktail of rum, honey and lemon juice.

Honigberg: German (Dromersheim, q.v.) white wine.

Honigsberg: German (Erbach, q.v.) white wine vineyard.

Hooch: American slang for liquor, especially illicitly distilled spirits. (Derived from 'hoochinoo', a spirit made by American Indians.)

Hooker: American term for a copious drink, esp. of spirits.

Hoop: A device displayed outside taverns in the Middle Ages to indicate that beer was on sale. See also Ale-Stake. Later it became the practice to display certain objects within the hoop in order to differentiate one tavern from another.

Hop: A perennial plant, *Humulus lupulus*, of the nettle family indigenous to Europe generally, which has been cultivated in England since the days of William the Conqueror. Oils and resins in the cones borne by the female plant are used to impart the bitter flavour and preservative values to beer. Hops were first used in English beer (then known as hopping beer) at the end of the 14th century, following the example of Eistrich beer (q.v.) which was then being imported from the Continent. For years after its introduction to England, hopping beer was not altogether popular and on several occasions the use of hops was banned. All beers nowadays contain the resins and oils of hops. See also Ale, Beer.

Hop Back: Brewery vessel into which the wort and hops are turned out after boiling. The wort is filtered through the hop petals as they lie on a false bottom before it passes to the cooling stage (q.v.).

Hop Bine: The growing stem of the plant.

Hop Cone: The strobile of the female plant. At the base of the petals of the cones are the seeds and resinous oils of the hops which impart the bitter flavour and preservative properties to beer.

Hop Diseases: Mould, Red Spider, Aphis, Mildew, Downy Mildew, and Verticillium Wilt. The latter disease began about 1935 and caused enormous losses to hop farmers particularly in Kent. New varieties of hops have been cultivated which are wilt-resistant.

Hope Valley: Australian (S.A.) wine centre.

Hop Farm: Where hops are grown. Approximately a quarter of the farm acreage is normally set aside for hop cultivation.

Hop Festival: An annual celebration of the hop harvest, held at Beltring, Kent, and consisting of two or three days' entertainment for the pickers and camp staffs.

Hop Garden: Field in which hops are cultivated.

Hopir: A 15th-century liquid measure.

Hôpital de Pourtalès: Swiss (Neuville) golden wine.

Hop Pickers: Men, women and children who come annually to the hop gardens to gather the harvest.

Hop Pillow: Pillow filled with hops and reputed to encourage sleep.

Hopping Beer: Said to be the early name for the first beer to contain hops, about 1400.

Hop Poles: These are of height 11 ft. to 14 ft. and used to support the wires and strings up which the bines are trained.

Hops Marketing Board: Under the provision of the Hops Marketing Scheme 1933, the Hops Marketing Board was set up to control all aspects of the growing, marketing, distribution and pricing of hops grown in Britain. It consists of four special members appointed by the Minister of Agriculture and fourteen representatives selected by the producers.

Hop Strings: During the early growth of the bines each year strings are strung from the hills to the overhead wires, up which bines can later be trained. Normally four strings are used for each plant and about $4\frac{1}{2}$ miles of string are used per acre of hops.

Hopstuck: White wine from Palatinate (q.v.).

Hop Tonic: The name given by old-fashioned staunch teetotalers to the home-brewed beer they prized so highly. Often it was more highly alcoholic than commercial beer.

Horace: His poetry abounds in praise of wine in general and of the wines of Caecuba, Chios, Lesbos, Falernum, Sabinum, Cales and Alba in particular. In the 37th Ode of the First Book he pens the glorious phrase '*Nunc est bibendum*' (The time to drink is now!)

Höreker: German (Canzem) white wine.

Horgengrund: German (Rheinhessen) white table wine.

Horn: In the sense of this book, an archaic drinking-vessel made from the horn of an animal; sometimes richly carved and mounted.

Horn: German (Kallstadt, q.v.) wine centre.

Hors d'Âge: When found on the label of a bottle of French spirits, this means that the contents are actually older than stated.

Horseradish Ale: This sounds horrible. Samuel Pepys the diarist drank it as a remedy against the stone!

Hörst: German (Hambach, q.v.) white wine.

Horstein: German (Franconian, q.v.) white wine.

Hospices de Beaujeu: French (Beaujolais) red wine.

Hospices de Beaune: Celebrated French (Burgundian) charitable institution commenced in the 15th century and still in very active operation for the care of the aged and poor sick. The income is almost wholly from the sale of wine. It owns many scattered vineyards of a total of nearly 150 acres, bequeathed from time to time by 30 or so benefactors. The wines are the subject of an annual auction. Each wine is sold under the *cuvée* (q.v.) or title of the original benefactor together with the name of the commune where the vineyard is placed. The auction is an important event, very widely attended, and is regarded as a sound pointer of the wine financial outlook for the year. Some of the names of the benefactors sound a trifle odd — Blondeau, Brunet and Docteur Peste.

Hot Deck: Cocktail of whisky, sweet vermouth and ginger.

Hotel: A later word for hostel, which in turn may have been a variant of hospital, especially in its implied meaning of a house for the entertainment and succour of the needy but not necessarily sick (cf. hospitality). In the British Empire there appears to be no strict legal definition of the term 'hotel'. See also Licensed Premises. Hotels may be licensed or not. In popular language the prefix 'private' means 'unlicensed'.

Hotte: The large wooden 'basket' so much a part of the French vineyard landscape, used for carting the grapes from vine to waggon.

Houghton: Western Australian large vineyard near Perth producing a variety of table and dessert wines.

Houringue, La: French (Médoc) red wine.

Housman, A. E. (1859–1936): 'Shoulder the sky, my lad, and drink your ale.' (*A Shropshire Lad.*)

Howell, James (1594–1666): Worthy of inclusion here because of his remarkable knowledge of alcoholic beverages. The long letter to Lord Cliff from his *Epistolae* has been freely quoted in this glossary. Oxford, Parliament and the post of Historiographer Royal seem to have combined to give him a nice discrimination and erudition. See also Music.

Hrad: Czechoslovakian red wine from Bzenec.

Hriato: Yugoslavian hot beverage of buttered slivovitz.

Hsiang Hsueh: See Shaohsing.

Huang Chiu: See Shaohsing.

Hübbaum: German (Kallstadt, q.v.) wine centre.

Hubertuslay: German (Kinheim, q.v.) white wine estate.

Huckle-My-Buff: An old English concoction of hot beer, brandy, and egg.

Huck-Muck: Old name for strainer used in brewing.

Huff-Cap: Obsolete term for particularly strong ale or other liquor.

Huguenot: South African centre for red and white wines.

Huhnerberg: German white wine from Rauenthal, Rheingau.

Huille: French (Anjou) white wine.

Hukster: A medieval term, alternative for 'ale-wife', woman who sold beer.

Humming Bird: Cocktail of gin, cranberry and lemon juice.

Hunding, King: Hunding, King of Sweden, joins Clarence and Fjolne (q.v.) as noblemen who are alleged to have been literally drowned in liquor.

Hungary: One of the great wine-making countries of the world and perhaps (statistics are difficult to obtain and interpret) the fifth in Europe. Red and white table wines in large variety are made, many of them excellent and cheap. Of course the really celebrated wine of Hungary is tokay (q.v.). Most of the better-known Hungarian wines are separately noted.

There is an annual wine production of nearly 120 million gallons. Much of this is common wine but there are some celebrated varieties, including Egri Bikaver. Somlai, Mori, Villanyer and Balatonfuredi are well known. Brandy called raki is widely made.

Hunger Stones: A group of rocks in the river Rhine, near Bingen, which are uncovered in years of drought. This means lean cereals but splendid wine, due of course to the 'higher gravity' or greater sugar content of the grapes. At a tangent, it can thus be seen that countries like South Africa, Australia, and California, with a fairly reliable summer climate, either have no 'great years' or can dub every year one, according to predilection.

Hunter River Riesling: The grape widely grown in Australia for the production of fine white table wines. This is a typical instance of the needless confusion surrounding much of the nomenclature of wines and vines. This grape is not the riesling but the sémillon (q.v.). Australia, South Africa and California have all, in the process of time, affixed false names to standard, well-known European vines. International agreement on nomenclature is necessary.

Hunter River Valley: Justly celebrated and old-established wine-growing region of New South Wales, Australia, now eclipsed in volume by South Australia but still supreme for the growth of reds and whites which are in the finest European tradition.

Hunt, Roope & Co.: Old-established (1735) shippers of port (q.v.).

Hurdenwein: German straw-wine. See also Vin de Paille.

Hütte: German (Dromersheim, q.v.) white wine.

Hydrogen Sulphide: Also known as sulphuretted hydrogen. The cause of the foul ('rotten egg') odour that is sometimes found in wine. It results from the reduction of the sulphur dioxide (q.v.) added to restrain wild yeasts.

Hydromel: This ancient name for mead (q.v.) is derived from the need to add water to honey before it can be fermented. Also an old hot beverage of apparently widely variable composition, but always containing honey. See also Metheglin.

Hydrometer, Sikes's: The instrument legalized in Great Britain for ascertaining the alcoholic strength of certain types of beverages, especially spirits, by observing the depth to which it sinks in the liquid.

Hymettus, Mount: An important wine area of Greece.

Hysteric Water: A strong alcoholic beverage common at least in Virginia in the late 18th century because it is specifically attacked as a generator of perjury and epilepsy in Rush's *Moral and Physical Thermometer*, a curious poster on the evils of excessive drinking issued by Benjamin Rush, a contemporary of Benjamin Franklin.

Ica: District in Peru noted for production of wine and of pisco (grape brandy, q.v.).

Idig: German (Königsbach, q.v.) white wine.

Ihringen: German (Kaiserstuhl, q.v.) white wine centre.

Ilbesheim: German (Palatinate) white wine centre.

Ile Margaux: French (Médoc) red wine.

Iles de la Gironde: The islands in the River Gironde on which are situated a number of important vineyards, mainly for red wine.

Illats: French (Graves) white wine centre, including vineyards of Clos du Tauzin, Château Cagès, and Château du Basque.

Im Herschtal: German (Niederingelheim, q.v.) white wine.

Immature Spirits Act: The beneficial U.K. legislation of 1915 which requires all spirits (q.v.) to be warehoused for at least three years.

Immi: Swiss wine measure of about one-third gallon.

Imperial: The term is used of liquid measures in the sense of actual as opposed to 'reputed'. Thus an imperial quart is four to the gallon and an imperial pint eight. An imperial gallon is British as against the smaller (five-sixths) American. See also Reputed.

Impériale: Large French bottle, holding six to eight ordinary bottles, used occasionally at Bordeaux for good wines though in general outsize bottles are not used for choice beverages. Useful for small-scale maturing of wine.

Im Pöll: German (Niederingelheim, q.v.) white wine.

Inches: The term, especially as used by excisemen, for the dip-stick. Dry and wet inches are the air and liquor content of the vessel.

India Pale Ale (I.P.A.): Name originally given to a fine pale ale made for export to troops in India. The term is still occasionally used for bottled pale ales by some brewers, especially if intended for export.

Inferno: Italian red table wine from Sondrio, Lombardy.

Infusion Process: A type of mashing (q.v.) in which the whole of the mash is heated in the mash tun until cooked. See also Decoction.

Ingelfingen: German (Württemberg) white wine.

Ingelheim: German town in Rheinhessen noted for production of red table wines.

Ingersheim: French (Alsatian) white wine.

Inghilterra: A grade of marsala dessert wine (q.v.), strong and heavy. As the name suggests, it is supposed to conform to British requirements.

Inglenook: American winery at Napa Valley, California.

Inglewood: Australian (Queensland) wine centre.

Inhaler: Large tulip-shaped 'snifter' glass for use, warmed, with fine brandy. The esoteric ritual is dying.

Ink Street: Cocktail of whisky, lemon juice and orange juice.

Inn: An English institution. A licensed residential house where beer and other refreshments can be obtained. Often the headquarters of local clubs and sporting occasions. See also Pub.

Innere Leiste: German Steinwein vineyard near Würzburg (q.v.).

Innerst: German (Gau-Bickelheim, q.v.) white wine.

Innkeeper: One who keeps an inn, the landlord.

Inn Sign: The traditional symbol of hospitality and welcome. For centuries the signs of English inns have excited artistic and literary curiosity and admiration. Many were, and indeed still are, beautifully designed and painted. The titles covered an enormous range and many of them have interesting histories. As an example, where the word 'butler' occurs, it has no reference to a domestic servant but refers to the celebrated recipe for medicated ale of Dr. Butler, physician to the Stuart monarchs. See also Piggin.

Inoculate: See Starter.

Inspissated Wine: The thick, heavily flavoured wine of Roman times, possibly a sign of degenerate taste.

Instituto do Vinho do Porto: The powerful and, on the whole, beneficial Portuguese Port Wine Institute, a government body charged with the general technological supervision of the great industry.

Inverness: Scottish centre for production of highland malt whisky.

Invert Sugar: A mixed monosaccharose obtained by enzyme action or weak acids on a disaccharose such as cane sugar or a starch (polysaccharide). All more complex carbohydrates must be converted into monosaccharoses before the zymase of yeast can ferment them. The monosaccharose is added to the wort before it is boiled with hops. It is not used at this stage to sweeten the beer, but to increase fermentability.

In Vino Veritas: This Latin maxim is a sound tribute to the observational powers of the Romans. It may be freely translated as 'There is truth in wine' or still more freely as 'When the liquor goes in the truth comes out'. It is an acutely accurate statement of the pharmacological action of alcohol as a depressant and remover of inhibitions. Just as the term 'truth serum' has been colourfully, if not strictly correct, applied to the

drug scopolamine, so it could be used with equal validity for alcohol. 'Drunken pig' on the one hand and 'Takes his liquor like a gentleman' on the other both illustrate the profound truth that a person shows his true colours under the influence of alcohol.
See also Alcohol, Physiological action of.

Iona: A native American grape used for making sparkling wine in the N.Y. Finger Lakes district (q.v.).

Iphofen: German (Franconian) white wine centre, including vineyards of Bettenberg, Kronsberg, Julius-Ekhesberg and Kalb.

Irish: Cocktail of Irish whiskey, triple sec, maraschino and absinthe.

Irish Coffee: Also known as Gaelic coffee. Mixed drink originally served at Shannon Airport, consisting of hot black coffee laced with Irish whiskey and topped with chilled whipped cream. It has become an advertising whimsy.

Irish Whiskey: Despite the much greater size of the Scotch whisky industry, that of Ireland is more ancient. There are only five whiskey distilleries in Ireland, all of considerable size. These are Jameson (1780), Old Bushmill (1784), Power (1791), Cork (about 1850) and Daly (1829). These are all noted separately. Most Irish whiskey is pot-stilled and the subject of three distillations. Note that Irish whiskey is spelt with an 'e'.

Irish Wine: Peter ('the Great', 1672–1725) stated 'Of all wine, Irish wine is the best'. He was speaking of whiskey. At that time Scotch whisky was hardly known but Irish (*usquebaugh*, q.v.) was already a valuable export commodity. The spirit of Ireland and the U.S. is spelt with an 'e', of Scotland without.

Irouléguy: Celebrated French red wine from the Basque country, Pyrenees. If the remarks of some are to be believed, the wine is trading not on its inherent merits so much as upon the romantic setting.

Irroy: Old-established champagne of Reims.

Isaiah, 29.9: 'They are drunken but not with wine' reveals profound psychology and pharmacology. Alcohol has been wrongly blamed for innumerable cases of emotional exaltation or shock and at least numerous cases of the effects of traumatic injury, diabetic coma and hypnotic drugs.

Ischia: Italian island near Naples, where some 'Capri' is grown. Some consider the wine is better than the real Capri from the much more celebrated neighbouring island.

Iskra: Bulgarian red sparkling wine.

Islay: An island off the west coast of Scotland noted for its heavy-flavoured pot-stilled whisky, in great demand by blenders.

Israel: Unlike their ethnic cousins the Arabs, the Jews have never had any religious objection to alcoholic beverages and the Old Testament contains many tolerant references, especially to wine. Together with the southern European peoples and the Chinese, the Jews are known as most temperate. A drunken Jew is a rarity. With the high concentration of technical and scientific talent in Israel and the rapid growth of viticulture under irrigation, one would have expected a wine industry of fine quality but it must be stated with regret that as yet production does not rise beyond the mediocre. The chief viticultural area is at Megiddo.

Issan, d': Red wine of Médoc region of Bordeaux.

Istria: Italian wine district noted for its sweet (dessert) Moscato. See also Terrano.

Italy: The world's second-largest wine-producer of nearly 1,000 million gallons. There is an immense range of liquors (red and white table wines, desserts, vermouths, sparkling wines, liqueurs and brandies), many of excellent quality. Large numbers of types and individual specimens are noted alphabetically.

Of recent years the quality of Italian wine has greatly improved, as the direct result of the efforts of both the government and the various trade associations. In particular the control of names and the enforcement of geographical limitations have had their good result, coupled with the gradual spread of modern efficient technology. Today Italian wines are, in general, excellent value though some still sell mainly because of the quaint shape of the bottle. The northern provinces make the best table wines.

Ivalikor: Herb-flavoured liqueur from Swiss Engadine.

Iwo Jima: Cocktail of Irish whiskey, curaçao, absinthe, maraschino and bitters. Joseph Rosenthal, who fought on Iwo Jima, indignantly repudiates this as a genuine invention of the time and place. 'We couldn't have made anything like this because we were out of cracked ice. As I remember, we were also out of whiskey, curaçao, absinthe, maraschino and bitters.'

Izarra: Liqueur from French Pyrenees with an intriguing flavour resembling sage and lavender.

Izsák: Hungarian white wine district.

Jack: A vessel to hold liquid (cf. Black Jack).

Jack Rose: American mixed drink (cocktail) of applejack, grenadine, lemon.

Jack Smithers: A lone drink; Australian term. See also Jimmy Woodser.

Jacob's Ladder: The conveyor which carries beer casks of fined beer from the brewer's cellars to the loading bank. The term is traditional and originated from the reference to Jacob's ladder in the Bible.

Jacob's Ladderman: The brewery hand responsible for the delivery of beers from the cellar to the loading bays.

Jahrgang: Term in Germany for the year of a wine.

Jailers: In 1776 William Smith, one of the first to try to bring medical care to English prisoners, wrote in his *State of the Gaols* that jailers made large profits by selling liquor. The trade was mostly in cheap and injurious substitutes for gin. These were variously known as vinegar, gossip, crank, mexico and sky-blue.

Jamaica: Large island in the West Indies which was one of the first centres of commercial production of rum. Jamaica rum is still one of the most esteemed. Highly flavoured.

Jamaica Swing: Cocktail of rum, orange juice and lime juice.

Jambava: Another name for slivovitz (plum brandy).

Jameson: Noted Irish (Dublin) whiskey, founded 1780.

Janneau: Established (1851) brand of armagnac (q.v.).

Jar: As used for beverages, a glass or earthenware cylindrical vessel, from one to ten gallons' capacity, and sometimes enclosed in wicker-work.

Jarnac: A townlet on the River Charente near Cognac, where many of the offices and plants of the principal shippers of cognac are situated.

Jarollières: French (Côte-d'Or) red wine.

Jarra: Mexican liquid measure of about 2 gallons.

Jarrons, Les: French (Côte-d'Or) red wine.

Jary-Boyer: Old-established (1863) brand of cognac (q.v.).

Jäsning: Swedish for fermentation (q.v.).

Jean du Mayne: French (St. Émilion) red wine.

Jechtingen: German (Baden) white wine.

Jefferson, Thomas: The third president of the United States was another (see Washington) who was deeply and sanely interested in alcoholic beverages. An advocate of temperance, he also became a commercial brewer. This is not the least interesting aspect of the life of this prince of men. See also Rush and Franklin.

Jenever: Dutch for juniper, the essential flavouring of gin (q.v.). By corruption this has become 'geneva', a common English synonym for gin though there is no connection with Switzerland.

Jerez de la Frontera: The town in Andalusia in S.W. Spain, the centre of a legally defined area in which alone sherry (q.v.) can be grown and made. This area is only about 25,000 acres. Also known as Xeres. See also Sherry.

Jerignac: Recently coined official name for Spanish brandy, obviously generated from Jerez (q.v.) and cognac (q.v.). See also Kanyak.

Jernozek: Czechoslovakian white table wine.

Jeroboam: A wine-bottle 8–12 times ordinary size (from the 'Mighty man of valour' of the Bible, who 'made Israel to sin').

Jeropiga: Portuguese concentrated must (q.v.) which is added to port wine with brandy and to which some of the special character of port is due. See also Port.

Jersey Lightning: A slightly opprobrious and probably undeserved synonym for applejack (q.v.) made in New Jersey.

Jesuitgarten: Winkel on the Rheingau and Forst in the Palatinate both have hock vineyards bearing this name. Fine wines.

Jezreel: The area where Naboth's vineyard was situated, a famous viticultural area mentioned in the Bible. Other famous grape regions were the Moabite Hills of Sibmah (Is. 16 : 8), Heshbon, Elealeh and Engedi.

Jigger: A term, originally American, for a small measure ($1\frac{1}{2}$ fluid ounces), particularly applied to spirits.

Jimmy Woodser: Australian slang term for a solo drink (without companions). A similar term is 'drink with the flies'. The origin of the term is misty but for what it is worth, one widely circulated theory is that it derives from a poem by Barcroft Boake about a lone drinker named Jimmy Woods. The 'poem' ends:

> His signature is on the scroll of fame.
> You cannot well forget him though you would, sir.
> The man is dead; not so his homely name.
> Who drinks alone drinks toast to Jimmy Woods, sir!

The celebrated Australian writer Henry Lawson had a ballad entitled *The Old Jimmy Woodser*, commencing:

> The old Jimmy Woodser comes into the bar
> Unwelcome, unnoticed, alone.

Jingle: Old drink of sweetened hot ale with nutmeg and apple. See also Lamb's Wool.

Johannesberg: German (Mülheim, q.v.) white wine.

Johannisberg: German (Laubenheim, q.v.) white wine.

Johannisberg: The name of both Moselle and Swiss vineyards not to be confused with those on the Rheingau. Hölle, Erntebringer and Klaus Johannisberger are amongst the best establishments.

Johannisberg: Celebrated German village on the Rheingau (q.v.) where fine white wine has been made continuously for over 1,000 years. The Schloss (or Castle) Johannisberg, founded as a Benedictine monastery, remained such for 900 years until 1807 when it was secularized. It is still a large vineyard by Rhenish standards (65 acres) and is still producing the finest wine.

The Schloss Johannisberg has long belonged to the Metternich family and the wines are sold under an elaborate system of labels which only a knowledgeable wine man will comprehend. There are five categories:

(1) Fürst v. Metternichscher Cabinet Wine Schloss Johannisberg, Spätlese.

(2) Fürst v. Metternichscher Cabinet Wine Schloss Johannisberg, Auslese.

(3) Fürst v. Metternichscher Original Abfüllung Schloss Johannisberg, Auslese.

(4) Fürst v. Metternichscher Original Abfüllung Schloss Johannisberg.

(5) Schloss Johannisberg. Wachstum Fürst v. Metternich.

For example, the second category means 'Fürst v. Metternichscher (the proprietor), Cabinet wine (good enough for the proprietor's own cabinet or sideboard), from the vineyard of Schloss Johannisberg, specially selected'.

It is interesting to remember that it was here that it is supposed was initiated the system of gathering grapes late and singly to produce the luscious trockenbeerenauslese (q.v.) wines.

Outside the Schloss are a considerable number of other good vineyards, the chief of which are separately noted.

Johannisberg Riesling: The Californian term for the genuine riesling grape of Germany and Alsace, to mark it off from the various other spurious and inferior 'rieslings'.

Johannislay: German vineyard at Wiltingen, Saar.

John Barleycorn: The personification of malt liquor.

John ('Johnnie') Walker: Old-established Scotch (Kilmarnock) whisky distillers, now part of D.C.L. (q.v.).

Johnson, Samuel: Everybody (who is anybody) knows that he said, or is supposed to have said something like 'Claret is for boys, port is for men, but he who aspires to be a hero must drink brandy'. A much finer dictum, also attributed to Johnson, is 'Wine gives great pleasure and every pleasure is of itself a good'.

Jordan: A term nearly obsolete but still occasionally used for a long-necked bottle. The name was originally given to bottles used to contain holy water brought back by pilgrims. Later applied to a long-necked vessel used by apothecaries and also to a chamber pot. (A Jordan almond, however, has no similar derivation but is a corruption of *jardin* — garden, e.g. a cultivated almond.)

Jordan: Large Canadian winemaker. See also Canada. Jordan Wines Ltd. has a capacity exceeding 6 million gallons.

Jorum: A half-pint measure, usually of pewter, named after Joram (2 Samuel 8: 10) 'who brought . . . vessels of brass'.

Josephshöf: Large vineyard at Graach, Moselle. White wine.

Joue: French (Touraine) red and white wines.

Joule: A name famous both in physical science and in brewing. The brewery was established at Stone, Staffs., in 1780 and acquired a high reputation for its celebrated 'Stone Ales' (q.v.). James Prescott Joule (1818–89), the famous physicist, inherited the brewery but devoted his life to scientific research in exact measurement.

Joyce: Padraic Colum was a friend of James Joyce. He said Joyce was a lover of white wine and was convinced that the proper sacramental wine was white. 'Joyce had a theory for everything and would willingly have set Rome straight on sacramental wine had Rome but asked.'

Juffer: German (Brauneberg, Moselle) white wine.

Jug: A deep vessel for holding liquids, fitted with a handle.

Jug, Toby: See also Bellarmine. Jug of stoneware in the shape of a portly man of the period (18th century). Many variants have since been produced, the most familiar depicting a cheerful rubicund fellow in a three-cornered hat.

Jug and Bottle Bar: The section found only in old hotels reserved for sale of liquor to be consumed off the premises. The modern equivalent is the bottle department.

Jugenheim: German (Rheinhessen) white wine district.

Jugful: A pleasing quantity.

Julep or Julup: Name (der. Arabic *julab*, rose water) of various beverages. This is a word of fascinating import. In the United States it means a cold, refreshing drink of spirits, sugar, bruised mint and ice. The exact composition and making of a julep is a subject upon which any two Americans (one of whom is not necessarily a true Southenah, sah) are prepared to do verbal battle instanter. However, the term is far more venerable than generally recognized. It is at least 300 years old and probably much more than that. Old-fashioned pharmacists still use (or recognize) it as a sweet, flavoured draft to disguise an unpleasant dose.

On 22 June 1660 Pepys noted in his diary: '. . . Had the great coach to Brigham's, who went with me to the Half Moon, and gave me a can of good julep.' Now the Half Moon Tavern was one of the favourite carousing places of Pepys and his friends. (6 July 1660: '. . . to the Half

Moon, and the house so full that we staid above half an hour before we could get anything.') This was no place for namby-pamby lolly water. It thus seems probable that julep for an alcoholic drink is a great deal older than southern American ritual.

Juliénas: Burgundian (Beaujolais) district. Sound red wine.

Julius-Ekhesberg: German (Iphofen, q.v.) white wine.

Juliusspital: Steinwein (q.v.) (Franconian) vineyard, a charitable foundation. The produce is called 'Holy Ghost wine'.

Jungfer: German (Hallgarten, q.v.) white wine.

Jungle Juice: Slang term for raw, crude spirit or for any supposedly harsh alcoholic beverage. From the Second World War slang for the liquor made by Allied troops in the East. A soldier's drink, often a mixture of anything alcoholic available.

Juniper: A shrub, *Juniperus communis*, bearing purplish berries used as a flavouring in the manufacture of gin. See also Gin.

Jura: French wine-growing district on the foothills of the Jura mountains opposite Burgundy. The celebrated Château Chalon comes from here, also Poligny and Arbois.

Jurançon: French (Pau) highly-prized and scarce amber dessert wine.

Kabinett: See Cabinet.

Kachetian: A celebrated Russian red table-wine from the Tiflis area, that region of reputed mighty drinkers.

Kadarka: Variety of red table wine produced in Hungary and Yugoslavia.

Kadarka: Bulgarian red wine, slightly sweet.

Kafels: German (Norheim, q.v.) white wine.

Kaffir Beer: See Beer, Kaffir.

Kaft: German (Ruppertsberg, q.v.) white wine.

Kagor: Russian red dessert wine.

Kahlenberg: German (Kröv-Kövenig, q.v.) white wine estate.

Kahlenberg: German (Nackenheim, q.v.) white wine.

Kaiserstuhl: Lit. 'King's Chair' or 'Seat of Kings', it is the name of more than one flat-topped hillock in the valley of the German Rhine. It is also the nostalgic name given by the first German settlers more than 130 years ago to the dominating site of their new village near Nuriootpa in the Barossa Valley of South Australia. Here descendants of the same settlers are working the same vineyards and still sending away wine that could make a valid claim of goodness for any wine-growing region of the world.

German wine-growing area in the Rhine Valley at Baden, a rocky, volcanic ridge where excellent wines are grown. The best areas include Lilienhof, Eichstetten, Ihringen, Endingen, Oberrotweil and Bötzingen.

Kaiserstüle: German (Hambach, q.v.) white wine.

Kalavryta: Greek (Morea) red wine.

Kalb: German (Iphofen, q.v.) white wine.

Kalkberg: German (Duttweiler, q.v.) white wine.

Kalkofen: White wine from Deidesheim, Palatinate (q.v.).

Kalkofen: German (Laubenheim, q.v.) white wine.

Kallstadt: German (Palatinate) red and white wine centre, including the vineyards of Steinacker, Hübbaum, Trift, Horn, Nill, Kobner, Saumagen and Kronenberg.

Kalmit: German (Palatinate) table wine.

Kalmont: German (Eller, q.v.) white wine of quality.

Kalmus: Bitter extract which is a common constituent of bitter liqueurs.

Kalmuth: German (Franconian) white wine.

Kalte Ente: German name (lit. 'cold duck') for hot-weather drink of sparkling white wine to which still red wine is added, together with soda, lemon and ice.

Kalterer: Red table wine from the South Tyrol.

Kaltererseewein: Italian (formerly Austrian) Tyrolean red wines, also called Lago di Caldaro.

Kaltern: Austrian wine district.

Kamaaina: Hawaiian mixed drink of gin, green coconut milk and lime juice. Delicious!

Kammer: German (Erden q.v.) white wine.

Kammerbau: German (Palatinate) system of training a number of vines over a low frame.

Kamptaler: Austrian wine district.

Kan: Japanese beverage made by heating sake (q.v.).

Kan: Dutch name for litre wine measure. The German version is *Kanne*.

Kanne: German name for litre wine measure.

Kantarah: See Amon and Nile Delta.

Kanyak: Recently coined name for Turkish brandy. The origin and intention are painfully obvious. See also Jerignac.

Kanzlerberg: French (Alsatian) wine estate at Bergheim. Esteemed white wine.

Kapelle: German (Gau-Bickelheim, q.v.) white wine.

Kapley: German (Eller, q.v.) white wine of quality.

Kappelenberg: German (Lorch, q.v.) white wine.

Kappellenberg: German (Münster, q.v.) white wine.

Karlowitzer: Sweet wine from Yugoslavia.

Karmelitergeist: German flavoured spirit made by Carmelite monastery.

Karthäuser: Swiss (Thurgau) red wine.

Karthäuser Hofberg: German (Ruwer) fine white wine estate, celebrated for many centuries. There are a number of satellite vineyards around the principal one at Eitelsbach. The wine label of the Eitelsbach wines is distinctive, incorporating a mitre, paschal lamb and shepherd's crook. These vineyards include Stirn, Orthsberg, Burgberg and Kronenberg.

Kasel: See Casel.

Kashmir: The area in the Himalayas where wine is reported to have been made continuously for five hundred years. One of the very few Asian wine regions.

Kastanienheide: German (Palatinate) table wine.

N

Kästenbuscher: German (Palatinate) white wine.

Kasthäuserhofberg: German (Ruwer, q.v.) white wine.

Katschel: German (Burg, q.v.) white wine.

Kattenwein: German (Nierstein, q.v.) white wine.

Katzenjammer: German for hangover (q.v.).

Katzenthal: French (Alsatian) white wine.

Kaulenberg: German (Müden, q.v.) white wine.

Kautzenberg: German (Kreuznach, q.v.) white wine estate.

Kava: A Polynesian intoxicating beverage made from the root of a shrub, *Piper methysticum*. The name is derived from the Maori *Kawa*, bitter. It is not only an alcoholic but also an alkaloidal beverage. It is prepared by village virgins who chew the root and spit it into a ceremonial bowl containing water.

Kaymagui: A Mexican liqueur of coffee flavour.

Kayserberg: French (Alsatian) white wine.

Kecskemét: Hungarian important white wine centre.

Keeve: A vat or tub, as used in brewing and fermenting. Also Kieve.

Keeving: The old-fashioned process, now replaced by mechanical filtration, of settling out debris, especially of apple pulp during manufacture of cider.

Kefir: Caucasian and Bulgarian beverage made by fermenting milk of cow, goat or sheep. It is both acid and alcoholic. See also Koumiss.

Keg: A small cask; usually of less than 10 gallons' capacity.

Kehr: German (Nierstein, q.v.) white wine.

Kehrenberg: German (Palatinate) white wine.

Kehrenberg: German (Kreuznach, q.v.) white wine.

Kehrnagel: German white wine estate of Casel (q.v.).

Keknyelü: Hungarian white wine from Badacsony (q.v.).

Keller: German for cellar.

Kellerabfüllung: German for cellar bottling, followed by the name of the estate of origin. The equivalent of the French château-bottled.

Kellerabzug: 'Bottled at the cellar of . . .', a German term rather wider than *Kellerabfüllung* as it can apply to a shipper.

Kellerberg: German (Gau-Bischofsheim, q.v.) white wine.

Kellermeister: German for cellarmaster. The French equivalent is *chef du chai*.

Kellerweg: White wine from Oppenheim. Rheinhessen.

Kelterberg: German (Canzem) white wine.

Kempten: German wine-growing parish of Rheinhessen.

Kensingen: German (Baden) red wines.

Kephesia: Greek (Attica) red and white table wines.

Kerbesberg: German (Östreich, q.v.) white wine.

Kerem: The Biblical (Hebrew) word for vineyards.

Kerndstbranntwein: German apple or pear brandy. See also Calvados.

Kerotim: Wine-growing region of merit mentioned in Bible as suited for the service of the sanctuary.

Kerz: German (Niederhausen-Schlossböckelheim A.D. Nahe, q.v.) white wine.

Kess, Kaas and Kos: A Hebrew adage claims that a person's character can be gauged by three things — his 'purse' (the way he spends his money), his 'wrath' (how he loses his temper) and his 'cup' (the way he drinks). See the entry In Vino Veritas.

Kesselring: German white wine from Rauenthal, Rheingau.

Kestener: German (Moselle) white wines including vineyards of Paulinsberg and Niederberg.

Ketones: A class of chemical compounds, related to the aldehydes (q.v.), that contribute to the flavour and aroma of alcoholic beverages.

Kette: German (Oppenheim, q.v.) white wine.

Keuchelberger: Red table wine from the South Tyrol.

Keyneton: Australian (S.A.) wine centre.

Kha: The chief vigneron of the Egyptian king Tutankhamen.

Khor: Celebrated wine region of Syria in classical age.

Khullar: District near Shiraz in Iran celebrated for the production of wine despite the religious (Moslem) disapproval of alcoholic beverages.

Kick: Alternative term for punt (q.v.), the pushed-in bottom of some glass bottles.

Kiechlinsbergen: German (Baden) white wine.

Kiedrich: German (Rheingau) white wine district, including vineyards of Graf Eltz, Gräfenberg, Berg, Wasserrose, and Sandgrube.

Kientzheim: Wine region of Alsace.

Kieselberg: German (Gimmeldingen, q.v.) white wine.

Kijafa: Danish sweetened alcoholic drink of cherry flavour.

Kilderkin: The standard British small transportable beer container, a cask holding 18 gallons. It was reckoned at one fourteenth of a tun (q.v.). Stainless steel kilderkins are rapidly replacing the casks of oak or other timber. There is still occasionally used a wine kilderkin of about 15 gallons.

Kill Devil: Old naval name for rum.

Kilmarnock: A centre of whisky distilling in Scotland.

Kiln: The part of the maltings in which the malt is dried after germination. The conical vents of the kilns are the distinguishing features of the maltings.

Kilning: The process of heating malt (q.v.) to arrest germination (q.v.) and to caramelize (q.v.) the grain.

Kimberley: English brewery founded in Notts. in 1832.

King's Peg: Cocktail of champagne and cognac. See also Champagne Cocktail.

Kinheim: German (Moselle) white wine district including vineyards of Petrusberg, Loewenberg, Hubertuslay and Rosenberg.

Kipling, Rudyard (1865–1936):

> Five and twenty ponies
> Trotting through the dark —
> Brandy for the parson,
> 'Baccy for the clerk.

Few mind safely bilking the liquor excise. The Churches of England and of Rome both have a realistically lenient attitude to drink.

Kippenheim: German (Baden) white wine.

Kirchberg: Another of the German wine names borne by many estates, including those situated at Lieser, Kirchhofen, Coenen, Ruppertsberg, Ostofen and Escherndorf. See the comments under Schlossberg.

Kirche: German (Burg, q.v.) white wine.

Kirchenberg: German (Hambach, q.v.) white wine.

Kirchenpfad: German vineyard at Zeltingen on the Moselle.

Kirchenpfad: German (Eibingen, q.v.) white wine.

Kirchenstück: The name of several fine German vineyards on the Rhine. Lit. 'church block'. Two of these are situated at Forst, Palatinate (q.v.) and Hochheim (q.v.).

Kirchheim: German (Franconian) red wines.

Kirchhofen: German (Freiburg) white wine centre, including vineyards of Höllbacken, Kirchberg and Bürgele.

Kirchlay: German vineyard at Zeltingen on the Moselle.

Kirrweiler: German (Palatinate) red and white wine centre, including vineyards of Amstgarten, Lerchelberg and Steingebiss.

Kirsch or **Kirschwasser:** German name for cherry brandy, a spirit (q.v.) made chiefly in the Black Forest district of Germany and in the Jura and Vosges districts of France. The best spirit is made from the wild cherry (*Cerasus avium*). After fermentation it is distilled, like cognac, in a pot-still.

It is a highly-flavoured spirit. The characteristic taste is due mainly to the small percentage of benzaldehyde and hydrocyanic acid formed by the hydrolysis of the glucoside in the stone of the fruit. It is the custom to crack some of the stones before fermentation to ensure the presence of these flavourings.

Prussic acid is, of course, one of the deadliest of poisons but in small amount it is used medicinally and some appreciate the sickly flavour. In

Alsace the stones are crushed but not in Switzerland, Austria and Germany. In Denmark a liqueur is made from kirsch some brands of which contain a minute amount of prussic acid. This liqueur is also confusingly called cherry brandy.

Kirschley: German (Osann, q.v.) white wine.

Kirschwasser: Syn. for kirsch, q.v.

Kirseboer: Danish for cherry brandy, a speciality of the country.

Kirwan: French (Médoc) red wine.

Kissamos: Cyprian red table wine.

Kissel: White wine from Wachenheim, Palatinate (q.v.).

Kissling: German (Erbach) white wine vineyard.

Kiwitani: Cocktail of gin, white wine and orange bitters.

Klamm: German (Niederhausen-Schlossböckelheim A.D. Nahe, q.v.) white wine.

Kleinbockenheim: German (Franconian) white wine.

Kleinbottwar: German (Württemberg) red and white wine.

Klein-Karbach: German (Württemberg) red wine.

Kleinmass: A German wine pot.

Klevovaca: Yugoslavian spirit made by re-distilling slivovitz (q.v.) after adding juniper berries. It is thus similar to gin (q.v.).

Klevner: Alsatian white grape and the wine made from it.

Klöch: Austrian (Steiermark) white wine.

Kloppberg: German white wine. See also Dittelsheim.

Klosterberg: Lit. 'monastery hill or mount'. The name of many German vineyards on the Rhine. See, for example, Wiltingen.

Kloster Eberbach: Fine white wine estate of Hattenheim, Rheingau.

Klostergarten: Lit. 'monastery garden'. The name of many German vineyards on the Rhine. See, for example, Östrich.

Klosterkiesel: German (Rüdesheim, q.v.) fine white wine.

Klosterlay: German vineyard of the Wehlen district (q.v.) on Moselle.

Klosterneuberg: The site near Vienna of the celebrated Austrian school of wine-making. Also good red and white table wines.

Klotten: German (Moselle) white wine district, including vineyards of Burgbeg, Wirges and Rosenberg.

Knickebein: German mixture of several liqueurs in layers. See also Pousse Café.

Knipperlé: Esteemed white grape used for some of the finest Alsatian wines.

Knitting-Cup: Drinking-vessel, usually of three handles and richly made, which was passed round the company after a marriage ceremony in Elizabethan England.

Knopf: German (Hahnheim, q.v.) white wine.

Kobern: German (Moselle) white wine district, including vineyards of Weissenberg, Uhlen and Fahrberg.

Kobner: German (Kallstadt, q.v.) wine centre.

Kochem: Also Cochem. German (Moselle) white wine.

Kohala: Sanskrit name of a spirit supposed to have been made from barley. Some writers believe this is the derivation of the Arabic term *al kohl* (al = the). However, see also Al Kohl.

Köhm: German (Ostofen, q.v.) white wine.

Koji: The Oriental steamed-rice culture of moulds used to ferment more rice to make sake (q.v.).

Kolben: German (Dromersheim, q.v.) white wine.

Komovitza: Yugoslavian brandy made from pressings. See also Dop, Grappa and Eau de Vie de Marc.

Könen: German (Saar) white wine district including vineyards of Fels, Nonnenberg and Rippchen.

Koniák: Greek name for local brandy. This, together with the Turkish kanyak and the Spanish coñac, might be regarded by a person with a nasty suspicious mind as an attempt to trade unfairly upon the name and reputation of the most celebrated French brandy.

Königsbach: German (Palatinate) fine white wine district including vineyards of Bender, Harlen, Mückenhaus, Weissmauer, Altenweg, Reiterpfad, Satz and Idig.

Königschaffhausen: German (Baden) white wine.

Königswinter: Most northerly German (Siegkreis) red wine estates.

Konjak: Albanian 'cognac', a courtesy title, of course unfair, for the local grape spirit.

Konsumwein: Cheap but wholesome bulk German wine. See also Vin Ordinaire and Consumo.

Kontuszowka: Polish liqueur of lavender flavour.

Kop Kaai: Chinese (Cantonese) medicinal wine containing fragments of dried red lizards.

Kopke, C. N., & Co.: Probably the oldest firm (established 1638) still operating as port shippers. Christian Kopke, son of the Hanseatic consul at Lisbon began trading in wine in 1638. He married an Englishwoman and his heirs owned the business until 1870. It is now under Portuguese ownership.

Korbel: Large vineyard in Sonoma, California, specializing in sparkling wines.

Korhelyeves: Hungarian 'drunkard's soup', a cabbage soup traditionally served on New Year's Day as a hangover cure.

Korkzeiher: German for corkscrew.

Korn: See Doppelkorn.

Kornbranntwein: Spirit made from fermented cereals, mainly rye, and thus resembling rye whiskey. Mainly German and Dutch.

Kornschnapps: Corn spirit, a sort of European whisky.

Kotnar: Romanian wine district.

Koumiss or Kumiss: Alcoholic beverage made from fermented milk. Koumiss seems to have originated in Mongolia and to have been prepared from mare's milk. According to recent report, it is still widely made in that country, Tartary and Siberia, and herds of milking mares are kept for the purpose. The making of koumiss spread over the whole of Central Asia and the extreme east of Europe. The milk of camels and cows is also used. Valuable medicinal properties are ascribed to koumiss but these may be mythical. The alcoholic content is very low, about 2% and hence less than beer. Koumiss contains unchanged milk constituents (some butterfat and milk sugar), hence has a considerable nutritive value. It is reputed to have a delicious and easily acquired taste for those who like an acidic beverage.

Kefir is stated to be similar to koumiss but is made from cow's milk and fermented with a mixed plant growth called kefir grains. The name koumiss is also given to the spirit (q.v.) distilled from the beverage.

Kranklay: German (Erden, q.v.) white wine.

Kranklay: Moselle vineyard near Uerzig (q.v.).

Kranzberg: German (Nierstein, q.v.) white wine.

Kranzler: White wine from Deidesheim, Palatinate (q.v.).

Kraski Teran: Yugoslavian wine area.

Krausen: The thick, frothy cover on a fermenting tun in the process of brewing beer.

Kräuterberg: German (Ahr) red wine estate.

Krems: Austrian (Danubian) wine district. Red and white.

Kreszenz: On a German wine label this means 'grown by', followed by the name.

Kreuz: Another of the German wine names borne by many estates, including those situated at Ockenheim, Ruppertsberg, Oppenheim, Nackenheim and Palatinate. See also Schlossberg.

Kreuzkirch: German (Niederingelheim, q.v.) white wine.

Kreuznach, Bad: Important German (Nahe) white wine centre, including the vineyards of Kehrenberg, Galgenberg, Kronenberg, Narrenkapp, Steinberg, Kautzenberg, Rittergut Bangert, Forst and Hinkelstein. Some unimportant red wine is produced.

Krk: Romanian red wine from the island of that name in the Adriatic.

Krohn: Old-established shippers of madeira (q.v.).

Kronenberg: Another of the German wine names borne by many estates, including those situated at Kreuznach, Kallstadt and Moselle. See also Schlossberg.

Kronsberg: German (Iphofen, q.v.) white wine.

Krötenbrunnen: German (Oppenheim, q.v.) white wine.

Kröv-Kövenig: German (Moselle) white wine district, including vineyards of Paradies, Kahlenberg, Niederberg, Steffensberg, Layen, Engelberg and Kahlenberg.

Krug: Old-established champagne of Reims.

Krupnikof: Caraway-flavoured liqueur sweetened with honey, a popular beverage in Poland, Lithuania and adjacent lands. Virtine is said to be somewhat similar.

Kuchelberger: Despite the name, this is the local wine of the Italian area of Merano.

Kugel: White wine from Oppenheim, Rheinhessen.

Kuibishev: Russian viticultural centre.

Kulmbach: Northern Bavarian strong beer of 7% alcohol by volume.

Kümmel: German liqueur of mixed aniseed and cumin flavour.

Kuppel: German (Nackenheim, q.v.) white wine.

Kützelborn: See Assmannhausen.

Kvass or Kwass: Widely used brewed beverage of Russia and eastern Europe, made by fermenting mixed cereals and stale bread, with addition of sugar or fruit. The word means 'leaven'. The alcoholic strength is said to be low, ranging from 1% to $2\frac{1}{2}$%, which is considerably less than that of most beer.

Kylix: A Roman-British bronze or silver drinking-cup, shallow on a long stem. Also known in Elizabethan times as a 'tazza' (q.v.).

Kymi: Greek (Eubean) red table wine.

Laacherberg: German (Ahr) red wine estate.

Labarde: French (Médoc) red wine which has long been sold under Margaux (q.v.).

Labégorge: French (Médoc) red wine.

Labels, German Wine: By both law and custom these are full, informative and accurate. If the grape (e.g., riesling) is shown the wine must be made from that alone. *Auslese* ('selection') means that the wine has been made from selected bunches of grapes with no added sugar. *Spätlese* means that the grapes are not gathered until the last stage of ripeness. *Beerenauslese* ('selected berries') means that the grapes are individually picked. *Trockenbeerenauslese* ('individually picked dehydrated berries') means that the grapes are half way to raisins. *Goldbeerenauslese* has the same meaning. *Kellerabzug* and *Originalabzug* both mean 'bottled on the estate', practically the same as the French château-bottled. *Wachstum* followed by a name means 'the growth of (Hans Schmidt)'. Occasionally one sees *Kabinett*, which means, or ought to mean 'This wine is superlative, fit for the owner's own cabinet or sideboard'.

Laberstall: German (Dromersheim, q.v.) white wine.

Laberstall: German (Ockenheim, q.v.) white wine.

Labouret-Moissac: French (Médoc) red wine.

Labrusca: The indigenous grape vine of North America (*Vitis labrusca*), used as grafting stock and for wine-making. The flavour is distinctive and disliked by some as 'foxy'. See also American Wine.

Lacaussade-Melon: French (Médoc) red wine.

Lacaze: French (Graves) red wine.

Lace: To fortify (q.v.) a drink by adding spirits (q.v.). The term is usually limited to the addition of alcohol to a non-alcoholic drink, e.g. adding rum to coffee.

Lach: German (Lorchhausen, q.v.) white wine estate.

Lachen-Speyerdorf: German (Palatinate) white wine.

Lacrima Christi: Lit. 'Christ's tear'. Also variously spelt *lagrima* and *lacryma*. An Italian, golden-hued, sweetish wine grown on the foothills of Mount Vesuvius. There is also a certain amount of red lacrima, but of lesser esteem. If the name puzzles, remember the words of the Italian poet Chiabrera:

> Who was the jesting countryman, I cry,
> That gave so fearsome and so dour a name
> To that choice vintage, which of all think I
> Most warms the heart's blood with its genial flame?
> Smiles, and not tears, the epithet should be
> Of juice wrung from so fair a vinery.

(Translation by H. M. Vaughan.)

Lactic Acid: The characteristic acid of wholesomely soured milk but also present in wine. See also Malo-Lactic Fermentation.

Lactic Acid Bacteria: Micro-organisms which convert a variety of materials such as other acids and carbohydrates to lactic acid, the pleasantly sharp acid found in sour milk. See also Malo-Lactic Fermentation.

Ladle: Instrument of china, pewter or silver used for serving punch.

Ladoix-Serrigny: French (Côte-d'Or) red wine.

Ladouys: French (Médoc) red wine.

Lady Godiva: Cocktail of rum, sweet vermouth, grenadine, apricot liqueur and lemon juice.

Lafaurie-Peyraguey: French (Bommes, Sauternes) sweet white wine.

Laffite: French (Entre-deux-Mers) red and white wines.

Laffite-Cantegric: French (Médoc) red wine.

Laffitte: French (Médoc) red wine.

Laffitte: Old-established (1848) brand of cognac (q.v.).

Laffitte-Saint-Estèphe: French (St. Estèphe) red wine.

Lafite-Canteloup: French (Bordeaux) red wine.

Lafite-Rothschild, Château: Celebrated wine estate on Médoc. It is close to Ch. Mouton-Rothschild, owned by another branch of the family.

Lafitte, Clos: French (Médoc) red wine.

Lafitte-Talence, Clos: French (Graves) red wine.

Lafon: The name borne by a number of vineyards of the Bordeaux, including Médoc, Graves and Blayais (red wine) and Sauternes (sweet white wine).

La-Gaffelière-Naudes: French (St. Émilion) red wine.

Lagar: Portuguese name for a large stone tub in which grape juices are pressed out. Especially applicable to the making of port wine.

Lagarde: French (Graves) red wine.

Lagen: German term for individually named vineyards, especially of the Rhineland.

Lager: Term properly applicable to beer or ale stored for a lengthy period in a lager or cellar, but today the name is loosely applied to a light type of beer.

Lagering: The almost obsolete process of ageing beer by holding it in large tanks, where it clarifies naturally by the settling out of yeast cells, coagulated proteins and other unstable substances. Here, too, the characteristic esters of the hop extract are reported to develop and to give to modern beer much of its pleasant tang.

Lagerreife: German term for period of maturation of wine in cask.

Lago di Caldaro: See Kaltererseewein.

Lagrange: French (Médoc) red wine, also the name of red wine vineyards in Pomerol and St. Émilion.

Lagrein-Rosato: Italian pink (*vin rosé*) table wine of the Bolzano area.

Lagrima: Spanish muscatel dessert wine from Malaga.

Lagune, La: French (Médoc) red wine.

Lahontan: French (Graves) red and white wines.

Lait de Poule: Nogg (q.v.) made in France from spiced brandy, rum and egg.

Lake Boga: Australian (Victorian) wine centre.

Lake Niagara: American sweetish table wine from New York State.

Lake Sevan: The romantic water in the centre of Transcaucasia, elevation nearly 7,000 ft., and the name of the best wine-growing centre of Armenia.

Lake Van: One of the important Turkish wine regions.

Lalande: Four French red wine estates of the Médoc bear this name.

Laman, Ch.: French (Bressan) red wine.

Lamarque: French (Médoc) wine commune whose produce is usually sold under the name Listrac, its neighbour.

Lamarzelle Figeac: French (Graves) red wine.

Lambeth Ale: Samuel Pepys the diarist records drinking this so it must have had special virtue. Already by 1650 in England there were many esteemed local brews of ale and beer. Some were brought to London from considerable distances.

Lambic: Beer made in Belgium by the simple process of spontaneous fermentation. Wort (q.v.) is run into a cask in winter, and slowly ferments owing to the chance ingress of yeast. Faro is a similar product, but weaker.

Lambrays, Clos des: Notable red wine of Burgundy.

Lambrusco: Italian red table wine from Modena (Bologna).

Lamb's Club: Cocktail of gin, two vermouths and benedictine. Still another variation on a familiar theme. See also Manhattan, Martini and Gin and Two.

Lamb's Wool or Brasenose Ale: Hot beer sweetened with sugar, spiced with nutmegs, and with roasted apples floating upon it.

Lämmerberg: Steinwein vineyard at Randersacker (q.v.).

Lamothe: A name borne by many French wine estates of the Bordeaux; all with the prefix *Château*. Both red and white wines are grown.

Lamothe-Bouscaut: French (Graves) red wine.

Lamothe-de-Bergeron: French (Médoc) red wine.

Lamothe-Lescure: French (Graves) red wine.

Lamothe-Montussan: French (Entre-deux-Mers) red wine.

Landau: German (Palatinate) white wines.

Landlord: Traditional name of the licensee, though he is, in fact, often the tenant installed by the brewer. The licensee of a free house (q.v.) is sometimes technically the landlord.

Landskroner Berg: German (Ahr) red wine estate.

Landwein: German for *vin du pays*, the sound but unpretentious 'wine of the country' which any sensible tourist in Europe drinks serenely with ordinary meals.

Lanessan: French (Médoc) red wine.

Langeberge: South African wine-producing area.

Langelonsheim: German (Nahe, q.v.) white wine.

Langenberg: German (Münster, q.v.) white wine.

Langenberg: German white wine of Cochem (q.v.).

Langenlonsheim: German white wine of Kreuznach, Nahe Valley.

Langenmorgen: German (Deidesheim, q.v.) white wine.

Langenmorgen: German (Forst, q.v.) fine white wine.

Langenstück: German white wine from Rauenthal, Rheingau.

Langenwingert: German (Erbach, q.v.) white wine vineyard.

Langestein: German (Nahe) white wine.

Langhe, Le: See Barolo.

Langhorne's Creek: Australian (S.A.) wine centre.

Langoa-Harton: French (Médoc) red wine.

Langoiran: French (Entre-deux-Mers) red and white wine district.

Langon: Red table wine of Bordeaux.

Langoon: The obsolete English term of the 16th century for the white wine of Langon, France.

Languedoc: The extensive southern French province (the 'Midi') which produces the ocean of *vin ordinaire*, the common, cheap and wholesome wine which is a staple article of Gallic diet. The Languedoc includes the Gard, Aude and Hérault *départements*. The finer wines are chiefly fortified, sweet dessert types.

Languettes, Les: French (Côte-d'Or) red wine.

Langweg: German white wine. See also Dienheim.

Lanson: Old-established champagne of Reims.

Larkmead: Californian (Napa Valley) vineyard. Mainly good red.

Larose: French (Entre-deux-Mers) red and white wines.

Larose-Perganson: French (Médoc) red wine.

Larose-Trintaudon: French (Médoc) red wine.

Larsen: Old-established brand of cognac (q.v.).

Lascombes: French (Médoc) red wine.

Lasenberg: German (Neumagen, q.v.) white wine.

Las Palmas: The capital of the Spanish archipelago in the Atlantic called the Canary Islands and the centre of the wine export trade. This is no longer important, as disease (*oidium*, q.v.) destroyed most of the vineyards in 1853 and other agriculture has replaced wine-growing. It is the origin of the name 'palm wine' (not to be confused with the beverage made from the sap of palms). See also Canary.

Last Drop Glass: Typical of the vessels used for practical jokes. Engraved on the bottom was the figure of a corpse on a gibbet and, even if the glass was turned upside down, the 'last drop' remained.

Last Orders, Please: Doleful sound, frequently accompanied by the ringing of bells and dimming of the light; not so final as 'Time gentlemen, please'.

La Tache: French (Côte-d'Or) fine red wine.

Latium: Italian province which produces a large volume of esteemed table wines. The fact that Rome is handy helps the industry.

La Tour-Blanche: See Tour-Blanche, La.

Latour Blanche: Esteemed French (sauternes) wine. See also Sauternes.

Latour-Blanche: No connection with La Tour-Blanche (q.v.). This is a white wine of Hermitage, Rhône Valley.

Latour-Blanche-de-Patiras: An island white wine vineyard in the River Gironde.

La Tour-Carnet: French (Médoc) red wine. Also rendered La Tour de Carnet or Latour de Carnet. A vineyard now over 600 years old.

Latour, Ch.: Celebrated French wine estate on the banks of the Gironde at Pauillac, Médoc, generally accepted by experts as one of the greatest clarets (q.v.). Some indeed state unequivocally that it is the standard by which all other clarets should be judged. It is an ancient vineyard and the tower was erected to protect the estate from water-borne attackers.

La Tour Charlus: French (Entre-deux-Mers) red wine.

La Tour Clanet: French (Gironde) red and white wines.

La Tour-Cordouan: French (Médoc) red wine.

La-Tour-de-Bessan: French (Médoc) red wine.

La Tour-de-By: French (Médoc) red wine.

La Tour-de-Grenet: French (St. Émilion) red wine.

La Tour-de-Lesparre: French (Médoc) red wine.

La Tour de L'Espérance: French (Bordeaux) red and white wines.

La Tour-de-Marbuzet: French (Médoc) red wine.

La Tour-de-Mons: French (Médoc) red wine.

La Tour de Périgal: French (Médoc) red wine.

La Tour-de-Pressac: French (St. Émilion) red wine.

La Tour des Termes: French (Médoc) red wine.

La Tour du Château Pinneau: French (Médoc) red wine.

La Tour du Fourneau: French (Médoc) red wine.

La Tour-du-Haut-Carmail: French (Médoc) red wine.

La Tour du Haut-Vignoble: French (St. Estèphe) red wine.

Latour-Dumirail: French (Médoc) red wine.

La Tour-du-Mont: French (Médoc) red wine.

La Tour-du-Pin-Figeac-Moure: French (St. Émilion) red wine.

La Tour-du-Roi: See La Tour.

La Tour-Figeac: French (Graves) fine red wine.

La Tour-Fourthon: French (Médoc) red wine.

La Tour-Gayet: French (Médoc) red wine.

La Tour Geyraud: French (Bordeaux) red wine.

Latour-Haut-Brion: French (Graves) red wine, not to be confused with Ch. Haut-Brion.

La Tour Haut-Vignoble: French (St. Estèphe) red wine.

La Tour-Jean-Faure: French (Graves) red wine.

La Tour-L'-Aspic: French (Pauillac) red wine.

La Tour Marcillanel: French (Médoc) red wine.

La Tour-Massac: French (Médoc) red wine.

La Tour-Négrier: French (Médoc) red wine.

Latour-Pibran: French (Pauillac) red wine.

La Tour-Pomerol: French (Pomerol) red wine.

La Tour-Pourret: French (St. Émilion) red wine.

La Tour Puymirand: French (Bordeaux) red wine.

La Tour-Rauzan: French (Médoc) red wine.

La Tour-Rouge: French (Médoc) red wine.

La Tour Saint-Aubin: French (Médoc) red wine.

La Tour-Saint-Bonnet: French (Médoc) red wine.

La Tour-Saint-Nicolas: French (Graves) red wine.

La Tour-Seran: French (Médoc) red wine.

La Tour-Sieujan: French (Médoc) red wine.

La Tour-Sigurd: French (St. Émilion) red wine.

La Tour-Surget: French (Bordeaux) red wine.

Lattice: In the Middle Ages, few taverns had glass windows. The aperture was covered by a trellis or lattice; this was painted red and served to distinguish the tavern from adjoining houses.

Laubenheim: German (Rheinhessen) white wine district including vineyards of Hitz, Dammsberg, Steig, Burg, Edelmann, Seckergrund, Steinerne Brücke, Kalkofen, Johannisberg, Heyl, Neuberg, Häuschen.

Laudamusberg: German (Neumagen, q.v.) white wine.

Laudenbach: German (Württemberg) white and Schillerwein (q.v.).

Laufen: German (Baden) white wine centre.

Lauffen: German (Württemberg) red wine centre.

Laujac: French (Médoc) red wine.

Laurentiusberg: German (Ruwer, q.v.) white wine.

Laurenzane: French (Graves) red wine.

Laurenzberg: German (Mertesdorf-Grünhaus, q.v.) white wine.

Lauter: A filter tub used in brewing.

Lautersberg: German (Oberemmel, q.v.) white wine.

Lautertrunk: Old German term for spiced wine.

Lavaux: Swiss (Vaud) wine region.

Lavrottes, Les: French (Côte-d'Or) red wine.

Lay: German (Eibingen, q.v.) white wine.

Lay: German (Niederemmel, q.v.) white wine.

Lay: German (Minheim, q.v.) white wine.

Lay: German (Rüdesheim, q.v.) fine white wine.

Layen: German (Kröv-Kövenig, q.v.) white wine estate.

Layon, Côteaux du: The Layon is a tributary of the Loire. Spread along about 30 miles of its banks or slopes (*côteaux*) are vineyards producing good white wines, including Quarts de Chaume, Faye, Beaulieu and Bonnezeaux.

Leacock: Old-established shippers of madeira (q.v.).

Leaguer: South African (Old Dutch) liquid measure equal to about 128 imperial gallons (153·7 U.S. gallons). In sailing ship days, the term was applied to a water cask of about 159 gallons. After Trafalgar, Nelson's body was placed in a leaguer with abundant spirit and safely brought back to England.

Leanyka: Hungarian white wine from Eger and Kecskemet. There are two types. Szaraz is dry and Edes is sweet.

Leather Bottle: Vessel long used for the transport and storage of beer most popular during the Restoration. It was made of seasoned hide, double-welted and cross-stitched with waxed thread. Pitch was sometimes used to seal the inside and make the vessel waterproof. There were varied shapes, though none would be recognized as bottles today: the most common were oblong, with flat base and ends, the rounded sides converging on the mouth at the top. Leather bottles were taken into the harvest fields until comparatively recent times. See also Black Jack, Bombard.

Leaven: Old-time English term for yeast. See also Lévure.

Leckerberg: German white wine. See also Dittelsheim.

Lees: The sediment or dregs from wine or other liquor.

Leeton: Australian (N.S.W.) wine centre.

Lefka: Table wine from a region of Cyprus.

Lehnchen: German (Östrich, q.v.) white wine.

Lehrensteinsfeld: German (Württemberg) red and white wines.

Leichentrunk: Old German rural custom of providing ample drink to mourners immediately after burial. See also Wake.

Leiderchen: German (Nittel, q.v.) white wine.

Leinhohle: White wine from Deidesheim, Palatinate (q.v.).

Leinsweiler: German (Palatinate) white wine.

Leisenheim: German (Baden) white wine centre.

Leistadt: German (Palatinate) red and white wine centre.

Leisten: Steinwein (q.v.) vineyard near Würzburg, Franconia. One of the State Steinwein establishments, with Randersacker, Hoerstein and Stein.

Leitacher: See Santa Giustina.

Lende: German (Hessloch, q.v.) white wine.

Léognan: Important wine-growing commune of the Graves district which includes many celebrated vineyards, e.g. Ch. Haut-Brion and Haut-Bailly.

Leonay: South Australian winery. Red and white table wines.

Léoville: The name borne by a number of noted red wines of the Médoc, France.

Léoville Barton: Fine red wine from St. Julien, Bordeaux.

Léoville-Las-Cases: French (Médoc) red wine.

Léoville-Poyferré: French (Médoc) red wine.

Lerchelberg: German (Kirrweiler, q.v.) wine estate.

Lesbos: An island centre of prized wines frequently mentioned by classical writers. Horace classed Lesbian wine as 'innocent'.

Lesigne: French (Anjou) white wine.

Lessona: Italian (Novara) red wine.

Lestage: French (Médoc) red wine.

Lett: German wine estate of Winkel, Rheingau.

Letten: German (Friedelsheim, q.v.) white wine.

Leutesdorf: German (Neuwied) white wine centre.

Leutschach: Austrian (Steiermark) white wine.

Leviticus: The rule of law in 19 : 9–10 and 23 : 22 prohibits wholly reaping a field at harvest in order to leave a gleaning for the poor. In southern Italy and elsewhere this hangover of Jewish custom impels some owners of vineyards to leave a vine unpicked to ensure a good vintage the following year.

Lévure: French term for yeast actually added (i.e. not present on the grape skins) to must (q.v.) prior to fermentation. In practice it is usually a substantially pure culture of a selected strain of *Saccharomyces ellipsoideus* (q.v.).

Leyenkaul: German white wine vineyard at Saarburg (q.v.).

Leyer: German (Ockenheim, q.v.) white wine.

Libation: Originally, a drink offering to a god.

Liber: Roman god of fructification, and, later, of the grape.

Libourne: French wine-market town of the River Dordogne, centre for Pomerol and St. Émilion.

Licence, Spirits on: Alternative term for a 'publican's' or 'full' licence. There is no minimum sale but the maximum that can be sold to one person at one time is two gallons. See also Licence and Wholesale.

Licence, Wholesale Spirits: In the United Kingdom this is the 'dealer's' licence which covers sales in quantities not less than two gallons or one dozen reputed quarts (q.v.) for consumption off the premises. Many other countries have similar legislation.

Licensed Premises: In the sense of this book, an establishment legally entitled to sell alcoholic beverages. Some system of licensing is in operation within every civilized country of the world and the variations, complexities, illogicalities and terminological confusion are so great that no book has ever fully covered the subject. Eminent lawyers have stated quite baldly that nobody really knows fully the licensing law for any English-speaking country. In Australia, for example, each of the six states has its own legal code and it is said that the same applies to every one of the states of the U.S.A.

There is not even uniformity in the legal or general use of names such as hotel, inn, public house, tavern, saloon, bar or pub (the last not necessarily a mere abbreviation of public house), licensed restaurant, off-licence, colonial wine licence, grocers' licence, wholesale licence and many more.

In most countries licences may seemingly be grouped under two broad headings:

A. *For consumption off the premises:* These licences include:
    (1) those of wholesale wine and spirit merchants (whose sales must be of or above a certain volume) and
    (2) retail establishments, which may sell by the single bottle.

O

B. *For consumption on the premises:* Restaurant and saloon licences are primarily to permit the consumption of liquor with meals and carry no residential or housing obligations. Hotel, inn and similar licences place a legal obligation upon the licensee to supply sleeping accommodation and meals to travellers.

The story of the evolution of licensed premises is one of fascination and covers every phase of human conduct. At that we must leave it.

Lichee Blossom: Cocktail of rum, pineapple juice, canned lichee juice.

Liebfrauenstift: German (Worms) white wine of which the best esteemed is L. Klostergarten. See also Liebfraumilch.

Liebfraumilch: The German name ('Blessed Mother's Milk') of the white table wine produced in more than 150 separate villages in Rheinhessen (q.v.). Naturally the quality varies and the name in itself means nothing. It was originally produced only in the small vineyard adjoining the Liebfrauenkirche (the Church of Our Lady) in Worms. So long as the wine is produced in Rheinhessen it can now be sold as Liebfraumilch, whatever the quality and whether it be dry or sweet. As Simon tersely says, 'formerly the white wine of Worms vineyards; now merely the name of a hock without any guarantee of origin or quality'. The genuine wine of the Liebfrauenkirche vineyards, near Worms, is sold under the name Liebfrauenstift (q.v.).

Liemenhohl: German (Rheinhessen) wine estate.

Lieser: German (Moselle) white wine centre including the vineyards of Kirchberg, Schlossberg and Niederberg.

Lieth: German (Harxheim, q.v.) white wine.

Lifter: Another name for filler (q.v.).

Light Ale: Pale ale. See also Ale.

Light and Mild: A mixture, pale ale and mild, half-and-half.

Ligist: Austrian wine district.

Lignières: French (Grande Champagne) wine commune where some of the best cognac is made.

Lignorelles: French (Chablis) white wine.

Ligré: French (Touraine) red wine.

Likörweine: The general German term for fortified dessert-wines. See also Fortified.

Lilienhof: German (Kaiserstuhl, q.v.) wine centre.

Lillet: One of the legion of French proprietary apéritif wines (q.v.).

Limassol: Table wine from a region of Cyprus.

Limoux: French (Aude) red and white table wines. See also Blanquette de Limoux.

Linderos: Chilean wine estate of quality.

Lingeaquavit: 'Travelled' aquavit (q.v.) or akvavit (q.v.).

Linsenbusch: German (Ruppertsberg, q.v.) white wine.

Lipari: The islands near Sicily noted for Malvasia di Lipari (q.v.).

Lipez: Russian mead (q.v.) made from honey gathered from the linden.

Liqueur Brandy, Whisky, Rum, etc.: A term applied indiscriminately to spirits as a trade puff of quality. The spirits are not sweetened and are in no sense liqueurs so the term has no real significance. It ought to mean (and sometimes does) a spirit of great age and so mellow that it can be drunk neat as a liqueur.

Liqueur de Dessert: The French term for the highly-flavoured beverages the first word of whose name has been adopted in England (rather foolishly) for the same substances. The meaning, of course, is merely liquor or alcoholic drink.

Liqueur d'Expédition: French term for the sweetening added to champagne just before it is despatched.

Liqueur Jaune and Liqueur Verte: These names are often used for imitations of yellow and green chartreuse respectively.

Liqueurs: Highly flavoured, sweetened spirits intended to be drunk in small amount with coffee at the end of a meal. For derivation of name, see Liqueur de Dessert.

Liqueurs are venerable beverages. They were originally made by adding brandy to fresh or dried fruits and herbs and were known as cordials. This name is still used occasionally for liqueurs so prepared though the word has come to mean in some countries a non-alcoholic flavouring syrup or a 'temperance' drink. A ratafia (q.v.) is a modern synonym for a true alcoholic cordial made by adding spirit to fruit juice.

Liqueurs vary in strength and can range from 60% down to 30% of alcohol by volume, according to the nature of the flavour.

The alcohol (spirit) used to make liqueurs should be either a highly-refined odourless alcohol made from grain or other suitable source or a brandy, whisky, rum or other spirit deliberately intended to contribute to the final blended flavour.

Liqueurs are made by any of three processes:

Distillation: This is the most expensive method and in general the one used for the finest products. The fruits, herbs, 'botanicals', and other ingredients are macerated in strong spirit and the mixture is then distilled. The alcohol and the volatile flavourings pass over. The distillate is sweetened and, if necessary, coloured. Obviously this process can only be applied to volatile (distillable) flavourings such as peppermint, raspberry, orange, caraway, thyme and many others.

Infusion: This is the process of adding fruits and other flavourings to spirit, filtering and sweetening. In general the infusion process results in liqueurs inferior to those made by distillation but it should be realized that some flavourings can only be incorporated by infusion.

The third method is the *essence process*, used chiefly, but not entirely, for the production of cheap and inferior liqueurs. This is the direct addition of natural or synthetic flavouring materials to spirit, with subsequent sweetening and colouring.

The nomenclature of liqueurs is sometimes fanciful. Especially sweet and strong ones are often called creams (*crèmes*). Those whose flavour is predominantly of one ingredient bear that name (banana, coffee, aniseed and many more). Some liqueurs are the result of a complex mixture of flavourings. Literally hundreds of herbs, barks, fruits, flowers and seeds are used.

Liquor: A word of great interest as an illustration of the complex and often absurd variation that may occur in a term. It is derived from the Latin *liquidus* and was originally more or less identical with 'liquid', a term that needs no definition to the layman though the physicist may have a little more difficulty in reaching an acceptable description. The word liquor is still used in pharmacy and technology in its rational sense of any liquid and especially of a solution in water, but it has gradually come to acquire the specialized meaning of any alcoholic beverage and names such as liquor trade, liquor laws and the like are without ambiguity. However, the adjective is often given a censorious twist, e.g., liquor traffic. To add to the confusion, even in the liquor industry itself the word has variable meaning. The brewer uses it as a synonym for water and speaks of 'a good brewing liquor'. For even worse confusion see Drink.

Liquor, Hard: See Hard Liquor.

Liquoreux: French wine term for sweet or luscious.

Lirac: Town near Tavel (q.v.) and also known as a centre of production of *vin rosé* (q.v.).

Lisbon Hock: The stupid and now mercifully obsolete name in England for Bucellas, a Portuguese dry white wine.

Lisbon Wines: A term now little used. In the trade it meant fortified sweet wine made on the Tagus and inferior to port (q.v.). There are also dry (table) wines made on the Tagus near Lisbon including Termo (white), Bucellas (golden) and Torres Vedras (red).

Listan: See Palomino.

Listrac: French (Médoc) wine-growing commune producing a great volume of sound but not superfine red wine. A number of adjoining communes are allowed by law to sell their wine under the better-known name of Listrac.

Litre: Metric unit of capacity. It is the volume of one kilogram of pure water, measured at a temperature of 4° C. and atmospheric pressure 76 centimetres. It is equivalent to 1·76 British imperial pints, or 2·1134 U.S. pints. An ordinary French wine bottle holds ¾ litre (75 centilitres).

Livener: Mixture of champagne and brandy, plus raspberry syrup, lemon and bitters. A typical confusion of the drink inventor.

Liversan: French (Médoc) red wine.

Livran: French (Bordeaux) red wine.

Ljaskowetz: Bulgarian centre for wine production.

Ljutomer: One of the principal wines of Yugoslavia, a dry white from the central region made from riesling grapes. Also known as Luttenberger.

Local: The Englishman's affectionate term for the pub round the corner. One of the mainstays of the English social system.

Lodge: The Portuguese term, applicable both to the Oporto and Madeira districts, for a storage place for wine. The predominant Anglo-Saxon ownership of the port and madeira trade is reflected in the word.

Loewenberg: German (Kinheim, q.v.) white wine estate.

Loggerhead: A tool for heating beverages consisting of a long iron handle terminating in a bulb. See also Flip. To be at loggerheads refers to the fierce arguments likely to be generated during drinking bouts.

Logroño: The nucleus of the Rioja (q.v.) vineyards of North Spain.

Loibner: Austrian table wine from Danube.

Loire Basin: This is an important French wine-growing region much less known outside France than areas such as Burgundy and Bordeaux. There are many hundreds of vineyards but reputations are mainly local and the wines usually do not bear estate names. The wines of Anjou and Touraine are somewhat similar. The whites are in general more highly esteemed than the reds and some are turned into sparkling wines by the true champagne system (q.v.). These include Saumur and Vouvray. There are also good *rosé* wines and some sweet growths. This is one of the most fertile and beautiful regions of France and many tourists return again and again to revel in the wine and food. The wines of the Loire are a large study in themselves and, a word to the wise, they are accounted particularly good value.

Lola Montez: Old Australian drink of gin, ginger, lemon and hot water. The name is that of the celebrated entertainer who toured the goldfields in the fifties.

Lombardy: One of the chief Italian wine-growing provinces. The most renowed wines are the Valtellinas.

Lomelino: Old-established shippers of madeira (q.v.).

London Dry Gin: General name for any unsweetened gin.

Longbeard: See Bellarmine.

Long Glass: See Yard of Ale.

Long John: Old-established Scotch whisky distillers, outside the D.C.L. combine.

Long Pull: Giving the customer rather more than he ordered. The opposite of short pull. For both these offences the British publican can be prosecuted.

Longuich: German (Moselle) white wine centre, of which the best-known estate is Probstberg.

Lorch: German (Rheingau) ancient white wine centre, including the vineyards of Kappelenberg, Bodingrube and Pfaffenwies.

Lorchhausen: German (Rheingau) white wine centre, including the vineyards of Galgenpfad, Rosenberg, Lach and Niederflur.

Lord of the Tap: An official appointed to visit all booths at which beer was sold during the annual fair at Cambridge and to test the quality by tasting. The custom survived until the 18th century, the first appointment being in the 15th. No doubt this appointment was keenly sought.

Lord Sugarcane: 18th-century sobriquet for rum.

Lorenzberg: German (Ruwer, q.v.) white wine.

Lorraine: Cocktail of kirsch, cherry brandy and lemon juice.

Lorraine, Gris de: Lorraine is not a wine region of distinction but her unpretentious local wines, lumped under this title, are pleasant enough.

Los Tercios: District of Jerez (q.v.), Spain, producing *fino* sherry.

Loudenne: Large wine estate north of Bordeaux producing red and white table wines for the English owners, a firm of spirit merchants.

Lounge: (Sometimes also lounge bar, saloon lounge.) An improvement even on the saloon bar; the best appointed and most expensive bar of the public house.

Loupiac: District near Barsac producing similar sweet wine.

Loupiac: French (Gironde) red and white wines.

Loupiac-Gaudet: French (Entre-deux-Mers) red and white wines.

Louvière: French (Graves) red and white wines.

Loving-Cup: A large drinking-vessel passed around a gathering of friends.

Lowland: General name for the single (q.v.) pot-stilled malt whiskies produced for blending purposes, mainly in the Edinburgh area.

Low Wines: The first bulk distillate in whisky production, containing practically all the alcohol of the wash (q.v.).

Loxton: Australian (S.A.) wine centre.

Ludes: French (Champagne) white wine.

Ludon: French (Médoc) wine-growing commune. Most of the wines of the six adjoining communes have the legal right to sell their wines under the better-esteemed name of Ludon.

Luginsland: White wine from Wachenheim, Palatinate (q.v.).

Lump: German (Escherndorf, q.v.) white wine.

Lunatic Soup: Australian slang for bad liquor, especially 'metho' (q.v.).

Lunel: Wine centre near Roussillon for *vins doux naturels* (q.v.).

Lupulin: The sticky powder in the hop cone, containing the oils and resins which provide the flavour and preservative properties.

Luther, Martin (1483–1546): Here is a shining example of giving somebody the benefit of a doubt. In the Luther room in Warburg is written:

> Wer nicht lieb Wein, Weib und Gesang
> Der bleibt ein Narr sein Leben lang.
> 'Who loves not woman, wine and song
> Remains a fool his whole life long.'

There is no actual proof that Luther was the author but Thackeray, for example, writes:

> Then sing as Martin Luther sang,
> As Doctor Martin Luther sang,
> 'Who loves not wine, woman and song,
> He is a fool his whole life long.' (*A Credo*).

Lutomer Sipon: One of the best-known Yugoslavian white wines. It is said to owe its name to the statement of the Crusaders that it was '*si bon*'.

Luttenberger: See Ljutomer.

Lüttje Lage: German mixed drink of schnapps and beer to be downed at one gulp. Ugh!

Luxembourg: The wines, as one would expect from the climate, are rather thin and acid but have their place. Amongst the better vineyards are Wormeldinger, Wintriger and Remicher. The vineyards are mostly on the left bank of the Moselle and in recent years the quality of the white wines has improved considerably. Some are made into sparkling wines.

Lynch-Bages: French (Médoc) red wine.

Lynch-Moussas: French (Médoc) red wine.

Lyndoch: Australian (S.A.) wine centre.

Lyne Arm: The wide pipe connecting the wash still (q.v.) to the condenser in distilling Scotch whisky. There is interminable argument amongst distillers as to the best shape for this pipe.

Lyon: The great gastronomic city of France. It is said, 'Three rivers bathe Lyon: the Rhône, the Saône and the Beaujolais'. See also Beaujolais.

Lys: French (Chablis) white wine.

Maasborn: German (Rauenthal, q.v.) white wine.

Macabeo: French (Pyrénées) sweet wine.

Macau: French (Médoc) wine-growing commune some of whose wines are permitted by custom to be sold as Ludon (q.v.).

Mac-Carthy: French (Yes! Médoc) red wine.

Macharndo: District west of Jerez (q.v.), Spain, where amontillado sherry (q.v.) is grown.

Machiavelli: A brand of chianti (q.v.) put out at Percussina in the actual building where Machiavelli wrote *The Prince*.

Machtumer Sylvaner: White table wine of Luxembourg.

Mackenzie & Co. Ltd.: Old-established (1850) shippers of sherry and port (q.v.).

McLaren Vale: Australian (S.A.) wine centre.

Mâcon: Important French wine market town of Lower Burgundy. The wines shipped from here, especially to England, are darker and heavier in type than those of the Côte-d'Or. Mâcon is the centre of a wine-growing district north of Lyon called the Mâconnais which includes the areas of Cluny, Tournus, Mâcon, Lugny and St. Gengoux. Though the Mâconnais is noted mainly for red wines there are also whites of which the reputed best is Solutré.

Madame Bishop: Mixed drink of port, sugar and nutmeg named after an Australian worthy of the 1850's.

Madara: 'Madeira', Bulgarian dessert wine.

Maddington: Australian (W.A.) wine centre.

Madeira: The name borne by wines of widely differing character from the island of that name. The word is Portuguese for timber and the forests which covered the island were burnt by the first settlers in the 15th century. The wine is made on the solera system (q.v.), but part of the process is the sustained heating or baking. (See also Rancio.)
   Almost as soon as the Portuguese settled on this island in the Atlantic the culture of the vine was commenced. In past times madeira was a celebrated, highly prized and expensive wine, a great favourite in England, the U.S. and the Royal Navy. Vine disease and other causes have

contributed to a great decline during the last 100 years not only in quantity but, according to oenophiles, also in quality, though at least a little modern madeira of superb properties is still made. The chief customer for the wines of Madeira today are the Scandinavians.

Madeira is a wine fortified with spirit mostly made locally from sugar residues and thus a type of rum, though highly rectified so that little or no flavour is added. The wine is made in a special way. The lightly fortified new wine is transferred to heated storerooms called *estufas* and kept there for some months. It is then fortified further and transferred to oak casks for long maturing. The longevity of madeira is proverbial. There are authenticated accounts of the wine being quite drinkable after 100 years. Whether present-day madeira would keep as long is doubtful.

Not all madeira is highly sweet. There are three recognized types or styles, being *sercial* (dryish), *verdelho* (half-way) and *bual* (typical sweet dessert wine). Bual is also known as 'malmsey', a name previously given in England also to similar wine made from the malvasia grape in Canary, Italy and Spain. The Duke of Clarence is supposed to have been drowned in the 15th century in a butt of malmsey. Whether madeira was really known in England at that time is, however, unlikely.

There are four principal vines, the verdelho, sercial, bual and malvasia. Each is separately fermented to produce a wine of marked characteristics. The verdelho is reported to be near extinction.

A style of madeira called Rainwater (q.v.) was once popular in the U.S.

The name madeira is falsely used for inexpensive sweet fortified wine in California, Australia and South Africa. Such wine bears no real resemblance to the true thing. Incidentally, genuine madeira will always be expensive.

Long periods of maturing are usual, and casks of madeira were formerly shipped as ballast on sailing-ships, as the wine was supposed to benefit from the rolling voyage.

Madère: French (Graves) white wine.

Madérisé also Maderization: A French term used frequently in England. When a white wine starts to develop a brownish colour and a curious musty smell, it is called *madérisé* and means that the wine is on the road downhill. The term is also applied to the weathering or maturing process applied to certain wines of the Midi (q.v.) involving exposure of the filled casks to the heat of the sun for a year or more. The result is supposed to resemble inferior madeira.

Madhulika: Sanskrit word stated to be for spirit made from wheat.

Madiran: French (Basque) red wine.

Madre Vino: Mother wine, the Spanish and Italian term for the concentrated (boiled-down) must (q.v.) added to other wines, such as marsala and malaga, to sweeten and tone them. See also P.X.

Magdalenegarten: German (Östreich, q.v.) white wine.

Magdelaine: French (St. Émilion) red wine.

Magnesian: Greek wine mentioned in classical writings.

Magnum: A large bottle, often used for champagne, holding two reputed quarts or $\frac{1}{3}$ gallon.

Mago: The Carthaginian agronomist frequently cited by Roman writers as a viticultural authority.

Mahogany: Cornish drink of gin sweetened and flavoured with treacle. The name clearly refers to the colour. The drink is alleged to have been the favourite of smugglers.

Mahua: Indian spirit made, as reported, from Bassia flowers.

Maiden: Old mixed drink of spirit, peppermint and cloves.

Maiden's Blush: Cocktail of gin, grenadine and curaçao.

Maiden's Prayer: Cocktail of whisky, dry vermouth, Swedish punch and lemon juice.

Maidstone: The English district reputed to produce the best hops in the world.

Maikammer: German (Palatinate) white wine.

Mailberger: Austrian white wine.

Mailly: French (Champagne) wine-growing district.

Main: Along this important tributary of the German Rhine there are important vineyards all the way from Franconia to Hochheim.

Maingebiet: German wine centre on River Main.

Mainz: Also Mayence. German wine-selling town.

Mainzer Michelsberg: Esteemed German wine from the Mainz area.

Mainzerweg: German (Bingen, q.v.) white wine.

Maison Brûlée: French (Côte-d'Or) red wine.

Maitai: Polynesian (esp. Tahitan) mixed drink of rum and lime juice.

Maître de Chai: French for cellarmaster, that all-knowing, all-powerful personage on whom the fate of the bulk rests.

Mai Tsau: Chinese (Cantonese) term for rice wine.

Maize Malt: The malt made from Indian corn used as a substitute for barley malt by the early settler in America.

Malaga: Spanish sweet dessert wine, long a favourite in France though the indigenous Roussillon (q.v.) seems largely to have replaced it. Malaga is or was, a manufactured wine, a blend of wines sweetened by concentrated grape juice and then heavily fortified (q.v.).

Malaga Blanc: An esteemed white table wine of Malaga, eastern Andalusia.

Malangin: French (St. Émilion) red wine.

Malartic-Lagravière: French (Graves) red wine.

Malbec: Red grape grown in Bordeaux for blending with cabernet (q.v.) for claret.

Malbec, Ch.: French (Bordeaux) red and white wines.

Malconsorts: Red table wine of Vosne, Burgundy.

Malescasse: French (Médoc) red wine.

Malescot: French (Bordeaux) red wine.

Malescot-Saint-Exupéry: French (Médoc) red wine. The second grade is or used to be curiously labelled '*Cru de la Colonie*'.

Malic Acid: This is the principal acid of apples and a number of other fruits but it also occurs in small quantity in grapes. It is always found in wine and may play an important part in the maturing process. See also Malo-Lactic Fermentation.

Malle: French (Sauternes) sweet white wine.

Mallia: Turkish wine centre.

Malmesbury: South African wine-producing area.

Malmsey: Best known of the Madeira wines, sweet and full-bodied. See also Malvasia and Madeira.

Malo-Lactic Fermentation: The bacterial (lactic acid bacteria, q.v.) decarboxylation of *l*-malic acid of grape juice to lactic acid and carbon dioxide gas. This is desirable if it occurs in bulk wines of high acidity but not in sweet or bottled wines. It may then lead to blown corks, cloudiness and other faults. The investigation of the phenomenon is recent and complex.

Malört: Swedish for wormwood (q.v.) and the basis of several compounded beverages and flavourings.

Malt: Cereal grain allowed to sprout, and subsequently dried; diastase (q.v.) is formed in the process, and converts the starch to sugar. Any grain can be malted, but the unadorned term usually means barley malt. See also Beer.

Malt, a glass of: A glass of beer.

Malt, Black or Roasted: Malt made by roasting in a cylinder.

Malt, Coloured: Known in the trade as amber, crystal, brown and black, according to the colour and flavour transmitted to the beer. The colour is largely determined by the extent of kilning (q.v.).

Malt, Crystal: Special barley malt of shortened growth used as a flavouring agent in brewing. Glucose sugar is usually added and the mixture is dried at high temperature to produce a flavour of caramel (q.v.).

Malt, Imperial: Special malt made by suddenly raising the drying temperature so that the malt swells and acquires a desired tar flavour.

Malta: A region at present of no consequence as a producer of wine but of much moment as a consumer.

Malting Process: The conversion of the insoluble proteins and starch contained in the barley grains into soluble matter and sugars of the malt grains. This is done by steeping the barley in heaps on the malting floor until it germinates and growth starts. When the growth has extended three-quarters of the length of the corn, the grains are removed from the floor and laid out in the kiln. There they are lightly cooked to prevent further growth and finally sieved to remove the rootlets or culms (q.v.). Malts for pale ale are now stored until required for brewing. The majority of the barley crop is dried at higher temperatures to provide malts of fuller flavour and richer colour, which are more suitable as malts for darker ales and stouts. These may be kilned over wood chips, heated in a gas oven, or fully roasted to provide a large range of malts for selection by the brewer. Wheat, rye and other cereals may also be malted.

Maltings: The buildings in which barley grains are converted into malt.

These buildings, with the long multi-windowed walls of the malting floors and the conical vents of the kilns, form a characteristic feature of the countryside in most English barley-growing areas. However, the modern malting is more of a huge city factory.

Malt Liquor: Generic term for all ales, beers, and other brewed beverages.

Maltroie, La: French (Côte-d'Or) red wine.

Maltster: The man who controls the malting process.

Malt Tower: The highest point of the brewery, from which the malt starts on its journey via the mills to the mash tuns.

Malvasia or Malmsey: A sweet, fortified wine that has been known for many centuries. The name is derived from Monemvasia, a town on the east coast of Morea, Greece, whence the wine was originally exported; the wine itself was produced mainly in Crete and the islands of the Aegean Sea. The malvasia or malmsey wine of modern commerce is mainly produced in the Portuguese islands of the north Atlantic, and in various districts of southern Europe. There is also a grape known as malvasia, white and luscious. See also Engaddi. The Malvasia grape was introduced into Italy by the Romans, into madeira (q.v.) by the Portuguese in the 15th century and into the Cape of Good Hope by the Dutch in the 17th.

Malvasia di Lipari: Italian dessert wine of the Lipari Islands.

Malvasia di Pantelleria: Italian dessert wine of the island of Pantelleria.

Malvoisie: French (Roussillon) amber dessert wine. Malvoisie is the French form of malvasia (q.v.)

Mamie Taylor: Highball of rye whiskey and ginger ale.

Manby: West Indian bitter drink.

Mancha: Spanish heavy table wines.

Mandarin: A liqueur with the flavour of mandarin oranges.

Mandarinovka: Vodka in which has been soaked dried mandarin peel, hence technically a gin (q.v.).

Mandel: German (Nahe) white wines.

Mandelacker: German (Ruppertsberg, q.v.) white wine.

Manhattan: Cocktail of whisky, sweet vermouth, bitters. There are many variants, e.g. brandy, rum or gin may be used. One of the few really basic cocktails. Also called Gin and It (q.v.). The birth of this celebrated cocktail is stated to have taken place at a banquet given by Lady Randolph Churchill, mother of Sir Winston, at the Manhattan Club in New York in honour of Samuel J. Tilden. The bartender mixed bourbon (q.v.) whiskey, vermouth and bitters as a special drink for the occasion.

Manicle: French (Bressan) white wine.

Mannberg: German (Hattenheim, q.v.) white wine.

Manta: Portuguese for the scum or cap that forms on the must (q.v.) during fermentation. This consists of skins, stalks and seeds.

Mantuo de Pilas: Also mantuo castellana. One of the lesser grapes used in Spain for sherry.

Manzanares: Spanish wine area north of Valdepeñas (q.v.). Heavy red, so-called burgundy-type.

Manzanilla: Sherry wine of *fino* type made at Sanlucar de Barrameda, a little northwest of Jerez de la Frontera (q.v.). Manzanillas are dry and pale with an esteemed slightly bitter aftertaste. The driest of all true sherries, manzanilla is mainly consumed in Spain. Appreciated by connoisseurs but not by the general public. The name is that of a village in the district. See also Sherry.

Maotai: Chinese strong pot-stilled (q.v.) spirit as celebrated in the Far East as is cognac in the Western world. Like cognac, the name is geographical. The spirit has been made for more than 200 years in the beautiful little town of the same name in the rugged mountains of Kweichow in SW. China. The principal or only industry is distilling maotai.

The spirit is made from a fermented mixture of kaoling and wheat. The former is the berry of a grain sorghum widely used for food in the Orient. The process of manufacture is traditional and quite complex. A Chinese official publication states 'it is fermented no less than seven times and distilled eight times in the course of a nine-month cycle. The liquor extracted each time is stored separately for three years.' However, the exact meaning of this description is obscure. One feature of the process is storage (i.e. ageing, q.v.) in large and rough pottery jars. These receptacles allow some air to enter through the pores. They are thus similar in action to the oaken casks used for maturing brandy and whisky. Maotai is reported to be a mellow and fragrant spirit which will undoubtedly eventually become appreciated in Europe.

Maqueline, La: French (Médoc) red wine.

Maranges: French (Burgundy) red wine.

Maraschino: A liqueur of fruit kernel flavour. (*Marascha* means 'small cherry'.) The taste is that of bitter almonds.

Marbuzet: French (Médoc) red wine.

Marc: The remains of grapes and other fruits after the juice has been pressed out. Also known as pomace. Marc is widely used for the production of an inexpensive brandy, usually inferior though Burgundy, *eau de vie de marc* and some Italian grappa (q.v.) can be quite good.

Marc de Bourgogne: The brandy produced in Burgundy from grape residues. Some marc brandies are of high quality and that of Bourgogne is probably the top.

Marchand de Vin: French for wine merchant.

Marchans: German (Ellsheim, q.v.) white wine.

Marchiafava's Disease: Degeneration of brain tissue (*corpus callosum*), supposed to be due to excessive consumption of alcohol and to be limited to the Italian 'race'. Now considered certainly wrong in latter and also highly probably so in former. One modern American textbook of neurology states dogmatically that it is caused by 'over-consumption of cheap Italian wine — Dago red'. Alcoholic fallacies exist in all quarters!

Marco Gallo: The trade mark of the Chianti Producers' Association. This consists of a black target with a rooster in the centre and will be found on the neck of every bottle of 'classic' chianti (q.v.). But this mark applies to but a small fraction of the wine legitimately labelled chianti.

Marconnets, Les: French (Côte-d'Or) red wine.

Marco Polo: Wrote in 1275 that the people of Peking enjoyed a clear, bright and pleasant wine made from rice, so well-flavoured with spices and so good that it made one 'drunk sooner than any other wine'.

He referred, of course, to a type of sake (q.v.). The spices would have produced the equivalent of a weakish vermouth (q.v.). The alcohol content would be considerably lower than that of our modern fortified (q.v.) vermouth. However, the Chinese have an astonishingly large list of scientific and technological priorities and may have practised commercial distillation and fortification earlier than Europeans.

Maréchaudes, Les: French (Côte-d'Or) red wine.

Mareotis: Wine of ancient Egypt praised by Athenaeus.

Mares, Les Bonnes: Red wine of Burgundy.

Marétel: White French wine from Savoy.

Marett: Old-established (1822) brand of cognac (q.v.).

Mareuil-sur-Ay: French (Champagne) white wine.

Margarita: Mixed drink made from tequila and citrus juice, drunk from vessel whose rim has been dipped in salt. Better than it sounds.

Margate: Samuel Pepys the diarist records his appreciation of the quality of Margate ale on several occasions.

Margaux: A celebrated French wine-growing commune of the Médoc containing some of the finest vineyards of Bordeaux. The adjoining commune of Cantenac and also those of Arsac, Soussans, Labarde and Avensan are all legally entitled to sell their wine as Margaux. The great wine of the region is Château Margaux itself, whose records extend over more than 600 years. With 225 acres of vines it is indeed a château. The fame rests, of course, upon red wine but since 1924 some excellent white wine has been made under the label Le Pavillon du Château Margaux.

In addition to the named wines of more than a dozen châteaux, there are many growths in the commune of quite good quality sold simply as Margaux.

Marienthal: German (Ahr) red wine.

Marigold 'Wine': Country wine (q.v.) flavoured with marigolds.

Maring-Noviand a.d. Lieser: German (Moselle) white wine district.

Marino: See Castelli Romani.

Maritza: Table wine from Bulgaria.

Markelsheim: German (Württemberg) white wine.

Markgraeffler: White table wine of Switzerland.

Markham, Gervase: In the *English House-wife*, published in the time of Shakespeare, Markham has given us what is still an excellent specification for true claret, the English name for the red wines of Bordeaux. 'See that in your choice of Gascoine wines you observe that your claret wines be fair coloured and bright as a ruby, not deep as an amethyst, for though it may show strength yet it wanteth neatness. Also let it be sweet as a rose or a violet. . . .' (Spelling modernized.) See also Claret, Bordeaux.

Markobrunn: German vineyard at Erbach, on Rheingau. One of the most highly esteemed Rhine white wines, a superb hock (q.v.).

Marlenheim: Bas-Rhin (q.v.) wine area.

Marnoz: French (Jura) white wine.

Maronean: Greek wine of high quality praised by Homer in the Odyssey.

Marque, La: Swiss (Martigny) table wines.

Marquis d'Alesme-Becker: French (Médoc) red wine.

Marquis-de-Terme: French (Margaux) red wine.

Marrying: In the beverage sense, the process of mixing together drinks and/or flavourings until they are effectively blended. Prolonged storage may be required.

Marsala: The best-known Italian dessert-wine amongst the English-speaking people. It is a comparatively modern wine, first made in the small Sicilian town of Marsala by an English merchant, John Woodhouse, in an attempt to imitate madeira (q.v.), but now made by a special technique which gives it an individual character. Some marsala contains egg.

Marsala all'uovo: Marsala with egg, the widely bottled sweet wine compound made by beating up egg-yolk with marsala wine and extra brandy. Some brands, alas, are quite innocent of egg, and are heavily perfumed.

Marsannay-la-Côte: French (Côte-d'Or) red wine.

Marsberg: Steinwein vineyard at Randersacker (q.v.).

Martell: Old-established (1715) brand of cognac (q.v.).

Martigné-Briand: French (Anjou) white wine.

Martigny: Swiss wine-producing area.

Martillac: French (Graves) wine-growing commune. The reds include Smith-Haut-Lafitte, Ferrand and Lagarde (q.v.).

Martinens: French (Médoc) red wine.

Martini: A mixed drink, or cocktail, in which the essential constituents are vermouth and gin. There are many variants. The name is derived from the name of a maker of vermouth of Torino, Italy.

Martinique: West Indies centre for rum production.

Martinsthal: German (Rheingau) village previously named Neudorf. White wine.

Maryland: American centre for whiskey production. One of the few regions still making straight rye whiskey.

Mary Queen of Scots: Deserves the gratitude of gourmets. She gave assent to an act prohibiting the watering of liquor or adulterating it by adding inferior material.

Marzelle, La: French (Graves) red wine.

Mascara: An Algerian wine-growing district near Algiers, producing red and white wines of robust type. Large quantities are exported to France.

Masdeu: French (Roussillon) red dessert wine.

Mash: A mixture of crushed malt grains and hot liquor (q.v.), which is run through the masher into the mash tun and from which is extracted liquid malt or wort (q.v.). See also Beer.

Mash Tun: A large cast-iron vessel in which wort is extracted from the grist (q.v.). The mash is run into the mash tun and lies on a false bottom consisting of perforated plates. It is then 'sparged' (sprayed) with hot liquor for several hours after which the wort is run off through the perforated plates and the spent grains retained. Modern mash tuns are of glass enamel.

Maslas: A type of tokay wine (q.v.).

Massalia: Classical name for Marseilles, which the Greeks are believed to have planted with vines nearly 3,000 years ago.

Massandra: The most important viticultural area of Russia, close to Yalta in the Crimea.

Massé: Champagne of Reims.

Massic: A wine from Campania, Italy, mentioned in classical writings.

Mastika: Greek flavoured spirit, technically a gin, made by adding resin (mastic). Some non-Greeks profess to like it. Like retsina (q.v.) it is very much an acquired taste.

Mataro: Grape of mediocre quality widely grown in warm climates for red wines. Also a fair Spanish (Catalonian) red table wine.

Matelotte: A Burgundian fish soup made with red wine, mentioned here to show that the alleged antagonism between fish and red wine has notable exceptions. *Meurette*, a stew of eels, also from Burgundy, is another.

Mateus: Portuguese pink table wine from Vila Real.

Matras: French (St. Émilion) red wine.

Matrimony: The name given in an earlier day to the mixed dregs of port and sherry decanters. Presumably it was consumed below stairs. The origin of this absurd name is a mystery.

Mattaru: Goatskin wine container. See also Zumzammim.

Matthew 9 : 17: 'Neither do men put new wine into old bottles.' Alas, observe the stars and letters and the name Napoleon upon certain bottles of cognac (q.v.).

Maturation: See Age.

Maury: French wine centre near Roussillon for *vins doux naturels* (q.v.).

Mauves: French (Graves) red and white wines. Also a wine commune of the Rhône Valley.

Mauvezin: French (Médoc) red wine.

Mavrodaphne: Greek dessert wine. Estimates of its worth vary greatly.

Mavrud: Bulgarian red table wine.

Max: Obsolete syn. for gin (q.v.). Possibly invented by Byron ('Oh, for a glass of max!' — *Don Juan*).

Maximiner Klosterlay: German (Detzem, Moselle) white wine.

Maximin-Grünhäuser: German (Mertesdorf-Grünhaus, q.v.) white wine.

Maybowl: (German Maibowle.) A festive compound of sweetened and flavoured wine, popular with continental students.

Mayence: Important German wine market town of Rheinhessen. Also Mainz.

Mayschoss: German (Ahr) red wine centre.

Mazer: Also Mazard. A wooden bowl (preferably of spotted or birds-eye maple) used in Elizabethan times and later especially to make a 'Christmas draught'. Pepys writes (4 January 1666) 'And, last of all, to have a flaggon of ale and apples drunk out of a wood cupp as a Christmas draught, made all merry!' The finest mazers were richly mounted in silver.

A variant of the mazer was the mether, an Irish drinking-vessel of wood, square in shape with four handles, so called because first made for drinking mead. Also a wooden drinking-cup used by the Saxons, probably for metheglin (q.v.).

Mazoyères-Chambertin, Le: Notable red wine of Burgundy.

Mazurka: Liqueur now obsolete but popular in Australia in the 1850's.

Mead: Alcoholic beverage made by fermenting a solution of honey. It is one of the oldest of liquors, perhaps as ancient as wine and beer. The name is derived from the Sanskrit *madhu*, honey; OE. *meodu*. Two thousand years ago mead was being made in India, Abyssinia and Scandinavia. It has long been a Welsh and Polish speciality. In this day and age little is made. It has become almost esoteric. Perhaps the high cost of honey is the reason.

Honey is not easy to ferment and it is remarkable that the technical tricks of yeast nutrition were discovered so long ago.

Many types of mead can be made and the alcoholic strength may be varied from about that of cider, say 7% of alcohol by volume, to that of a 'big' wine, 14%. Sparkling mead may be made by the champagne process (q.v.). Various types of flavoured mead may be made, employing fruit, juices, spices, herbs and other botanicals. These include cyster, pyment and so on.

Metheglin, derived from the Welsh word *meddyglyn*, is a spiced mead. The Roman beverage hydromel ('honey water') was apparently identical with metheglin. This word was also used as a synonym for plain mead.

There is little commercial honey brandy. However Taliesin, a Cymric bard of the 6th century, is reported to have written a *Song of Mead* which says 'Mead distilled I praise. Its eulogy is everywhere'. (This is a pretty but highly improbable story. See also Distillation.)

The bee and honey held high place in early Indian history. Some 5,000 years ago there was written in Sanskrit in the *Rig-Veda* (Macdonell's translation):

In the wide-striding Vishnu's footstep
There is spring of mead.

One thing is sure. There ought to be far more mead available in this troubled period.

Mealie Beer: Beverage made by South African natives from corn or other grains.

Meather: Ancient Irish timber drinking vessel. See also Mazer.

Meckenheim: German (Palatinate) white wine district, including the vineyards of Neuberg, Spielberg, Fautenböhl and Vierzehnmorgen.

Meddersheim: German (Nahe) white wine centre.

Medicinal Wine: Usually sweet, fortified wine to which this and that, ranging from quinine to meat extract to vitamins, has been added to produce a tonic. One important virtue of such compounded wines is that they allow strict teetotallers to drink them copiously under the euphemism of medicine. Wines containing drugs such as quinine, ipecacuanha and iron citrate are official in some pharmacopoeias.

Médoc: An important part of the French wine-growing region generally called the Bordeaux country or Bordelais, and consisting of a narrow strip of land along the left bank of the River Gironde, about 50 miles long and 6 miles wide. Here is produced much of the truly fine red wine of the world.

In 1855 the French Chamber of Commerce asked the Bordeaux Syndicate of Winebrokers to draw up a list of the best Médoc wines, in order of merit. After more than a century, with minor changes, this list of about 60 wine estates remains in use today. It is still regarded as sacrosanct by an army of wine people though it contains and perpetuates many anomalies and errors. It has even been contended by some that the classification has done as much harm as good.

For example, Ch. Haut-Brion (q.v.), is not in the Médoc at all but its merits were recognized as so outstanding that it was felt it could not be overlooked! On the other hand Mouton-Rothschild was placed in the second category though actually this wine often fetches the highest price in the whole world for red table wine and explains the estate motto, 'First I cannot be, second I disdain to be, Mouton I am!'

Experts agree that today a number of the wines are classed too low or too high but apparently nothing can be done in the face of conservatism and vested interest to revise the hallowed order.

It should be freely admitted, however, that after more than a century it is astonishing that the list remains as accurate as it does despite the changes in ownership and technique and the ravages of *Phylloxera* and other diseases.

One of the principal evils of such a crystallized list as the Médoc Classification is the injustice done to hundreds of wines not mentioned. Below the Fifth Growths are the 'Bourgeois Supérieurs', 'Bourgeois', 'Artisans' and 'Paysans'. Many of these, especially in good years, are markedly better wines than some of the classified châteaux wines.

For what the list is worth, it is reproduced below:

RED WINES

Names	*Communes*
First Growths	
Lafite-Rothschild	Pauillac
Margaux	Margaux
Latour	Pauillac
Haut-Brion	Pessac
Second Growths	
Mouton-Rothschild	Pauillac
Rausan-Sègla	Margaux
Rauzan-Gassies	Margaux
Léoville-Lascases	St. Julien
Léoville-Poyferré	St. Julien
Léoville-Barton	St. Julien
Durfort-Vivens	Margaux
Gruaud-Larose-Sarget	St. Julien
Gruaud-Larose-Faure	St. Julien
Lascombes	Margaux
Brane-Cantenac	Cantenac
Pichon-Longueville, baron de Pichon	Pauillac
Pichon-Longueville, Ctesse de Lalande	Pauillac
Ducru-Beaucaillou	St. Julien
Cos-d'Estournel	St. Estèphe
Montrose	St. Estèphe

RED WINES

Names	*Communes*
Third Growths	
Kirwan	Cantenac
Issan	Cantenac
Lagrange	St. Julien
Langoa-Barton	St. Julien
Giscours	Labarde
Malescot-St. Exupéry	Margaux
Boyd-Cantenac	Cantenac
Cantenac-Brown	Cantenac
Palmer	Cantenac
La Lagune	Ludon
Desmirail	Margaux
Calon-Ségur	St. Estèphe
Ferrière	Margaux
Marquis d'Alesme-Becker	Margaux
Fourth Growths	
Saint-Pierre	St. Julien
Talbot	St. Julien
Branaire-Duluc	St. Julien
Duhart-Milon	Pauillac
Pouget	Cantenac
La Tour-Carnet	St. Laurent
Rochet	St. Estèphe
Beychevelle	St. Julien
Cantenac-Le Prieuré	Cantenac
Marquis de Termes	Margaux
Fifth Growths	
Pontet-Canet	Pauillac
Batailley	Pauillac
Grand-Puy-Lacoste	Pauillac
Grand-Puy-Ducasse	Pauillac
Lynch-Bages	Pauillac
Lynch-Moussas	Pauillac
Dauzac	Labarde
Mouton-d'Armailhacq	Pauillac
Le Tertre	Arsac
Haut-Bages-Libéral	Pauillac
Pédesclaux	Pauillac
Belgrave	St. Laurent
Camensac	St. Laurent
Cos-Labory	St. Estèphe
Clerc-Milon	Pauillac
Cantemerle	Macau
Croizet-Bages	Pauillac

WHITE WINES

Names	*Communes*
First Growths — Supérieur	
Yquem	Sauternes
First Growths	
La Tour Blanche	Bommes
Lafaurie-Peyraguey	Bommes
Haut-Peyraguey	Bommes
Rayne-Vigneau	Bommes
Suduiraut	Preignac
Coutet	Barsac
Climens	Barsac
Guiraud	Sauternes
Rieussec	Fargues
Rabaud-Promis	Bommes
Sigalas-Rabaud	Bommes
Second Growths	
Mirat	Barsac
Doisy-Daëne	Barsac
Doisy-Dubroca	Barsac
Doisy-Védrines	Barsac
D'Arche	Sauternes
Filhot	Sauternes
Broustet	Barsac
Nairac	Barsac
Caillou	Barsac
Suau	Barsac
Malle	Preignac
Romer	Preignac
Lamothe	Sauternes

Médoc, Ch: French (St. Julien) red wine. Bourgeois growth. Not included in the 1855 Médoc Classification. An example of the danger of such lists. See also Médoc.

Médoc Mousseux: French sparkling red Bordeaux wine (claret) made locally by genuine bottle fermentation (champagne process, q.v.). Alas, whatever the merits of sparkling wines made outside the Reims region, competition is hard. The chief centre for Médoc Mousseux is Bourg-en-Gironde.

Meersberg: German (Baden) white wine.

Meerspinne: German (Gimmeldingen, q.v.) white wine.

Megaspileon: Greek (Morean) red wine.

Megiddo: Israeli wine region.

Mehrhölzchen: German (Hallgarten, q.v.) white wine.

Mehring: German (Moselle) white wine.

Meisenberg: German (Ruwer, q.v.) white wine.

Meisenheim: German (Nahe) white wine.

Meix, Les: French (Côte-d'Or) red wine.

Meix-Bas: French (Côte-d'Or) red wine.

Meix-L'Allemand: French (Côte-d'Or) red wine.

Meix-Molnot: French (Côte-d'Or) red wine.

Meix-Remiers: French (Côte-d'Or) red wine.

Meleto: A brand of chianti (q.v.).

Melikraton: The Greek name for mead (q.v.).

Melitites: Greek drink of classical times made by sweetening wine with honey. See also Myritis.

Melnik: Czechoslovakian red and white wines.

Melnik: Bulgarian red table wine.

Melomeli: Roman beverage said to have been made from honey and fruit juices. If fermented, this would be a type of mead (q.v.).

Memel: Also known as Russian oak. The finest oak from the Danzig area, used for port casks. The small top-line is called Crown Memel. Danzig oak is now almost unobtainable.

Mendaean: Greek wine mentioned in classical writings.

Mendoza: One of the chief Argentine wine-growing districts.

Menthe, Crème de: Liqueur of peppermint flavour. Perhaps the most popular of all liqueurs to end a meal.

Merbein: Australian (Victorian) wine centre.

Mercurey: French (Côte Challonais) fine red and white wines.

Mercurol: French (Rhône Valley) white wine.

Mergerei-Ketterhausberg: German white wine. See also Briedel.

Merignac: Parish of the Graves (q.v.) district of France renowned for red table wine.

Merissa: Sudanese brewed beverage.

Merlot: French grape widely grown in the Médoc (q.v.). Blended with cabernet (q.v.) it produces excellent clarets.

Merry-Goe-Downe: Old English term for strong ale. John Taylor in 'Drink and Welcome' (1637) states, 'It (ale) is called Merry-goe-downe for it slides down merrily. It is fragrant to the sent. It is most pleasing to the taste.' The term seems also to have been used for malt-liquor in general.

Merry Widow: Cocktail of gin, dry vermouth, absinthe and benedictine.

Mersin: Turkish liqueur of orange flavour.

Merta: Greek wine from island of Chios.

Mertesdorf-Grünhaus: German (Ruwer) white wine centre, including vineyards of Spielberg, Laurenzberg, Herrenberg and Maximin-Grünhauser.

Merxheim: German (Nahe) white wine.

Mescal: See Mezcal.

Mescaline: See Mezcal.

Mesek: Also Mesech, Mimsak and Mimsach. Biblical (Hebrew) word for wine to which has been added spices to improve the flavour. It is thus manifest that the manufacture of vermouth (q.v.) is no recent innovation. See also Mimsak.

Mesnil, Le: French (Champagne) white wine centre.

Messias: Portuguese dry white wine.

Mesure: Old-established (1850) brand of cognac (q.v.).

Metallic Contamination: Owing to the increasing mechanization of brewing and wine-making and the greater use of metallic containers, filters and other machines, the introduction of traces of iron, copper and other metals has become a serious problem. The traces of heavy metals cause turbidity, objectionable flavours and other faults and call for a wide range of preventives and correctives. These include the use of inert metals and the removal of soluble traces by a variety of chemical methods. See also Blue Fining.

Metheglin: A word meaning 'spiced drink', and derived from the Welsh *meddyglyn*. Applied also to a type of spiced mead (q.v.). The term is especially used of mead flavoured with mace, ginger, cinnamon, cloves and pimento. Hydromel seems to have been identical.

Metho: Australian slang for methylated spirit (q.v.) used by the depraved as beverage alcohol. See also Lunatic Soup and White Lady.

Méthode Champénoise: The 'champagne method'. See also Champagne.

Méthode Charentaise: The traditional and legally compulsory method of distilling cognac brandy (q.v.).

Methodists: Although total abstinence seems to be a tenet of modern Methodism, even to the extent of advocating unfermented grape juice for communion, John Wesley wrote in his *Journal* on 9 September 1771: 'Wine is one of the noblest cordials in nature.' There have been half-hearted attempts to contend that Wesley did not really mean *ordinary* wine!

Methuen: Mentioned here as the author of the celebrated commercial treaty with Portugal in 1703 which preserved for that country the exclusive right to the use of the name port for that wine on the English market. The Methuen Treaty operated until 1914. See also Portuguese Treaty.

Methuselah: Outsize bottle holding 8 reputed quarts or nearly $6\frac{1}{2}$ litres. Mainly for display though a little Bordeaux wine is so bottled as a novelty.

Methyl Alcohol: Synonyms methanol, wood alcohol, Columbia spirit. Formula CH_3OH. It is the first (lowest) member of the homologous series of alcohols of which common or ethyl or beverage alcohol, C_2H_5OH, is the second. Although the chemical or structural difference is slight, the physiological difference between the two alcohols is profound. It is sufficient to say that methyl alcohol is highly poisonous and the drinking of any considerable quantity may lead to blindness and death, as frequently happened in the U.S. during the period of prohibition.

A very small amount of methyl alcohol is usually produced during the fermentation of cereals and this is, of course, much concentrated during distillation. The first fraction (the foreshots) of whisky and most other spirits contain all the methyl alcohol. Long before the period of accurate chemical analysis, distillers had recognized that this fraction should not be consumed as such. See also Whisky.

Methymnaean: Roman wine of antiquity.

Mettenheim: German (Rheinhessen) white wine centre including vineyards of Michelsberg, Schlossberg, Goldberg, Hellborn, Wolfskaut, Mulde, Kaloschenberg, Börnchen, Platte.

Metzingen: German (Württemberg) Schillerwein (q.v.).

Meuhlberg: German (Östrich, q.v.) white wine.

Meukow: Old-established (1862) brand of cognac (q.v.).

Meung: French (Orléans) red wine.

Meunier: Black grape of no special quality.

Meursault: Important French (Burgundian) wine centre of the Côte de Beaune, noted especially for white.

Mexico: Despite the Spanish and general Latin influence, Mexico is not an important wine-growing country. The climate — mainly arid and hot — is against this. The more important wine-growing regions are in the Western and Atlantic states, with a certain amount of development in the Central section, including Aguas Calientes. There is, of course, a large importation of wine from Europe and elsewhere for use by the well-to-do. Good beer is made in the larger towns and there are a number of liqueurs and other native specialities.

However, the predominant alcoholic beverage sociology and industry of Mexico is based upon 'pulque' as a light drink and mescal or mezcal (q.v.) as a spirit, together with the more expensive tequila (q.v.). The pulque of Mexico is the true counterpart to the workers of Mexico of beer to the Britisher and wine to the Latin. Pulque is an ancient drink, well-established for more than 1,000 years prior to the Spanish invasion. The action of pulque is not entirely alcoholic. It is a very weak drink (usually less than 3% of alcohol by volume) but it also contains a little of a rather powerful hallucinant drug, mescaline.

Mexico: See Jailers.

Meyney: French (Médoc) red wine.

Mezcal, Mescal or Mercal: Mexican spirit (q.v.) distilled from pulque. It thus stands in the same relation as brandy to wine or whisky to beer. It is a strong spirit of about 50% alcohol by volume (100° proof American). It contains a small amount of an alkaloid (mescaline) with marked pharmacological action (hallucinant). It has for many centuries formed part of the indigenous religious ceremonies.

Michelmark: German (Erbach, q.v.) white wine vineyard.

Michelsberg: German (Dürkheim, q.v.) white wine.

Michelslay: Moselle vineyard near Uerzig (q.v.).

Mickey Finn: A drugged alcoholic beverage — one which contains a sleep-producing substance. Origin obscure but possibly from a publican of San Francisco alleged to be willing to shanghai sailors.

Middy: Popular name in N.S.W., Australia, for a hotel glass (half-pint) of beer.

Midi: The French Midi, including the *départements* of Gard, Hérault and Aude, produces a vast volume of wine, mostly red. This is the *vin ordinaire* that appears on every French table, wholesome and undistinguished. It is largely blended with Algerian (q.v.).

Midus: Lithuanian name for mead (q.v.).

Mignotte, La: French (Côte-d'Or) red wine.

Migraine: This curiously named French (Burgundian) centre makes good red wine.

Milawa: Wine district in N.W. Victoria, known especially for dry reds.

Mild: The English term for a lightly-hopped beer, more or less contrasted with *bitter*.

Mild and Bitter: A mixture of ales or beers, originally of beer (hopped and bitter) and ale (unhopped and mild).

Mildew: A dreaded disease of the vineyard. The fungus attacks both leaves and fruit. Fortunately it can be controlled by spraying with copper salts or the modern organic fungicides.

Mildura: Australian (Victorian) wine centre. Despite the use of irrigation, excellent table wines as well as desserts and flor sherries are produced.

Miliana: Red table wine from the region of that name in Algeria.

Milk and Cream: These words are hallowed by usage when linked to alcoholic beverages. 'Bristol Milk' has been used of sherry in that city for over 300 years. Cream is now a common trade puff for any sweet 'sherry' and is also used of whisky where special quality is rightly or wrongly claimed by the vendor. There seems no objection to such innocent whimsy and certainly no reasonable support for the action by a zealous person in the British Ministry of Food who warned a Bristol merchant in 1949 that he was liable to be prosecuted for selling cream sherry not made of cream.

The word cream in its French form *crème* is also widely used of extremely sweet liqueurs (q.v.).

Milk of the Aged: The fanciful term applied to genuine claret (the red table wine of Bordeaux) in the pious belief that it can be drunk freely with no effect on kidneys and arteries. Well, there are worse excuses for drinking sound wine.

Mill: Machine in which malt is cracked at the brewery.

Millandes, Les: French (Burgundy) red wine.

Millendon: Australian (W.A.) wine centre.

Millésimé: The accepted French term for the date of a wine vintage. *Millésimé* means dated.

Millet: French (Graves) red and white wines.

Mill Hand: Brewery hand in charge of the mill machines.

Mimsak: Spiced wine of Biblical times, apparently a synonym for Mesek (q.v.).

Minard: Old-established brand of cognac (q.v.).

Minchinbury: A vineyard in New South Wales, producing mainly white sparkling wines.

Mineral Water: A vague term originally restricted to natural waters impregnated with mineral salts, later extended to artificial substitutes, and now, especially in the U.K., used generally for all carbonated temperance drinks, such as soda water, ginger ale, and lemonade. Most natural mineral waters and all artificial ones are bottled carbonated (q.v.). Examples of natural mineral waters sold under geographical names are Vichy, Selters, and Daylesford.

Mineral Waters, Natural: Amongst the common ones are the following:
    (1) Aperient Waters: Apenta, Arabella, Cheltenham, Leamington, Montmirail, Seidlitz.
    (2) Alkaline Waters: Aix-les-Bains, Malvern, Bouillens, Chantilly, Contrexéville, Evian, St. Galmier, Selters, Vichy.
    (3) Chalybeate Waters: Auteuil, Flitwick, Homburg, Marienbad, St. Alban, Spa Vittel.
    (4) Sulphurous Waters: Aix-la-Chapelle, Bonnes, Cauterets, Enghien, Harrogate.
    (5) Table Waters: Apollinaris, Buxton, Couzan, Godesberger, Kronthal, Reginaris, Malvern.

Minervois: French (Languedoc) pink wine. Also white.

Minheim: German (Moselle) white wine centre, including vineyards of Lay, Grauberg and Rosenberg.

Minho: Portuguese wine area.

Minorca: Wine has been grown in the Balearic Isles for thousands of years. The best Minorcan is Alba Flora but by all reports it is nothing remarkable.

Miodomel: A medieval Polish beverage said to be mead flavoured with hops, a speciality of the Polish monks of St. Basil.

Mirabelle: Liqueur made from the Alsatian yellow plum.

Miraflores: District of Jerez (q.v.), Spain, producing *manzanilla* (q.v.) type sherry.

Mirin: Japanese sweet wine.

Misa, Manuel: Old-established (1792) shippers of port and sherry (q.v.).

Mis en Bouteille au Château: Also *mise du Château*. This phrase on the label of a bottle of French wine and more notably still stamped on the cork inside the neck, is a guarantee of authenticity and usually of a respectable minimal quality. It is a certification that the wine has been estate-bottled, that the owner and grower of the wine also bottled it at his (or her or its) winery. Usually, at any rate, the owner of a château or estate will not allow wine to be bottled under the name unless the quality is acceptable. Otherwise, the wine is bundled off to a dealer to sell under no special name, though sometimes the château-proprietor also owns another winery near by of secondary reputation, or worse, to receive the rejected of the great.

Mishteh: Biblical (Hebrew) term for a banquet of wine such as that given by Queen Esther. The feast of Abraham at the weaning of Isaac is called a *mishteh gadol* or great drinking.

Misket Karlovo: Bulgarian white (yellowish-green) wine from the misket (muscat) grape.

Misshu: Korean brandy said to be made from honey.

Mission: An unidentified Spanish wine grape brought to Mexico some centuries ago, and subsequently taken to California.

Mission-Haut-Brion: See Haut-Brion.

Mista: Greek wine from island of Chios.

Mistela: See Dulce Apogado.

Mistelle: A North African wine in which the fermentation of the freshly pressed grape juice is arrested by adding alcohol. Also, 'mistela' from Spain. The name is also applied to the white wine similarly made in the Midi (q.v.) as the base of vermouth (q.v.).

Miteado: Spanish equal mixture of alcohol and mature sherry, used in fortifying.

Mitidja: Algerian red and white wines.

Mittelber: French (Alsatian) white wine centre.

Mittelbergheim: Bas-Rhin (q.v.) wine area.

Mittelhaardt: German (Palatinate) white wine centre.

Mittelheim: Wine parish of the Rheingau (q.v.).

Mittelwihr: Wine region of Alsace.

Mittlere Reitel: German (Ostofen, q.v.) white wine.

Mixed Drinks: There appears to be an irresistible temptation to try to produce new flavours by mixing this ingredient with that and the other. Cocktails, punches, sours, highballs, fizzes, sangarees, coolers, rickeys, slings, pegs, cups, smashes, caudles, syllabubs and more embrace a legion of beverages. The various types of mixed drinks are separately noted.

Mobbi: Also Mobby and Mobbie. The West Indies name for a variety of beverages, including a spirit distilled from sweet potatoes and a fruit brandy. Howell (1634) writes 'In the Barbado Island the common drink among the English is Mobbi made of Potato Roots'.

Moco: Well-masticated corn used as a 'converter' in making chicha (q.v.). It is, of course, the ptyalin (q.v.) of the saliva that brings about the change.

Modbury: Wine estate near Adelaide, South Australia. Good white wines.

Modern: Cocktail of whisky, rum, absinthe, lemon juice and orange bitters.

Modius: Roman measure of capacity. The volume is disputed but seems to have been about an English peck. Also a 15th-century liquid measure.

Moelleux: French wine term meaning soft, velvety, mellow.

Moeslinger Finings: See also Blue Finings. Trade name for potassium ferrocyanide, used in Germany to remove traces of heavy metals from white wine. A dangerous process prohibited in most or all other countries.

Moët (Moët et Chandon): Old-established (1743) champagne of Epernay.

Moi Kwai Lo: Chinese rose wine, said to be rice wine (saki) scented with rose.

Mojito: Mixed drink of rum, lime mint and soda served in large glass with cracked ice.

Moka, Crème de: Liqueur of coffee flavour.

Molasses: By-product of sugar manufacture and the raw material for rum (q.v.).

Monastine: Another of the many French liqueurs made by monks.

Monbazillac: French sweet golden wine from the Dordogne. Sometimes damned unfairly with the name 'poor man's sauternes'.

Mönchberg: German (Hahnheim, q.v.) white wine.

Monchhof: Austrian (Burgenland) white wine.

Mondeuse: French (Bressan) red wine.

Monferrato Hills: Italian (Piedmont) centre producing some of the finest wines of the country.

Monforte: See Barolo.

Monica: Italian (Sardinian) dessert wine.

Monlerens: French (Gradignan, q.v.) red and white wines.

Monmousseau: French (Vouvray) still white wine.

Monongahela: River in Pennsylvania, U.S. stated to be the first region of whiskey production in the U.S. Monongahela Rye became a celebrated beverage and the subject of history, as the Western Pennsylvanians forcibly opposed the tax on spirits imposed by the newly created congress.

Monopole: French term for proprietary brand.

Monschberg: German (Ahr) red wine estate.

Montagna: Italian (Valtellina) red wine.

Montagne, Ch.: French (Sauternes) white wine.

Montagne: French (St. Émilion) red wine.

Montagnieu: French (Bressan) white wine.

Montagny: French (Côte Chalonaise) white wine.

Montagu: South African (Cape) wine centre.

Montbrun: French (Médoc) red wine.

Montbrun-Goutte-d'Or: French (Graves) white wine.

Montcontour, Château: The best of the Vouvray wines.

Mont de Milieu: French (Chablis) fine white wine.

Mont d'Or: Swiss fine white wine.

Montebello: Champagne of Ay.

Montecarlo: Italian (Tuscanian) dry white wine.

Montedonato: Italian (Bolognese) table wine.

Montée Rouge: French (Beaune) wine centre.

Monteferrato: Italian (Turin) red and white wine.

Montefiascone: Italian (Piedmont) red wine.

Monte-Napoleone: Italian (Lombardian) red wine.

Montenegro: Mixed drink of maraschino and cherry brandy.

Monteneubel: German (Enkirch, q.v.) fine white wine.

Montepulciano: A fine wine of Tuscany (Italy). Even in early days it was highly esteemed, for Francesco Redi concludes his poem 'Bacco in Toscana' (1685) with 'Montepulciano's the king of all wine'.

Montforte: Italian (Piedmont) red wine.

Montgiraud: French (Médoc) red wine.

Montgomery: A martini (q.v.) of surpassing dryness (15 parts of gin to 1 of dry vermouth). F. M. Montgomery is a total abstainer, i.e., wholly dry. Perhaps the ultimate achievement will be a glass of straight gin over which has been waved the cork from a bottle of vermouth. Martini whimsy appears to be limited to the U.S.

Monthélie: French (Côte-d'Or) wine centre for fine red.

Montibeux: Swiss (Valais) white wine.

Monteith: An early form of punch bowl, with a scalloped rim in which glasses could be rested. Said to be named after an 18th-century eccentric who wore a coat with scalloped tails.

Montilla: The sherry (light, dry, delicate) grown on the Montilla Hills in Spain, about a hundred miles from the true sherry centre of Jerez (q.v.). Some contend that from its geographical position it has no right to the name sherry. The celebrated sherry called amontillado (meaning 'from Montilla') has no true link with Montilla. Montilla is mainly consumed within Spain and one supposes the Spaniards know a good sherry when they find one.

Montlouis: French (Touraine) red wine. Sometimes rather sweet, according to season. Also white wine.

Montmélian: French (Savoy) red wine.

Montmurat: French (Cantal) red wine.

Montpelier: Cocktail of gin and dry vermouth identical with dry martini except for lesser proportion of gin.

Montpellier: The so-called Wine University of France.

Montrachets, Les: A group of French (Côte-d'Or) white wine vineyards of which the celebrated Le Montrachet is one. There are also vineyards in the adjoining communes of Chassagne and Puligny which use the name. In all, caution in buying is needed. Dumas has said that Le Montrachet should be drunk bare-headed, on one's knees.

Montrose: French (Médoc) red wine.

Monts de Milieu: French (Chablis) white wine.

Monts Luisants: A group of good French vineyards of the Côte-d'Or.

Montsoreau: French (Anjou) white wine.

Mont Vully: Swiss (Fribourg) red and white wines.

Monzingen: German (Nahe) white wine.

Moonshine: The self-explanatory American name for illegally distilled spirit, usually of the whisky type. It is a derogatory term and is sometimes applied to a commercial, strictly legal, duty-paid spirit if the quality is, or is supposed to be poor. Moonshine is usually made on the small scale in the mountain areas of the Southern States of the U.S. Actually the quality is generally inherently high because the primitive stills are necessarily pot-stills (q.v.) of much the same design as those used in France for the production of cognac and armagnac. The trouble is lack of maturation. Illegal spirit obviously cannot be stored in porous wood and mellowed for the necessary period of years. It is not improbable that much moonshine could be aged into a connoisseur's spirit. However, as peddled almost straight from the delivery tube of the still, it is deplorable stuff. See also Whisky.

Moonshine Whiskey: Amongst the American vernacular synonyms are popskull, red-eye, panther-sweat, bust-head, tarantula juice, mountain lightning, fighting soup, tonsil paint, embalmer's special, ignorant oil, moose milk, wolf bran, and white mule.

Moore's Diamond: A native American grape from which table wine is made.

Moorook: Australian (S.A.) wine centre.

Mooroopna: Australian (Victorian) wine centre.

Moosberg: German (Hahnheim, q.v.) white wine.

Moqueguar: Peruvian wine centre.

Mor: Hungarian parish near Budapest where Ezerjó wine is grown.

Moranean: The dark-red, sweet wine of antiquity praised by Homer.

Morange: French (Médoc) red wine.

Morat: Ancient drink of mulberry juice sweetened with honey. Probably mead or wine was added.

Moray: Scottish centre for the production of single (q.v.) malt whisky for blending purposes.

Morbisch: Austrian (Eisenstadt) white wine.

Morey-St.-Denis: French wine-growing commune of the Côte-d'Or producing much fine red burgundy. It includes the celebrated Clos de Tart.

Morgan: Australian (S.A.) wine centre.

Morgan Bros. Ltd.: Old-established (1715) shippers of port (q.v.). This firm was the purveyor of the D.D. port immortalized by Dickens. ('A magnum of the Double Diamond, David, to drink the health of Mr. Linkinwater.')

Morgeots, Les: French (Côte-d'Or) white wine centre.

Morgon: French (Beaujolais) red wine.

Morin: French (Médoc) red wine.

Morning Draft: Pepys frequently alludes to this. At the Restoration it was unusual to sit down to breakfast. The custom was to repair to a tavern and there take a 'morning draft' of ale or wine.

Morocco: Despite the teaching of Mahomet there is a large and still-expanding growth of wine. A large volume of concentrated grape juice is also exported to England for conversion to wine.

Morphett Vale: Australian (S.A.) wine centre.

Morra, La: Italian (Piedmont) red wine. See also Barolo.

Morzheim: German (Palatinate) white wine.

Moscate, Moscatel, Moscatello, Moscato: The general names for the sweet dessert wines made in Latin and Latin-American countries from the Muscatel grape.

Moscatello di Montefiascone: Italian (Latium) sweet dessert wine made from muscatel grapes.

Moscato di Noto: Italian sweet dessert wine.

Moscato di Pantelleria: Italian sweet dessert wine.

Moscato di Salento: Italian sweet dessert wine.

Moscato Fior d'Arancio: Italian sweet dessert wine.

Moscato Passito: The sweetest of the Moscati (q.v.).

Moscato Secco: See Moscate. Not really dry but less sickly sweet than usual.

Moscato Zucco: Italian (Palerman) sweet dessert wine.

Mosco Spumante: Italian sparkling wine of no especial merit.

Moscow Mule: Cocktail of vodka, ginger beer and lime. The concoction is reported to be unknown in Russia. It is an American invention and presumably to be classed as a weapon.

Moselblümchen: The word means 'Moselle floweret' and is a pretentious name applied to blended wine from obscure vineyards. It is often made from sugared wines.

Moselle: An important German wine-growing area stretched along the valley of this tributary of the Rhine and of its own tributaries. There are about 140 established wine-growing parishes and more than 20,000 separate vineyards, some only an acre or two in extent. Moselle wine is predominantly white and is traditionally put into tall bluish-green bottles, as distinct from the Rhenish brown. The more important Moselle wines are separately noted. In England Moselle wines are held to include those of the Mittelmosel, Untermosel, and the valleys of the Ruwer and Saar rivers.

Moslinger: Syn. for 'blue fining', q.v.

Mosser: The most vicious, stupid and destructive implement ever invented to debase fine wine. It is the English name of the small spatula or fork used to beat the bubbles out of champagne or other sparkling wine.

Why anybody should be willing to pay the necessarily high price required for the process of turning an indifferent still white wine into a sparkling one, involving as it does literally years of work and heavy investment, merely to reverse the process in a matter of seconds, is a sad reflection upon human fallibility.

The name is obviously a corruption of the French *mousseux*, foaming or sparkling.

Most: German for must (q.v.).

Mostaganem: Red table wine from the region of that name in Algeria.

Mosto: The Italian (and also the Spanish and Portuguese) word for must or grape juice. It may also mean newly fermented grape juice, i.e. new wine.

Mosto Cotto: Concentrated must (q.v.) used for sweetening marsala and other dessert wines.

Mosto de Yema: The best must (q.v.), Spanish for the first pressing of grape juice in making sherry. The second pressing is called *aguapie*. There is a final and inferior pressing, *prensa*.

Mostzuckerung: The German term for addition of sugar before fermentation to weak musts (q.v.) in bad years. See also Chaptalization and Amelioration. The process is illegal in many countries.

Mother-in-Law: Cockney drink of mixed stout and beer.

Mother's Milk: Slang 19th-century name in England for gin (q.v.).

Moto: The intermediate stage of manufacture of sake (q.v.).

Mouillage: French for watering wine.

Mould Ale: The hot ale which it was customary to drink at funerals.

Moulerens: French (Graves) red wine.

Moulin-à-Vent: There are many French vineyards which bear the name 'Windmill'. The most celebrated is the fine red wine of the Beaujolais (Burgundy), produced by 32 vineyards, all entitled to use the title Moulin-à-Vent Grand Cru. In the Bordelais there are five similarly named vineyards producing claret and/or white wine.

Moulin-à-Vent de Lavau: French (Pomerol) red wine.

Moulin-Blanc: French (Branne) white wine.

Moulin de Calon: French (Médoc) red wine.

Moulin-de-Soubeyran: French (Médoc) red wine.

Moulin d'Issan: French (Médoc) red wine.

Moulin-du-Bourg: French (Médoc) red wine.

Moulin-du-Cadet: French (St. Émilion) red wine.

Moulin-Riche: French (Médoc) red wine.

Moulin-Rompu: French (Bourg) red wine.

Moulin-Rouge: French (Branne) red wine.

Moulis: French (Médoc) red wine.

Mountain: Another of the intriguing archaic English wine names. This was the name given in the 18th and early 19th centuries to malaga, the sweet red Spanish dessert wine once so popular. The origin of the name is obscure but may relate to the vineyards of the high ground round Malaga.

Mount Carmel: Israeli white wine.

Mount Pleasant: See O'Shea, Maurice.

Mourisco: One of the best grapes grown for port (q.v.). There is also a white variety, mourisco branco.

Mousseux: French for 'sparkling', as applied to wine. Vin mousseux relates to all sparkling wines but only the wine made in a particular way in a particular place may bear the name *champagne* in France.

Moustique: Liqueur from St. Catherine's Monastery, Mount Sinai, said to have been made by the monks continuously since the 6th century.

Moût: French for the must (q.v.) of grapes or the wort (q.v.) of beer.

Mouton-Blanc: French (Médoc) white wine.

Mouton Cadet: The label used for the bottles of Mouton-Rothschild (q.v.) which do not reach the highest standards of the château.

Mouton-d'-Armailhacq: French (Médoc) red wine, under the same owner-ship as Mouton-Rothschild (q.v.).

Mouton-Rothschild, Ch.: Celebrated wine estate of Médoc. This red wine is so esteemed that it is probably the most consistently expensive of its type in the world. Curiously enough, it is still graded into the second class of the famous original classifications of 1855. See Médoc. The owners were justly indignant and adopted the motto: 'First I cannot be, second I disdain to be, Mouton I am.' Time has proved the proud truth of this. The wine is made exclusively from cabernet sauvignon grapes and each bottle is numbered.

Moutwyn: Dutch term, lit. 'maltwine', for the pot-stilled spirit (q.v.) made at Schiedam and used for the manufacture of gin (q.v.).

Moyet: Old-established (1864) brand of cognac (q.v.).

Moyston: Australian (Victorian) village, centre for growth of good dry red wine of same name.

Mskhali: Russian grape vine of Lake Sevan (q.v.) said to be indigenous.

Muchen: Australian (W.A.) wine centre.

Müchenhaus: German (Königsbach, q.v.) white wine.

Muddle: To mix thoroughly, if necessary by crushing. Used of mixed drinks.

Müden: German (Moselle) white wine district, including vineyards of Funkenberg, Radein and Kaulenberg.

Mudgee: Australian (N.S.W.) wine centre.

Mud in Your Eye, Here's: A toast.

Muehlberg: Dry white wine from Östrich (q.v.).

Mug: Cylindrical drinking-vessel, with or without handles.

Mughouse or Mugroom: (c. 1740) an early form of English music hall. Only ale or stout was sold and a chairman presided over the songs, speeches (often political) and toasts.

Mugwort: Vernacular English name for beer flavoured with *artemisia* (related to absinthe). See also Wormwood.

Muhl: German (Rheinhessen) white wine from Aspisheim.

Mühle: German (Deidesheim, q.v.) white wine.

Mühlenberg: German white wine vineyard of Saarburg.

Mühlstein: German (Rüdesheim, q.v.) fine white wine.

Mui Guy Loo: A Chinese flavoured spirit, technically a gin (q.v.) apparently distilled from fermented rice and flavoured with lichee.

Muid: French cask of capacity about 60 gallons.

Mulberry 'Wine': Country wine (q.v.) made from sugar and mulberries.

Mülheim: German (Moselle) white wine district, including vineyards of Himmelsleiter, Elisenberg, Bitsch and Johannesberg.

Mull: To prepare a hot drink from any liquor by adding sugar, spices, beaten egg-yolk, and so on.

Mullayhofberg: German (Reil, q.v.) white wine.

Muller: Copper, conical vessel used for heating liquor intended to be 'mulled'.

Müller-Thurgau: White hybrid grape widely grown in Switzerland and the Rhine.

Mullet or Ale Mullet: Copper funnel with handle, but closed at the narrow end. It was filled with ale and heated in the embers of the fire.

Mullheim: German (Baden) white wine.

Mulsum: An alcoholic beverage of classical and later times, wine apparently flavoured with honey.

Multum: An extract of quassia and licorice, formerly used to adulterate beer. If it also contained cochineal, it was called Hard Multum.

Mum: An old English brewed beverage prepared from various grains and pulses together with a hotch-potch of aromatic vegetable matter. Also strong ale or beer, said to be derived from Christian Mumme, who first made it in Brunswick, Germany, in 1489. A favourite of Samuel Pepys. See also Gruit.

Mumm: Old-established champagne of Reims.

Mundelsheim: German (Württemberg) red wine.

Munich Beer or Bavarian Beer: Of sweet taste and malty flavour, with little hop characteristic. Used generically.

Münster: German (Nahe) white wine district, including vineyards of Langenberg, Kapellenberg, Pittersberg, Sendel and Dautenpflänzer.

Munzingen: German (Baden) red wine.

Münzlay: German (Graach, q.v.) white wine.

Murcia: Spanish wine district. The best wine is yecla.

Murets, Les: French (Hermitage, q.v.) white wine.

Murets de Sion, Les: Swiss (Valais) white wine.

Murettes, Les: Swiss (Fendant) white wine.

Murrumbidgee: The river that supplies the great irrigation area of New South Wales, where there is a high production of wine of moderate quality.

Murs: French (Loire) white wine.

Muscadelle: White grape which used to be the source of Constantia wine (q.v.).

Muscadet: French white wine from the Loire.

Muscadine: Native American grape from which is made a wine of strong flavour. It is related to the scuppernong.

Muscat: A sweet, fortified wine made from overripe muscat grapes, and produced in many countries. Also called 'muscatel' and 'muscadel'. Heavy muscat wines of pronounced flavour are sometimes called 'liqueur muscat'.

Many wines bear the name, all presumably made predominantly from the highly-flavoured muscat grape. These include the Greek wine Muscat de Samos (popular in Northern Europe) and Muscat de Frontignan, the French dessert wine. The Muscat d'Alexandrie grape is a delicious table variety not used for wine-making in Europe but widely grown in California for sweet fortified types. It is probably the same grape as the gordo blanco, a coarse and heavy yielder of Australia.

The true muscat grape of Alexandria is a romantic vine. It was indigenous to Egypt, then moved to Spain and thence to England for cultivation in hothouses. The ripe berries are excellent for dehydration. See also Frontignac and Vitis Apiana.

Muscatel, Sparkling: A rather coarse *vin mousseux* (q.v.), sometimes made by carbonation and doctored with flavouring.

Muselet: French term for the wire network used to anchor the corks of sparkling wine. The wiring process is called 'muselage'.

Musenhang: German (Forst, q.v.) fine white wine.

Music: There is ample scope and perhaps an aesthetic and scholarly need for a book upon the relation of alcohol and music. Since the pharmacological action of alcohol is that of a depressant and a remover of inhibitions, the reason is clear why slight tipsiness leads to song. Moreover, a moderate drink of an alcoholic beverage quite often enables the shy, stammering, tight-throated singer to surpass by far his or her usual form. Alcohol also usually generates love of one's fellows and singing is the natural result. Is there any authentic record of an abstaining major composer?

There is a rich and extensive musical literature of drinking songs, bacchanalian revels and the like. It is astonishing that no extensive collection of this material, some of it of high artistic value, seems to have been made.

James Howell (q.v.) in 1634 wrote, 'The Greek will drink as many glasses as there be Letters in his Mistresse's Name and the German will drink the number of his years and though he be not apt to break into Singing, being not of so Airy a Constitution, yet he will drink often Musically a Health to every one of these 6 notes Ut, Re, Mi, Fa, Sol, La, which, with this reason, are all comprehended in this Hexameter:
Ut Relivet Miserum Fatum Solitosque Labores.'

Musigny: Celebrated French red wine region of the Côtes-d'Or. Amongst the noted vineyards are Les Amoureuses, Les Charmes, Les Bonnes Mares and Le Musigny. This fine red burgundy is especially praised by critics as possessing 'a fragrance of violets with an undertone of truffle', but why wine should be especially valued for resembling something else is obscure. There is also a little white wine of high esteem.

Muskotály: Hungarian (Villány) white wine which is made, as the name suggests, from the muscat grape (q.v.).

Mussbach: German (Palatinate) white wines.

Mussbien: German (Ruppertsberg, q.v.) white wine.

Must: Newly-pressed grape juice ready for fermentation. Fr. *moût*. Ger. *Most*.

Mustum Lixivum: The name given by the Romans to grape juice intended to be turned into everyday wine.

Musty: The unpleasant, mouldy taste acquired by wine exposed to decayed casks or corks.

Mutenice: Czechoslovakian white wine.

Muting: The process of stopping fermentation of cheap sweet wine by sulphuring or heating.

Mycoderma Vini: Botanical name for the Spanish *flor* (q.v.) of sherry.

Myrat: French (Barsac) sauternes (q.v.) sweet white wine.

Myritis: Roman beverage made from wine flavoured with myrtle berries and sweetened with honey. See also Melitites.

Nachgärung: The German term for the slow second fermentation after the main one is over.

Nackenheim: German (Rheinhessen) white wine centre, including the vineyards of Kreuz, Rotenberg, Fenchelberg, Engelsberg, Weyersborn, Rheintal, Fritzehöll, Platte, Kuppel, Kahlenberg, Dieterkapp and Schmidtskapelle.

Nacktarsch: German dry white wine from Moselle alleged to be sold not on quality but on the label depicting a boy being smacked on his bare bottom.

Nagelprobe: German equivalent of 'bottoms up' or 'no heeltaps'.

Nahe: German red and white table wine district in the valley of this tributary of the Rhine. There are more than 30 wine-growing parishes whose commercial centre is Kreuznach (q.v.). Amongst the finer vineyards are Winzenheim, Bad Kreuznach, Burgsponheim, Heddesheim, Münster, Langenlonsheim, Niederhausen, Norheim, Schloss and Böckelheim.

Nairn: Scottish centre for production of highland malt whisky.

Nalivka: Russian flavoured beverage on vodka base.

Nallys: See Châteauneuf-du-Pape.

Nantz: Another of those interesting English object-names derived from a shipping port. Nantz was a name common in England in the 18th century as a synonym for French brandy. The name is a corruption of the English idea of the pronunciation of Nantes, the French city on the River Loire, near the Atlantic, from which much brandy was shipped to England prior to the rise of cognac and armagnac (q.v.).

Napa: Wine-growing region of northern California reputed, with Sonoma (q.v.), to be responsible for the major part of the high-grade table wines of the United States.

Napa Golden Chasselas: See Palomino.

Napareuli: Russian (Caucasian) white wine.

Napoleon: A name given to certain French brandies as implying great age or special merit, but it does not appear to have any real significance. See also Stars.

Nappy: As applied to ale, means foaming, heady or strong. Also means slightly intoxicated.

Narrenkapp: German (Kreuznach, q.v.) white wine estate.

Nasha: Northern Indian (Rajasthan) term for intoxication. The term is not censorious.

Nassberger: Austrian table wine from Vienna.

Nathan System: A proprietary brewing process consisting, *inter alia*, in the use of filtered air and other methods of avoiding micro-biological contamination.

Natural Conditioning: A rather vague brewery term meaning that beer is clarified by storage and 'dropping clean' instead of being subjected to mechanical filtration. 'Sedimentation' is more or less a synonym. Naturally-conditioned beer is beer produced by the old system of bottling direct from the cask. There is a slight second fermentation in the bottle, resulting in a small sediment of yeast, but the flavour of the beer is often much relished.

Natural Wine: The unadulterated vinous product of grape juice that has been allowed to ferment naturally, without the addition of other substances, and has not been fortified with added alcohol. However, see V.D.N.

Nature: French term for a wine which has not had sugar added to it. The term is also applied to champagne. Originally it meant that no sweetening had been added, i.e. that the champagne was entirely dry or *brut*. Today it may mean that the champagne is not so sweet as 'extra dry'. See also Champagne.

Naturwein: On a German wine label this means 'wholly natural', i.e. that no sugar has been added to the original grape juice (must) and no other 'assisted' wine has been blended with it. *Natur* and *Naturrein* have the same broad significance. See also Chaptalization.

Naturweinversteigerer: Association of German wine auctioneers who sell only pure wines.

Navarra: See Rioja.

Naxos: The largest of the Cyclades islands of the Mediterranean, was also known in classical times as Dia or Strogyle. A famous centre for fine wine and a celebrated place of worship of Bacchus (q.v.).

Nazir: The Biblical (Hebrew) term for the unpruned grape vine in the sabbatic year, when wine-making was proscribed.

Neat: Not diluted. Synonymous with straight.

Nebbiolo: Fine red Italian (Piedmont) wine grape, generally considered the country's best.

Nebouana: Romanian red table wine.

Nebuchadnezzar: Another of the huge bottles with Biblical names. It holds 20 quarts, has no practical value and is merely a novelty for show purposes.

Neckarsulm: German (Württemberg) wine district for red and white.

Nectar: The drink of the gods, in Greek mythology. See also Ambrosia. The French sometimes use the word for liqueurs to suggest fine quality.

Nederburg: South African winery. Red and white table wines.

Nef: An old table-appointment of the wealthy in the shape of a ship on wheels that whistled as it transported a bottle of wine or other material from one part of the table to another.

Négociant en Vins: French for wine merchant.

Negro Rancia: Spanish golden wine from Zamara.

Negus: Old English beverage of mulled wine said to have been invented by one Colonel Negus during the reign of Queen Anne. It is hot port with lemon and spiced with nutmeg and the like. Madeira or sweet sherry may be substituted for port. See also Mull.

Nektar: Modern Greek (or something like it) for nectar. When it appears, as it often does, on a wine label, it means precisely nothing.

Nelson's Blood: The name — it is hardly slang by now — used in the British Navy for rum.

Nemes Kadarka: Hungarian red table wine.

Nenenberg: German (Ellsheim, q.v.) white wine.

Nénin: French (Pomerol) red wine.

Nerthe, Château de la: One of the Châteauneuf (q.v.) red wines.

Nerveux: Another of the flowery French wine terms. This means vital or lively.

Neuberg: Amongst the many German white wine estates bearing this some-what trite name are those situated at Trittenheim, Gau-Bickelheim, Meckenheim, Hochheim, Oestrich, Laubenheim and Gimmeldingen.

Neuburger: Austrian grape and wine.

Neuchâtel: Swiss wine canton whose reds and whites are highly esteemed. The red Cortaillod is renowned.

Neudorf: German (Rheingau) white wine.

Neuenahr: German (Ahr) red and white wines.

Neumagen: German (Moselle) white wine district, including vineyards of Hambach, Lasenberg, Engelgrube, Rosengärtchen and Laudamusberg. It is reputed to be the oldest-known wine centre in Germany. The Roman poet Ausonius sang the praise of Neumagen (as Nociomagus) or so it is reported.

Neumorgen: German (Harxheim, q.v.) white wine.

Neuquén: The reputed finest beverage wine of Argentina.

Neustadt: White wine from Palatinate (q.v.).

Neustadt: German (Württemberg) red wine.

Neutral Brandy: The legal term in the U.S.A. for brandy distilled at more than 170° proof. See also High-Proof Brandy.

Neutral Spirits: American term for purified alcohol. Also known as cologne, silent or velvet spirit. The U.S., which has been a leader in pure-food legislation, has curiously reversed its policy to allow neutral spirits with the addition of as little as 20% of the genuine material to be labelled 'blended whisky' or 'whisky, a blend'.

Neuville: Swiss (Berne) golden wine.

Neuweg: German white wine. See also Dienheim.

Neuweier: German (Baden) red and white wines.

New England Rum: Rum made on the mainland of the United States, mainly on the East Coast though the term was originally used for American rum irrespective of origin.

New England Triangle: The name for the grim journey of the ships which carried slaves from Africa, molasses to Boston and rum to Europe.

Newfoundland Port: A term now obsolete. In earlier days some of the English port shippers of Oporto also gained a monopoly of the cod-curing business of Newfoundland. They exported the cod (*bacalhau*) to Portugal and wine from Portugal to England. Wine which crossed the Atlantic in these ships was supposed to have a special virtue. See also East India.

New Norcia: Australian (W.A.) wine centre owned by a Spanish order of monks.

New Orleans: Cocktail of bourbon, orange bitters and absinthe.

New South Wales: The genesis of the Australian alcoholic beverage industry. Beer was made here from the date of the first settlement towards the end of the 18th century. The first wine on a commercial scale was made more than 150 years ago. The Hunter River Valley north of Sydney has long been a renowned area for the growth of fine red and white table wines with a marked resemblance to the wine of Burgundy. In recent years the large vineyards of the Murrumbidgee region have shown that irrigation and reasonable quality are not incompatible. See also Rum Currency.

News Room: A name still found in some old-fashioned English public-houses in place of tap-room (q.v.), though it seldom now contains newspapers.

New York: Cocktail of whisky, grenadine and lemon juice.

New York Muscat: Hybrid grape, a cross of muscat hamburg (*Vitis vinifera*) and ontario (*V. labrusca*). Dark grape, very sweet, of muscatel flavour with the hardy qualities of indigenous U.S. vines. Mentioned here as typical of the many hybrid vines now being developed for wine-making or the table in the commendable hope of combining the best of two worlds. Schuyler is another, a cross of zinfandel (q.v.) and ontario.

New Zealand: Predominantly a beer-drinking country, New Zealand makes only a little wine in the Auckland region of the North Island. The volume is too small for New Zealand to be shown in the list of world producers. This fertile, well-watered sub-continent has much land eminently suited to the grape. There should be a moral to be extracted somewhere, despite the fact that the local beer is excellent.

Nezmély: Hungarian white table wine.

Ng Ka Pei (or Pay): Chinese brandy, so-called, though derived from rice, not grapes.

Niagara: Native American grape used mainly for sweet wines of sauternes type.

Niederberg: 'Low Mountain', a common name of German wine estates, including those of Kestener (q.v.) and Kröv-Kövenig (q.v.), all white wines.

Niederemmel: German (Moselle) white wine district, including vineyards of Lay, Hinterslay, Hohlweid and Traubengarten.

Niederflur: German (Lorchhausen, q.v.) white wine estate.

Niederhausen-Schlossböckelheim A.D. Nahe: German (Nahe) white wine district including vineyards of Schlossböckelheimer Kupfergrube, Schlossböckelheimer Felsenberg, Niederhäuser Steinberg, Niederhäuser Hermannsberg, Hermannshölle, Klamm, Kerz, Rosenbeck and Steiger.

Niederhäuser Hermannsberg: German (Niederhausen-Schlossböckelheim A.D. Nahe, q.v.) white wine.

Niederhäuser Steinberg: German (Niederhausen-Schlossböckelheim A.D. Nahe, q.v.) white wine.

Niederheimbach: German (Moselle) white wine.

Niederingelheim: German (Rheinhessen) white wine district, including vineyards of Am Bruderweg, Am Klopp, Kreuzkirch, Im Pöll, Am Höllenweg, Im Herschtal, Am Steinacker, Nonnenberg, Am Langenberg.

Niederleuken: German (Saar) white wine district, of which the best vineyard is Stirn.

Niedersaulheim: German (Rheinhessen) white wine district, including vineyards of Goldberg, Hauben, Westerberg, Probstei, and Seidenberg.

Niederstetten: German (Württemberg) white wine district.

Nieder-und-Oberwalluf: German (Rheingau) white wine district, including vineyards of Walkenberg and Steinitz.

Nierstein: The principal wine region and town of Rheinhessen. The best of the Nierstein wines are entitled by general consent to the name great. There is an old German saying that 'all Liebfraumilchs (q.v.) would be Niersteiners if they could!'

Amongst the better lagen (q.v.) are Niersteiner, Rehbach, Hipping, Glöck, Orbel, Floss, Pettental, Heiligenbaum, Fuchsloch, Schnappenberg, Spiegelberg, St. Kiliansberg, Auflangen, Flächenhahl, Kehr, Kranzberg, Streng, Oelberg, Brudersberg, Gutes Domtal, Rohr, Hölle, Fockenberg, Findling, Schmitt, Pfuhlweg, Berg, Bergkirch, Galgenberg, Gemarkgasse, Hinkelstein, Hintersaal, Kattenwein, Rehgasse, Rosenberg, Schlangenberg and Warte.

Nieschen: German (Ruwer, q.v.) white wine.

Nieschen: German white wine estate of Casel (q.v.).

Nig: This mystic word used to appear on the silver name plates of 18th-century gin decanters. Gin was considered 'low'. Apparently it became elevated by spelling the word backwards.

Night-Cap: Beverage (usually diluted and sweetened hot spirit) taken to induce sleep.

Nile Delta: The region of ancient Egypt from which came the best wines, as recorded in the tomb of Tutankhamen. See also Amon, Aton and Kantarah.

Nill: German (Kallstadt, q.v.) wine centre.

Nimmo: Old-established (1826) English brewery of Durham.

Nine Men's Monies: An old inn game, played in Elizabethan times, with counters or pebbles on a marked board. Possibly an ancestor of 'shove ha'penny'.

Ninepins: A form of skittles (q.v.).

Nin Ka Si: The reported Babylonian goddess of brewing.

Nip: Name given to a quarter-bottle or 'baby', containing half a reputed pint. Also an obsolete term meaning a half-pint of ale.

Nippitatum: Obsolete term for especially strong and good ale.

Nismes-Delclou: Established (1832) brand of armagnac (q.v.).

Nittel: German (Moselle) white wine district including vineyards of Weisert, Gipfel and Leiderchen.

Niykub St.-Georges: French (St. Émilion) red wine.

Noah: Indigenous American green grape widely used as grafting stock (*Phylloxera*-resistant). A very old wine is sometimes called a 'noah'. The first recorded viticulturist was Noah ('. . . he planted a vineyard: and he drank of the wine. . . .'—Gen. 9: 20–21).

Nobbler: Australian term for a small serving (dram or fluid ounce) of spirits.

Noble Rot: (*pourriture noble.*) A particular fungous growth permitted to develop on overripe grapes, especially in the making of sauternes and certain other sweetish wines. Ger. *Edelfäule*. See pourriture noble.

Noé: French (Médoc) red wine.

Nog: Strong beer brewed in East Anglia. Also applied to a drink containing beaten egg, e.g. brandy nog.

Noggin: (1) A small mug. (2) A small quantity of liquor, about 5 fluid ounces.

Nomenclature of Wine: Alex. Atkinson, in his entirely imaginary but delightful and wise *By Rocking Chair Across France*, retails a lucid explanation given to him by a bearded vineyard proprietor seated waiting to sample his crop being harvested. 'I asked him if he would be good enough to explain about red and white wine to me. "But certainly", he replied, "It is really very simple. Burgundy, you must understand, is red, and so is claret. Chablis, however, is Burgundy although it is not red at all, but white — or even yellow. Bordeaux, too, is red because it is claret, but Graves is also sometimes called claret although it is white. On the other hand I cannot deny that some Graves is not in fact white but red, and it is also Bordeaux." "Thank you", I said, "And what would you drink with a grilled herring?" "For myself, monsieur, a cup of nice strong tea, with plenty of sugar".'

Non-Deposit Beer: Various methods are adopted to treat beer so that it will not form a cloud or haze when chilled. One is to cool the beer, hold until the protein precipitates, filter to brightness and bottle. Another is to add a proteolytic enzyme (q.v.) which acts upon the protein to make it permanently soluble. See also Beer, Chillproof.

Nonnenberg: A name borne by a number of German wine-growing estates producing good white, including properties situated at Niederingelheim, Coenen and Wehlen.

Nonnengarten: German (Dürkheim, q.v.) white wine.

Nonnenstuck: German (Deidesheim, q.v.) white wine.

Non Spumante: Italian for 'still' or non-sparkling, applied to wine.

Noondrink: Medieval term for ale consumed at noon when trading was slacker. Previously 'high noon' had been popular; this was drunk at about three o'clock, when street trading was finished.

Noonschenche: The 15th-century noon drink of ale. The *nones* was the 'high-noon' or three o'clock drink. See also Elevenses.

Nordheim: German (Neckar) red wine.

Nordheim-am-Main: German (Franconian) white wine.

Norheim: German (Nahe) white wine district, including vineyards of Kafels and Hinterfels.

Norman and Pring Ltd.: Owners of the old-established (1807) English brewery at Exeter.

Normandin: Old-established brand of cognac (q.v.).

Norois: Calvados (q.v.) from Foucarmont, Normandy, France.

Northdown Ale: Samuel Pepys the diarist approved of this. On one occasion he writes of the pleasure of drinking it with neats' tongues, oysters and anchovies. See also Margate.

Nostrano: Swiss red wine from Tessin Canton.

Nötsmak: Scandinavian equivalent of nutty (q.v.).

Nouchet: French (Graves) red wine.

Noval: Renowned Portuguese *quinta* (q.v.).

Noyau: Liqueur (q.v.) made from brandy flavoured with fruit kernels. (Lat. *nux*, nut.)

Nu: French wine term of price. It means that the price is that of the wine bare or alone and thus does not include the container, handling charges or freight.

Nube: Defect (cloudiness) of sherry.

Nuits (Côte de Nuits): A district in Burgundy, which produces some of the finest red wines of France.

Nuits-Saint-Georges: Important French wine-growing commune and town of the Côte-d'Or, Burgundy. It is the chief town of the Côte de Nuits and includes some of the finest red burgundies. Amongst the celebrated vineyards are Les Saint-Georges, Les Cailles, Les Vaucrains, Les Porrets, Les Boudots, Les Pruliers and Les Corvées.

Nuriootpa: Australian (S.A.) wine centre for some of the finest table wines of the Commonwealth.

Nussbein: White wine from Palatinate (q.v.).

Nussberg: Austrian wine district.

Nussbrunnen: German (Hattenheim, q.v.) white wine.

Nussdorf: Austrian white table wine.

Nussdorf: German (Palatinate) white wine.

Nusslikor: Liqueur made by steeping walnuts in brandy and sugar.

Nuts and Bolts: Local term, principally used in East Anglia, for mild-and-bitter (q.v.).

Nutty: Term applied to sherry (q.v.) to describe the characteristic, desirable pungency of some types.

Oast: The kiln in which hops are dried. The oast consists of a boiler at ground level, a slatted floor above covered by a horsehair blanket on which the 'green' hops are laid, and a conical chimney surmounted with a cowl and a vane. Hot air and sulphur fumes from the boiler are driven or sucked up through the slatted floor by fans, thereby drying out the moisture content of the hops, and the fumes are expelled through the cowls. The drying takes from 8 to 12 hours and the moisture content is reduced to between 7 and 9 degrees.

An oasthouse is a conical brick building containing two or more oasts, and consisting of an arrival gantry, where the hops are received, the oasts, and a cooling floor where hops are cooled and pressed into pockets (q.v.).

Oatmeal Stout: A brew of fanciful virtues in which a little of the barley malt is replaced by oats.

Oberbergen: German (Baden) white wine.

Oberdiebacher: German (Moselle) white wine.

Obere Hahl: German (Rheinhessen) wine estate.

Oberemmel: German (Saar) fine wine district, including vineyards of Rauler, Rosenberg, Falkenstein and Lautersberg.

Oberetsch: Wine district of South Tyrol.

Oberfell: German (Moselle) white wine.

Oberheimbach: German (Moselle) white wine.

Oberherrenberg: German white wine. See also Avelsbach.

Oberingelheim: German (Rheinhessen) red wine.

Oberkirchen: Austrian (Gairnfarn, q.v.) red wine.

Obernai: Bas-Rhin (q.v.) wine area. Good white.

Oberrotweil: German (Baden) white wine.

Oberrotweil: German (Kaiserstuhl, q.v.) wine centre.

Oberstenfeld: German (Württemberg) red wine.

Ober-und-Nieder Walluf: Wine parish of the Rheingau (q.v.).

Obscuration: The extent to which the determination of alcoholic content by means of a hydrometer (q.v.) is obscured, or rendered inaccurate through the presence of non-volatile substances. See also Sikes.

Ochsle Grade: German scale for sugar content of grape juice. See also Baumé.

Ockenheim: German (Rheinhessen) white wine district including vineyards of Hölle, Rechweg, Gehaneweg, Hockenmühle, Laberstall, Schanz, Leyer, Kreuz and Ringelzell.

Ockfen: German white wine from the Saar. Amongst the vineyards are Herrenberg, Bockstein, Heppenstein and Geisberg.

Octave: A small cask, so named as having one-eighth the capacity of a 'pipe'. However, the cask known as an 'octave' may vary in capacity from 12 to 18 imperial gallons.

Octave of Sherry: The interesting but disappearing London habit of ordering eight half-filled glasses of sherry with a small piece of mild cheese between each. The first was *manzanilla* (q.v.), that driest of all wines, then in turn a *fino*, a *vino de pasto* and so on up to the almost saccharine P.X. The rite was both educational and promotional. May it regain popularity!

October Brews: The specially strong beers brewed in late autumn in 18th-century England and treated by the citizens with the same respect as good wine.

Ocucaje: White table wine of Peru.

Odenas: Red wine of Beaujolais, France.

Odenburg: Hungarian wine centre.

Odyssey: Homer makes frequent reference to wine, e.g.
 . . . ripe bunches gave it grace.
 . . . Pramnian wine she mingled.
 . . . fifty rows of vines that were to be mine.

Œil-de-Perdrix: Lit. 'partridge eye', a French term for the colour variously described as the pinkish-grey or brownish-red tint of certain wines. This tint sometimes develops in champagnes made from black grapes (*blanc de noir*, q.v.). The term is also applied to pink wines of any type.

Oenology: The study of wine. An oenologist is one versed in wines; an oenophile is a wine-lover, in the aesthetic sense.

Oeonotria: Lit. 'wine-land', the Greek vernacular name for Sicily and Southern Italy. A magical term.

Offenbach: German (Glan, q.v.) white wine.

Offenburg: German (Baden) wine centre.

Offley, Forrester Ltd.: Old-established (1737) shippers of port (q.v.).

Oggau: Austrian wine centre.

O'Halloran Hill: Australian (S.A.) wine centre.

Ohligberg: German (Bingen, q.v.) white wine.

Ohligsberg: German wine estate of Wintrich, Moselle.

Oidium: Dreaded grape-vine fungus disease, also known as powdery mildew. It apparently first appeared about the middle of the 19th century in Europe. The remedy is to dust with elementary sulphur in fine powder.

Oinos: Greek for wine and the word commonly used in the New Testament, as at the marriage feast at Cana. Obviously most of the common European words for wine are derived from this, e.g. wine, *Wein* (Ger.), *vin* (Fr.), *vino* (It.), *vinho* (Port.), etc. The bare word meant wine made from grapes but it could be qualified as required. Thus, barley wine (beer), apple wine (cider). See also Low Wines.

Ojen: Spanish type of absinthe (q.v.).

Okelehau: Also variously spelt. Whatever the original precise meaning, the term is now applied to spirit from any source distilled on a small scale in Hawaii.

Okuzgoza: 'Bull's Eye', the celebrated red Turkish wine from Elazig which is supposed to be the most deeply coloured wine in the world.

Ölberg: German (Nierstein, q.v.) white wine.

Old Ale: A name sometimes used for a strong ale. Hence 'old-and-mild' (mild and Burton mixed half-and-half).

Old Brown: English name for dark, sweet sherry (q.v.).

Old Bushmill: Noted Irish (Antrim) whiskey, founded 1784.

Olde Cheshire Cheese, Ye: London (Fleet St.) inn rebuilt 1667. It has always been patronized by journalists and other writers.

Old East India: A name given to sherry that has made the round trip to India, as ballast in a sailing-ship, to assist maturing.

Old-Fashioned: Cocktail of sweetened rye whiskey with bitters and fruit.

Old Tom Gin: General name for gin sweetened with sugar or glycerin. For possible origin see the entry Broadsheets.

Old Trousers: This is alleged once to have been sold in London taverns. The price was very low but would still have shown a profit, as the drink consisted of the mixed dregs of the customers' glasses.

Oleloth: The Biblical name for the gleanings of grapes which were required to be left for the stranger, the widow and the fatherless.

Oliena: Sardinian red table wine.

Olivier: French (Graves) red and white wines.

Olmeto: French (Corsican) red and white wines.

Oloroso: Spanish sherry, sweetish, dark and full-flavoured. The sweetening is usually added to dry (fermented out) wine in the form of *arrope* (q.v.). Olorosos are not *finos* and not made by the flor process (q.v.). The existence and popularity of olorosos is a complete answer to the wine snobbery that regards only bone-dry sherries as worthy.

Olympus: Red table wine from Cyprus.

Omar Khayyám: No English-speaking oenophile is ignorant of the praise of wine in *The Rubáiyát*. Few have not heard:

> And much as Wine has play'd the Infidel,
> And robb'd me of my Robe of Honour — well,
> I often wonder what the Vintners buy
> One[half so precious as the Goods[they sell.
>
> (FitzGerald's Translation.)

Hackneyed this may be but it remains the best aphorism in English, and possibly in any language, on the use of alcoholic beverages. It is a triumphant recognition of the deep truth that the good achieved by alcohol far outweighs the evil.

Ombiaux, Maurice des: This Belgian writer on gastronomy observes: 'The owner of a fine wine cellar can be recognized merely by the way he smiles and puts out his hands to his friends.'

One for the Road: Usually the last drink before leaving a house or pub.

One-Two-Three: Cocktail of whisky, honey and cream.

Opimiam: Roman wine supposed to have been vintaged in 121 B.C. when Opimius was Consul. There was obviously a lot of nonsense talked in Imperial Rome about old wine. Wines were labelled Opimiam for a century! The term was applied to any very old liquor.

Oporto: The shipping port in the north of Portugal, which gives its name to port wine.

Oporto Factory: See Factory House.

Oppenheim: Celebrated German (Rheinhessen) white-wine district, including the vineyards of Steig, Sackträger, Herrenberg, Zuckerberg, Schlossberg, Kreuz, Goldberg, Kugel, Krötenbrunnen, Reisekahr, Daubhaus, Kette, Garten, Berg, Hockbrueck and Kellerweg. Wine has been made here for more than 1,000 years.

Optic: A measuring and dispensing bar-liquor device widely used for spirits. It is usually inserted into the neck of an inverted bottle. A 'six-out optic' is one-sixth of a quartern (q.v.) or 32 to the bottle. A 'five-out' is one-fifth of a quartern or 26 to the bottle.

Orange: The dominant flavour of many celebrated and delectable liqueurs. In general it is not the juice that is used but the skin, which contains a potent essential oil rich in citral and is highly odoriferous. Curaçao uses the dried peel of the local green-skinned fruit. Cointreau, triple sec, dubb orange, van der hum, grand marnier, cristal floquet and many more are all variants.

Orange: Australian (N.S.W.) wine-growing district around the town of that name.

Orange Bitters: Compound of orange oil, quinine and additives, used as an apéritif.

Orange Blossom: Cocktail of equal parts gin and orange juice.

Orange Wine: Made from fermented orange juice. Brazilian industry.

Orbel: German (Nierstein, q.v.) white wine.

R

M.D.D.

Ordinaire: *Vin ordinaire* is the common red and white wine of France, produced in enormous volume, especially in the Midi, and sold at trifling
price for daily appearance at the French table. Countries such as
Australia and the United States will never become wine-drinking until
they produce cheap, wholesome, light 'ordinary' wine.

Ordinary: An English term of much interest as illustrative of change of
meaning. In current usage, the effect of the word is commonplace or of
small value. In earlier times the ordinary was the meal served at a tavern
at a fixed time and price to all comers. It was the equivalent of the
modern *table d'hôte*, as distinct from the meal *à la carte* where each dish
is charged separately. From Pepys onwards literate Englishmen have
enjoyed the ordinary of the London tavern. In the English ordinary
unlimited ale or beer was included in the fixed price. In the Latin
countries it is wine.

Ordonnac-et-Potensac: French (Médoc) commune. Clarets of moderate
quality.

Orgeat: A beverage made of pounded almonds, sugar, orange-flower water
and brandy. Tastes better than it sounds. Used mainly as a flavouring
agent.

Oriental: Cocktail of whisky, vermouth, triple sec and lime.

Oriental Gimlet: Cocktail of gin and lime juice.

Original Bottling: This phrase in various forms is found on the labels of
hock of superior quality and indicates that the bottling was effected on
the premises of the actual grower. It is a guarantee (if truthful) of
authenticity but not necessarily of quality, although a vineyard which
values its reputation will not allow the label to be used on other than
fine wine. It is almost exactly equivalent to the French *Mise du Château*.
The German phrases *Originalabfüllung*, *Originalabzug*, *Kellerabzug* and
Kellerabfüllung all mean substantially the same.

Original Gravity: The strength of a wort or beer expressed as the specific
gravity of the unfermented wort at $15\cdot5°/15\cdot5°$. The original gravity is the
basis of assessment of excise duty in Great Britain and is found by distillation and reference to an official table. The merit of the system is
hard to see.

Orkney: Scottish centre for production of Highland malt whisky.

Orlando: Large vineyard in Barossa Valley, South Australia, in continuous
production since 1847. Like most Australian wine establishments, a
large range of wines and brandies is made. The general quality is good.

Orlenberg: German vineyard of Bisserheim (q.v.).

Orme: French (Côte-d'Or) red wine.

Orveaux: French (Côte-d'Or) red wine.

Orvieto: One of the best-known Italian wines. This is the celebrated pale
yellow wine of high bouquet from the town of Orvieto in Umbria. Dry
Orvieto has a flinty after-taste reminiscent of a chablis (q.v.). There is
also a dessert Orvieto.

Osann: German (Moselle) white wine district, including vineyards of Kirschley, Hofberg and Rosenberg.

Osborne Park: Australian (W.A.) wine centre.

Osborne y Cia: Another of the old firms of sherry shippers established in Spain by English families. The Osborne and the Duff, Gordon (q.v.) concerns are twin firms under the same directorate.

Oschelskopf: German (Freinsheim, q.v.) white wine.

Osey: A wine designated in Shakespeare's *Richard II*, Act v. It is also spelled Oseye, Osoye and Ossoy. It is considered to have been a sweet wine grown in Alsace, apparently because Osoy or Auscois was a common ancient name for that region. This theory of the origin has been disputed. Simon states it was a Peninsular wine similar to Bastard (q.v.).

O'Shea, Maurice: Australian *vigneron* who died in 1956. His name will live long in Australian wine history. He produced superb red table wines on his Hunter River Valley (Mount Pleasant) property and added wit, *bonhomie* and generosity to his viticulture.

Osiris: The Egyptian God of Agriculture is supposed to have taught man the art of making barley wine (ale).

Osoye: See Osey.

Osterberg: German (Harxheim, q.v.) white wine.

Osterfinger: Swiss red wine.

Osterlaemmchen: German (Ediger, q.v.) white wine.

Osterwein: German term for special wine drunk at Easter.

Ostofen: German (Rheinhessen) white-wine district, including vineyards of Köhm, Mittlere Reitel, Rosstal, Goldberg, Hasenbiss, Kirchberg, Schnapp and Wölm.

Östrich: Important German white wine-growing district of the Rheingau, including the vineyards of Doosberg, Lehnchen, Eiserweg, Klostergarten, Eiserpfad, Gottesthal, Kerbesberg, Neuberg, Pfaffenpfad, Pflänzer, Magdalenegarten and Meuhlberg.

Otard: Old-established (1795) brand of cognac (q.v.).

Othello: Red table wine from Cyprus.

Other Half, The: The second of two drinks.

Otibaba: Central African beer made from guinea or purple corn.

Otraqua: Writing in 1634 James Howell states: 'In the Philippines there is a drink called Otraqua that comes from a Nut and is the more general drink.' No further information is available.

Ouillage: French term for keeping a wine cask full. The almost universal practice is to add enough sound wine of the same vintage. However, in a few areas of France the volume is made up by adding clean pebbles. The word is related to the English ullage (q.v.).

Ouzo or **Oyzo:** A Greek unsweetened spirit heavily flavoured with aniseed, and therefore technically a gin. The laity are always intrigued by the milky effect on dilution with water, due, of course, to precipitation of the essential oil of aniseed.

Over-Proof or O.P.: See Proof Spirit.

Over the Walnuts and Wine: To linger at talk after dinner.

Oyster Bay: Cocktail of gin and triple sec.

Oysters: Samuel Chamberlain observes 'Whenever an oyster is to be eaten, it seeks the companionship of a dry chablis'. Most gourmets agree with this. See also Chablis.

Ozyat: Old beverage brewed from sugar, crushed almonds and orange flower water. See also Orgeat.

Paarl: South African (Cape Province) wine-producing area. Good white wine.

Paceta: Spanish (Rioja) red wine.

Padarnac: French (Médoc) red wine.

Padarnac-Belle-Rose: French (Médoc) red wine.

Paddy Whack: Cocktail of Irish whiskey, sweet vermouth, lemon juice and bitters.

Pago: Spanish term for a group of sherry vineyards.

Pahit: Malay Club term for long gin drink.

Paikan: Chinese (Pekinese) name for potent white spirit distilled from kaoliang or sorghum.

Pajarete: See Paxarete.

Palat: French (St. Émilion) red wine.

Palatinate: The better-known name of the celebrated German wine-producing district called the Pfalz or Rheinpfalz. It is a small region of entrancing beauty yet there are 40,000 acres of vineyards. The district was for long ruled by the Counts Palatine. The tall green bottles of the Pfalz wines are characteristic. The Palatinate is a plateau on the left bank of the Rhine. The fame of the Palatinate wines rests wholly upon the whites. Some of the finest hocks are from this region. The best Palatinate wines are all the subjects of separate entries. The area is also called the Bavarian Palatinate.

Pale: A curious term indeed as applied to liquor. Often it is used as denoting special merit, for example, the letters V.S.O.P. appearing upon some cognacs, and supposed to mean 'Very Special Old Pale'. However, cognac as freshly distilled (like all other spirits) is colourless and derives its brown tint partly from material extract from the oak storage casks but mainly from the subsequently added caramel (q.v.). Similar considerations apply to *fino* sherry.

Pale Ale: Made of the highest quality malts, the driest and most highly hopped beer. Sold as light ale or pale ale in bottles, or on draught as bitter.

Palermo: The market and shipping centre for marsala and other Sicilian wines.

Palestine: Wine was made here for some thousands of years until the advent of the Turks, who uprooted the vineyards. The vine is believed to be indigenous to Palestine. Under the leadership of Rothschild vineyards were re-established at the end of the 19th century. Since the formation of the State of Israel there has been a great expansion in wine-production but as yet the quality is not impressive and the use of European place names does not improve the situation. See also Engeddi and Israel.

Palette, La: French wine district north of Marseilles, producing strong reds, whites and *rosé*.

Palheite: Portuguese dry white wine.

Pallas Athena: Cocktail of brandy and ouzo.

Palma: In Spain the chief of a sherry *bodega* (q.v.), as he makes the rounds, chalks a traditional sign like a palm upon the cask as an indication of its destiny. There are usually five grades of acceptability for blending — *una palma, dos, tres* and *cuatro palmas* and 'crossed palms' for something unusually excellent.

Oloroso sherries, which are not destined for flor treatment (q.v.), are marked with a *palo cortado*, a long chalk line with a short one, making a cross.

Palmer: Another of the Médoc red wines which has long been popular in England.

Palm Wine: Wine made from sweet sap of palms, also from dates, especially in equatorial regions.

Palo Cortado: The chalk-mark (up to four) consisting of a slanting line with a cross-bar at top used to designate casks of *oloroso* sherry (q.v.). See also Palma.

Palomino: Grape most widely used for sherry in Spain, both for *finos* and *olorosos*. It is also known as Listan in Spain. In California it is called Napa Golden Chasselas and in Australia Sweet Water. The word is Spanish for little dove or pigeon. The grape lacks acidity, hence the widespread use of plaster (q.v.) in palomino must (q.v.).

Paloumey: French (Médoc) red wine.

Palus: The area on the low sides of the River Gironde (Bordeaux) from which come the cheap bulk clarets.

Paluswein: German name for wine made from grapes cultivated on poles.

Pamid: Bulgarian red table wine.

Pansy: Cocktail of grenadine, absinthe and bitters.

Pantelleria: The muscat and other wine of this island between Sicily and Tunis.

Panyers: 14th-century term for beer sold at 1d. a gallon, as opposed to 'better' beer at 4d. a gallon.

Papaskarasi: Turkish red table wine put up in characteristic squat bottles. It is said to be one of the best, if not the best of the Turkish wines.

Pape, Le: French (Léognan, q.v.) red wine.

Pape-Clément: French (Graves) red wine.

Pape-Léon: French (Graves) red wine.

Paphos: Table wine from a region of Cyprus.

Pappen: German (Rheinhessen) wine estate.

Paradies: German (Kröv-Kövenig, q.v.) white wine estate.

Parempuyre: French (Médoc) red wine.

Parisian: Cocktail of gin, dry vermouth and cassis.

Parliament Brandy: The curious popular name for the unflavoured spirit which was able to evade the tax placed on gin by the Act of 1729.

Parlour: Also known as the lounge or saloon. The traditional name for the 'best' room of an English pub. Here the same drinks cost more.

Parnay: French (Anjou) good white wine from an area near Saumur (q.v.).

Paros: Wine from island of Greek Archipelago.

Parsley: This herb was believed in classical times to be capable of warding off intoxication and was therefore woven into wreaths and worn by Greeks and Romans at their banquets.

Parsley Wine: See Country Wines.

Parsnip Wine: See Country Wines.

Pascal Combeau: Old-established (1838) brand of cognac (q.v.).

Passe-Tous-Grains: The French term for the undistinguished wines made from a blend of pinot and gamay grapes in Burgundy.

Passion Fruit: Liqueur based on this unique fruit, Australian by adoption. The flavour is delicate, elusive, almost orgiastic. The juice of this fruit makes interesting cocktails.

Passito: Italian dessert wine made from semi-dried grapes almost to the stage of raisins. It is also used to flavour other wine such as marsala (q.v.). Widely used as a supposed tonic in Italy.

Passulated: The action of partly drying wine grapes on the stem. See also Vins de Paille.

Pasteur, Louis: A hallowed name in the wine industry, both as chemist and microbiologist. See also Arbois.

Pasteurization: The process of destroying undesirable micro-organisms in a liquid by raising the temperature to a suitably high degree, usually around 140° to 150° F., for the necessary time. The method was originated by the noted scientist, Louis Pasteur, who carried out his early researches with French wines. The process is never applied to fine wines.

Pastis: French imitation absinthe with strong flavour of aniseed.

Pastoso: Italian sweetish wine.

Patent Still: The continuous distillation (q.v.) equipment invented in 1832 by the Irish distiller Aeneas Coffey which has revolutionized the manufacture of certain spirits. The old pot-still (q.v.) is a discontinuous apparatus but the patent still allows a steady stream of wine, beer, rum-wash or other liquid containing alcohol to be fed into it and a continuous stream of alcohol-enriched liquid (as whisky, brandy, rum or industrial alcohol) to be discharged. For details a specialized text should be consulted. The distiller can keep a close control over his product. Unwanted fractions or constituents are readily removable. A spirit made in a patent still is much purer than a pot-stilled one and therefore needs less maturing. The ultimate quality of pot-stilled spirits is, by general consent, superior. Cognac, armagnac and much rum are wholly pot-stilled. Scotch whisky is a standard, judicious and acceptable blend of pot and patent-stilled whiskies.

Pativiloa: Peruvian wine centre.

Patras: The best Greek white table wine.

Patrimonio: Best-known red table wine of Corsica.

Pauillac: Wine-growing commune of the Médoc (q.v.) which produces many of the finest clarets, including Lafite, Latour and Mouton-Rothschild.

Paulinsberg: German (Kestener, q.v.) white wine.

Pavie, Château: Red wine of St. Émilion district of Bordeaux.

Pavie-Decesse: French (St. Émilion) red wine.

Pavie-Macquin: French (St. Émilion) red wine.

Pavilion Château Margaux, Le: See Margaux.

Pavillon-Cadet: French (St. Émilion) red wine.

Paxarete: Spanish compound wine, also known as Pedro Ximénez, made by fortifying *arrope* (concentrated grape juice). It is widely used for blending with sweet sherries to give body and colour, especially with *oloroso* (q.v.) to make brown sherry. The name is derived from the small Spanish town of Paxarete. It is said to be widely used in the U.S. to impart a fictitious 'age' to whisky. Also known as *pascarete* and *pajarete*.

Paycharmant: French red wine of Bergerac (q.v.).

Pays, Vin de: See Vin.

Peach Brandy: Not a brandy (q.v.) but a liqueur consisting of sweetened brandy flavoured with peach.

Pea Pod Wine: Country wine (q.v.) made by fermenting sugar and young pea pods.

Pearl: General name in English for mildly sparkling wine, usually made by the closed-tank process. It is broadly synonymous with *Perlwein* (q.v.), *perlant, frizzante, reciotto, crémant* and *crackling*. Since about 1930 there has been a large increase in the consumption of these slightly-effervescent, inexpensive and wholesome wines, which are now being made in most of the wine-growing countries. They cannot, of course, compare with champagne (q.v.).

Peat Reek: The Scots term for the characteristic flavour of their best whisky.

Pechstein: German (Forst, q.v.) fine white wine.

Pécs: Hungarian wine district.

Pédesclaux: French (Médoc) red wine.

Pé de Vinha: Portuguese *rosé* wine.

Pedro Ximénèz: Spanish white grape whose juice is used mainly to boil down to make the liqueur wine paxarete (q.v.). Also a synonym for paxarete itself. Sometimes drunk as a liqueur in Spain. Also known as Pedro Jimenez and P.X.

Peg: A measure of wine. Also a small drink of spirits. *Chota peg* is the Anglo-Indian term for a small drink of spirits. (*Chota*, Hind. small.) This would have the literal meaning — a small small drink! Actually it means an ordinary drink of spirits, a 'nobbler' (q.v.), especially of brandy or whisky and soda.

Also a pin in a drinking vessel (see Peg Tankard) hence the quantity measured by the pin, i.e. a small drink.

Peg Tankard: Wooden drinking-tankard (also known as a 'pin tankard'), divided into sections by pegs driven into the inner surface, the idea being to prevent a member of a convivial gathering drinking more than his share from the common vessel. Archbishop Anselm prohibited priests 'drinking to pins'.

Pekmez: Turkish sweetmeat or sweetening agent made by boiling down a mixture of grape juice and honey.

Pellen: German (Erbach, q.v.) white wine vineyard.

Pelletan: French (St. Émilion) red wine.

Pelure d'Oignon: French for onion skin and the term used to denote the characteristic shiny brown hue that aged red wines may acquire. Not unattractive. Especially applied to wine of Arbois, in the French Jura, whose brownish pink hue is just that.

Pélures, Les: French (Côte-d'Or) red wine.

Penang Cooler: Cocktail of gin, crème de menthe, pineapple juice.

Pennie-Hweep: Weak ale, in the central Ayrshire dialect of Robert Burns.

Peparetherian: Greek wine mentioned in classical writings.

Peralta: Spanish dessert wine of Navarre.

Perapedhi: Turkish wine centre.

Perdrix, Aux: French (Côte-d'Or) red wine.

Perelada: Spanish (Catalonian) red wine.

Pergos: Greek (Morean) red wine.

Pérignon, Dom: A Benedictine monk of the Abbey of Hautvillers (q.v.), who is said (on slender evidence, but what of it?) to be the originator of champagne wine. See also Champagne.

Periquita: Portuguese dry red wine from Setubal.

Perkeo: The German medieval dwarf jester who was celebrated for his immunity to alcohol. His wooden statue stands next to the celebrated Heidelberg Fass (cask), which is one of the largest vessels in the world.

Perla: Bulgarian white sparkling wine.

Perlant: French term (lit. 'pearly') for a slightly sparkling wine. See Pearl, also Pétillant.

Perlwein: German term for mildly sparkling wine made by the tank (bulk) process and bottled under pressure. Under 'pearl' and other names, wine of this type is now being made in many countries outside Germany. These wines are slightly gassier than pétillant or spritzig (q.v.).

Pernand-Vergelleses: Notable red wine of Burgundy.

Perno: See Barolo.

Pernod: French aniseed-flavoured apéritif, one of the modern harmless substitutes for absinthe (q.v.).

Perrano: One of the lesser grapes used in Spain for sherry.

Perrier: Old-established brand of champagne of Chalons, not to be confused with Perrier-Jouet.

Perrières, Clos des: French (Meursault) white wine. Part of the 42-acre vineyard of Les Perrières.

Perrières, Les: Large Burgundian vineyard (42 acres) divided into a number or proprietorships. Fine white wines.

Perrier-Jouet: Old-established champagne of Epernay.

Perry: Pear wine. The name is derived from the Fr. *poiré*, perry. The beverage is the exact counterpart of apple cider and is made in identical fashion. Cider and perry are equally delicious but for some obscure reason the latter has never achieved comparable esteem in the English-speaking world. Little, if any, of the surplus tonnage and the waste of the pear orchards and canneries is put to the commerical production of perry. Anybody who has drunk the *poiré* of northern France may well wonder why this is so. See also Cider.

Pear brandy, the counterpart of applejack and calvados (q.v.) is still less a commercial product. Well-made pear brandy is an attractive spirit with a delicate, characteristic flavour.

Persia: Despite the tradition that this was one of the cradles of wine-making, none is exported and in modern times, according to report, the quality is low.

Persico: Liqueur of peach flavour. Also an old beverage made from sweetened spirits in which is steeped lemon peel, cinnamon and red currants.

Perth: Town in Scotland with several important whisky distilleries and blending plants.

Pertuisots: French red wine of Beaune (q.v.).

Peru: Small wine-producer (only 3 million gallons) and the quality is not notable. However, Pisco brandy (q.v.) has long had a high reputation. This appears to be a freak industry. However, it should be remembered that the wine of Cognac is valueless as a beverage.

Pessac: One of the most important of the wine-growing districts of the Graves. It produces many renowned clarets, including Haut-Brion (q.v.). Pessac is now virtually a suburb of the city of Bordeaux.

Pessan: French (Graves) red and white wines.

Peterhohle: German (Deidesheim, q.v.) white wine.

Petersberg: German (Gau-Odernheim, q.v.) white wine district.

Pétillant: French term, meaning crackling or sparkling, applied to slightly sparkling wines, much less heavily charged than mousseux (q.v.). The equivalent German term is spritzig.

Petit: Small, often used in France of wine as inferior. See also Small.

Petit-Bosc: French (Graves) red and white wines.

Petite Bière: The Norman term for small cider (q.v.) made by fermenting watered apple residues.

Petite Champagne: Grade of cognac (q.v.).

Petite Sirah: Red wine grape widely grown in France (Rhône Valley).

Petit-Faurie-de-Soutard: French (St. Émilion) red wine.

Petit-Faurie et Nulon: French (St. Émilion) red wine.

Petit-Mangot: French (St. Émilion) red wine.

Petit-Moulinet: French (St. Émilion) red wine.

Petit-Pontac: French (Graves) red wine.

Petit Sirah: Californian name of a black grape said to have no link with the Syrah (q.v.) but to be another name for the Duriff vine.

Petits Musigny, Les: A group of renowned red burgundy vineyards of the Côte-d'Or.

Petit-Village: French (Pomerol) red wine.

Peto: West African (Togoland) beer made from Guinea corn.

Petrus: Wine centre of Graach, Moselle.

Pétrus: French (Pomerol) red wine.

Petrusberg: German (Kinheim, q.v.) white wine estate.

Pettental: German (Nierstein, q.v.) white wine.

Pewter: An alloy of tin and lead and other metals, used in the manufacture of tankards and beer drinking vessels. It was well known to the Romans but was not heard of in England until the Middle Ages, when it provided a cheap substitute for silver. The term is now commonly applied to metal beer-mugs, whether made of this old-fashioned alloy or not.

Peycharmant: French (Dordogne) light red wine.

Peyraguey: An esteemed sauternes wine. See also Sauternes.

Pezerolles: French (Côte-d'Or) red wine.

Pezinok: Czechoslovakian white wine. Also known as Bösing.

Pfaffenberg: German (Hattenheim, q.v.) white wine. There are other hock (q.v.) vineyards at Rauenthal and Ediger of the same name.

Pfaffenpfad: German (Östrich, q.v.) white wine.

Pfaffenrötter: German (Hahnheim, q.v.) white wine.

Pfaffenwies: German (Lorch, q.v.) white wine.

Pfalz: The usual German name for the Palatinate (q.v.).

Pfalz-Wein: The German term for Palatinate wine.

Pfandloch: German (Hochheim, q.v.) white wine.

Pfeiffer: White wine from Forst, Palatinate (q.v.).

Pflänzer: German (Östrich, q.v.) white wine.

Pflaumenbranntwein: German term for plum brandy, of which the best known is slivovitz (q.v.). See also Quetsch.

Pfuhlweg: German (Nierstein, q.v.) white wine.

Pfülben: Steinwein vineyard at Randersacker (q.v.).

Phanean: Roman wine of antiquity.

Pharaoh: Obsolete term for strong ale.

Phélan-Ségur: French (Médoc) red wine.

Phénix-Haut-Brion: French (Graves) red wine.

Phylloxera: The most dreaded of all diseases of the European grape vine, *Vitis vinifera*. The indigenous Eastern American stocks, *Vitis ruparia* and *rupestris*, are highly resistant. *Phylloxera vastatrix*, an aphid commonly called a plant louse, was introduced into Europe in the 1860's when American vines, which were somewhat resistant to the disease *oidium* (q.v.), were imported for grafting purposes. Grimmer irony can hardly be imagined. *Phylloxera*, though native to the U.S., does little damage there and *oidium* (downy mildew) is a much less serious disease and one that can be controlled with a bit of effort. Within a decade or two *Phylloxera* had killed most of the vines of Europe, Africa and Australia. *Phylloxera* lives on the roots, sucks the sap and finally kills the plant. The vines are stunted, the leaves yellow and wither and galls form. Any grapes that grow are quite useless.

After long years of suffering and experiment a cure was found. The European vines were grafted on roots of American stocks, the disease thus constituting its own remedy. No other practical cure has yet been found though the Russians have recently reported promising experiments in harnessing radioactivity to kill the insects.

Fierce argument is still proceeding as to whether the wine made from grafted grapes is the equal of the old vines. On general evidence there does not seem to be any marked difference, though some stoutly assert that the grafted vines give a larger yield of wine of shorter life.

There are still considerable areas which have never experienced the scourge of *Phylloxera*. These include small patches throughout Europe.

The most astonishing free region is the whole vast Australian State of South Australia, the most important wine-producer of the Commonwealth. This is despite the fact that the adjoining State of Victoria was an early and extreme sufferer. It is one of the romances of viticulture that the State of South Australia has long maintained an extensive nursery on the contaminated Victorian soil at Rutherglen, ready to rush millions of pieces of grafting stock to affected areas. A large monetary fund has been accumulated from the levy imposed on South Australian wine-growers.

Piada: French (Barsac, Sauternes) sweet white wines.

Pian, Le: French (Médoc) red wine centre whose wines are legally allowed, by custom, to be sold under the better-known commune of Ludon. How French!

Piatria: Romanian sweet dessert wine.

Picardan: French (Pyrénées) dessert wine.

Picard-Canteloup: French (Bordeaux) red wine.

Piccadilly: Cocktail of gin, dry vermouth, dash of absinthe and grenadine.

Pichon-Longueville: French (Médoc) red wine.

Pichon-Longueville-Lalande: French (Médoc) red wine.

Pick-Me-Up: A term variously used. It can mean any alcoholic beverage of alleged restorative value. It is also used for any nostrum supposed to remove the effect of drunkenness, or a 'run-down' state.

Picpoul: The best wine under this name is a dessert. See Picardan. The same name is given to the inexpensive sweet white wines of the Aude Département which are largely used for the production of vermouth (q.v.).

Picton Junction: Australian (W.A.) wine centre.

Piece: The maltster's term for barley undergoing germination. It can be No. 1, 2, or 3 Piece according to stage.

Pièce: The large Burgundy barrel containing the equivalent of 288 bottles.

Piedmont: Perhaps the most important of the Italian wine-growing areas from the aspect of quality. Here are the renowned reds — Barolo, Cortese, Nebbiolo, Barbera. The best white wine is Castello di Canelli.

Pierry: One of the best wine-growing centres of the Marne (Champagne).

Piesport: German (Moselle) wine region. Amongst the best known of the fine white wines are Gunterslay, Goldtröpfchen, Grafenberg and Falkenberg.

Pig, Drunk As a: The saying is said to be derived from the use of a piggin (q.v.).

Pigg or **Piggin:** Archaic term for drinking-mug. The oft-seen inn-sign 'Pig and Whistle' is said to be a corruption of the ancient phrase 'piggen wassail' or celebration with mugs. It was a drinking-vessel of medieval times, made of earthenware or metal, holding about a pint. Originally made from pig-skin. See also Black Jack and Bombard.

Pigment: Apparently identical with 'pyment' and 'piment' (q.v.). Medieval beverage, a sweet, spiced wine or mead.

Pig's Ear: Colloquial phrase (Cockney rhyming slang) for beer.

Piledriver: Mixture of vodka, orange liqueur and bitters.

Pilsener (or Bohemian Beer): Of pale colour, with pronounced hop flavour and odour. The term is now generic rather than geographical.

Piment, Pyment or Pigment: Wine or mead (q.v.) flavoured with honey and spices. See also Hippocras, Bishop, Cardinal and Pope. From at least the 9th century piments have been popular among the clergy, for an order condemning their use was made at Aix-la-Chapelle in A.D. 817. The use spread to the laity and it was not until the 17th century that the growing use of spirits ousted piments from popularity. See also Clarre.

Pin: Miniature beer cask of 4½ gallons, i.e. half a firkin or a quarter kilderkin. The smallest beer cask in general use.

Pinard: French soldier's slang for the coarse wine supplied as part of the food ration. Samuel Chamberlain has put it better than anybody else: '. . . *le bon pinard*, the all-but-universal ordinary red wine which appears on every French bourgeois table twice a day. *Vin ordinaire* is usually a nameless, yearless fluid, adequate in strength, deep in colour, acceptable in taste. It is the backbone of French morale, the cornerstone of their nourishment. Most of it comes from the Languedoc. In a normal year one sixth of all the wine of France is produced by the fertile vineyards of the single *département* of the Hérault.'

Pineapple Milk: Cocktail of brandy, ripe pineapple pulp, milk and vanilla.

Pineau des Charentes: Beverage, a type of liqueur (q.v.) made in the Cognac area by adding brandy to fresh grape juice (must). See also Angelica.

Pinga: Syn. for 'cachasa' (q.v.), crude rum distilled by Indian peasantry in Amazon valley.

Pink Champagne: A novelty of no special value usually made by adding a small percentage of red wine to the white.

Pink Gin: A mixed drink of gin and bitters, the latter conferring a pink tint. A British Navy favourite. Ashore ice and lemon are usually added.

Pink Lady: Celebrated American festive mixed drink of gin, applejack, grenadine and egg white.

Pink Milk Punch: Mixture of whisky, rum, grenadine and milk.

Pink Wine: See Rosé.

Pinnerkreuzberg: German white wine of Cochem (q.v.).

Pinot: Many viticulturists contend that the pinot is the finest of all wine grapes. In France most of the great burgundies and three-quarters of the champagnes derive from the juice of the pinot. There are red and white pinots. The latter is sometimes called the chardonnay and is the source of Montrachet, the most esteemed dry white wine of all France. There is a so-called 'grey pinot' widely grown in Alsace.

Pinot Blanc: Also known as white burgundy. White grape which is widely used for white burgundies and champagne.

Pinot Chardonnay: Commonly known as chardonnay. The French fine white grape responsible for chablis, Montrachet and some champagne.

Pinot Noir: Black grape, the basis of some of the finest red wines in the world, especially of Burgundy. Also used for champagne (q.v.).

Pin Stage: In hop growing the first of the three final stages before picking.

Pint: Measure of capacity. The British imperial pint, one-eighth of a gallon, contains 20 fl. oz.; the reputed pint is one-twelfth of a gallon or 13⅓ fl. oz. The U.S. pint, one-eighth of a U.S. gallon, is approximately five-sixths the volume of an imperial pint.

Pin Tankard or Peg Tankard: Vessel divided into eight sections, each marked by a peg driven into the wood on the inside. They were made on the order of King Edgar in the 10th century, in an effort to restrain heavy drinking; any person drinking past the pin at a draught was to forfeit a penny. Hence the phrase 'to drink to pins', a deep draught, and a peg as a measure (still used today for whisky). See also Peg Tankard.

Pipe: A large cask of varying capacity, usually 100 gallons or more. As a unit, the English wine pipe is 105 gallons, the nominal subdivisions being two hogsheads, three tierces, four quarter-casks, or eight octaves.

Piper-Heidsieck: Old-established (1785) champagne of Reims.

Pipette: Syn. for 'vellinch' (q.v.).

Pipkin: Small earthen pot, also a piggin, also a 7-pint beer can.

Piqué: French term for sour (acetified or vinegary) wine. Much of the rough, common wine of all wine-drinking countries, i.e. the *vin ordinaire, consumo*, etc. is more or less *piqué*. No harm to health results. See also Piquette.

Pique-Caillou: French (Graves) red and white wines.

Piquette: French name for a crude, cheap wine of low alcoholic content made from the residues or marc (q.v.). Also known as *piqué* or *vinade*. In Germany the corresponding beverage is called *Tresterwein, Nachwein* or *Haustrunk*. In Italy it is called *vinelli*.

Piqueur de Vin: French for wine taster or grader.

Piron: This witty French poet, when told that he would lose his sight if he did not cease to drink burgundy, replied (the translation is free) 'Hell, I have seen enough but I haven't drunk enough'.

Pisadores: The wine-treaders of Spain who crush the grapes under their nail-studded shoes.

Pisco: Brandy from Peru, some of it of excellent quality. See also Peru.

Pisco Punch: Celebrated mixed drink dating from 1850's in Parker's Bank Exchange Bar, San Francisco. See also Pisco.

Pisco Sour: Cocktail of Pisco brandy, honey, egg white, lemon juice and soda.

Pitcher: A leather vessel so called because it was treated with pitch on the inside to make it waterproof.

Pitching: The operation of adding yeast to a carbohydrate-containing solution (fruit juice, cereal mash, etc.), to cause fermentation.

Pitlochry: Scottish centre for production of Highland malt whisky.

Pittersberg: German (Münster, q.v.) white wine.

Piva: The home-brew of the Aleutian Islands, also known as quas, and which may be made from potatoes, raisins or any other fermentable material.

Plagnac: French (Bordeaux) red wine.

Plaisance: French (Médoc) red wine.

Planig: German wine-growing parish of Rheinhessen.

Plastering: The process of adding plaster of paris (a form of calcium sulphate) to must (q.v.) deficient in acidity in order to increase this. Plastering is an essential process of making sherry in Spain, where about 20 lbs. of *yeso* (q.v.) per ton of grapes is used. Most countries prohibit or strictly limit the addition of plaster to wine but recognize that the Spanish sherry process is traditional. However, some Spanish sherry wineries are now substituting the addition of tartaric acid for part or all of the plaster.

Plat: French wine term meaning flat, dull, uninteresting and a host more opprobria.

Plâtrage: French term for the process of adding gypsum (calcium sulphate) to must to increase acidity. This is standard procedure in making sherry. See also Plastering.

Platte: German (Nackenheim, q.v.) white wine.

Plattensee: Hungarian wine centre.

Pleven: One of the important Bulgarian wine regions.

Plevna: Bulgarian wine-growing centre.

Pliska: Bulgarian brandy of good quality.

Plonk: Australian derisive term for wine, especially sweet fortified type. Cridland states the term is a corruption of *vin blanc* and is soldiers' slang from the Australians in France in the First World War.

Plough, The: English inn at Worcester Park, Surrey, established in 15th century.

Plum Port: The foolish name fastened to a beverage made by fermenting sugar and plums and fortifying with brandy. See also Country Wines.

Plymouth: Variety of gin of special flavour originally made in west of England. The name is now generic.

Pmorie: Bulgarian dessert wine.

Pocket: A large sack made to contain roughly one and a half cwt. of dried hops. The hops are pressed into the pockets after cooling, and are thus stored until their arrival in the brewery.

Poculum: Roman drinking cup. See also Cyathus.

Podensac: French wine-growing commune of the Gironde whose white wines are better esteemed than the reds.

Podersdorf: Austrian (Burgenland) white wine.

Poggibonsi: Italian (Tuscanian) red wine.

Pointes d'Angles, Les: French (Côte-d'Or) red wine.

Poiré: The French name for perry (q.v.).

Pokolbin: Townlet of the Hunter River Valley region of New South Wales. Pokolbin is the Australian equivalent of, say, Gévry (q.v.).

Poligny: French (Jura) white-wine centre. Here are also made 'straw' wines such as Ch. Chalon (q.v.).

Polishing Filtration: The final clarifying process of wines, ales and other liquids, usually consisting in the forcing of the liquid under heavy pressure through mechanical filters. There are many designs of these filters, but all employ the same basic principle. The liquid passes slowly through a medium whose pores are fine enough to hold back even colloidal particles. This 'polishes' the liquid to brilliancy.

Polka: Liqueur now obsolete but popular in Australia in the fifties.

Pol Roger: Old-established (1849) champagne of Reims.

Pomace: The mass of crushed or pulped fruit from which the juice is extracted in the making of beverages.

Pomal: Spanish (Rioja, q.v.) red wine.

Pombe: Uganda beverage said to be made from fermented bananas.

Pombo: African brewed beverage from millet grain or sorghum.

Pomerol: One of the finest red wine-growing districts of the Bordeaux. There has never been an official classification of the Pomerol wines as of those of the Médoc (q.v.), hence almost all the vineyards claim to be in the top class. However, there are indeed many renowned Pomerol clarets. They are all supposed to taste of truffles!

Pomeys: French (Médoc) red wine.

Pomies-Agassac: French (Médoc) red wines.

Pomino: Italian (Tuscany) red wine.

Pommard: Important French (Côte-d'Or) red burgundy commune. The quality of the Pommard wines is very variable. It is the name of the particular estate that counts.

Pommarède: French (Graves) red and white wines.

Pommeraie, La: French (Anjou) white wine.

Pomys: French (Médoc) red wine.

Pontac: South African (Cape) dark red, very sweet, fortified dessert wine. It is largely used to blend with other wines to increase colour and sugar.

Pontac is also the name of a white bordeaux and the area was once also celebrated for bordeaux red (claret, q.v.).

Though today none of the Pontac clarets is highly regarded, things were different in England in the 17th century. Locke wrote in 1677: 'The Vin de Pontac, so much esteemed in England. . . .' Evelyn (the

S   M.D.D.

contemporary and friend of the still more famous diarist Samuel Pepys) wrote in 1683, about meeting Pontac, 'the son of the famous Bordeaux President, who owns the excellent vineyards of Pontac and Haut-Brion, whence the best Bordeaux wines come from'. See also Haut-Brion.

Pontac-Lynch: French (Médoc) red wine.

Pontac-Monplaisir: French (Graves) red wine.

Pontac-Pinot: French (Graves) white wine.

Pontet-Canet: One of the largest vineyards of the Médoc producing 15,000 or more cases of claret annually; owned by a Bordeaux wine merchant.

Pontet-Pachan: French (Médoc) red wine.

Pony: Conventional liquor measure for spirits of 1 fl. oz. Also a small glass of about 4 fl. oz. It originated during the 19th century when landlords served saloon bar customers with five measures to the pint and four measures to public bar customers, charging each the same price.

Pop: Any aerated or carbonated beverage which expels the cork with popping sound.

Pope: A spiced drink made from tokay (q.v.), ginger, honey and roasted orange. See also Bishop, Cardinal and Negus.

Poppy: Cocktail of gin and crème de cacao.

Pop-Skull: U.S. slang for crude, strong spirits (q.v.).

Populo: An old-standing Italian liqueur (q.v.) originally made in the 16th century of cinnamon, aniseed and other flavourings. There is a modern very different version.

Porlond: William Porland is remembered as the Clerk of the Brewers who took up his appointment in London in 1418 and promptly commenced to keep a very informative set of records, still available.

Porphyry: An Australian, sweetish, white beverage wine.

Porrets, Les: French (Nuits-Saint-Georges, q.v.) red burgundy.

Porrón: Glass vessel with two spouts used by the Spanish to drink wine by pouring direct into the mouth. Also a Spanish wine-measure, variable but in Barcelona about 1·7 gallons.

Port: Fortified sweet dessert wine. The name should be restricted to wine made from grapes grown in the Douro valley of Portugal and shipped from Oporto. The Portuguese government has laid down exhaustive regulations for the growth, harvesting, fermenting, fortifying, storing and shipping of the wine and in the U.K. only the produce of Portugal can legally bear the name. Under the Methuen Treaty port long enjoyed special privilege and protection in England. However the name has been unfairly adopted by many other countries for their sweet dessert wines, though some bear little resemblance to the genuine thing. Some governments have the grace to require the name port to be preceded by the country of origin or the word 'style' added.

The hard schistose soils of the Douro are broken up by explosives and pickaxes and the steep slopes terraced.

The vines used are the native touriga, the tinta, bastardo and others.

Fermentation continues for a day or two but long before the sugar is gone brandy is added, 'silent spirit' for cheap wines and good brandy for better ones. At the same time jeropiga is added. This is the concentrated grape syrup similar to the arrope of Spain and it gives to port much of its flavour and character. No other country makes 'port' in the same way.

The sweet, fortified wine remains in the vats for some months. In spring the boats are loaded with filled barrels (pipes containing 115 gallons). The boats (or motor lorries or railway trucks) take the filled pipes down to Vila Nova, on the river opposite Oporto. Here the wine matures for years in the wine lodges until it is shipped away, mainly to English-speaking countries.

Port contains about 20% of alcohol and, according to style, from 5 to 10% of sugar. The port-drinking squires of 18th-century English literature were more abstemious than may be thought. Port as we know it is a modern drink and fortification dates back only to the early years of the 19th century. Those 'two-bottle men' were drinking a dry table wine.

In the early days of fortification port was faked and adulterated, especially as concerns the colouring with elderberries. Today, however, the quality of true port is rigidly controlled.

Vintage port is wine of a single year, and is made only from suitably fine vintages. Thus there was no vintage port made from 1936 to 1941.

All ports other than vintage are called blended. Ruby port is wine bottled young and still retaining the natural red colour, which alters very slowly or not at all in bottle. Tawny port has been long stored in wood (oak); the red colour is slowly changed to a brownish tint supposed to resemble the hair of a tawny lion.

Tawny ports do not improve in the bottle, but vintage and ruby ports are the better for a few years (up to twenty) of bottle age.

Fine port is one of the great drinks of the world. Contrary to popular belief, less than a third of Portuguese wine production is port.

Port: Foundation dates of some of the older British firms in the Oporto wine trade (Ernest Cockburn):

1638	C. N. Kopke & Co. Ltd.
1670	Warre & Co.
1678	Croft & Co.
1680	Quarles, Harris & Co.
1692	Taylor, Fladgate & Yeatman
1715	Morgan Bros. Ltd.
1730	Butler, Nephew & Co.
1735	Hunt, Roope & Co.
1737	Offley, Forrester Ltd.
1750	J. W. Burmester & Co. Ltd.
1784	Smith, Woodhouse & Co.
1790	Sandeman & Co.
1814	Cockburn, Smithes & Co. Ltd.
1815	Feuerheerd Bros & Co. Ltd.
1820	W. & J. Graham & Co.
1835	Gonzalez, Byass & Co.

Port, Late-Bottled Vintage: Wine of one vintage, usually of a 'declared' year, i.e. a year agreed upon by port shippers (q.v.) as such. Unlike ordinary vintage port, it is stored in cask for three years or more, before bottling. It thus has less colour and body but matures faster in bottle.

Port, 'Mark': Port wine of commerce sold under hundreds of different trade labels. A Mark port is the laudable attempt of a merchant to produce a standard, unvarying blend.

Port, Newfoundland: See Newfoundland Port.

Port, Off-Vintage: Wine of actual or alleged high quality made from a single vintage but not in a vintage year.

Port, Ruby: Wine bottled young. The comparatively short life in wood does not result in the change of red pigment to 'tawny'.

Port, Vintage: The wine of a single year bottled early. See also Port, Late-Bottled Vintage. Vintage port needs declaration of the associated port shippers of Douro that the produce of a particular year is of quality high enough to merit this grade. At any rate that is the theory of the matter.

Port, White: See White Port.

Porter: A brew popular in the late 18th and early 19th centuries, equivalent to a mixture of ale, beer and twopenny. It is reputed to have been so called because of its popularity amongst London market porters. See also Entire. It is now dark ale, sweeter in taste than usual, brewed from black malt.

Porterhouse: A house at which porter was retailed.

Porterhouse Steak: Choice cut of beef to be obtained at a porterhouse (q.v.).

Portet: French (Béarn) white wines, dry and sweet, of local esteem. Some red is also made.

Portets: French (Graves) red and white wines.

Porto Flip: Cocktail of port and whole fresh egg.

Port Royal: Cocktail of rum, coffee, lemon juice and syrup.

Port Shipper: A link with the port wine industry of Portugal and much more than a mere profit-taking middleman. Not infrequently the shipper owns his own *quinta* (q.v.). He must be a man of substantial wealth to be able to grow or buy and mature stocks of port. He must be a skilled blender and maturer. He must also be commercially sagacious. Many of the wine shippers of Spain and France as well as of Portugal are of British origin.

Portugal: One of the important wine-growing countries of the world. Despite the small area available the production is relatively enormous and Portugal is about the fifth largest world-producer. We ordinarily think of port (q.v.) as the one wine of Portugal but this is a wine-drinking country and there is a big production of red and white dry table wines. Some of these are very good and are exported. The best are separately noted. Colaro, Mateus, Setubal and Sadao are some of the principal areas outside the port region.

Portuguese Treaty: The important agreement between Great Britain and Portugal, signed in 1914, which recognizes that port wine can come only from the Douro District. Prior to this the Methuen Treaty (q.v.) operated.

Porusot: French (Côte-d'Or) white wine.

Posset-Pot: A two-handled vessel used for making posset, which is a drink of hot milk curdled with ale or other liquor, and often flavoured with spices. Possets used to be drunk as a remedy for colds and were highly regarded by the diarist Samuel Pepys.

Pot: A popular term for a large mug of liquor, especially ale or beer. Pot is also the name of liquid measures in other countries. In Switzerland it is about 2¾ pints, in Scandinavia about 1¾ pints and in Belgium half a litre. In Portugal the *pote* is about a gallon, but variable. Also a rounded drinking-vessel; hence pot of pewter.

Potable: Fit or suitable for drinking.

Pot-Ale: The curious and misleading term for the exhausted residue in the whisky still after the low wines (q.v.) have been distilled from the wash. Sometimes fed to cattle but usually run to waste.

Potation: Drinking, especially of alcoholic beverages. Also the draught of liquor itself.

Potato: There is no one well-known and characteristic alcoholic beverage based upon potato but because these tubers are so rich in starch, much alcohol is made from them. This can take the form of industrial spirit, or after rectification become the basis of vodka, akvavit and Kornbranntwein (all q.v.). Flavouring is usually added, e.g., caraway, cumin, anise, etc. Beverage alcohol from the potato is a large industry in Scandinavia, Germany, Russia and elsewhere.

Pot Crown: A drinking-vessel similar to a fuddling-cup (q.v.) placed on the head of a village bride, and from which her male admirers drank.

Poteen: Derived from *poit'in*, a pot, this is the Irish term for any spirit (q.v.) distilled illicitly. The usual pronunciation is 'pocheen' and the word is variously rendered 'potsheen', 'potyeen' and 'potheen'. The distillation is invariably carried on with small and primitive plant and the ingredients and fermentation process may show wide variation. With malted barley a true whisky is made. Sugar as base, especially if unrefined, yields a type of rum. It is generally assumed that poteen is a very poor, crude and fiery spirit, but this is by no means necessarily so. The principal defect of illicitly distilled spirit is lack of maturing. All such spirit is made in a pot-still (q.v.) as is cognac (q.v.) and the finest 'single' Scotch whisky. Adequately aged poteen may therefore be very good stuff. See also Moonshine.

Potell: 15th-century liquid measure.

Potensac: French (Médoc) red wine.

Pot-House: Opprobrious term for a low-grade public drinking establishment whose sole interest is selling liquor for immediate consumption. An inferior inn, tavern or hotel. An ale-house.

Pot Knight: One who has been made bold by liquor.

Potman: A publican's assistant.

Pot-Pal: Drinking companion.

Pot-Still: See Still, Pot.

Pottle: A wine measure. As so frequently happens, America has retained the obsolete English pottle of 3·33 imperial pints, though since 1826 the English pottle has been 4 imperial pints.

Pot Valour: Archaic name for the courage of a man who has emptied numerous pots of liquor. Hence also 'pot valiant' for drunk and boastful. See also Pot Knight.

Pouget: French (Médoc) red wine.

Pougets, Les: French (Cote-d'Or) red burgundy.

Pouilly: A Burgundian commune adjoining Fuissé where good white table wine is grown and sold as Pouilly-Fuissé.

Pouilly-Fuissé: The French white wine from the twin Burgundian communes of those names. There are various picturesque legends surrounding this wine, which may account for its popularity as an export item.

Pouilly-Fumé: French white table wine from Loire. The origin of the name ('smoky') is obscure as it has no such flavour. Like many other French wines, it is claimed to have a flavour of truffles.

Pouilly-sur-Loire: The central French town which is the focus of a large trade in the local dry white wines. Wine bearing only this name on the label is sound but undistinguished, is made from the sauvignon blanc grape (also termed blanc-fumé locally) and bears the name Pouilly-Fumé (q.v.) or Sancerre. There is no connection with the Pouilly-Fuissé (q.v.) of Burgundy.

Poujeaux: French (Médoc) red wine.

Poujeaux-Marly: French (Médoc) red wine.

Poulaillères: French (Côte-d'Or) red wine.

Poulsard: Species of grape vine grown in the Juras at Arbois from which an esteemed local red is made. Said to be indigenous.

Pourriture Noble: French for 'noble rot' and synonymous with the German *Edelfäule*. It is the result of the greyish mould, *Botrytis cinerea*, growing on ripe grapes. This is an astonishing fungus, quite common in temperate, moist European climates. When, for example, it occurs on most soft fruits it is accounted an agricultural enemy. However, in parts of France and Germany, especially the Rhineland and those parts of the Bordeaux that produce sweet wines, *Botrytis* is not merely a friend but an essential partner in wine-making. Its filaments can penetrate the soft skin of ripe grapes, thus allowing water to evaporate and the juice to concentrate and rise in sugar. At the same time complex and subtle changes occur in the composition of the juice, especially by the removal (consumption) of part of the potassium. From the exceedingly rich juice of such grapes are made regal sweet unfortified table wines such as sauternes, barsac and the sweet Rhine beverages. The essential feature of manufacture is that these musts (q.v.) may contain 50% or more of sugar. The yeast can ferment only about 30% and thus 20% or more of sugar remains in the wine. *Botrytis* cannot flourish in the hot dry climates of Spain, California, Australia and South Africa, hence it is not possible for these countries to produce true wines of the sauternes type. These *Botrytis*-produced wines always contain a considerable amount of glycerine.

Pousse: The 'pushing' disease of wine, so called because the carbon dioxide gas generated may force corks and bungs. Also called tourne. The disease is the result of using mildewed grapes.

Pousse-Café: A term of varied meaning. The commonest is a glass of liqueurs of different colours, carefully added so that the layers remain unmixed in the vessel. There are even practitioners in the art of mixing who contend that the number of rings must always be odd, 3 to 7.

It can also mean a glass of a single liqueur taken with the coffee at the end of a meal.

Pousse-l'Amour: A layered drink. Pour cherry brandy (liqueur), then whole fresh egg yolk, finally any other liqueur. See also Pousse-Café.

Pousse d'Or: French (Côte-d'Or) red wine.

Power: Noted Irish (Dublin) whiskey, founded 1791.

Power Drury: Old-established shippers of madeira (q.v.).

Poysdorfer: Austrian white table wine.

Pöytävüna: Finnish spirit of whisky type.

Prairie Oyster: Supposed pick-me-up or restorative made by breaking a raw egg into a glass of dry red wine and drinking without mixing.

Prälat: German (Erden, q.v.) white wine.

Pramnian: A wine praised by Homer, and evidently esteemed in ancient Greece.

Preignac: French parish of the Bordeaux producing sauternes (q.v.).

Prémeaux: French (Burgundy) wine centre. The town is near Nuits (Côte-d'Or) and the wines are usually named Nuits-St. Georges-Prémeaux.

Prensa: See Mosto de Yema.

Pressburg: Czechoslovakian red and white wine centre also known as Bratislava. The chief vineyards are Andreich, Füchsel, Honehei and Goldfuss.

Preuses: French (Chablis) white wine. See also Chablis Grand Cru.

Priban: French (Médoc) red wine.

Pricked Wine: Wine soured by acetification (q.v.).

Prieur: Champagne of Vertus.

Prieuré, Le: French (Médoc) red wine whose name originates in the fact that the vines were planted centuries ago by the Priors of Cantenac.

Prieuré-Lichine: French (Médoc) red wine. Previously called Prieuré. The name Prieuré is borne by a number of wine estates of the Bordeaux.

Priming: The process of adding an additional small quantity of sugary material to already fermented liquor to set up a further fermentation. This is sometimes done with beer and is standard procedure in making sparkling wines.

Priming House: Section of the brewery where the sugar is dissolved prior to adding to the fermented beer or stout. See also Priming.

Princeton: Cocktail of gin, port wine and orange bitters.

Priorato: Spanish dry red wine from Tarragona.

Prisage: The former 'right' of English kings to make a levy in kind on any shipment of wine entering the country.

Probstberg: German (Longuich, q.v.) white wine vineyard.

Probstei: German (Niedersaulheim, q.v.) white wine.

Probus: The Roman emperor of hallowed memory who, in A.D. 280, ordered vines to be planted in Champagne in the Marne Valley and also told his legionaries generally to spread the culture of the vine.

Prohibition: In the sense of this book, prohibition is the legal system which totally forbids the use of alcohol as a beverage. All such systems and attempts have failed in the past and are likely to fail in the future owing to the fact, readily observed by the citizenry, that the supposed evil effects of alcohol do not manifest themselves under moderate usage. In other words, the movement, law or policy lacks public support.

The most celebrated attempt to enforce prohibition was, of course, the Volstead Act passed by the U.S. Congress in 1919. This was repealed in 1933 after nearly fifteen years of unparalleled crime, bloodshed and official corruption.

India and some other Asiatic and Moslem countries have a nominal prohibition in force but the provisions of the law seem to be readily surmountable.

Since the American repeal, there has been no further serious effort to introduce prohibition in any country of western civilization though Canada and Scandinavia have passed restrictive legislation, apparently with varying success.

Proof and Proof Spirit: The complicated and archaic system of expressing the alcoholic content of beverages in the British Commonwealth. The term (but based on a simpler system) is also used in the U.S.A.

Before the 19th century accurate chemical or physical methods for calculating alcoholic strength were not available and rough and ready tests were employed. In particular a mixture of alcohol and water which would just burn or allow gunpowder to explode after wetting, was taken as standard. This was called 'proof' spirit. The test was supposed to constitute 'proof' that the mixture contained a minimum percentage of alcohol. With the advance of analytical chemistry, greater precision became possible. In England a statute of George III defines proof spirit as that which, at 51° F., weighs exactly 12/13ths of an equal measure of distilled water. This is equal, for all practical purposes, to 57·10% of alcohol by volume or 49·28% by weight. Stronger and weaker spirits are described as over and under proof respectively (O.P. and U.P.). Thus pure (absolute) alcohol is 75·35 O.P.

To convert the percentage of alcohol by volume to percentage of proof spirit, multiply by 1·7535.

To ascertain the proof strength of spirits, Sikes's hydrometer has been made official in the U.K. and adopted generally in the Commonwealth. See also Hydrometer.

In the U.S.A. mixtures of alcohol and water and the alcoholic content of beverages are still expressed in terms of proof spirit but the system is much simpler and more rational. American proof spirit contains equal volumes of alcohol and water, i.e. a beverage of proof strength contains 50% of alcohol by volume. Thus 90 proof whisky is 45% alcohol by volume.

Proof Gallon: A gallon of proof spirit. It is customary in the excise of the English-speaking world to collect revenue in terms of proof gallons, but the system is long overdue for replacement by a more rational scale. See also Proof.

Proppenstein: German (Dürkheim, q.v.) white wine.

Prosecco: Italian (Venetian) sweet white wine. Also a liqueur (q.v.).

Provence: This French region produces a large volume of pleasant but hardly choice wines of various types — red, white, *rosé* and dessert. The best are separately noted.

Pruliers, Les: French (Nuits-Saint-Georges, q.v.) red burgundy.

Pruna: French spirit distilled from plums. See also Slivovitz.

Prunella: Pale green plum liqueur.

Prunelle: French liqueur of sloe flavour.

Prunet: Old liqueur made by soaking wild plums in spirit, said to be similar in flavour to sloe gin (q.v.). Also 'prunet cup', a vessel to serve the same.

Prunier: Old-established brand of cognac (q.v.).

Prussia: The vineyards owned by the State of Prussia are the largest in the Rheingau (q.v.) and are rigorously maintained as models.

P's and Q's: These initials headed the columns of 18th-century tavern account books to indicate the number of pints and quarts debited. Hence — 'Mind your P's and Q's' — Do not forget to enter up the debts.

Ptyalin: The enzyme of human saliva that converts starch into sugar. See also Moco and Kava.

Pub: An affectionate diminutive for the most democratic of all British institutions, the public house. An establishment licensed to sell beer and alcoholic liquors for consumption on or off the premises. A social centre which is frequently the meeting place of local sports clubs and associations. A native product which is unexportable.

Pub-Crawling: British slang for a series of visits to licensed premises.

Pubgoer, Pubman: One who knows the value of the public house.

Puerto de Santa Maria: Once the chief sherry port at the mouth of the River Guadalete and still a main centre for *bodegas* (q.v.).

Puerto Rico: West Indian island, now an American possession. Despite small size it ranks second in world production of rum. The spirit is deliberately made light in flavour by adopting rapid fermentation, and the rum is therefore popular in the U.S. as an ingredient of cocktails and other mixed drinks.

Pulchen: German (Filzen, q.v.) white wine.

Puligny-Montrachet: The French commune of the Côte-d'Or (Burgundy) that is credited with producing the finest dry white wine of the whole country, Montrachet. Le Montrachet is the most celebrated vineyard but there are numerous others separately noted.

Pulque: The national light alcoholic beverage of Mexico made from the sweet agave or century plant, which stands in the same relation to Mexico as does the vine to Spain and barley to England. It has an alcohol content intermediate between beer and wine. The agave is a cactus.

    The corresponding spirits (q.v.) of pulque are mezcal and tequila (q.v.).

Pulque Curado: Mixed drink made by sweetening pulque (q.v.) and adding pineapple.

Punch: Any mixed alcoholic drink containing fruit juice (usually hot and spiced). The word is of uncertain derivation. Some authorities hold that it comes from the Hindu or Persian word *panch* for five (denoting the number of ingredients) while others derive it from 'puncheon' (q.v.). But be the derivation what it may it is true, alas, that the brewing of punch is a rarity in these hurried times.

    There are hundreds of recipes for punch, some of which are separately listed. Almost all punches contain lemon juice and sugar in addition to the other ingredients. For example:

Ale: Ale, sherry, brandy, spices.

Fish House: Rum, brandy, peach brandy.

Loganberry: Orange, pekoe tea, salt, loganberry juice, ginger ale, mint. (This curious, indeed outrageous, recipe makes no mention of spirits, the very *fons et origo* of a punch. Presumably brandy, rum, whisky or s.v.r. will withstand salt, tea and the rest.)

Milk Punch: Milk, brandy, rum.

Mississippi: Brandy, whisky, rum.

Old Melford: Rum, brandy, claret, tea, orange, pineapple. Add champagne!

Peabody: Rum, cognac, madeira, guava jelly, tea, limes.

Roman: Whisky, champagne, orange, lemons, egg whites. (Surely a studied insult to the refined Roman gastronomy.)

Royal: Green tea, brandy, rum, white curaçao, arrack, limes, calve's foot jelly. (A mess! Calve's foot jelly has long ago been debunked as a restorative.)

Puncheon: Large cask, capacity variable. However, the word is still used as a measure of volume. The English wine puncheon was formerly 84 wine or 70 imperial gallons. In earlier times a beer puncheon was 2 barrels each of 36 gallons. Now usually around 100 gallons. Used largely in the West Indies for rum, lime juice, etc.

Punching: The process of breaking up the cap (q.v.) of actively fermenting wine or other liquid so that it is kept immersed and also so that the carbon dioxide gas can escape.

Punch-House: Old Indian term for inn or boarding house for seamen.

Punderich: German (Lower Moselle, Zell) white wine.

Punt: The mound or well (according to which end one looks at) of a bottle, designed to give extra strength and to help collect sediment. The punt is an essential for bottles to hold sparkling wines and distinctly useful for others.

Pupillin: French (Jura) white wine centre which produces wine similar to Arbois (q.v.).

Pupitres: The 'pulpits' or special tables used in champagne manufacture. They are the wooden structures on which the bottles are stored during processing.

Purl: Old name of ale or beer to which has been added wormwood (q.v.). Also hot beer laced with gin (and perhaps sugar and spices), formerly popular as a morning draught, also known as 'dog's nose' (q.v.). It was matured for about a year. Purl was much in vogue up to the end of the 17th century.

Pussyfoot: A synonym for a prohibitionist, much used in the twenties when Tom E. Johnson, an American teetotaller nicknamed Pussyfoot, was active.

Puttonyo: See Butto.

Puyblanquet: French (St. Émilion) red wine.

Puzzle Jug: Form of practical joke popular in England until about a hundred years ago. Puzzle jugs were made in a variety of shapes and were usually presented to the newcomer to an inn. Many had concealed holes which spilled beer over various parts of the drinker's body. In some ways, civilization has advanced.

P.X.: The Spanish winery name for the wine made from Pedro Ximénèz grape and used for sweetening some types of sherry. See also Paxarete.

Pyrmont Water: German naturally sparkling (gaseous) medicinal water, much esteemed and very expensive in England in the 18th century.

Qarabas: Persian (Iranic) large ceramic jars used for wine storage. The name is probably the origin of 'carboy' (q.v.). See also Amphora.

Quaff: To drink in large draughts or to drink from a quaich (q.v.) or cup.

Quaich: Scottish drinking-vessel of varying size of characteristic bowl-shape with double handles, often made of silver, richly engraved. See also Quaff.

Quai des Chartrons: The row of buildings on the Bordeaux waterfront where most of the powerful and renowned wine merchants have their cellars and offices. To the wine-lover it is an almost hallowed place.

Quarles Harris: Old-established (1680) shippers of port (q.v.).

Quart: Measure of capacity. The British imperial quart, one-quarter of a gallon, contains 40 fl. oz.; the reputed quart is one-sixth of a gallon or $26\frac{2}{3}$ fl. oz. The U.S. quart, one-quarter of a U.S. gallon, is approximately five-sixths the volume of an imperial quart.

Quart de Chaume: A distinctive French white wine from Rochefort-sur-Loire, noted for bouquet and strength.

Quarter-Cask: A medium-sized cask, so named as the quarter of a pipe. However, the vessel known as a 'quarter-cask' may vary in capacity from 25 to 35 imperial gallons.

Quarter Deck: Cocktail of rum, dry sherry and lime juice.

Quartering: A term used in coopering to describe the part of the cask between the chime (q.v.) and the bouge (q.v.). The quarter hoop is placed midway between the chime and the bouge.

   Also a term for one method of sawing timber suitable for use as cask staves (q.v.). This method tends to waste some of the timber as only a small proportion can be used for staves.

Quartern: A liquor measure, lit. 'one-quarter' but conventionally $5\frac{1}{3}$ to a standard British bottle.

Quas: The home-brew of the Aleutian Islands, also known as piva (q.v.). The name is clearly derived from the kwass (q.v.) of the Russians.

Queen Elizabeth: Cocktail of gin, cointreau and absinthe.

Queen's College, Oxford: The oldest brewery in the British Isles.

Queensland: Centre for rum production of good quality.

Quelle: White wine from Palatinate (q.v.).

Quelle Vie: Cocktail of brandy, kümmel, or absinthe.

Quelltaler: Australian (Waterdale, S.A.) white wine of hock character, one of the esteemed domestic estate wines.

Quema: The Spanish term for the defective acid wine destined to be converted to vinegar.

Quetsch: Alsatian or other plum brandy.

Quick-Ageing: This is a contradiction in terms but the meaning will be obvious — the acceleration of the maturing of alcoholic beverages. For many years technologists have laboured to reduce the years needed to mellow and improve wines, spirits and other alcoholic beverages. Understandably, if any success has been achieved the process is kept secret at all cost. Heat incubation, electric discharge, ozonation, alternate heating and freezing and numerous other processes and devices are said to be used or to have been tried. Whether any process is effective is doubtful for it is still common for less scrupulous merchants to fake the age of brandy by adding vanilla, the age of whisky by adding oak extract and so forth.

Quick One: A quick one.

Quinas: French term for the various proprietary apéritif wines which have a slightly bitter taste due to the presence of a little quinine.

Quincié: Red wine of Beaujolais, France.

Quincy: Wine region of the Loire.

Quincy Fumé: French (Berry) white wine. Still another of the allegedly 'smoky' wines of France. The reason for the name is unknown.

Quinine Wine: Sweet fortified wine to which is added a little quinine and perhaps other 'botanicals' to give a bitter taste. Their brands are legion, e.g., Quinquina (French). See also Quinas.

Quinsac: French wine centre of the Gironde. Also a château wine (red and white) of the same place.

Quinta de Agueira: Portuguese dry white wine.

Quintas: Portuguese port wine-growing estates along the Douro, many of which are of great extent and age. Some of the famous quintas are Ferreira's Quinta do Vesuvio, the Quinta Roriz, Cockburn's Quinta do Tua, Graham's Quinta dos Malvedos, Silva and Cosen's Quintas Zimbro, Bomfim-Offley's Boa Vista, Feuerheerd's La Rosa, and Da Silva's Quinta do Noval. Note the many English names.

A *quinta* is the close equivalent of a French *château* (q.v.).

Quintigny: French (Jura) white wine.

Rabaud-Promis: French highly esteemed (first-growth) sauternes (q.v.), sweet white wine of Bommes.

Rabbit: Obsolete name for a wooden drinking-vessel.

Rablay: French (Anjou) white wine.

Rabo de Ovelho: Portuguese grape grown for white port (q.v.).

Raboso: Italian (Veneto) red wine.

Race: French wine term for high-grade.

Racimo: Spanish for bunch of grapes.

Rack: To fill a cask or container with beer in a brewery, hence 'racking cock, racking machine'. The term is also used for bulk wines.

However, the commonest use of the word is to draw off wine to clear it from dregs or lees, hence 'racked wine'. 'Racked beer' is beer which has been fined (see Finings) in bulk in the brewery and then racked into casks for distribution and immediate consumption.

Racky or Raky: Austrian plum brandy of type of slivovitz (q.v.). Derived from rakia (q.v.).

Racquet Club: Cocktail of gin, dry vermouth and orange bitters.

Radda: Chianti (q.v.) from Tuscany.

Radein: German (Müden, q.v.) white wine.

Radgona: Yugoslavian wine area.

Raicilla: Mexican strong cactus spirit distilled from the maguey plant and reported to contain 90% alcohol by volume.

Rainwater (Madeira): This was originally a term applied to a light, dry madeira clarified in a special way but is now merely a commercial trademark of one firm.

Raise: A term used in coopering to describe setting up cask staves into a chime (q.v.) hoop in readiness for trussing (q.v.). An ash hoop is placed over the bouge (q.v.) as a measure to ensure that the cask will ultimately hold the correct amount of beer.

Raisin Wine: Wine made, especially in non-vine-growing countries, by fermenting imported raisins. See also Seder Wine.

Rajah: Cocktail of champagne laced with brandy.

Raki: Balkan spirit. The name is apparently general for spirit from any source — wine, orchard fruits, grain or potatoes. It is usually very fiery (too strong).

Rakia: Yugoslavian brandy, the common spirit of the country.

Rambaud: This name is borne by a number of Bordeaux red wines.

Ramos Fizz: Mixed drink of gin, lemon, cream, egg white and orange flower water.

Rancio: The flavour in sweet dessert wines induced by 'baking' (q.v.), extensively used in California, but also to some extent in Madeira, Marsala, Malaga and elsewhere. The word is also used for wine with a defective flavour of old age and of the woody taste of very old cognac brandies. Obviously a word of usage so wide has little real utility and should be abandoned, especially as it means 'rancid' in its native Spanish.

Randersacker: German Steinwein (q.v.) district in Franconia on River Main. Amongst the best vineyards are Spielberg, Marsbert, Teufelskeller, Lämmerberg and Pfülben.

Randersacker Lämmerberg: German Steinwein vineyard near Würzburg (q.v.).

Rangen: Ancient Alsatian vineyard near Thaun. Fine table wine.

Ranina: Yugoslavian (Radgona) dessert wine. Syn. 'Tiger's Milk'.

Rappis: An Elizabethan cordial or apéritif wine whose recipe called for, *inter alia*, cinnamon and cloves.

Rasade: French term for a brim-full glass, especially of wine. A bumper.

Rasaki: Turkish white table grape widely grown in Australia and known both as Malaga and Waltham Cross.

Rasch: The oldest German writer on wine, about 1582.

Rasteau: Wine centre near Roussillon for *vins doux naturels* (q.v.).

Ratafia: Any liqueur made with a fruit or fruit kernel base. The process is simple, usually consisting in adding fruit juice, etc., and sugar to brandy, filtering after a lapse of time, and storing to mature. Ratafias are readily made at home. The origin of the name is unknown.

Ratsch: Austrian (Steiermark) white wine.

Rauchloch: German (Hochheim, q.v.) white wine.

Rauenthal: German (Rheingau) district producing some of the finest hocks of the country. Amongst the best vineyards are Berg, Baiken, Wieshell, Rotheberg, Langenstück, Gehren, Pfaffenberg, Maasborn, Wulfen, Siebenmorgen, Steinhausen, Burggrafen and Kesselring.

Rauler: German (Oberemmel, q.v.) white wine.

Rausan-Ségla: French (Médoc) red wine. This is one of the oldest châteaux of the Médoc whose wine has been esteemed for hundreds of years. Now owned by a Bordeaux wine merchant.

Rausch: German white wine vineyard at Saarburg.

Rauschbier: German (esp. Franconian) smoked beer made by fermenting malt which has been exposed on shallow trays to smoke.

Rauscher: German sparkling cider, especially from Frankfurt area.

Rauzan: French (Médoc) red wine.

Rauzan-Gassies: French (Médoc) red wine. It is even older than Rausan-Ségla (q.v.) and equally esteemed.

Raya: The mark made by the Spanish sherry expert on the butt of wine after the first racking, to indicate the general group of quality. This is the third lowest classification of Spanish wine whose ultimate destination is uncertain. See also Sherry.

Raymond-Lafon: French (Sauternes) sweet white wine.

Raynal: Old-established (1840) brand of cognac (q.v.).

Rayne-Vigneau: First-growth sauternes (Bommes). See also Sauternes.

Ream: An English provincial word for cream or froth. As a verb, applied to beer, it means to froth or foam.

Rebèche: The final pressing of champagne grapes, made into *vin ordinaire* (q.v.).

Rech: German (Ahr) red wine.

Rechweg: German (Ockenheim, q.v.) white wine.

Recioto: A special sweetish Valpolicella (q.v.) wine made from partly dried grapes. It has something of the character of sauternes (q.v.). Also sweetish deep red still and sparkling wines from Veneto.

Récolte: French for vintage. Practically synonymous with 'vendange'.

Recoulles, Les: French (Hermitage, q.v.) white wine.

Rectified Spirit: Alcohol of a comparatively high degree of purity except for the presence of up to 10% by volume of water. 'Rectification' is the process of purifying any volatile liquor by fractional distillation. The term 'rectified spirit' is not a precise one. It is sometimes applied to the final product of a patent still (q.v.), which contains about 94% of alcohol free from odorous materials. The official rectified spirit of the British Pharmacopoeia contains 90% of alcohol. Sometimes the term 'white spirit' is used in commerce as a synonym for rectified spirit, but this is undesirable, as the term is also commonly applied to a petroleum fraction. See also Vodka and Spirit.

Rectifier: In the distillation of alcohol, the second column of a patent still, which further purifies and concentrates the spirit after it leaves the column known as the 'analyser'.

Redcliffe: Australian (W.A.) wine centre.

Redox System: A brewing process whereby conditioning, chilling and cold storage is carried out in a single vessel.

Red Rowanberry Vodka: In *Doctor Zhivago*, Pasternak writes of frosted bottles of this on the ballroom supper table splendidly set for a feast. Not all vodka is unflavoured diluted alcohol. These flavoured vodkas are technically gins (q.v.).

Refosco: Mediocre Italian red wine grape. In California called 'Crabb's Black Burgundy'.

Refosco: Italian sparkling red wine from Trieste region.

Regauge: The exciseman's term for the reduced volume of spirits in a cask, by reason of evaporation.

Regnié: Red wine of Beaujolais, France.

Regua: Port wine district of Alto Douro.

Regular: A customer who is a regular visitor to a licensed establishment. He may have special privileges.

Rehbach: German (Nierstein, q.v.) white wine.

Rehgasse: German (Nierstein, q.v.) white wine.

Rehoboam: An outsized wine-bottle for show purposes, larger again than jeroboam (q.v.) and holding six reputed quarts or about a gallon.

Reil: German (Moselle) white wine centre, including the vineyards of Goldlay, Mullayhofberg, Falklay, Weingrube, Heisenstein.

Reims or Rheims: The picturesque French city that is the heart and centre of the champagne industry, both for production and sales. With its vast underground galleries and ancient buildings, it is a focus for the wine-lovers of the world.

Reinhartshausen: Celebrated German (Rheingau) vineyard for hock, owned by Prussian ex-royalty.

Reisbranntwein: German spirit made from fermented rice, thus essentially a type of whisky.

Reisekahr: German (Oppenheim, q.v.) white wine.

Reiterpfad: German (Königsbach, q.v.) white wine.

Reiterpfad: German (Ruppertsberg, q.v.) white wine.

Remicher: Dry white wine from Luxembourg.

Remitente: Spanish for shipper (q.v.).

Remueur: The craftsman who daily twists and slightly shakes the bottles containing champagne in the making. An important functionary. After weeks of work the bottles are upside down and the sediment rests on the cork ready to be disgorged. The process is termed *remuage*. See also Champagne.

Rémusat: Old-established brand of cognac (q.v.).

Renmark: Australian (S.A.) wine centre.

Resin: Greek and other wines stored in pine casks acquire a resinous flavour. In some cases resin is actually added. See also Retsina.

Resins, Hop: Constituents of the hop flower mainly responsible for the pre-servative action, also for the bitter flavour in beer.

Resolute: Cocktail of gin, apricot cordial and lemon juice.

Respide: French (Langon) sweet table wine of sauternes type. Another estate of similar name makes dry red and white wines.

T

Retsina: Resin-flavoured wine of Greece. A quaint taste that can be acquired. See also Resin.

Retz: Austrian wine centre.

Reuilly: Wine region of the Loire.

Reversées, Les: French red wine of Beaune (q.v.).

Rex Convivii: The Roman 'King of the Feast', chosen by casting dice to take charge of a drinking bout. The *Arbiter bibendi* had broadly similar duties.

Reynella: Venerable (1838) South Australian vineyard. Good dry reds and sherries.

Rheingau or **Rhinegau:** German district on right bank of the Rhine, generally accepted as the producer of the finest white wines (hocks). The principal areas are Assmannshausen, Lorch, Lorchhausen, Rüdesheim, Eibingen, Geisenheim, Johannisberg, Winkel, Mittelheim, Östreich, Hallgarten, Hattenheim, Kiedrich, Erbach-Eltville, Rauenthal, Ober-und-Nieder Walluf, Wiesbaden and Hochheim. See also Hock. These names will bring a sparkle to the eye of any lover of Rhenish wines, which many furiously insist are the finest in the world, without qualification.

The grape chiefly used is the riesling, with about a quarter sylvaner. A hybrid of the two is named Müller-Thurgau, from the breeders' names. A limited amount of fine red wine is also made.

Rheinhartshausen: German (Rheingau) vineyard. Fine hock.

Rheinhell: German (Erbach, q.v.) white-wine vineyard.

Rheinhessen: German wine-growing district on the Rhine, nearly opposite the Rheingau (q.v.). The quality is generally very high. The chief centres are Alzen, Bingen, Mainz, Oppenheim and Worms. The many more important Rheinhessen estates are separately noted.

Rheinpflicht: German wine estate of Winkel, Rheingau.

Rheintal: German (Nackenheim, q.v.) white wine.

Rhenish: The obsolete English name for the wines of the Rhine, especially the whites, which was used until the 18th century, when they commenced to be called hocks (q.v.). One could wish for the return of this good, expressive place-name. See also Rhine Wines.

Rhenish Wine: See Ascham, Roger, for typical Elizabethan opinion.

Rhin: An esteemed Chilean wine.

Rhine Riesling: Australian name for the true riesling vine of Germany as distinct from the so-called Hunter riesling, which is really the sémillon (q.v.).

Rhine Wines: Wine has been grown on the banks of the Rhine for 2,000 years. Somebody (of course an Englishman) has said that there are only two growers of superb white wines and Germany is both of them! There are vineyards on the Rhine from Switzerland, where the river rises, down to Koblenz. It is generally stated that the finest wines are grown in the Rheingau on the right side of the river from Rüdesheim to Wiesbaden, and also on the opposite bank in Rheinhessen.

Rhine wine is the general term for the produce of the valley of the River Rhine and adjacent areas. These are mainly white and red table wines, though sparkling and dessert wines are also produced. Climate is uncertain and suitable soil is limited, hence production is comparatively small. Some connoisseurs hold that the finest German Rhine dry white wines (commonly known as hock, q.v.) are the pinnacle of the wine-maker's art. The Rhine vineyards are smaller than those of other countries. There are perhaps over 50,000 peasant farmers or others growing vines as a sideline whose production is from 1 to 3 acres and these are organized into co-operative wineries which turn the grapes into wine. As in other countries the great bulk of German wine is for local early consumption, the equivalent of the French *vin ordinaire* (q.v.). Hundreds of the best German estate wines are separately noted alphabetically.

The white wine production of the German Rhine is characteristic. For the hocks (q.v.) the grapes are the riesling and sylvaner, with the former predominating for the finer wines. A cross called 'Müller-Thurgau' is also used. For some perfumed wines, the traminer grape is used. In unpropitious years the German law allows sugar to be added to the otherwise unduly acid must. This is prohibited in other wine-growing countries and it undoubtedly results in a poorer wine. However, it is useless to sidestep the fact that without the addition of sugar to some Rhine musts, they simply could not be turned into drinkable wines.

The labelling of Rhine wines is very full and characteristic. See also Labels, German Wine.

Rhodes: Island of the Greek archipelago that has been noted for wine for three thousand years or more.

Rhodian: Roman wine of antiquity.

Rhône: This splendid river of France has vineyards on almost the whole length of its banks. It actually rises within a few miles of the Rhine but there the comparison ends. The Rhône wines cannot compare with Rhenish. Nevertheless some of the Rhône wines are of great merit. The best are generally accepted as coming from between Lyons and Avignon. Here are the Côte Rôtie, Hermitage and Châteauneuf-du-Pape (all q.v.). Many of the wines are sold under the general name Côtes-du-Rhône.

Rhubarb Wine: See Country Wines.

Rhymney: Australian white table wine from Victorian hamlet of that name.

Ribeauville: Good white wine from Alsace.

Ribera: Spanish heavy red table wine from Galicia.

Ricaud: French (Entre-Deux-Mers) white wine.

Riceys: French (Aube) wine centre.

Richebourg: One of the most celebrated red wines of France and hence of the world. It is a small vineyard — a mere 12 acres, of Vosne-Romanée (Côte de Nuits, q.v.), Burgundy. Small though it be, it is divided among several owners.

Richelieu: This French duke, who lived to 92, was a lover of red bordeaux, especially Château Haut-Brion (q.v.). He said of it: 'If drinking were forbidden, would God have made this wine so good?' Even to free-thinkers this should be sound reasoning.

Rickey: American mixed drink of variable composition. Usually it is similar to a Collins (q.v.) but without sweetening. It is thus rum or other spirit served with lemon or lime and ice in a tall glass.

Riegel: German (Baden) white wine.

Riesling: The white grape responsible for the finest dry wines of Germany, Austria, Hungary, Alsace and a number of other countries. It is claimed by the Germans as *their* grape and they contend with some vigour that it does not produce the best results grown away from the Rhine. Be the fact what it may, the riesling is the basis of delightful white wines in cool climates in Australia, South Africa and elsewhere.

It closely resembles the pinot blanc grape (q.v.) but is definitely distinct. It is commendable that so many makers now use riesling as a wine name for this has none of the geographical dishonesty of such names as chablis for a wine made outside France. Under the name Hunter Riesling another grape is the foundation of some of the best Australian dry white wines. The so-called riesling grape grown on the Upper Murray region of Australia is actually the sémillon (q.v.) of the graves and sauternes regions of France. There are, however, a few acres of true Rhine riesling in the area, brought from the Rheingau in 1838. In Switzerland this grape is known as Johannisberg.

No country outside Germany is able to produce the syrupy wines from late-picked riesling grapes (see Edelfäule) but the table wines sold under the varietal name have much in common with sound moselle.

Riesling, Hunter River: See Hunter River Riesling.

Rieussec, Ch.: French (Sauternes) sweet white wine.

Rigailhou: French (Graves) red and white wines.

Rilly-la-Montagne: French (Champagne) white wine.

Rince-Cochon: 'Pig swill', the French nickname for chilled white wine with a dash of cassis (q.v.). It does have a dim colour!

Rincette: The French (Normandy) term for 'just another glass' of spirits.

Ringelzell: German (Ockenheim, q.v.) white wine.

Rio Grande do Sul: The Brazilian wine region which produces more than three-quarters of the national output but the quality is not high.

Rioja: Spanish table wines, red and white, from the north (Navarre). They are delightful wines, clean and delicate, some put up in slender bottles covered with a fine wire network. The Rioja wines have been renowned for five hundred years. They are perhaps the fine flower of Spanish light wines and reasonably priced.

Rioja, La: Argentine wine district.

Rion: Russian viticultural centre in Georgia.

Rio Negro: Argentine wine district. Moderate quality.

Rions: French commune on the River Garonne south of Bordeaux where much pleasant but not fine wine is grown.

Ripeau: French (Graves) red wine.

Rippchen: German white wine of Coenen (q.v.).

Riquewihr: French (Alsatian) white wine centre. The chief vineyard is Clos du Moulin.

Rittergut Bangert: German (Kreuznach, q.v.) white wine estate.

Riva, Anto de la: Old-established shippers of sherry (q.v.).

Rivero, J. M.: Old-established shippers of sherry (q.v.). The firm absorbed Cabeza y Zarco, which was founded in 1650.

Rivesaltes: French wine centre around the town on the foothills of the Pyrénées, near the Mediterranean. The wine production is almost entirely a sweet white dessert. This has become popular throughout France (like Roussillon, q.v.) for drinking as an apéritif. This lays still another British myth that wine-drinkers despise sweet apéritifs.

Rjabinowka: Russian flavoured spirit, one of the many variations of vodka (q.v.).

Roadster: Cocktail of gin and orange liqueur.

Robertson: South African wine-producing area.

Robertson Bros.: Established (1847) shippers of port (q.v.).

Robin: Old-established brand of cognac (q.v.).

Rob Roy: Cocktail of Scotch whisky, sweet vermouth, bitters.

Rocca: One of the innumerable European proprietary apéritifs of the vermouth type, in this case Italian and bitter-sweet.

Roche-aux-Moines, La: French (Anjou) white wine.

Rochecorbon: French (Touraine) red and white wines.

Rochefort-sur-Loire: French (Anjou) white wine.

Rochelle: The medieval name for the wines of Poitou, from the port from which they were shipped to England. The name survives in Rochelle Salt (sodium potassium tartrate, $NaKC_4H_4O_6$), derived, of course, from wine. See also Argol.

Rochemorin: French (Graves) red wine.

Rochet: French (Médoc) red wine.

Rochusberg: German (Bingen, q.v.) white wine.

Rochusweg: German (Bingen, q.v.) white wine.

Rock and Rye: A species of American liqueur made from rye whiskey and containing large sugar crystals (rock candy).

Rocks, on the: American term for a beverage, especially spirits, poured over much ice contained in a substantial glass.

Rödelsee: German (Franconian) white wine.

Roederer: Old-established champagne of Reims.

Roffignac: Old-established brand of cognac (q.v.).

Rohfäule: The German term for 'acid rot', the defect that develops in grapes grown in northern areas when the summer is cut short prematurely.

Rohr: German (Nierstein, q.v.) white wine.

Roma: Australian (Queensland) wine centre.

Romanèche-Thorins: French fine red wine (burgundy) of Beaujolais.

Romania: Most people will be surprised to learn how high up on the world list of wine production is Romania. This, of course, applies to quantity, though under modern technology there are now some excellent wines of all types. Some of the better-known wines are separately listed. Development and change are rapid.

Romanée-Conti: A French tiny (4-acre) vineyard situated in the commune of Vosne-Romanée, near Dijon, which many knowing ones confidently claim produces the finest of all red burgundies. Until 1946 the vines, having resisted *Phylloxera* (q.v.), had never been grafted. Naturally some of the diehards contend the wine is not now what it was but this is apparently mere prejudice. The name Romanée is borne by other equally and less distinguished red wine estates in the same locality. The simply-named La Romanée of 2 acres is equally famed as Romanée-Conti. Romanée la Tâche is another celebrated growth. The largest of the vineyards, Romanée-St. Vivant, is reputed to be just a little below the others.

Romer: French (Sauternes) sweet white wine.

Römer: Also Römerglas. Large German wine glass of characteristic shape.

Romney: Greek wine, mentioned by Holinshed (*Chronicles*) in Elizabethan period.

Rompope: Also Ronpope. Mexican mixed drink of sweetened rum, orange juice, cinnamon, cream and eggs.

Ron: Spanish for rum. Ron Carta, white rum, is pale and lightly flavoured. Ron Oro, golden rum, is of heavier colour and flavour.

Ronceret: French (Côte-d'Or) red wine.

Roob: A mash (q.v.) of juniper berries which was separately fermented in the original Dutch process of making gin.

Rooty Hill: Australian (N.S.W.) winery.

Roriz: One of the best port *quintas* (q.v.) of the Douro.

Rosa: Bulgarian liqueur flavoured with genuine attar of roses.

Rosala: South African (Stellenbosch) semi-sweet *rosé* wine.

Rosato, Vino: The rose-tinted wine of Italy. See also Chiaretto.

Rose: Cocktail of gin, kirsch and cherry brandy.

Rosé: The generic name for pink wines. Those of Tavel (q.v.) are the original and most celebrated. They are variously made. Originally the method was to remove the skins of red grapes before much colour has been extracted but some are now made by blending red and white wines. They are, of course, merely a fad and subject to the good-humoured contempt of serious oenophiles. Sometimes a touch of cochineal (q.v.) works wonders in a poor white. Pink champagne explains itself.

In France, *vin rosé* must be produced under recognized and legally controlled conditions. It is not made from a mixture of black and white grapes, and most definitely not from a tinted white wine. It is largely made from grenache grapes and is a pleasant, short-lived wine from which more should not be expected.

Rose Brandy: Oriental (especially Chinese) rectified rice spirit, flavoured with rose and lichee fruit extract.

Rose Hip Wine: Country wine (q.v.) flavoured with rose hips.

Rosemary: The familiar shrub whose leaves were used to flavour ale in the 16th and 17th centuries.

Rosemont: French (Médoc) red and white wines.

Rosenbeck: German (Niederhausen-Schlossböckelheim A.D. Nahe, q.v.) white wine.

Rosenberg: A name borne by many German vineyards, with inevitable confusion to all but experts in German wine labelling. There are Rosenbergs at Wiltingen (q.v.) Saar, Oberemmel, Palatinate, Rheinhessen, Klotten, Nierstein, Minheim, Lorchhausen, Osann and in the Wehlen district (q.v.) of Moselle. These are all white wine (hock, q.v.) estates.

Rosenbuckel: German (Freinsheim, q.v.) white wine.

Roseneck: German white Rhine wine from Rüdesheim, Rheingau.

Rosengarten: 'Rose Garden', the name of many German vineyards on the Rhine, including Neumagen and Ellsheim.

Rosenthal: German (Ahr) red wine estate.

Rose Petal Wine: Country wine (q.v.) flavoured with rose flowers.

Rose Wine: Classical spiced wine of Roman times, with rose flavour.

Rosolio: Greek sweet wine of golden hue from Samos. The name is also given to an Italian liqueur, originally made from mulberry juice.

Rossberg: German Steinwein vineyard near Würzburg (q.v.).

Rossesse: Red wine from Liguria, Italy.

Rossolis: Almost extinct home-made French liqueur of sweetened brandy flavoured with any available fruit.

Rosstal: German (Ostofen, q.v.) white wine.

Rosswiese: German white wine. See also Dienheim.

Rosteisen: German (Gau-Bischofsheim, q.v.) white wine.

Rostov: Russian centre for sparkling wine production.

Rota Tent: Also known as Tintilla de Rota. Rich, dark-red Spanish wine, widely used as altar wine. From Rot, near Cadiz. See also Tent.

Rotenberg: German (Mackenheim, q.v.) white wine.

Roterd: German (Dhron) white wine.

Rotgipfler: Austrian grape which, despite its name, is used for white wine.

Rot-Gut: A name vulgarly applied to an inferior liquor or one that is otherwise regarded as deleterious.

Rothberg: German (Ruwer, q.v.) white wine.

Rotheberg: German (Rauenthal, q.v.) white wine.

Rotkirch: German (Erden, q.v.) white wine.

Rotlay: German vineyard at Zeltingen on the Moselle.

Rottland: German (Rüdesheim, q.v.) fine white wine.

Rouges du Bas: French (Côte-d'Or) red wine.

Rough: The beer in the drip-cans, also overflows from draught beer or the residue from bottles. This is also called ullage (q.v.).

Roumieux: French (Sauternes) sweet white wine.

Round: An order for drinks for more than one person.

Rousing: The brewery term for agitation, either mechanically or by a stream of air. Also the process of vigorous stirring of wines and spirits to assist blending. A 'rouser' is a long-handled instrument, often in the form of a wooden stick, used to 'rouse' or stir the yeast and wort in the fermenting vessels (q.v.), thereby aerating the yeast and promoting maximum fermentation.

Roussette de Frangy: White French wine from Savoy.

Roussette de Seyssel: French (Bresse) white wine.

Roussette de Virien, La: French table white wine (Bresse).

Roussillon: An area in France near the Spanish border where fortified sweet wine is made, used as a substitute for port. Much Roussillon wine is now drunk in France as apéritifs. See also Rivesaltes. The name Roussillon is also borne by a Pomerol château producing claret.

Route du Vin, La: The road through Burgundy which traverses many celebrated wine centres. Of course Bordeaux, the German Rhine and many other regions would hotly dispute the validity of this name.

Rouyer: Old-established (1801) brand of cognac (q.v.).

Rowland Flat: Australian (S.A.) wine centre.

Roxheim: German (Nahe) white wine.

Rubin: Bulgarian dessert wine.

Ruby: The term applied to port (q.v.) bottled young whereby it retains its bright, rich hue.

Rüdesheim: German (Nahe) white wine estate. No connection with the wine centre of the Rheingau.

Rüdesheim: This is the most north-westerly town of the Rheingau (q.v.) proper. It is the rightful pride of Germany and the centre of production of some of the best hocks. The finest vineyards, terraced on the slopes of the river, are known under the general geographical name Rüdesheimer Berg. Amongst the best estates are Schlossberg, Engerweg, Burgweg, Roseneck, Bischofsberg, Bronnen, Zollhaus, Lay, Rottland, Mühlstein, Häuserweg, Hinterhaus and Klosterkiesel.

Rue: Perennial evergreen shrub whose bitter leaves are believed to have been used by the ancient Egyptians to flavour their beer.

Rueda: Spanish (Valladolid) red wine.

Rufina: Italian (Tuscany, Chianti) red wine.

Rug: An obsolete English term for a kind of strong liquor, apparently ale.

Rugiens-Bas et Hauts, Les: Group of French vineyards of Pommard (Côte-d'Or) producing fine red burgundy.

Ruhlander: White grape mainly grown in cool climates.

Ruinart: Old-established (1868) champagne of Reims.

Rully: French white burgundy centre of the Côte Chalonnaise.

Rum: Spirit (q.v.) made from sugar-cane. The origin of the name is doubtful. It was originally called 'Barbados waters' because possibly it was first made there. It was also called rumbustion, rumbo and rumbullion, any of which may be the genesis of the name. Another possibility is *saccharum*, Latin for sugar.

Rum is made wherever sugar cane is grown. The chief distilling centres are in the West Indies, the United States, Australia, South Africa, British Guiana, Madagascar and the East Indies. However, there are many more.

The source material of rum is the residues or the by-products of the sugar industry, especially molasses.

The technology of rum production varies greatly according to locality and the size of the distillery. Fermentation may be fast or slow, ranging from two to ten days. The stills may be old-fashioned simple pot-stills (q.v.) or modern patent stills (q.v.). The residue of a previous distillation, a thick yellowish paste called 'dunder', is often added to the new fermentation.

When freshly distilled, rum is colourless and a small amount is sold as such. However, in the process of long ageing in oak containers (up to ten years and occasionally twenty) colour is extracted. It is customary to add caramel (partly charred sugar) to produce the familiar brownish-red colour of rum.

The characteristic and pronounced flavour of rum is due to a comparatively high percentage of esters (q.v.), especially ethyl butyrate. It is, unfortunately, fairly simple to make a synthetic rum essence which can be used to produce an artificial rum ('Hamburg Rum').

Until recent times rum (together with gin) bore a low social reputation. It was accounted the tipple of sailors and was correspondingly reprobated. Fortunately better counsels have prevailed and rum is now respectable and increasingly prized as an ingredient of mixed drinks.

Amongst the important centres of distillation of rum are Cuba, Barbados, Jamaica, British Guiana, the New England area of the U.S., Hispaniola, Puerto Rico, Trinidad, Virgin Isles, Mexico, Brazil, Martinique, Haiti, Bolivia, Queensland, South Africa, Antigua, Guadaloupe and Peru.

See also Ron.

Rum, New England: The recognized legal term in America for straight rum produced in the U.S.A. and distilled at less than 160° proof. The term is no longer geographical.

Rumbullion: Possible derivation of name rum. See also Rumbustion and Saccharum.

Rumbustion: Possible derivation of name rum. See also Rumbullion and Saccharum.

Rum Currency: In the earliest days of Australian history, owing to the scarcity of coin or suitable commodities, rum was actually used as a medium of exchange in commercial transactions. The commerce was a monopoly of the military regiment, the New South Wales Corps, who flagrantly abused it.

Rummager: The moving chain of a whisky still which scrapes the bottom of the chamber to prevent burning and bumping.

Rummer: A traditional English glass of the 18th century long associated with the inn. It has a large bowl and a squat stem and was especially used for holding punch.

Rumney: Sweet Greek wine used in England in Elizabethan times.

Rundlet: Also Runlet. An obsolete English liquid measure from Fr. *rondelle*, a little tun (q.v.). It was variable but eventually came to be recognized as about 15 imperial gallons or 18½ wine or U.S. gallons. Often of earthenware, used mainly for storage of wines and spirits. 'Somebody this day from Portsmouth has sent me a Runlett of Tent' — Pepys, *Diary*, 3 December 1663.

Ruppertsberg: German (Palatinate) white wine centre, including the vineyards of Hoheberg, Reiterpfad, Spiess, Achtmorgen, Mandelacker, Gaisböhl, Goldschmidt, Linsenbusch, Hofstück, Mussbien, Kreuz, Kaft, Helbig, Hofstuck, Kirchberg, Stickelpfad, Weinbach.

Rush, Benjamin: The celebrated physician, who was one of those who signed the Declaration of Independence and professor of medicine of the University of Pennsylvania, was a strong advocate of beer, cider, and wine in the interests of temperance (q.v.). See also Franklin, Jefferson and Washington.

Ruskin, John: This most English of Englishmen was the son of a wine merchant whose speciality was sherry. The writer-aesthete had a proper appreciation of the finest products of Jerez.

Russia: The characteristic alcoholic beverages of Russia have been, in the past, the light brewed liquor kvass and the spirit vodka (q.v.). However, there has always been a certain production of wine and in recent years this has greatly expanded. It is stated officially that it is expected that by 1970 Russia will be second only to France as a wine-producer.

In the South of Russia (where, of course, economical vine growth alone is possible) there are vast areas which are suitable for the growth of any sort of wine. The oldest and best-established areas are in the Crimea, but there are other extensive wine regions in Bessarabia, the Caucasus and Central Asia.

Large volumes of wines — table, dessert and sparkling — are made.

The absence of these wines on the world's market is almost certainly an indication that, with the steady rise in living standards, there is none to spare outside Russia.

Russian Chambertin: A pretty example of vinous credulity. Chambertin was the favourite wine of Napoleon, who carried cases of it on his Russian campaign. During the retreat the stocks were lost. At the Restoration the gullible bought wine at fancy prices guaranteed 'from the Emperor's wine-cellar, back from Russia'. Think, too, of Napoleon brandy, of which enough has been sold to float not a battleship but fleets.

Russian Cocktail: Another of those American insults, a mixture of vodka, dry gin and chocolate liqueur.

Russian Stout: Type of heavy stout previously brewed in England, or so it is reported, especially for the Russian Royal Family.

Rüst: German (Rheinhessen) wine estate, also an Austrian white-wine centre.

Ruster: Austrian white table wine.

Rustschik: Also written Ruschuk. Bulgarian wine-growing centre. Mainly red.

Rutherford and Miles: Old-established shippers of madeira (q.v.).

Rutherglen: Australian region in the River Murray Valley, (Victoria and New South Wales). Perhaps the last important wine-growing area of Victoria and even this is rapidly declining in output though fortunately not in quality. The Rutherglen vineyards are a century old and were first planted by the miners after the gold rush. Rutherglen, Wahgunyah and a few adjoining villages still produce the finest Australian sweet fortified wines and also perhaps the best of the local dry flor sherries. There is also some good heavy dark-red so-called burgundy produced.

It is regrettable that the names of Rutherglen and Wahgunyah have not replaced port and other European place and type names. Here are made some fine dessert wines which might become celebrated if given a geographical name in place of 'port', 'madeira', 'tokay', etc. See also Wahgunyah. Rutherglen is the seat of the Government Viticultural Station. Here is also maintained a large collection of stocks for the South Australian Government and wine industry, to be used in case there ever comes an outbreak of *Phylloxera* (q.v.) in that state.

Ruubus-Vünake: Finnish apéritif (q.v.), flavoured with cloudberry.

Ruwer: German white wine centre on the tributary of the Moselle of that name. The cool climate results in the production of rather tart wines. They are light, graceful wines sold as moselles. Amongst the finest vineyards are Laurentiusberg, Meisenberg, Ehrenberg, Nieschen, Taubenberg, Hitzlay, Dominikanerberg, Kasthäuserhofberg, Eitelsbacherhofberg, Sonnenberg, Rothberg, Maximin Grünhäuser, Herrenberg, Lorenzberg and Spielberg.

Rye Whiskey: American and Canadian spirit. By American law it is required to contain not less than 51% of whiskey made wholly from rye and to be aged in the traditional manner in warmed warehouses.

Saar: German white wine district on the river of this name, a little tributary of the Moselle. The vineyards are on both sides of the river. The wines are grouped with those of the Ruwer and Moselle (q.v.). The flavour of the Saar wines is valued by experts and is generally called 'steely', a term that seems to mean delicate, tart, but with marked bouquet. Amongst the best Saar centres for vineyards are Saarburg itself, Ockfen, Ayl, Wiltingen, Scharzhof, Canzem, Oberemmel, Wawern, Serrig and Filzen.

Saarburg: The principal town and wine market of the Saar (q.v.). The chief vineyards are Mühlenberg, Leyenkaul, Rausch, Schlossberg and Antoniusbrunnen.

Sabinum: A wine often mentioned in classical writings, light in nature and recommended to be kept 7 to 15 years in a cool cellar.

Sabor a Botella: The characteristic taste ('bottle taste') that Spaniards claim develops in some sherries after bottling. See also Bottle Stink.

Saccharification: The process of converting starch to sugar by malting or otherwise. The process is also known as 'converting'.

Saccharomyces Apiculatus: See Yeast.

Saccharomyces ellipsoideus: The true wine yeast, so called from the shape of the cells. They are vigorous fermenters and can produce up to 16% of alcohol by volume in favourable circumstances though they usually die out at about 13–14%. As the wild yeast (*apiculatus*, q.v.) is much more sensitive to sulphur dioxide than *ellipsoideus*, it is common practice to dose the must (q.v.) with this gas.

Saccharomyces ellipsoideus occurs naturally on the skins of ripe grapes and some other fruits, contained in the pretty 'bloom'. There are numerous varieties of *S. ellipsoideus* which produce varying amounts of substances which give a special character to this wine or that. Thus it is becoming increasingly common for the modern wine-maker to employ a pure culture of the variety of yeast on which he pins his faith. See also Yeast.

Saccharum: Brewer's term for invert sugar used in making beer. It is the name the Romans gave to the sugar collected from reeds and is thought by some to be the derivation of the name 'rum', the spirit made from sugar. No connection with saccharin, a synthetic sweetening agent never used in brewing.

Sack: A venerable English wine name of disputed origin and meaning. It is generally supposed to be derived from the Spanish *seco*, dry but it is also stated to originate in the Spanish word *saca*, export. It is now obsolete as a general name for a type of wine, though used as a trade-mark by some English wine merchants. It has been widely believed that it was the old English name for sherry (q.v.) but Markham (1568–1637) writes: 'Your best sacks are of Xeres in Spain; your smaller of Gallicia and Portugal; your strong sacks are of the islands of Canaries and Malligo.' The truth seems to be that the name 'sack' was applied in England to all the white wines imported from southern Europe. Wines from Spain were called 'sherris-sack' as distinct from 'canary-sack' and others. As hot-climate wines they could be considerably stronger in alcohol than those of France and Germany but this was long before the period of fortification (q.v.) and thus they would be merely ordinary dry wines, considerably lower in strength than modern sherry.

Shakespeare was obviously fond of sack and makes many references to it. However, he was certainly guilty of an anachronism in making Falstaff a 'sack-bibber'. Falstaff's time was long before sack came into England.

An Elizabethan and later drink made by sweetening wine with honey was also called sack.

Sack Pot: A 17th-century squat glass mug used to bring wine from cask to table.

Sackträger: German (Oppenheim, q.v.) white wine.

Sacramental Wine: Although Christians and Jews employ wine in religious exercises, all that can be said with certainty is that the requirements of the nature of the wine are quite uncertain. There is a general edict that it must be 'pure' but there is no clear definition of purity or indeed of wine.

Some of the more extreme teetotal Nonconformist Protestant Christian sects have tried to adduce authority for the statement that the Bible requires unfermented grape juice to be used for the sacrament. However, this doctrine is contemptuously and indeed violently rejected by Roman Catholic, Anglican and other scholars and indeed the Bible itself gives no real support to so preposterous a belief. As a matter of commonsense, in the Biblical era it would have been a sheer impossibility to keep unfermented grape juice.

Also known as altar wine.

Sacrantino: Italian (Umbrian) red table wine from Montifalco.

Sage Ale: An infusion of sage leaves used in the 17th century for medicinal purposes. (See also Scurvy Grass Ale.)

Sahler: German (Gau-Bischofsheim, q.v.) white wine.

Saint-Aignan: French (Bordeaux) red wine.

Saint-Albe: French (Graves) red wine.

Saint-Amand: French (Sauternes) sweet white wine.

Saint-Amour: The French red wine of this Burgundian estate is pleasant enough but far less distinguished than its intriguing name.

Saint-André-Corbin: French (St. Émilion) red wine.

Saint-Aubin: French (Médoc) red wine, sold usually under Ludon.

Saint-Aubin: French (Côte-d'Or) red burgundy wine.

Saint-Aubin-Richard: French (Médoc) white wine.

Saint-Augustin-la-Grave: French (Graves) red wine.

Saint-Avertin: French (Touraine) red wine.

Saint-Bris: French (Graves) red and white wines.

Saint-Christoly: French (Médoc) red wine.

Saint-Christophe-des-Bardes: French (St. Émilion) red wines.

Sainte-Croix-du-Mont: French (Gironde) white wine district for sweet white wines of the Sauternes type (q.v.).

Saint-Elie: Greek (Santorin) red wine.

Saint-Émilion: An important wine-growing district of the Bordeaux, on a plateau about twenty miles east of the city. It is a compact area in the middle of a group of hills. St. Émilion wines are heavier and more coloured than the Médoc wines and some judges say they resemble burgundy. The most celebrated wine of St. Émilion is Château Ausone (q.v.). Many others are separately noted herein.

Saintes: French town which is one of the important commercial centres for the sale of cognac (q.v.) brandy.

Saint-Estèphe: Important French wine-growing commune of the Médoc (q.v.).

Saint-Étienne-la-Varenne: Red wine of Beaujolais, France.

Saint-Étienne-les-Ouillières: Red wine of Beaujolais, France.

Saint-Georges: A name borne by a number of French wine-growing communes in both Bordeaux and Burgundy. The vineyards are separately listed. The Burgundian (Nuits) Saint-Georges also makes red sparkling wine. The most important wine is in the St. Émilion region.

Saint-Georges-Côte-Pavie: French (St. Émilion) red wine.

Saint-Georges-de-Montagne: French (Saint-Georges) red wine.

Saint-Georges-Macquin: French (Saint-Georges) red wine.

Saint-Germain: French (Bordeaux) red wine. There are at least four Bordeaux estates of this name.

Saint-Germain-de-Grave: French (Bordeaux) table wines.

Saint-Jacques, Le Clos: Red wine of Burgundy.

Saint-Jean-d'Angély: A town of the Charente which is one of the commercial centres of the cognac trade. See also Saintes.

Saint-Jean-de-Braye: French (Orléans) red wine.

Saint-Jean-de-la-Porte: Red French wine from Savoy.

Saint-Julien: Of the several French wine-growing places bearing this name, by far the most important is the commune in the Gironde (Bordeaux).

Here are a number of the finest classed growths of the Médoc (q.v.), including Léoville-Lascases, Léoville-Poyferre, Léoville-Barton, Gruaud-Larose, Gruaud-Larose-Faure and Ducru-Beaucaillou, in addition to various 3rd and 4th growths. Some of the wines of adjacent communes are traditionally sold under the name of Saint-Julien.

There are Saint-Juliens of lesser importance in the Rhône and the Meuse. There is a Château Saint-Julien in St. Émilion producing good red wine.

Saint-Lager: Red wine of Beaujolais, France.

Saint Landry: French red wine of Beaune (q.v.).

Saint-Laurent: This is a name borne by a number of French table wines of varying merit and from widely separated areas. The only commune which contains vineyards of real worth is that in the Médoc. Here are, for example, La-Tour-Carnet, Belgrave and Camensac.

Saint-Laurent-des-Combes: French (St. Émilion) red wine.

Saint-Leger-de-Montbrillais: French red wine from Poitiers.

Saint-Magdalena bei Bozen: Now Bolzano. South Tyrolean white-wine district. Usually the wines are now known as Santa Maddalena.

Saint-Martin: French (St. Émilion) red wine.

Saint-Nicholas-de-Bourgueil: French (Touraine) red wine.

St. Patrice: See Châteauneuf-du-Pape.

St. Patrick: Finds a place here as the first reported manufacturer of spirits by the freezing process, though to be sure, according to report, he regarded alcohol as poison. By all account, when St. Patrick returned from Gaul to Ireland about A.D. 435 his great adversaries were the druids. On one occasion a druid poured poison into Patrick's cup of wine. Patrick promptly blessed the wine, which froze to ice, while the 'poison' (i.e. the alcohol) remained liquid. He poured off the poison, thawed the 'wine' and drank it.

American farmers on the North Atlantic Coast and French farmers in Brittany still carry out the same process except that they throw away the (apple) wine and drink the 'poison'. See also Freezing Process.

Saint-Péray: French (Rhône Valley) white-wine commune. Here sparkling and still wines have been made for centuries. Despite the proud local claim that sparkling St.-Péray was a great favourite of the composer Richard Wagner, the wine remains a minor affair. Those who are not Wagnerites will be unimpressed by the story that the composer consumed a hundred bottles while writing *Parsifal*.

Saint-Pierre-Bontemps: French (Médoc) red wine.

Saint-Pierre-de-Mons: French (Sauternes) white wine.

Saint-Pierre-Servaistre: French (Médoc) red wine.

Saint-Pourçain: French (Loire) white wine.

St. Raphaël: Another of the numerous proprietary French apéritif wines of the vermouth type made from sweet white wine and herb extracts.

Saint-Satur: French (Sancerre, q.v.) white wine.

Saint-Sauveur: French commune of the Médoc whose red wines have acquired by custom the legal right to be sold under the name of the adjoining more celebrated St. Estèphe (q.v.).

Saint-Seurin-de-Cadourne: See Saint-Sauveur. The same facts apply.

Saint-Thibault: French (Sancerre) white wine.

Saint Vincent: The patron saint (but mainly in France) of wine-makers. He is supposed to have preferred to be allowed to drink the wine of La Mission Haut-Brion (q.v.) rather than to go to Paradise.

Saint-Vivant: French (Côte-d'Or) red wine, one of the celebrated Vosne-Romanée vineyards.

Saint-Yzans: French (Médoc) red wine.

Sakana: The Japanese relishes which almost invariably accompany sake (q.v.).

Sakazuki: Japanese name for the small china-ware or lacquered wood cups used for drinking sake (q.v.).

Sakazuki-Goto: 'Events of the cups.' The Japanese ceremony of sealing promises between two parties with sake (q.v.).

Sake: Alcoholic beverage made from fermented rice. It is the national beverage of Japan and to a less extent, under a wide variety of local and fanciful names, of China also. It is commonly called rice wine but although the alcoholic content is high (17% to 18% by volume) it is in no real sense a wine but more of the character of a brewed (q.v.) beverage. The process of manufacture is characteristic and complex.

Rice is steamed to make *koji*. This is then mixed with a traditional mould (*Aspergillus oryzae*) which turns the starch of the rice into fermentable soluble sugars. Lactic acid is usually added to reduce the risk of bacterial spoilage. The mass is then kneaded to an impalpable mixture and water is added. A special yeast, *Saccharomyces sake*, may be added to accelerate fermentation. After about a month *moto* (alcohol about 11%) results. More *koji* is then added. A second fermentation results and is complete in about a week.

After a short period of 'resting' or maturing the sake is clarified by filtering and then bottled. Sake is drunk in small amounts but the total production is large. There are many artistic ceremonies associated with the drinking of sake, some of which are separately noted. The taste of sake suggests a dry sherry or madeira.

Saladin System: Process of storage and mechanical turning which has virtually replaced floor malting.

Salerno: This was once the centre of the world for medical studies. Vaughan quotes one famous precept:

> If a carouse at night do make thee ill
> For morning medicine drink of wine thy fill.

But perhaps the reader prefers the terser 'hair of the dog that bit him'.

Salignac: Old-established brand of cognac (q.v.).

Salins: French (Jura) white wine.

Salle de Breillan, La: French (Médoc) red wine.

Salmanazar: Another of the outsize bottles of variable capacity with Biblical names. Usually the size is about that of a dozen reputed quarts or two imperial gallons.

Saloon: An American term whose legal significance seems to vary. It is an establishment licensed to supply liquor to be consumed on the premises. Many states require food to be supplied as well, if ordered, but a saloon differs from a licensed restaurant in that the emphasis is strongly towards the beverage. The term has become opprobrious.

The British and Dominion saloon bar provides the same liquor but in better surroundings than the ordinary bar and, of course, at a higher price. There is a saloon lounge in the larger and more fashionable hotels of Australia and some other countries.

Samaria: Important wine region in Biblical times.

Samarkand: Asiatic ancient city of U.S.S.R. and now a rapidly developing centre of viticulture for both raisins and wine.

Samogon (Russian): Vodka distilled and sold illegally. See also Moonshine and Poteen.

Samos: On this Greek island are grown sweet tawny dessert wines which have long been popular in Scandinavia and Holland. A wine from Samos was esteemed in classical days. This, of course, was a dry wine.

Byron (*Don Juan*) writes: 'Fill high the cup with Samian wine' and 'Dash down yon cup of Samian wine'.

Sam Shiu: The general Chinese term for spirits, whether or not of domestic origin. What is known to Europeans as samshu is a beverage brewed from rice resembling the Japanese sake.

Sanary: French wine region near Toulon.

San Casciano: Italian (Tuscanian) red wine (chianti).

Sancerre: French white wine of Berry. It is wine of the moselle character — tart, fruity and light. Packed in bottles of distinctive shape, it has been widely and vigorously boosted.

Sancocho: Grape juice boiled down to a third of the original volume and used in the manufacture of sweet sherry (q.v.). See also Arrope.

Sandbichler: Italian red table wine of the Ortisei district. As with many of the other names of the area, this remembers the previous Austrian affiliations.

S and C: Cocktail of Scotch whisky and chartreuse.

Sandeman: Name of the venerable firm founded in 1790 and still active as shippers of port and sherry.

Sanderson: Well-known (since 1863) firm of Scotch whisky blenders, now part of D.C.L. (q.v.), whose principal brand, Vat 69, is world-wide.

Sandgrube: German (Kiedrich, q.v.) white wine. The name ('sand quarry') is borne by many Rhine vineyards.

Sandy Creek: Australian (S.A.) wine centre.

San Francisco: Around this bay and its tributaries are many of the finest Californian wine-growing areas, including Napa, Sonoma, Alameda and Santa Clara.

Sangaree: Mixed drink of sherry, spirits, port, etc., served with ice, lemon and nutmeg.

Sängarei: German (Dhron) white wine.

San Gimignano: Italian (chianti) red wine.

Sangiovese: Italian table wine from the Bologna region. It is also the name of the Italian grape largely used for the production of chianti wine (q.v.). It is the only wine of the tiny Republic of San Marino.

Sangioveto: Italian black wine grape of fine quality, used for chianti (q.v.).

San Giustino: Italian red table wine of the Bolzano area.

Sanglot d'Amour: This French cocktail with the provocative name ('sob of love') is said to be a favourite in the Touraine but if it really exists its composition remains obscure.

Sangre: Mexican mixed drink of tequila (q.v.) and tomato juice. At least it sounds superior to Turkish Blood (q.v.). See also Bloody Mary.

Sangria: Portuguese wine drink of red wine, sugar, orange and lemon juice with iced soda.

Sangue di Giuda: Italian (Lombardian) red wine.

San Joas da Foz: Portuguese wine district along Douro producing not port but common table wine.

San Juan: Argentine wine district.

Sankt Georgen: German (Pressburg) red and white wines.

Sankt Johann: German (Rheinhessen) white wine.

Sankt Justina: Wine district of South Tyrol.

Sankt Magdalena: Wine district of South Tyrol.

Sankt Martin: German (Palatinate) white wine.

San Lucar de Barrameda: This Spanish town is one of the principal centres for the production and sale of sherry (q.v.), especially manzanilla (q.v.).

San Miguel: Portuguese dry white wine.

San Rafael: Argentine wine district.

San Sadurni de Maya: Spanish centre near Barcelona, especially noted for sparkling white wine of champagne (q.v.) type.

Sansankudo: Lit. 'three-nine-nine cups'. The Japanese ceremony of drinking sake at the Shinto wedding service.

San Severo: Southern Italian white table wine.

Sansonnet: French (St. Émilion) red wine.

Santa Barbara: Californian wine-growing county.

Santa Giustina: Italian (Tyrolean) white wine. Before the First World War this wine from Bolzen, South Tyrol, was called Leitacher.

Santa Maddalena: Northern Italian red table wine from Bolzano, Trentino.

Santa Rita: Chilean wine estate of quality.

Santenay: French (Côte-d'Or) wine commune for red burgundy. The chief vineyards are Les Gravières and Tavannes.

Santenot-Milieu: French (Meursault) red wine.

Santenots, Les: The name borne by a group of French vineyards of Meursault, Côte-d'Or, whose products are variously put in order of merit by experts. These vineyards are Santenots Blancs, du Dessous and du Milieu. All make red burgundy.

Santiago: The principal Chilean city. It is surrounded by vineyards. Red and white wines of excellent quality are made and the world has started to recognize their value.

Santo d'Umbria: Italian (Umbrian) table wine, mainly red.

Santorin: Greek island, one of the Cyclades, which, for its small size, produces a variety and a large volume of wines, including the white Saint-Elie.

Santo Tomas: Reputed to be one of the best Mexican dry red table wines.

Santo, Vin: Italian table wine from Tuscany.

São Paulo: The chief wine-growing state of Brazil. Quality does not yet reach that of Chile (q.v.).

Sarab: A type of Turkish grape brandy.

Saragossa: A medieval wine known in England, said to have been spiced with rue and fennel.

Saransot-Dupré: French (Médoc) red wine.

Sarap: Turkish red wine.

Sardinia: Of no great consequence as a wine-producer. *Giro* and *Monica* are well-known sweet wines.

Sari: Vineyard area of Corsica.

Sarigim: The Biblical term for the new shoots of the vine sent out in March.

Sarmsheim: German (Nahe) white wine.

Saronitic Wine: In Biblical times this had the reputation of great strength, needing two parts of water to dilute it.

Sarrazin: Old-established brand of cognac (q.v.).

Sartene: French (Corsican) table wines.

Sasbach: German (Kaiserstuhl) white wine.

Sassari: Italian (Sardinian) red wine.

Sassella: Italian red table wine from Sondrio, Lombardy.

Satz: German (Königsbach, q.v.) white wine.

Saulcet: French (Allier) red wine.

Saum: Swiss wine measure equal to about 33 imperial gallons.

Saumagen: German (Kallstadt, q.v.) wine centre.

Saumur: The ancient French city on the Loire noted for its horse museum housed in a rambling old castle and for its sparkling wines. The wine is made of a mixture of grapes, of which two-thirds is white chenin and the resulting wine is rather fruitier than champagne, though made in a similar manner. Saumur also uses a vast collection of tunnels for maturing.

It is unfortunate and stupid that most countries tax sparkling wines not on price but on mere volume. This militates against the sale of sparkling saumur which, with all its merits, is not the equal of the proud champagne of the Champagne. The same applies, of course, to all other sparkling wines.

Incidentally, it is to the credit of Australia and one or two other wine-producing countries that there is no tax at all upon local sparkling and other wines.

Sausilles: French (Côte-d'Or) red wine.

Sautchoo: Chinese spirit of whisky type, which is stated to have been distilled for over 2,000 years.

Sauterne, American: See American Sauterne.

Sauternes: This celebrated French district of the Bordeaux gives its name to the renowned sweet white wine there grown and made. The district includes not only the wine estates of the Commune of Sauternes but those of the adjoining Communes of Barsac, Bommes, Fargues and Preisac. The white wine of St. Pierre de Mons (q.v.) may also legally be sold as sauternes.

The wine itself is remarkable and it has been said that the finest sauternes, Château Yquem or d'Yquem, is the most expensive wine in the world. (Before the First World War Tokay Essenz (q.v.) had that doubtful honour.) Sauternes wine is carefully limited by French law to wine grown in a defined region from defined grapes and made in a defined manner. There can be few products so fully protected legally. Sauternes is a pale, golden, sweetish table wine, luscious and inimitable. It is not, like dessert wines, fortified (q.v.) and is prone to undergo secondary fermentation in the bottle.

The finest sauternes are made from a blend of about two thirds sémillon and one third sauvignon and other white grapes. The heart of the process consists in allowing the grapes to become over-ripe and be attacked by a mould called *Botrytis cinerea*. This softens and attacks the skin of the grape without producing an unpleasant flavour. It is called *pourriture noble* or 'noble rot'. The opening of the skin allows some evaporation to occur and the grapes go part of the way towards raisins. Further, the mould consumes some of the potassium and phosphorus. These are essential ingredients in the process of alcoholic fermentation and thus the stoppage of the production of alcohol is achieved.

In the vintaging for the finest sauternes, the pickers go over the vines several times, removing only single grapes at the proper stage. Cheaper sauternes are dosed with sulphur dioxide to arrest fermentation and sometimes sweetening is added.

In propitious seasons a similar wine is made on the Rhine. The grapes are attacked by the same mould and the process is called *Edelfäule*, the exact equivalent of *pourriture noble*.

Genuine sauternes and similar wine can only be made in a country of suitably moist autumn climate and cheap labour. Outside Europe a mongrel wine labelled Sauterne is made by sweetening white wine and dosing with sulphur dioxide or by fortifying. Such wine is an insult to a great name.

Some French wine is labelled Haut Sauternes. This may mean that the wine was grown on better land than usual but the term has no legal significance.

The celebrated Sauternes wines are listed below:

Château Yquem — considered supreme — in a class of its own.

First Growths

Estate Name	Commune
Château La Tour-Blanche	Bommes
,, La Faurie-Peyraguey	,,
,, De Rayne-Vigneau	,,
,, De Suduiraut	Preignac
,, Coutet	Barsac
,, Climens	,,
,, Bayle-Guiraud	Sauternes
,, Rieussec	Fargues
,, Rabaud-Promis	Bommes

Second Growths

Château De Myrat	Barsac
,, Doisy	,,
,, D'Arche	Sauternes
,, Filhot	,,
,, Broustet-Nérac	Barsac
,, Caillou	,,
,, Suau	,,
,, De Malle	Preignac
,, Romer	,,
,, Lamothe	Sauternes

Sauvignon: See Cabernet.

Sauvignon Blanc: French white grape widely-grown in Graves, Sauternes and Loire Valley. In the last area it is called blanc fumé. Highly esteemed for production of great wines. It is the basis of sauternes (q.v.) and is also grown abroad for fine table wine where quality is more important than quantity.

Savennières: French (Anjou) white wine.

Saverne: French (Alsatian) white wine.

Savigny: French (Côte-d'Or) red wine centre.

Savigny-les-Beaune: Notable red wine from Burgundy.

Savoy: Cocktail of gin, grenadine, dry vermouth and absinthe.

Savuto: Red table wine from Calabria, Italy.

Sazerac: Cocktail of whisky, pernod, bitters, lemon peel and syrup.

Scandinavia: This is a beer-drinking population. All the Scandinavian countries and Denmark in particular make superb beer. Danish beer is exported all over the world. There has always been a tradition of wine-drinking in the wealthy classes but in recent times consumption of wine has greatly expanded and is no longer confined to the well-to-do. Some of the lesser European wine countries are generally dependent upon Scandinavia as their customers and this particularly applies to sweet fortified wines.

As would be expected of people of a cold climate, the Scandinavians have a high consumption of spirits. Scotch whisky is for those with well-lined pockets but the universal spirit is the home-made aqvavit (q.v.).

In earlier days the general beverage of the country seems to have been mead (q.v.). There is no doubt of the wide consumption of this beverage and Scaldic verse ascribes the gift of mead to Odin. Mythological poetry abounds in descriptions of the gods drinking ale, mead and wine. All the warriors in Valhalla drank wine.

Scantling: Timber stage used for holding casks of beer.

Schäferlay: German white wine. See also Briedel.

Schaffhausen: Swiss red and white wines.

Schafsbohl: German (Deidesheim, q.v.) white wine.

Schallenberg: German (Gau-Odernheim, q.v.) white wine district.

Schank: German white wine. See also Bergzabern.

Schanz: German (Ockenheim, q.v.) white wine.

Scharlachberg: German for 'scarlet mountain' and centre for white wines. The vineyards are at the junction of the Rhine and the Nahe.

Scharzberger and Scharzhofberger: White wines of the Saar Valley, Germany.

Schaumwein: German term for sparkling wine.

Schenk: Beer made for prompt consumption and not stored like lager (q.v.).

Schenke: German for public-house.

Schenkenböhl: German (Dürkheim, q.v.) white wine.

Schenkenböhl: White wine from Wachenheim, Palatinate (q.v.).

Schiedam: Strongly flavoured Dutch gin from the town of that name. Chief centre for gin. The spirit is also known as hollands and schnapps.

Schild: German (Gimmeldingen, q.v.) white wine.

Schild: German (Franconian) white wine.

Schillerwein: German pink ordinary wines, especially of Baden and Württemberg, made from mixed red and white grapes. A sort of inexpensive *rosé* for local and copious drinking.

Schlangenberg: German (Nierstein, q.v.) white wine.

Schlangengraben: German vineyard at Wiltingen, Saar.

Schlarlachberg: German (Bingen, q.v.) white wine.

Schloss: Castle in German and the equivalent of the French château. As often as not both Schloss and château are very humble buildings.

Schloss: German (Nahe, q.v. and Braunberg, Moselle) white wines.

Schlossabzug: German equivalent of 'château-bottled'.

Schlossberg: Many German white wine estates along the Rhine bear this rather trite name. It is surprising that some effort has not been made to re-christen some or all of these places. See also Rosenberg for a similar situation.

    Some of the better-known Schlossbergs are situated at Oppenheim, Lieser, Cochem, Saarburg, Rüdesheim, Wiltingen, Wachenheim and Bingen.

Schlossberger: Swiss (Aargau) white wine.

Schlossböckelheimer: German (Nahe) white wine.

Schlossböckelheimer Felsenberg: German (Niederhausen-Schlossböckelheim A.D. Nahe, q.v.) white wine.

Schlossböckelheimer Kupfergrube: German (Niederhausen-Schlossböckelheim A.D. Nahe, q.v.) white wine.

Schlossgarten: German (Dürkheim, q.v.) white wine.

Schlossgarten: German (Friedelsheim, q.v.) white wine.

Schloss Johannisberg: See Johannisberg.

Schloss Vollrads: Celebrated German wine estate of Winkel, Rheingau. See also Vollrads.

Schmeck: The German term for the characteristic smack of wine from a particular locality, derived from the soil. See also Goût de Terroir.

Schmidtskapelle: German (Nackenheim, q.v.) white wine.

Schmitt: German (Nierstein, q.v.) white wine.

Schnait: German (Württemberg) white wine.

Schnapp: German (Ostofen, q.v.) white wine.

Schnappenberg: German (Nierstein, q.v.) white wine.

Schnapps: Dutch spirit prepared from potatoes, usually flavoured with juniper and other aromatics, thus a type of gin. Many 'abstainers' drink schnapps as a medicine. It is essentially the same as hollands and schiedam (q.v.). The word schnapps is also used loosely in Germany for spirits resembling whisky, vodka, etc.

Schnepfenflug: German (Forst, q.v.) fine white wine.

Schochu: Japanese spirit made from sweet potato, the equivalent of vodka (q.v.).

Schoenenberg: French (Alsatian) white wine.

Schomlau: See Somlay.

Schonhele: German (Rheingau) vineyard. Fine hock.

Schönhell: German (Hallgarten, q.v.) white wine.

School: Collective noun for group of drinkers for whom a 'round' (q.v.) is bought.

Schooner: A large, tall drinking-glass, usually about 15 fl. oz.

Schoongesicht: South African table wine of hermitage type.

Schoppen: German, Austrian and Swiss liquor measure, variable but about half a litre or tenth of a gallon. Also known as a Seidel.

Schoppenwein: About the same as a French *vin de carafe*. It is the freely-dispensed restaurant wine of the Palatinate (q.v.).

Schorlemorle: Widely-known German beverage, usually equal parts of wine and mineral water.

Schozach: German (Württemberg) white wine.

Schriesheim: German (Baden) white wine.

Schutzenhausen: German (Hattenheim, q.v.) white wine.

Schuyler: Hybrid U.S. black grape. See also New York Muscat.

Schwabsburg: German (Rheinhessen) white wine.

Schwaigern: German (Württemberg) red and white wines.

Schwarzes Kreuz: German (Freinsheim, q.v.) white wine.

Schwarzlay: Moselle vineyard near Ürzig (q.v.).

Schwätzerchen: German (Bingen, q.v.) white wine.

Schweinfurter: German (Franconian) white wine (Steinwein, q.v.).

Schwenker: A large, thin-walled glass goblet for serving brandy, the purpose being to enable the spirit to be warmed by the hand and swirled around so that it will give out its aroma. Also known as a balloon (Fr. *ballon*).

Schwund: The German equivalent of ullage (q.v.).

Scintillation: Obsolete American term of the 1850's for a small glass of whiskey.

Sconce: Originally the ancient challenge at Oxford. To sconce was, *inter alia*, to inflict a forfeit of beer for an offence against table etiquette. Other English universities adopted the term and sconced in beer or money any breach of the rules.

Scopelo: Another of the small wine-growing islands of the Greek archipelago. The principal growth is sweet, heavy dessert wine.

Scot Ale: An extortion by medieval English forest officers who kept ale-houses and compelled travellers to drink there.

Scotch: This bald word is used in the U.S. for genuine Scotch whisky, i.e. whisky (q.v.) made wholly in Scotland according to recognized Scotch practice.

Scotch Ale: Draught or bottled Burton type brewed in Scotland.

Scotch Mist: Cocktail of Scotch whisky and lemon peel.

Scott System: A modern method of bulk-handling yeast in breweries under micro-biologically controlled conditions to avoid bacterial and other contamination from the air.

Screwdriver: Mixture of vodka and orange juice.

Screw Stopper: A now obsolete form of sealing bottles introduced about 1885 but superseded by corks.

Scuppernong: An American wine from the native grape of that name.

Scurvy Grass Ale: Infusion of watercress.

Scythian: Roman wine of antiquity.

Sean O'Farrell: Obsolete U.S. vernacular name of a shot of whiskey followed by a pint of beer. Apparently it originated in the mining town of Butte, Montana. See also Chaser and Boilermaker.

Sebennytus: Wine of ancient Egypt praised by Strabo.

Sec: French word meaning dry. It is often misused. Thus when applied to champagne it actually means sweetish!

Secchio: Italian liquid measure of about $2\frac{1}{2}$ gallons.

Séchet: French (Chablis) white burgundy wine.

Sechsmorgen: White wine from Forst, Palatinate (q.v.).

Seckergrund: German (Laubenheim, q.v.) white wine.

Seder Wine: Wine for the Jewish Seder service, usually prepared on the domestic scale from raisins.

Sediment: The general term for the solid matter which sinks to the bottom of containers of liquids. Lees are the sediment of bulk containers and consist of vegetable debris, together with the argol or tartar (acid potassium tartrate) that comes out of solution as alcohol forms.

Crust is the deposit formed in bottles of wine on long-standing and consists mainly of argol. Red wines deposit more sediment than white.

Seedy: Term applied to brandy to denote inferior flavour supposed to be caused by weeds amongst the vines.

Seeweine: Name applied to the Swiss wines grown around Lake Constance.

Segonzac: One of the brandy-making centres of the Cognac.

Ségur: French (Médoc) red wine.

Seibel: Red grape giving light wine, reported being planted in the south of England in a brave attempt to produce wine commercially.

Seidel: Large beer glass or mug, often with a hinged lid. Originally Austrian but widely used in the U.S. (Capacity $\frac{3}{4}$ pint.)

Seidenburg: German (Niedersaulheim, q.v.) white wine.

Sekt: German for sparkling wine, especially the whites (hock and moselle). If made by the champagne process they can be excellent.

Sellers, G. H., & Ferro: Old-established shippers of port (q.v.).

Seltzer (water): The name is a corruption of Selters, a natural German mineral water (q.v.). Now used as a synonym for mineral water (q.v.) generally.

Selzen: German (Rheinhessen) white wine.

Semeillan: French (Médoc) red wine.

Semichon Method: A method of preventing the action of wild yeasts in wine by mixing about a quarter of finished wine with three quarters of must (q.v.). Also called the superquatre or superquattro method.

Sémillon: A variety of grape which, with sauvignon, is grown for the fine white wines of Sauternes, France.

Sendel: German (Münster, q.v.) white wine.

Sénéjac: French (Médoc) red wine.

Senheim-Senhals: German (Moselle) white wine.

Sennchen: German (Rheinhessen) white wine from Aspisheim.

Sentiers: French (Côte-d'Or) centre for fine red burgundies.

Seppeltsfield: Huge (1,400 acres) South Australian vineyard near Tanunda, now over a century old. As is usual with Australian wineries, a large range of wines is produced.

Sequillas: Spanish term for the inferior grapes removed from the bunches before treading.

Sercial: The name of the driest (or more accurately the least sweet) of the various types of dessert wine from Madeira (q.v.). It is often drunk as an agreeable apéritif. It is also the name of the Portuguese grape from which the wine is made. This grape is now becoming rather rare.

Serein: The little river in Chablis above whose right bank are placed the grand growths of the wine. See also Chablis.

Serene Highness: Cocktail of brandy, orange and pineapple liqueurs.

Serra: The name Junipero Serra is honoured in California as that of the Franciscan monk who introduced the vine. See also Busby.

Serralunga: See Barolo.

Serre, La: French (St. Émilion) red wine.

Serrig: German (Saar) white wine.

Serrigny: French (Côte-d'Or) red burgundy wine.

Sesame Wine: The wine supposed to have been drunk at the meeting of the gods of Assyria. For example, the Assyrian god Marduk attended a council of war of the gods where sesame wine was drunk. It would hardly be possible to make an alcoholic beverage from sesame seed (the source of the widely used sesame oil) but possibly the Assyrians flavoured wine with the ground seed or the flowers.

Sester: Old British measure of about 16 gallons levied on certain brewers from each batch.

Setina: Roman wine of classical times, grown in Campania.

Setinum: Roman wine, highly prized and stated to be the favourite drink of Augustus Caesar.

Setubal: Portuguese sweet wine (muscatel) from Estremadura.

Seurey: French (Côte-d'Or) red burgundy wine.

Sève: French wine term (lit. 'sap') denoting liveliness, savour, general good quality.

Sevenhill: Australian (S.A.) wine centre.

Sex and Alcohol: There is a widespread belief that alcohol heightens the sexual urge. There is a certain basis of fact in this but there are important qualifications. Alcohol, as a depressant drug, releases or minimizes the brakes on emotion we call inhibitions. It may therefore be broadly pro-vocative in action. However, much depends upon the emotional back-ground of the subject.

As the research physician Lolli has sagaciously observed, from time immemorial the link between alcohol and sexual activity has been known but has been described more frequently by poets and writers than by scientists. As usual, the playwright and psychologist Shakespeare reveals sound knowledge in the subject. 'Lechery, Sir, it provokes and unprovokes; it provokes the desire but it takes away with performance. Therefore much drink may be said to be an equivocator with lechery.' (*Macbeth*)

It has been said that alcohol, by lessening inhibition, permits women to act as they wish to act. The American Ogden Nash has written: 'Candy is dandy, but licker is quicker.'

Sextarius: Roman liquid measure of capacity one sixth of a *modius* or *congius*.

Seyssel: French white wine centre on the River Rhône near Lake Geneva. There are two villages, on either bank of the river. The most esteemed wine is called Roussette.

Seyve-Villard: A recent hybrid white grape whose early-maturing and frost-resisting claims have led to plantings in the south of England in a brave attempt to establish commercial wine-production.

Shades: Cellars of a bar below ground level (see also Dive).

Shakespeare: The Bard was manifestly a wine-lover and he also had what seems to be an encyclopaedic knowledge of the wines and other bever-ages of his day. Presumably an inference can be drawn from the fact that he frequently mentions sack (q.v.). Indeed one authority writes that the name sack occurs in the plays more than all the other wine names put together. As to historical accuracy, that is another matter. Shakespeare makes Falstaff drink sack on many occasions but although it was a popular drink in Elizabethan times, it was certainly not known in Falstaff's lifetime. Who cares? Amongst the wines mentioned by Shakespeare are bastard, canary, charneco, claret, Greek wine, malmsey, madeira, muscadel, rhenish, sack and sherris (sack). These are subjects of separate entries. There are many pieces and comments upon wine in general and, of course, ale, contained in the plays.

Shakespeare also had an astonishing knowledge of the pharmacology of alcohol. His allusions to liquor and its effects would fill many pages. For example 'A good Sherris-Sack hath a two-fold operation in it; it ascends me into the brain; dries me there all the foolish, and dull, and crudy vapours which environ it, makes it apprehensive, quick, inventive, full of nimble, fiery and delectable shape, which delivered o'er to the voice which is the birth, becomes excellent wit. The second property of your excellent Sherris is the warming of the blood; which before cold and settled left the liver white and pale, which is the badge of pusillanimity and cowardice; but the Sherris warms it, and makes it course from the inwards to the parts extreme.' (*Henry IV*, *Pt.* 2, Act IV, Sc. iii, 103.) See also Sex and Alcohol.

'A man cannot make him laugh; but that's no marvel; he drinks no wine.' (*Henry IV*.)

'The wine of life is drawn, and the mere lees
Is left this vault to brag of.' (*Macbeth*.)

'Dost thou think, because thou art virtuous, there shall be no more cakes and ale?' (*Twelfth Night*.)

Shakespeare's father was appointed an ale-conner (q.v.) of Stratford-on-Avon in 1557.

Shamrock: Cocktail of Irish whiskey, dry vermouth and crème de menthe.

Shandy or Shandy Gaff: A drink of beer mixed with ginger beer; sometimes served as a mixture of beer and lemonade, though this is perhaps more correctly termed 'lemon shandy'. The modern meaning is a mixture of beer and any soft drink.

Shaohsing: Town in China in northern Chekiang province, known for over 2,000 years as the centre of manufacture of rice 'wine' of the same name. The beverage is, of course, not wine but a type of sake (q.v.) flavoured with herbs. It is also known as huang chiu (yellow wine) because of its amber colour. There are three types of shaohsing: Shan Niang is full-bodied; Chu Yeh Ching or Bamboo Green gets its colour and mild fragrance from the new bamboo leaves added during fermentation; and Hsiang Hsueh or Fragrant Snow is a light, sweet variety.

Shebeen: The Irish name for an establishment where liquor is sold illegally (i.e. without a licence). See also Sly Grog.

Shekar or Schechar: The general Biblical word for strong drink. It occurs 23 times in the O.T. It was variously said to be made from palm juice, wheat, fruit juice, grapes or honey. It is, however, clearly not grape wine because it is often coupled with wine as if that were another intoxicating beverage. Strong drink was to be given to those about to perish, which has been supposed to refer to the deadening of the pain of execution. The Yiddish word *shikkered* for drunk has spread into general use. Shekar is also said to be the origin of the name 'cider'.

Shekete: Central African beer made from maize. See also Mealie.

Shemahrin: Biblical term for wine of undoubted purity and quality.

Sheoak: Generic name for crude liquor, originally Australian slang for coarse beer.

Sheoak Net: A net slung at the ship's gangway, originally to prevent returning drunken sailors falling into the water.

Shepparton: Australian (Victorian) wine centre.

Sherris: The Elizabethan English name for sherry (q.v.) which is said exactly to reproduce the old pronunciation of the name of the town Jerez (q.v.). See also Sack and Shakespeare.

Sherry: A wine perhaps more discussed by drinkers than any other. The only definition that will not be subject to furious argument is a fortified (q.v.) wine. Admittedly this does not tell us much.

The name is almost certainly derived from the Spanish town Jerez, pronounced approximately 'Haireth'. The Elizabethan name of the wine was 'Sherris' and this is believed to have been the current pronunciation of Jerez or, to give it the full title, Jerez de la Frontera. Jerez was and still is the recognized centre of Spanish sherry production.

Sherry in its many forms is a Spanish wine. Under Spanish law only wine made from certain grapes grown within a defined area and produced in a defined way may be called sherry. That area is a portion of the Spanish province of Cadiz in Andalusia, about 400 sq. miles. The only exception is that a small proportion of grapes are traditionally allowed to come from a district about a hundred miles north of Jerez, in the province of Estremadura.

Sherry is essentially a drink of the English-speaking countries and at that more British than American. Great businesses and fortunes have been built in England on bottling and selling sherry. It is said that there is much more sherry bottled in England than in Spain. See also Bristol.

There are broadly two types of sherry. The first is dry sherry made by the flor process. The second is sweet sherry. Sweet sherry is a dessert wine which fills much the same gastronomic role as, say, port. Flavour and appearance of sweet sherry vary widely and wine under that name is made in all warm-climate, wine-growing countries.

Dry sherry is made by a secondary fermentation, using a special film-forming yeast called *flor* ('flower'). The process and technique are characteristic and complex and although now more or less successfully imitated in other countries, the finest dry sherries are still those of Spain. Dry flor sherries bear the general name of *finos*.

The true sherry grape is the palomino ('little dove') a small sugary berry. Another prolific and sweet grape, the Pedro Ximénèz, is also used for blending. The best soil for vineyards is the dramatically light, chalky *albariza*. Where this is mixed extensively with clay it is called *barros*. The exceptionally dry manzanilla (q.v.) sherry is grown on sandy soil called *arenas*.

The grapes are carefully picked as they ripen, perhaps being gone over three or four times. They are spread out in the full hot sun to dry partially on coarsely woven *esparto* mats. The grapes are trodden out in shallow timber vessels called *lagares*, the men wearing special boots (*botas de Jerez*). The juice is 'plastered' (q.v.) to increase the acidity. The juice or must is then fermented in casks of about 100 gallons and a few months later is 'racked' (q.v.). It then may start to grow the crinkled film (*flor*) of special yeast on the surface which will eventually turn the wine into dry sherry by acting on some of the alcohol and residual sugar to form the aldehydes and other compounds which give to flor sherry its very characteristic 'mushroomy' or *rancio* taste. Not all sherries develop the flor growth. Those that fail are either converted to sweet sherries or distilled to make brandy or fortifying spirit.

The most promising flor sherries are divided into classes — palmas, cortados and rayas and varying percentages of brandy are added.

The maturing and blending are effected in a *solera* (q.v.) a system of containers in tiers which is the subject of a separate entry. The many types of sherry are noted alphabetically.

There is no such thing as a vintage sherry. It is by definition a blended wine. It is also obvious that a true flor sherry can never be cheap.

Australia, South Africa and to a lesser extent California are all making excellent dry sherries, though as noted not quite up to the standard of the finest Spanish. The French wine Château Chalon (q.v.) is made by a flor process and the best closely resembles a fine dry sherry.

Sherry, Brown: A sweet sherry, actually a dessert wine, made especially for the Anglo-Saxon trade by blending *paxarette* (q.v.) and *oloroso* (q.v.). Also known as East Indian.

Sherry, Californian: See Californian Sherry.

Sherry Cobbler: Mixed drink of variable composition but it always contains sweet sherry. Served cold and decorated with fruit. Port, spirits, curaçao, etc., may be added.

Sherry Cocktail: Dry sherry, dry vermouth and orange bitters.

Shipper: In the specialized sense of this book, one who ships wine or spirits away from its country of origin. The work is especially connected with the export of sherry, port, madeira, burgundy, claret, cognac, rum and Rhine wine. It is not a happy term, for a shipper is much more than a cartage contractor or a middleman. Often or usually he selects wine and spirits with skill, matures and blends them and is an integral part of the industry. In some cases the shippers are also actual vignerons or distillers. The number of shippers with British names in Spain, Portugal, Cognac, etc., tells a story.

Shippers' Lodges: The establishments at Vila Nova de Gaia, opposite Oporto, from which port is sent off.

Shipshape: Cocktail of whisky, sherry, rum, prune syrup and orange bitters.

Ship's Stores: The picturesque term applied, *inter alia*, to alcoholic beverages loaded free of excise duty on a ship or aircraft destined outside the country. Such ships must be 'outward bound'.

Shiraz: Originally a rich, fortified wine from the Persian (Iran) district of Shiraz, which has sometimes been claimed as the cradle of viticulture. A variety of grape known as shiraz, said to have been introduced from Persia, has long been cultivated in the Rhône Valley of France and in other parts of the world. See also Khullar. In some countries it is believed the local grape called hermitage is identical with the shiraz.

Shirosake: Japanese weak, colourless sake (q.v.), of about 5% alcohol.

Shirozake: The Japanese Dolls' Festival at which white sake is ceremoniously drunk.

Shive: A circular wooden or cork plug, partly bored in the centre, which is hammered into the bush of a cask when it has been filled. A solid shive or bung, smaller in diameter and with a countersunk centre, is used to seal the tap hole.

Shochu: Japanese spirit distilled from sake (q.v.).

Short: A colloquial name for a gin or whisky drink, usually taken before a meal. See also Snifter.

Shortridge Lawton: Old-established shippers of madeira (q.v.).

Shot: This is one of the widely-used half-slang words for a serving of liquor, especially of spirits (q.v.). Other cognate words are spot, snifter, slug, and tot. Each has its sphere of meaning but this varies with locality.

Shouting: Term, probably originally Australian, synonymous with 'treating', i.e. paying for another's drink. 'Shouting for the mob' is treating in the grand manner — paying for everybody in the bar. The origin of the term is unknown but is presumably connected with the loud invitation of him who pays. It has now been extended in Australia beyond liquor to include anything, almost.

Shove Groat: The parent of 'shove ha'penny' played in the days when the groat was a coin of the realm.

Shove Ha'penny: A popular inn game. Metal disks the size of a halfpenny are balanced on the edge of a small board marked laterally in sections. The discs are 'shoved' by a smart tap with the palm of the hand. The object is to steer three discs into each section or 'bed'.

Shrub: 18th-century English beverage of spirits (usually brandy or rum), spice, sugar and fruit juice. There has been a revival of interest in shrub, especially in the Scilly Isles.

Shuked or Shooked: Staves of casks bundled together for economy of transport.

Siblinger: Swiss (Schaffhausen) white wine.

Sicard: Old-established brand of cognac (q.v.).

Sicasse: The slang French (Normandy) term for crude spirits. There are many English and American equivalents, e.g., popskull, chain lightning, redeye. See also Moonshine.

Sicera: Vulgate form of the Hebrew word for strong drink. Related to shikar (q.v.).

Sichelsberg: German (Erbach, q.v.) white-wine vineyard.

Sicily: A renowned wine-producing region. Perhaps none of the Sicilian wines is in the top compartment but for all that there are many excellent ones. Sicily has been a huge vineyard from the earliest Graeco-Roman times and there are many allusions in classical writings to the quality of the produce. Sicilian wines run the gamut of type from light, bone-dry table wines to heavy, luscious desserts. The most celebrated Sicilian wine is, of course, marsala (q.v.). Other esteemed wines are Syracuse muscat (*moscato di Siracusa*), zucco, corvo, albanello and etna.

Sidecar: Cocktail of brandy, orange liqueur and lemon juice.

Sidra: Spanish sparkling cider.

Siebenmorgen: German (Rauenthal, q.v.) white wine.

Siederich: German (Duttweiler, q.v.) white wine.

Siefersheim: German (Rheinhessen) white-wine centre.

Sierre: Swiss (Valais) white wine.

Sievering: Austrian white table wine.

Sifone: The Italian evaporated grape juice boiled down by two-thirds and used to flavour and colour marsala (q.v.). It resembles the Spanish arrope (q.v.).

Sigalas Rabaud: First-growth sauternes (Bommes). Highly valued.

Signa: Wine-growing region of merit mentioned in Bible as suited for the service of the sanctuary.

Sikes's Hydrometer: See Proof Spirit.

Silberberg: Austrian (Steiermark) white wine.

Sillerbor: Hungarian *rosé* wine.

Sillery: French wine centre in the Champagne district. It is one of the few important places of the area not producing solely sparkling wine (champagne). It is a blanc de noirs (white wine made from black grapes). See also Verzenay and Catawba.

Silva, Antonio Jose da: Old-established shippers of port (q.v.).

Silva & Cosens: Old-established shippers of port, a sister firm of *Warre & Co.* (q.v.). The daughter of Edward Silva married the nephew and heir of Disraeli.

Silver Bullet: Cocktail of gin, kümmel and lemon juice.

Silver Fizz: Gin fizz (q.v.) plus egg white.

Silvergrogg: Swedish long drink of unflavoured spirit and soda-water.

Silzbrunnen: German white wine. See also Dienheim.

Simard: French (St. Émilion) red wine.

Simonds: English brewery established 1774 at Reading.

Simple: As a noun, this is an archaic word one meaning of which was a medicine made of a single vegetable ingredient. It has, however, often been used by old writers as synonymous, or practically so, with liqueur or cordial (q.v.), perhaps by confusion owing to the fact that many such medicinal simples were tinctures, or alcoholic extracts.

Singapore Gin Sling: Cocktail of equal parts dry gin, cherry brandy and benedictine. Add ginger beer.

Single: The expressive native term for a Scotch whisky entirely unblended, the product of one still and usually of one 'run'. A fully-matured pot-stilled single probably represents the pinnacle of the Scotch whisky distiller's art. A single is not a practical commercial proposition for several reasons. The run is too small and there is no guarantee of continuity. Moreover the long maturing time needed to mellow a pot-stilled single makes the cost riskily high. Nevertheless the really discerning Scot and some of his customers are sometimes able to find and buy 'single' whisky. The flavour may be equivalent to a fine cognac or armagnac. The term is also applied to a drink of spirits consisting of one measure, as opposed to a double.

Singlings: Crude brandy of the first distillation, which is usually subjected to re-distillation. See also Armagnac.

Sinzheim: German (Baden) red wine.

Sion: One of the most important Swiss (Valais) wine centres. The red wine (Dôle de Sion) and the white (Fendant de Sion) are named for the grape varieties used.

Siracusa, moscato di: Fruity Sicilian dessert wine.

Sir John: The name in Stuart times for an outsize Black Jack (q.v.).

Sistova: One of the important Bulgarian wine regions.

Sitges: Golden muscatel wine shipped from Spanish port south of Barcelona.

Sixain: French liquid container of 120 litres.

Six Out: Measure used today principally for spirits, which gives six out for a gill (q.v.). See also Optic.

Sizer, La: French (Hermitage, q.v.) red wine.

Sizies, Les: French red wine of Beaune (q.v.).

Sizing: Old term for food and drink, especially the latter, ordered by a student from a college buttery. At Harvard in the 17th century the sizing of beer was a pint, sold to the student for a farthing. See also Bever.

Skekszard: Hungarian red table wine from the village of that name.

Skhou: Central Asiatic spirit distilled from koumiss (q.v.).

Skimming System: English brewing method in which the complete fermentation is effected in a single large vessel, the yeast being periodically skimmed off. If the wash is subsequently run off to a 'cleansing' vessel the system is called 'skimming and dropping'. See also Dropping System.

Skittle Board: An adaptation of skittles, popular in the West Country. Sometimes called 'Devil among the tailors', since there are nine skittles and 'nine devils make a tailor'. A small wooden ball is attached by cord to a pole set on the left-hand side of a large tray. In this tray are nine skittles placed in a box. The ball is swung to the left, round the pole and the object is to knock down as many skittles as possible. See also Dadloms.

Skittles: A traditional inn game, revived in recent years. It is played in an alley (a narrow space enclosed with wooden guards) and heavy wooden cheeses are directed at nine pins (skittles).

Sky-Blue: See Jailer.

Skye: Island off west coast of Scotland. A centre for production of highland malt, a heavy pungent whisky for blending.

Slanthorpe: Australian (Queensland) wine centre.

Slavjanka: Bulgarian dessert wine.

Sling: A vague term for a mixed spirit drink. It used to be confined to hot drinks of this sort flavoured with nutmeg, and hence resembling a heated sangaree (q.v.), but it is now also used for cold mixed spirit drinks of any composition (e.g. gin sling).

Slivovica: Syn. for 'slivovitz' (q.v.).

Slivovitz: Plum brandy made in central Europe, especially Hungary.

Sloe Gin: A spirit of blackthorn flavour.

Slop: The de-alcoholized residue after distillation of spirits. The disposal of slop to avoid nuisance is often a troublesome matter.

Slug: A curious word and an example of a standard term taking the backward route to become slang. It has a large variety of meanings but for the present purpose it usually denotes a dram, draught or other moderate serve of spirits. However, it can also mean a large and hurried one. Use was largely limited to the U.S. but is now widespread.

Sly Grog: Liquor illegally retailed by a non-licensed person.

Small: Obsolete synonym for light or low alcoholic content, e.g. small beer.

Smash: A small julep or cobbler (q.v.).

Smeller: A brewery employee whose important function is to smell the interior of casks before they are filled with beer to ensure that they are in sound condition. An experienced man acquires an expert nose.

Smith-Haut-Lafitte: French estate of Martillac, Graves, which has a large production of good red and white wines.

Smith, Woodhouse & Co.: Old-established (1784) shippers of port (q.v.).

Smoke: Moonshine (q.v.) straight from the still.

Snifter: The large glass used for the better enjoyment of brandy. See also Ballon. The idea is to expose a large surface of the fragrant spirit to the heat of the hand, and to sniff the volatile flavour. Also U.S. slang for a dram or other small drink of spirits. Now widespread colloquial for a quick drink of anything alcoholic.

Snug or **Snuggery:** Semi-private apartment in the pub, reserved usually by custom for the regulars. Similar to the bar parlour.

Soave: The reputed best white wine of Veneto (Italy), from the small town of that name.

Sobe: Biblical (Hebrew) word for intoxicating drink in general. See also Yayin, Tirosh, Shekar, Hemer and Asis.

Sochu: Chinese spirit distilled from sake.

Soda Water: Water containing dissolved carbon dioxide gas, always made artificially as distinct from some mineral waters (q.v.). It contains no soda, and the misleading name is derived from the common small-scale method of preparing the gas from sodium carbonate and acid.

Sofia: Bulgarian centre for wine production.

Soft Drink: A non-alcoholic or so-called temperance beverage, usually sweet and carbonated.

Sohlbrunnen: German white wine. See also Dienheim.

Soleil de Sierre: Swiss (Sierre, Valais) 'straw wine' (*vin de paille*, q.v.).

Solera: The Spanish term for a collection of casks used for the production of certain types (not all) of sherry wine (q.v.). The term also means the characteristic process used to mature the wine by systematic movement of wine from one row of casks to the next lower. Though originally an exclusively Spanish process, it has now been adopted by some other countries making *fino* (q.v.) sherries. Though the system has undeniable merit, especially for large producers who aim to keep their wine uniform over the years, excellent dry sherry can be made without a solera.

The solera consists of a pile of casks each of about 120 gallons. There may be perhaps 12 casks in a row and up to 6 such rows, making 72 casks in all and a total volume of over 8,000 gallons. The top row contains young wine, the bottom the wine that has graduated through the system and some of which is ready to be run off for disposal. As the wine is removed from the bottom row the ullage (q.v.) is made up by filling the vacant space with wine from the next layer and so on in succession. It usually takes about six years for wine to pass right through the system. No row of casks is ever fully emptied. During the process the flor (film yeast) is carefully kept from disturbance.

The solera system is also used to some extent for the production of malaga (q.v.). See also Sherry.

Solera is thus not the name of a particular wine but of a process and is equivalent to vatting or blend. Less than half is ever withdrawn in any one year so old wine is always present and in theory a solera which was started a century ago still contains some wine over 100 years old. However, a little schoolboy mathematics will soon prove that the original wine will not be present to a much greater extent than the proverbial drop in the ocean.

To establish and maintain a solera requires great skill in selection and operation, great patience and a large capital outlay. For these reasons the solera remains an exclusive Spanish process though of course not all Spanish sherry 'goes through the tiers'. In some establishments the solera is used to produce a sherry of supreme quality a little of which will enhance lesser breeds. How long the romantic solera will endure in the face of competition and mass-production is anybody's guess.

Solitude, La: This beautifully-named smallish French red wine vineyard is in Martillac, Graves.

Solomon: Irrespective of who in fact wrote the Song of Solomon, surely the supreme compliment to wine is 'Let him kiss me with the kisses of his mouth: for thy love is better than wine'.

Solutré: French Burgundy (Maçon) white wine. The better-known Pouilly and Fuissé are neighbours and the wine is usually sold as Pouilly-Fuissé.

Sol-y-Sombra: Spanish drink (sun and shadow) of equal parts brandy and gin.

Soma: Classical, perhaps mythical, intoxicating beverage of ancient India used in sacrificial rites in honour of Indra. Some scholars believe it was mead (q.v.). Also supposed to be a Persian beer, said to have been brewed as early as 1,000 B.C. Also the name of an Italian liquid measure of a hectolitre or 22 gallons.

Something Short, Drop of: A tot (q.v.) of spirits as opposed to a glass of beer.

Somlauer Auslese: Although Somlauer is said to be the best Hungarian white wine (see Somlyo) and the pride of the local wine-growing industry this German name, meaning 'selected Somlyo wine' is still widely used as the title.

Somló Furmint: Table wine from Hungary.

Somlyo: The finest white wine district of Hungary. By general consent Somlauer (q.v.) can stand comparison with the good white wines of the world.

Sommelier: A drink-waiter or butler, especially of wines. He usually wears a special costume, consisting of a heavy silver chain and perhaps a decorated leather apron.

Sommerach: German (Franconian, q.v.) white wine.

Sommerhalde: German (Hambach, q.v.) white wine.

Sommerhäuschen: German (Rheinhessen) wine estate.

Sommerheil: German (Hochheim, q.v.) white wine.

Sommerseite: German (Herxheim, q.v.) wine estate.

Sondrio: North Italian (Lombardian) red wine centre. The best is called Valtellina (q.v.).

Songurlar Valley: One of the principal wine producing regions of Bulgaria, noted for white wines of the Misket (Muscat) type.

Sonnenberg: German (Rheinhessen) white wine from Apisheim. Also a white wine estate on the Ruwer (q.v.).

Sonnenkuests: Bulgarian white wine from Rekazeteli grapes. The name means 'sunny coast'.

Sonnenuhr: German vineyard (fine wine) of the Wehlen district (q.v.). The name means sundial ('sun clock') from the huge sundial cut out on a rock in the vineyard. It is a fairly common German vineyard name. There is a Sonnenuhr at Zeltingen and several others of lesser quality in the Moselle.

Sonnseite: German wine estate of Wintrich, Moselle.

Sonoma: District (county) of northern California, U.S.A., noted for wine production. It is stated to produce the largest volume of wine in the U.S. Most of the production is of ordinary quality but there are individual estates producing very fine wines.

Sontheim: German (Württemberg) red and white wines.

Sophistication: As applied to liquor, means adulteration.

Sopron: Hungarian centre for production of a dessert wine called Valtellin (q.v.).

Sops-in-Wine: Intriguing popular name for the carnation because the fragrant, clove-scented petals of the blossoms were once used to flavour wine.

Sorbet: Water ice which may contain spirits.

Sorek: Special variety of grape vine with dark-red grapes mentioned in Bible (e.g. Is. 5 : 2, Jer. 2 : 21).

Soubya: Egyptian rice beer. See also Sake.

Souche: French for stump or stem, especially of old grape vine.

Soulaines: French (Loire) white wine.

Sour: A clear distinction must be drawn between the terms sour and acid applied to wines and also some brewed beverages. All acid beverages are sour in the lay sense but the acid is wholesome and desired. In wine it is due to tartaric acid, in cider to malic and some beers are acidified with a little lactic or other organic acid. Defectively sour beverages are so because some of the alcohol has been converted by micro-organisms to acetic acid or vinegar, always a fault. See also Acid.

Sour: U.S. term for iced long drink made from a mixture of spirits, lemon and other fruit juice, sugar and mineral water with ample ice. All manner of variants are possible on this theme. Wine may be added, slices of fruit used for decoration, and there is even an egg sour using the yolk. Some of the stock recipes are separately mentioned. The sour is usually essentially a sweet drink. See also Acid.

Soussans: French (Médoc) red wine area whose produce is usually sold under the more renowned adjacent commune of Margaux (q.v.).

Soutard: French (St. Émilion) red wine.

South Africa: Old-established wine-producer. Wine has been grown at the Cape for over 300 years. All types are made. The quality has risen steadily and the best South African wines, like those of Australia, can now stand comparison with all but the finest European products. Most of the wine is now made and sold by growers' co-operative organizations. The vineyards are almost all established within a radius of 200 miles from Cape Town itself. One celebrated and ancient establishment of Constantia is actually part of the city. Here both dessert and dry red wine are made. The former, under the dignified and accurate name Constantia, has been prized in Europe for generations.

There are important vineyards at Paarl, Stellenbosch, Malmesbury, Tulbagh, Worcester, Robertson, Montagu, Langeberge and Swartberg.

Much brandy of fair quality is distilled. The liqueur Van der Hum (q.v.) has a large sale beyond South Africa. Much light beer for native consumption is brewed. See also Mealie.

South America: Every country of South America makes wine. Argentine makes the most and Chile, by common consent, makes the best. Since the South American population of European origin is principally from vinous countries — Spain, Portugal and Italy in particular, and as there are large areas suitable for viticulture, it is surprising that quality is not generally higher.

In total volume (over 600 million gallons), South America is a major wine-producer. Although wine has been grown for some hundreds of years, the quality of South American wine has been mediocre or worse. However, in recent years modern methods have resulted in a big lift in the quality of the best wines, especially of Chile and Argentina, though the bulk of the South American production is still *vin ordinaire* (q.v.) and is nearly all consumed locally. See entries for individual South American states.

South Guildford: Australian (W.A.) wine centre.

Soutirage: French for racking (q.v.).

Souzão: One of the dark-red grapes grown for port (q.v.).

Spa: Syn. for 'mineral water' (q.v.). Strictly, it should be limited to a natural water but the meaning has been extended to any unsweetened mineral water or 'tonic'.

Spain: Probably about the third largest wine-producer in the world, the annual make being normally about 450 million gallons. All types of wine are made and much of it of fine quality but sherry overshadows all the rest just as port does in Portugal. This is unfortunate. Many of the red and white table wines of Spain are a credit to the industry. The chief of these are separately noted. There is, of course, a large trade in wine with South America but France is also a considerable importer. The French wine merchant has a keen sense of a bargain. See Rioja, Malaga, etc. Spain is a large producer of excellent cider, both still and sparkling.

Spalato: Dalmatian red wine, also known as Split.

Spangenberg: German (Rheinhessen) white wine from Apisheim.

Spanish Clay: Lebrija clay (*tierra de lebrija*), a silicate of the type of bentonite which is added to sherry as a filtering and clarifying agent.

Spanna: Alternative name for nebbiolo vine.

Sparge: To spray hot liquor (q.v.) on the grist (q.v.) in the mash tuns (q.v.). This is to ensure that the 'goods' (q.v.) remain suspended in the wort during the extraction process.

Sparkling: The general English term for a wine charged with carbon dioxide gas (q.v.). It is never applied to the finest of such wines, champagne. It is used, perhaps unfortunately, for both the naturally-sparkling wines made by the champagne process (q.v.) such as sparkling burgundy, hock, moselle (and cider) and for artificially carbonated beverages. The finest burgundies, hocks, etc., are never used for sparkling wines but the products may be very agreeable nevertheless. In their own countries these sparkling wines are comparatively inexpensive but as non-wine-producing countries unfairly levy the same tax on them as on champagne, they are not usually good value.

It has long been recognized that the true champagne process produces a longer and more controlled sparkle than does carbonation effected by pumping in the gas. This is probably due to the actual chemical combination of the carbon dioxide gas with the alcohol in champagne-process wine to form the unstable compound ethyl pyrocarbonate. In carbonated wines the gas is merely dissolved and escapes more rapidly. See also Sparkling Wine.

Sparkling Bordeaux: French sparkling wine of limited demand and production. Also called Bordeaux Mousseux.

Sparkling Burgundy: In France this is a wine of high quality, legally required to be made by the true champagne process (q.v.). It may be red, white or *rosé*. In other countries the name is limited to red sparkling wine and the quality may vary from good to damnable.

Sparkling Wine: See also Champagne. Although it is said that a rough, poor sparkling wine of sorts called Refosco was made in Italy long before the advent of champagne, it was this wine alone that ushered in the true sparkling wine that we know today. Champagne was the first true sparkling wine and although such wine is now made in all countries of Europe and also in all other wine-growing lands, the best of it is still made by the champagne process.

Sparkling wines are those which contain dissolved carbon dioxide gas, which causes the wine to effervesce when opened and to give an agreeable tingle on the palate. There are three ways of making sparkling wine. In descending order of merit they are the champagne process, the bulk, tank or Charmat method and the impregnation process. These can be broadly described respectively as fermentation in individual bottles, fermentation in bulk in closed tanks and the artificial process of pumping carbon dioxide gas into bulk wine.

The best sparkling wines of Burgundy, Germany and other centres may approach champagne in quality and are made in exactly similar manner. The grapes are fermented to produce an ordinary 'still' wine, usually of an acid character. This is 'fined' (q.v.) and filled into the familiar specially strong bottles with punt (pushed-in bottom). Some sugar and a pure-yeast culture are added; usually with a little tannin. Corks are inserted and securely wired on. The bottles are stored at

60° F. to 65° F. Fermentation takes place in the bottle, developing considerable pressure from the imprisoned gas. Prior to the end of fermentation the temperature is lowered to about 40° F.

Now commences the long and difficult job of removing the dead yeast cells and other debris to leave a crystal-clear wine without losing the precious gas or 'sparkle'. Several times a week a skilled worker called a *remueur* gives each bottle a twist and a slight downward cant. After two or three months the bottles are standing upside down and all the sediment is on the cork. Next follows the most difficult of all operations, disgorging or *dégorgement*. The object is to remove the cork and let the sediment fly out with the least possible loss of gas and clear liquid. It is highly skilled and highly paid work. A modern variant is to freeze the neck of the bottle and eject the little plug of sediment-containing ice.

We now have dry or *brut* sparkling wine, fit for connoisseurs but not generally popular. For the wide market it needs to be dosed or sweetened, the process called dosage (q.v.). This varies for different markets. The Russians like it very sweet, the English fairly dry with other buyers in between. The dosage may be with pure cane sugar solution (syrup) or with a little good brandy added.

The tank method produces a wholesome but lower grade wine.

The impregnation method is used only for cheap wines. The gas rapidly escapes on opening the bottle. Unlike the champagne-type and to a lesser extent the bulk-process wine, the carbon dioxide gas is not combined but merely dissolved. See also Sparkling.

Spätlese: German for late-picked. This term on a wine label indicates special quality resulting from the process of sorting over the vines several times in the finer German vineyards, each time picking only the most mature grapes. Late-harvested grapes are more luscious and sugary, yielding a superior wine. See also Auslese and its related terms Beerenauslese and Trockenbeerenauslese.

Spearwood: Australian (W.A.) wine centre.

Spent Liquor: General name for the alcohol-free residue after distillation. See also Slop.

Spey: The river in Scotland that cuts through some of the most famous whisky-distilling centres, including Glen Grant, the Glenlivet, Glenfiddach, Glenlossie, Glen Rothes and Mortlach. The Valley of the Spey is generally considered the birthplace of modern whisky and the region is dotted with distilleries.

Spice: The use of spices for flavouring wine is a very ancient practice. The Bible and other ancient books have many references to the art. Wines were flavoured with spices and herbs not only to mask rank flavours of defective wines, but to give a distinctive taste valued *per se*. Common spices of ancient times were ginger, clove, cinnamon, cassia and nutmeg. Possibly all those were used as well as aromatic herbs such as anise, dill, sage and many more. As noted elsewhere (see Retsina) the Greek practice of flavouring wine with pine resin is an ancient practice. Vermouth and other spiced appetizer wines are more popular than ever.

Spider: Archaic term for mixed drink of lemonade and brandy.

Spielberg: Another of the German wine names borne by many white-wine estates, including those situated at Mertesdorf-Grünhaus (q.v.), Randersacker, Meckenheim, Dürkheim, Ellsheim and Ruwer. See also Schlossberg.

Spiess: German (Ruppertsberg, q.v.) white wine.

Spigot: A small plug for stopping a vent hole in a cask. Also a faucet that can be plugged into a cask.

Spike: To add spirits to wine or brewed liquor. Syn. with 'lace'. See also Dog's Nose.

Spile: A small peg of wood or cane which fits into a hole in the shive (q.v.). It is loosened to facilitate the drawing of the beer from the cask, or tightened to thumb pressure to keep the beer in condition, when not in use. To 'spile a cask' means to bore a small hole in it. (The boring of spile holes is not always done with honest intent.)

Spirit: As ordinarily used, this word means any distilled liquor (e.g. brandy, rum). It is also employed vaguely as a synonym for unflavoured alcohol of any strength.

Spirit, Cologne; — Neutral; — Silent; — Velvet: These are all synonymous terms applied to rectified, odourless, tasteless spirit (alcohol), irrespective of source, used for manufacture of beverages. See also Rectified.

Spirit of Wine: Ethyl alcohol.

Spirit Still: The vessel used in Scotch whisky-making for the second distillation whereby the low wines (q.v.) are further concentrated.

Spiritus Frumenti: U.S. pharmaceutical term for whisky.

Spiritus Tenuior: British pharmaceutical term for proof spirit (q.v.).

Spiritus Vini Gallici: British pharmaceutical term for brandy. In spite of the '*gallici*', it is not necessary that French brandy be used.

Spiritus Vini Vitis: The brandy of the U.S. Pharmacopoeia; required to be a true grape brandy containing not less than 54% by volume of alcohol, and stored (aged) in wood for not less than four years.

Spittert: German (Palatinate) table wine.

Spitze: German (Brauneberg, Moselle) white wine.

Spitzenwein: German term for a super-excellent wine. Such a wine is often served with a garland around the neck of the bottle.

Splash: The mark, usually of whitewash, placed on unlabelled bottles, mainly to show on what side they have been resting in the bin.

Splice the Main Brace: To gain a merited alcoholic drink. One of the most strenuous and urgent jobs aboard a sailing man o' war was to repair the main brace controlling the main yard. The job done, the captain traditionally ordered a double issue of rum.

Split: See Spalato.

Spontaneous Combustion: The rollicking myth, persisting into the second half of the 19th century, that heavy drinkers are liable to burst into flames, with fatal results. This folkway, one of the most stupendous pieces of nonsense of all ages, was chiefly propounded by American non-conformist preachers of the hell-fire school but Charles Dickens, per-haps the most realistic of British writers, is said to have been a strong supporter of the doctrine. See *Bleak House*.

In 1827 Johnathan Kittredge, a reformed drunkard, at a public meeting in New Hampshire, described 'well-authenticated cases attested by living witnesses, examined by learned men and published in the journals of the day without contradiction'. Other instances of spon-taneous combustion were cited in the *Georgia Journal* of 15 May 1830, the *Massachusetts Spy* of 12 May 1830 and many more.

Sporen: Alsatian vineyard planted about A.D. 1400. White wine.

Spot: British colloquialism for a friendly drink.

Spot: See Shot.

Sprendlingen: German (Rheinhessen) white wine.

Springvale: A region in South Australia noted for light, white wines.

Spritzer: German term for Rhine wine with soda water.

Spritzig: A German wine term that means lively. It is applied to wines that contain a little carbon dioxide gas, not enough to class the wine as sparkling but just sufficient to give the tongue a gentle prickle. A wine can be *spritzig* either from very early bottling or from undergoing a slight secondary fermentation. See also Pétillant.

Spruce Beer: Not a beer or other brewed beverage, since it uses no barley or other cereal. It is essentially fermented molasses flavoured with spruce twigs and cones. It is reported to be made (and liked!) by the fisherfolk of Newfoundland.

Spumante: Sparkling in Italian, the equivalent of the French *mousseux*, the Spanish *espumoso* and the German *sekt*.

Square-Face: Name of a bottle of characteristic shape, especially used for hollands (q.v.).

Sremski Karlovci: Yugoslavian red beverage wine, also known as Carlo-witz.

Staatsweingut: German (Erbach, q.v.) white wine.

Stablay: Wine centre of Graach, Moselle.

Stadecken: German wine-growing parish of Rheinhessen.

Stand of Ale: A large barrel. Now obsolete.

Star: English brewery established 1777 at Eastbourne.

Starboard Light: Popular name given to crème de menthe on account of the green colour, and adopted as a trade-mark by one proprietary line.

Stars: It has long been customary for blenders and shippers of cognac brandy to use stars and letters on the labels and each firm has its own esoteric system. It is said that the star was used to denote quality because it represented Halley's Comet of the year 1811, when the wines happened to be of unusually high quality, supposed to be an undoubted example of cause and effect.

The star was used after *Phylloxera* when some wise person decided that brandy of extra quality needed a sign. The system soon became quite unworkable. According to Lichine, a 3-star brandy usually means the firm's cheapest, from 3 to 6 years old and broken down to 42% alcohol. Today it can be safely accepted that the star system is valueless and often grossly misleading. It is no longer limited to the Cognac region but is copied by every brandy firm in the world. The only criterion is taste. See also Brandy, Age of, and V.S.O.

Stars: Dom Pérignon (q.v.) is alleged to have said: 'I am drinking stars' on first tasting sparkling wine. If this story were not true it would be necessary to invent it.

Starter: The pure culture of yeast added to a liquid (must, wort, etc.) to ensure a satisfactory fermentation. The process is technically known as inoculation and in the brewery as pitching (q.v.).

Stave: A constituent of a cask, carefully shaped to make a watertight joint with its neighbours. To stave wine or beer is an obsolete term meaning to destroy defective liquor by knocking in a stave and letting the contents of the cask run to waste.

Steel Wine: Old-fashioned tonic medicine consisting of wine, usually sherry, in which steel or iron filings had stood for some time.

Steely: The maltster's term for hard barley grains which fail to germinate effectively.

Steeping: The first part of the conversion (q.v.) of barley in the malting process (q.v.), i.e. soaking the grain in large cisterns at the maltings. 'Steep ripe' describes the steeped barley when it has absorbed approximately 60% of water.

Steep Ripe: The maltster's term for barley which has been soaked ('steeped') until it has absorbed about 60% water and is ready to germinate.

Steffensberg: German (Enkirch, q.v.) fine white wine.

Steffensberg: German (Kröv-Kövenig, q.v.) white-wine estate.

Steiermark: Austrian wine region.

Steig: German (Guntersblum, q.v.) white wine.

Steig: German (Laubenheim, q.v.) white wine.

Steig: German (Oppenheim, q.v.) white wine.

Steiger: German (Niederhausen-Schlossböckelheim A.D. Nahe, q.v.) white wine.

Stein: The patent still (q.v.) invented in 1826 by Robert Stein, a cousin of the Haigs (q.v.), which was superseded in 1831 by the Coffey still (q.v.).

Stein: German Steinwein vineyard near Würzburg (q.v.).

Stein: German (Worms) wine estate. See also Bechtheim.

Stein: German (Hochheim, q.v.) white wine.

Stein: An earthenware beer-mug.

Steinacker: German (Kallstadt, q.v.) wine centre.

Steinberg: German (Herxheim, q.v.) wine estate.

Steinberg: German (Kreuznach, q.v.) white-wine estate.

Steinberg: Celebrated German (Rheingau) wine estate of 60 acres at Hattenheim belonging to the Prussian government. The Steinberg wines are made at Kloster Eberbach (q.v.) and are always sold by public auction. They are divided into the eight classical and time-honoured German wine categories, starting at simple Steinberger and ending at the almost hallowed Steinberg Kabinett or personal selection of the original owner, the Duke of Nassau.

Steinbrucher: Swiss (Villingen) white wine.

Steinbühl: German white wine. See also Bergzabern.

Steinchen: German wine estate of Winkel, Rheingau.

Steinerne Brücke: German (Laubenheim, q.v.) white wine.

Steinert: German (Gau Algesheim, q.v.) white wine.

Steingebiss: German (Kirrweiler, q.v.) wine estate.

Steingrubler: Ancient vineyard of Wettolsheim, Alsace. Whites.

Steinhausen: German (Rauenthal, q.v.) white wine.

Steinitz: German (Nieder-und-Oberwalluf, q.v.) white wine.

Steinländ: German (Rheinhessen) wine estate.

Steinmauer: German (Moselle) vineyard near Zeltingen.

Steinmorgen: German (Erbach, q.v.) white-wine vineyard.

Steinweg: German (Gau-Bickelheim, q.v.) white wine.

Steinwegen: German (Erbach, q.v.) white-wine vineyard.

Steinwein: Highly individual German wine from Würzburg, on the Main. The wine is sold in dumpy bottles called *Bocksbeutel*. Steinwein is the produce of about 350 acres of the Steinmantel area. Buergerspital and Juliusspital are charitable foundations. The German government is an important Steinwein producer.

Stellenbosch: The oldest and one of the best South African (Cape Province) wine districts. Reds, whites and brandies.

Stellenrood: South African heavy-bodied red table wine of merit, grown near Stellenbosch (q.v.).

Stengah: Malay States Club version of stinger (q.v.).

Stepony: A 17th-century London beverage made from lemons, raisins, and spirits.

Stevenson, William, 1530–75: The reputed author of the celebrated comedy *Gammer Gurton's Needle*, which contains the song:

> I stuff my skin, so full within,
> Of jolly good ale and old
> Back and side go bare, go bare,
> Both foot and hand go cold:
> But belly God send thee good ale enough,
> Whether it be new or old.

Stickelpfad: German (Ruppertsberg, q.v.) white wine.

Still: An apparatus for the production of spirits (q.v.). See Distillation. The word is derived from the Latin *stillare*, to drop or drip, which exactly describes the appearance of the spirit as it emerges from a small and simple piece of distillation equipment. See also Still, Patent and Still, Pot.

Still, Patent: Commercial distilling equipment (based on the original patent of Aeneas Coffey, and sometimes even today called a 'Coffey still'), consisting of apparatus for the continuous distillation of spirit of a high degree of purity, and thus directly opposed to the action of a pot-still (q.v.). See also Distillation.

Still, Pot: A simple distilling appliance in which the distillate is not unduly refined or separated as in the patent still. In general, the finest potable spirits are those made from a pot-still. Cognac and armagnac legally must be pot-stilled. See also Distillation.

Stillage: Bench or shelving for holding liquor bottles, *inter alia*.

Stillion: The wooden cradle in which the casks are stood in the cellars of a public house or vats in a brewery. Also known as thrawls.

Still-Room: The housekeeper's storeroom in a country mansion in which the cordials (q.v.) and herb preparations were made. Also, the building or room in a distillery in which the still (q.v.) is housed.

Still Wine: One that does not effervesce, as opposed to a sparkling wine (q.v.).

Stinger: Cocktail of brandy and crème de menthe. Surely a degradation of both and also of a hallowed name.

Stinger (syn. Stengah): British slang for whisky and soda, especially in Malaya. Said to be derived from Malayan *sa* (one) and *tenah* (half).

Stingo: A strong English beer. Originally brewed in Yorkshire.

Stirn: German (Niederleuken, q.v.) white wine.

Stirrup-Cup: A drink handed to a parting guest, when his feet were already in the stirrups ('One for the road'). Sometimes, however, the term is applied to a drink given on arrival.

Stockheim: German (Württemberg) white wine.

Stof: Russian liquid measure of about a quart.

Stolzenberg: German (Detzem, Moselle) white wine.

Stolzenberg: German (Gau Algesheim, q.v.) white wine.

Stone-Fence: Obsolete term for mixed drink of ginger beer and brandy, presumably from the conventional 'stone' (earthenware) bottles.

Stonsdorfer: Silesian brandy produced by a characteristic method.

Stonyfell: South Australian vineyard close to Adelaide, producing a range of wines.

Stooming: Howell writes (1634) that this is the process used by the 'cunning Hollander' to improve 'hard green Wine that grows about Rochel . . . and he hath a trick to put a bag of Herbs . . . to give it a whiter tincture and more sweetness, then they re-embark it for England where it passeth for good Bachrag' (i.e. Bacharach, q.v.) 'and this is called stooming of wines'.

Stop Close: The old term for covering mead or ale after the first main fermentation is completed, to allow time for final 'fermenting out' and maturing.

Stoup or Stope: Elizabethan term for a drinking vessel (*Twelfth Night*, Act II, sc. iii), also its contents, which could apparently range from half a pint to half a gallon but mainly meant a large drink.

Stout: Strong porter (q.v.) with heavy malt flavour.

Straight: A straight spirit is an unblended one, i.e. the product of one distillation only. To drink any liquor 'straight' means to take it as it comes from the bottle, without adding water or other diluent.

Strasse: German (Deidesheim, q.v.) white wine.

Stratzenberg: German (Rheinhessen) wine estate.

Straw: Apart from the material still used for packing, the name straw is applied to the tube used to drink by sucking. Today straws are invariably made of paper or plastic. Babylonians are stated to have drunk their beer through jars by inserting reeds and other tubes.

Strawberry Fizz: Mixed drink of gin, ripe strawberries, cream and lemon.

Straw Wine: Sweet wines (*vins de paille*) are made by half-drying grapes on straw mats to increase sugar strength. Straw wines under various names are made in many countries, e.g., in France for sauternes, the Rhine for sweet white dessert wines, in Italy and Spain for addition to dessert wines and sherries and in Portugal for ports. The process is expensive, involving much labour, and in general is applicable only to the better-quality wines.

Strega: Italian liqueur, one of the many proprietary lines. Exceedingly sweet and highly flavoured. The name means 'witch'.

Streng: German (Nierstein, q.v.) white wine.

Strength, Alcoholic: There is a vast literature on this subject. Most laymen's beliefs and estimates of alcoholic potency are fanciful. There have been many quaint claims by tavern-keepers. The Chinese novel *Water Margin*, written in the 14th century, describes the banner fluttering over an inn on which was inscribed 'After Three Bowls of Our Wine You Can't Cross the Bridge'. In 18th-century London a prominent sign was displayed outside a tavern to advertise its gin. 'Drunk for threepence. Dead drunk for fourpence. Clean straw to lie on free.' The following table gives a summary of the facts;

STRENGTH OF ALCOHOLIC BEVERAGES

Type	Examples (not exhaustive)	Approximate Percentage of Alcohol by Volume
Brewed beverages	Beer, ale, stout, porter	5%. Very light continental beers may be as low as $2\frac{1}{2}$%, and strong English ales 7%
Wine — beverage, to be drunk with meals	Claret, burgundy, chablis, sauternes, hock, moselle, rioja (Spanish), chianti (Italian), and similar wines made in other countries	10%, varying from 8 to 14%. The wines of warmer climates (Australia, California, etc.) are usually higher than those of temperate European climates, owing to the greater sweetness of the must
Wine — fortified or dessert	Sherry, port, muscat, marsala, madeira	18 to 20%. The extra alcohol comes from added brandy or other form of alcohol
Wine — sparkling	Champagne, sparkling burgundy, sparkling hock, sparkling moselle, asti spumante	13%. (Part of the alcohol derived from added sugar)
Vermouth	French and Italian	16 to 20%
Wine — fruit	Cider, perry, pineapple, apricot, plum and many others	Extremely variable: anything from 3 to 12%, according to sugar-content of fruit and added sugar
Spirits	Brandy, whisky, rum, gin, vodka, applejack, calvados	Rather variable — 45%, but ranging from 40 to 55%
Cereal and other 'wines'	Sake	Up to 18%
Liqueurs or cordials	Chartreuse, benedictine, crème de menthe, cherry brandy, and very many others	Very variable: from 30 to 65%

(Quoted by permission of George Allen & Unwin Ltd. from *The Earnest Drinker*, by O. A. Mendelsohn.)

Stringing: The hopgrower's term for the process of affixing the supports for the hop vines.

Stromboli: Italian sweet wines from the Lipari island of that name, off Sicily. The best known is Malvazia di Lipari.

Strong Waters: An archaic term for alcoholic beverages in general but especially for spirits (q.v.).

Stübchen: German wine measure, variable but about 6½ pints.

Stückfässer: German (Rhine) cask or tun of 1,200 litres. The Halbstücke and the Viertelstücke are a half and a quarter this capacity. The last is the most commonly used vessel.

Stuck Wine: Material in which alcoholic fermentation has prematurely ceased, due to change of temperature or other cause.

Studebaker: A term for a large beaker (q.v.) said still to be used in Heligoland. Studebaker was a pirate, a native of Heligoland, noted for his mighty thirst. His habit was to drink down a vast volume and invert the container on the tavern counter as a mute challenge.

Stuff, Hard: See Hard.

Stum: Almost archaic English word of various meanings. It could signify ordinary must (q.v.) and in particular must whose fermentation had been arrested by adding an antiseptic. It also meant partly fermented wine whose action had been revived by adding fresh must. To stum wine was to preserve it.

Sturm: Austrian wine still in last stage of fermentation ('stormy'). See also Federweisser and Heuriger.

Stuttgart: The German market centre for the red and white wines of Württemberg.

Suau: French (Barsac) sweet white table wine. See also Barsac.

Succeeded: One of those quaint English wine terms. This one means that the wine has come up to expectations. Why so obvious a description is needed by oenophiles is obscure.

Sucrage: French term for the addition of sugar to the must (q.v.) to increase the alcohol in bad wine years. French law prohibits the addition of both sugar and acid together. Also known as amelioration and chaptalization.

Suds: American slang for beer. An inept term. Foam is not limited to soap solution and beer.

Suduiraut: French (Sauternes) fine sweet white table wine. It is almost as renowned as the adjoining Yquem (q.v.).

Suisse: Cocktail of anisette, absinthe and egg white.

Suites, Les: French term for the later pressings of wine which go to make poorer grades of wines, as opposed to *vins de goutte* from the first pressings.

Sukindol: Bulgarian wine-growing centre.

Sulfatado: Spanish term for the frequent treatment of grape vines with sulphur.

Sulphur: In one form and another sulphur has long been a great friend of the wine-grower. It had been usefully employed empirically centuries before the era of microbiology. In 1630 Howell (q.v.) noted the use of brimstone in Rhenish wines. The use of powdered elementary sulphur as a dust to prevent or destroy mildew literally saved some of the European wine industry from destruction. Burning sulphur gives rise to the germicidal gas sulphur dioxide and it has long been common practice to fumigate casks in this manner, though today more convenient solutions of sulphur compounds (sulphites, etc.) are used.

The same or equivalent sulphur compounds are also widely used to add to must to delay fermentation and to new wines, especially whites, to preserve them before bottling. A regulated amount of sulphur dioxide in the form of *potassium metabisulphite* is also added to the cheaper sweet table wines of the sauternes type (q.v.) or substitutes to prevent secondary fermentation in the bottle.

Sulphur dioxide is also commonly added to the poorer bottled dry white wines and many people who are sensitive to sulphites find such wines nauseous. In general sulphur, like fire, is a good servant and a bad master. All wine-producing countries have wise laws regulating the amount of sulphites and sulphates that wine may contain.

Sultana: Seedless grape, also known as Thompson's Seedless, widely grown for dried vine fruit. In some countries it is also used for white wine.

Sumshu: Manchurian beverage reported to be made from fermented kaoliang, a type of sorghum.

Sunday Morning: Cocktail of brandy, port, black coffee, whole egg and sugar.

Sundown: Cocktail of gin, apricot cordial and lemon juice.

Sundowner: A drink taken at dusk, especially the Malayan planter's pre-dinner cocktail. Also a term imported from South Africa used for the first glass of beer in the early evening.

Sup: Swedish for dram. *Supbroder*, boon companion.

Superquatre Method: A French wine-making process due to Semichon, designed to reduce the activity of wild yeasts by mixing together fully-fermented wine with unfermented must.

Superquattro Method: See Superquatre. This is the Italian version of the term.

Suresnes: Another of those maligned places. Brillat-Savarin (in 1830) describes it as a pleasant village on the Seine to the west of Paris, famous for its poor wine. The saying was that it needed three men to drink a glass of Suresnes wine — one to swallow and two assistants to keep him up and prevent him from losing heart.

There are many places of unjustly evil reputation. In Melbourne the inhabitants of the dull, respectable and innocuous suburb of Footscray are for ever dogged by cruel jest about smells, the truth being that these emanate wholly from the fellmongeries and slaughter-houses of the adjoining suburb of Newmarket, which escapes scot-free! Poor Suresnes! See also Bercy.

Surrentinum: Wine of Roman times recommended by physicians but Tiberius thought it little better than vinegar.

Süsskratzer: German sparkling wine (Schaumwein).

Susuyari: The Chinese immigrant who is supposed to have taught the Japanese to make sake.

Sutler: A follower who sells provisions and liquor to soldiers. Sutlers have been put out of business in most armies by the establishment of official canteens (q.v.). Madame la Cantinière is a well-known identity of the French army and the subject of many ribald songs.

Sutter: Californian wine-growing county.

S.V.R.: The common abbreviation of *spiritus vini rectificatus* or rectified spirit, the alcohol of medicinal and commercial use, which contains about 94% of alcohol by volume. See also Rectified Spirit.

Swan: Old-established Australian (Perth) brewery with subsidiaries at Kalgoorlie and Darwin.

Swartberg: South African wine-producing area.

Swats: An old, provincial word for ale, especially newly brewed.

Swedish Beer: This is not Scandinavian but English, dark in colour and lightly hopped.

Swedish Punch: See Caloric Punch.

Sweet Martini: Cocktail of gin and sweet vermouth, usually served with a cherry. In England this is known as Gin and It (-alian vermouth).

Sweets: A curious English legal term in the Finance Act which, according to Halsbury's Laws of England, 'means any liquor which is made from fruit and sugar or from fruit and sugar mixed with any other material and which has undergone a process of fermentation in the manufacture thereof, and includes British wines, mead and metheglin'. The definition is technologically absurd for it would cover all wines, beers, liqueurs and perhaps every form of alcoholic beverage.

Sweet Water: See Palomino.

Sweet Wines: A general and imprecise term. Such wines can be unfortified (q.v.), such as sauternes, or fortified such as port and sweet sherry. The method of manufacture can also be variable. In some cases brandy is added to arrest fermentation, leaving much unchanged sugar in the must (q.v.). In other wines, concentrated grape juice may be added. The lusciously sweet Tokay Essenz is unique in lack of fortification. Sweet wines, except sauternes, are usually drunk at the end of the meal, as sugar destroys appetite.

Swig: Slang term, probably of Australian origin, for a drink, usually alcoholic and usually rapid. Also used as verb.

Swipes: Poor, thin or spoiled beer, also slang for beer in general.

Switzerland: Much good and a little fine wine is grown here, though the acreage of vineyards is steadily contracting. It is a tribute to man's love of wine in general and Swiss pertinacity and skill in particular that wine is made at all. The climate is at about the upper limit of temperature for wine-growing, soil is scarce and the country is so highly industrialized that only the true lover of the soil remains to practise viticulture. Cistercian monks established the vine in Switzerland about 600 years ago. Holdings are small and are mainly around the Lake of Geneva. Many of the noted Swiss growths are separately noted. The best wines are the table whites though the red wine of Dôle is celebrated. Lake Geneva, Ticino, Lake Neuchâtel, Zurich, Lavaux, Le Chablais, La Côte, Commugny, Bex, Valais, Fendant, Martigny, Visp, Sierre and Cortaillod are all wine-producing areas.

Switzerland produces much excellent beer but little or no gin. The common term *geneva* for gin has nothing to do with the Swiss lake or city but is a British corruption of the Dutch work *jenever*, juniper. See also Gin.

Swizzle: In addition to being the name of a mixing or beating rod, the name swizzle is given to cocktails not containing ice and not mixed in a 'shaker'. Also a West Indian drink of milk strongly laced with rum.

Swizzle Stick or Swizzle: Small rod used to beat or agitate a sparkling beverage to facilitate the escape of the carbon dioxide gas. The use of a swizzle for this purpose is perhaps the prime example of human foolishness. Why anybody should wish or be willing to pay the high price reasonably demanded by the maker of champagne for the enormous work of putting the gas into the wine merely to beat out the sparkle and thus convert it into an indifferent still drink must remain a mystery for the psychologist to unravel. The name is also applied to any small stirring-rod.

Sybillenstein: German (Rheinhessen) wine estate.

Sygate: A village in Norfolk which deserves to be remembered for the inscription in the church:

> God speed the plough
> And give us good ale enow,
> Be merry and glade,
> With good ale this walk was made.

See also Church Ales.

Syllabub, also Sillabub and Cillabub: A milk drink which came into fashion at about the end of the 16th century. One form was a third Spanish wine and two-thirds milk, either hot or cold. A mixture of milk and alcoholic beverage (rum, brandy, port, etc.) is still much appreciated, especially hot and spiced in winter. *Floreat syllabub!* A favourite of Samuel Pepys.

Sylvaner: A German rather prolific white grape which is the basis of much good Alsatian and Rhine wine. It is a lesser grape than the riesling (q.v.) though it is sometimes called Franken Riesling. Much Alsatian wine is labelled Sylvaner. The wine is light, tart, dry and lacking the marked aroma of the riesling. However, much white wine made from the sylvaner outside Europe is legally sold as riesling.

Sylvius: Dutch 17th-century chemist of Leyden, reputed to be the inventor of the modern type of gin.

Symposium: The Greek drinking bout, especially after a dinner party.

Syphon: Container for carbonated water said to have been invented by Savaresse in early 19th century.

Syracuse: Italian (Sicilian) town that is the centre of a large wine-making industry. See also Moscato.

Syrah: Black grape variety used to make red hermitage wine.

Szamorodni: One of the Hungarian tokay wines.

Szaraz: Hungarian for dry.

Szekszárd: Hungarian (Tolna) red wine.

Szesz: Hungarian for alcohol or spirit.

Szilva: Hungarian plum brandy. See also Slivovitz.

Taberna: Latin for a hut or tavern. During Saxon times *tabernae* were erected on the Roman roads. If wine as well as mead and ale were sold, an ivy-bush was displayed. This is supposed to be the origin of the tag 'Good wine needs no bush'.

Table-Wine: A beverage- or unfortified wine, of the kind usually taken with meals. Also known as beverage wine.

Tâche, La: Fine red burgundy from Vosne-Romanée (q.v.).

Tadcaster: Old-established (1758) Yorkshire brewery.

Tafelberg: South African table wine of hock type.

Tafelstein: German white wine. See also Dienheim.

Taffea: Rum from Guadeloupe.

Tafia: French for rum, especially that of Guiana. See also Taffea.

Tahbilk: Victorian vineyard established over 100 years ago on the Goulburn river, one of the few remaining large table wine estates of the state. Both reds and whites of considerable quality are made. The use of varietal names is a commendable feature.

Taillan: French (Médoc) red wine usually sold under the label of the neighbouring commune Ludon (q.v.).

Tailles: The pressings after the first of champagne grapes, made into second-quality sparkling wine. See also Champagne.

Tain: French township on the Rhône where the celebrated hill of the Hermitage (q.v.) rises. Hence the place is often called Tain l'Hermitage.

Taittinger: Old-established champagne of Reims.

Talbot: French (Médoc) red wine. Because of the name, Château Talbot is a popular wine in England. See also Médoc.

Talcahuanol: Chilean wine region.

Talcy: French (Touraine) wine estate celebrated for its vast wine press.

Talence: French (Graves) red-wine centre.

Taliesin: This Cymric bard is reported to have written a Mead Song in the 6th century which contains the line 'Mead distilled I praise. Its eulogy is everywhere.' However distilled mead (honey brandy) is not a commercial product. The reason is obscure. See also Mead.

Tamjanka: Bulgarian dessert wine.

Tanais-Clapeau: French (Médoc) red wine.

Tango: Cocktail of gin, dry and sweet vermouth and orange juice.

Tan Hill Inn, The: Reputed to be the highest in England, on a moorland road between Yorkshire and Westmorland.

Tankard: Originally a pint or quart size drinking-vessel made from wood, leather or pewter with either one or two handles, and occasionally fitted with a lid. It is more usual nowadays for tankards to be made of pewter, silver or glass in ½-pint or pint sizes.

Tank-car Wine: American term for bulk wine, usually made from the aramon grape. It is the equivalent of the French *vin ordinaire*. Only wine snobs will condemn this worthy trade.

Tannin: The name of a wide group of vegetable constituents, also known as tannic acid. The word is derived from the ability of these substances to convert animal skins (hides) to leather. The tannins are important constituents of grapes and hence of wine. Tannins assist in the maturing process of wine and play an important part in the production of a bright, clean flavour. Wines lacking tannin are flat and often fail to clarify. It is often necessary and a quite legitimate procedure to add tannin to musts (q.v.) deficient naturally. On the other hand, wines containing too much tannin (as may occur in reds which have remained too long in contact with skins and stalks) have a disagreeably sharp and astringent taste. This can be at least partially corrected by treatment with albumen and other agents.

Tantalus: A locked stand for holding bottles of spirits or wine, so called because the contents are visible but not attainable without a key (after, of course, the mythical tortured son of Zeus). The obsolescence of the tantalus is one sign, at least, of the advance of civilization.

Tanunda: Australian (S.A.) wine centre.

Tap: This word has numerous meanings in relation to brewing. It is the cock through which beer is drawn from cask. The term is also used in the sense of a particular brew or guile, e.g. an excellent tap. This use is now uncommon. To tap a cask is to drive the wooden or brass tap into the cask in preparation for serving draught beer, i.e. 'drawn from the wood'. The word is also an abbreviation of 'tap-room', the room where beer is served direct from the cask. See also Tap-Room.

A brewery tap was a bar or public house attached to a brewery from which beer could be bought on draught. The name is no longer in common use although a few public houses retain the title.

Tapas: The 'nibbles' of cheese, shrimps, olives, almonds and whatnot served free in Spanish cafés and inns with the wine. An excellent custom. Produced automatically when sherry is ordered.

Tappit Hen: A drinking-vessel of earlier times containing two Scottish pints or more. The name was supposedly derived from the resemblance of the knob of the lid to the crest of a hen. The vessel was traditionally used for dispensing a hot drink to departing guests.

Tap-Room: The traditional name for the room in an old-fashioned English pub, usually intermediate in social status between vault (q.v.) and parlour (q.v.). See also Tap.

Tapster: An old-fashioned name for barman or cellarman.

Tarantula Juice: Opprobrious American term for low-grade (or supposedly low-grade) spirits (q.v.). See also Moonshine, Valley Tan and White Lightning.

Tarija: Bolivian wine-growing centre.

Tarragona: The correct name for the dark-red Spanish dessert wine previously known in England by the draggletail and unjust term 'poor man's port'. This was, of course, an illegal description, as the name port (q.v.) is legally restricted in England by the Methuen Treaty to certain produce of Portugal. These cruel trade nicknames! Excellent Australian matured dessert wine was contemptuously invoiced in England as Australian Sweet Red. Commodity nicknames are like anonymous letters and drug-addicts. They rarely contain any truth.

Tart, Clos de: One of the most renowned red burgundy wines of the Côte-d'Or. It was planted by an order of nuns hundreds of years ago.

Tartar: See Tartaric Acid.

Tartaric Acid: The characteristic and principal acid of the grape. As the fruit ripens there is a corresponding conversion of acid to sugar. In hot climates this action proceeds almost to completion. As a reasonable amount of tartaric acid is essential to flavour and stability, these hot-climate wines deficient in acid may need correction, either by replacing or by plastering (q.v.). On the other hand, some cold climate wines, such as Rhines and Swiss, may be unduly sharp, especially to the unsophisticated palate. Hence some countries permit the addition of a reasonable amount of sugar to the must (q.v.).

Acid potassium tartrate or cream of tartar occurs in grape juice and wine. It is less soluble in dilute alcohol than in water and therefore slowly precipitates or falls out of solution, forming the deposit called 'argol' or tartar. This is also the 'crust' that forms in some wines after bottling. Argol is the raw material for the refined cream of tartar used in self-raising flour. See also Sediment.

Tartuguière: French (Médoc) red wine.

Tashkent: Asiatic ancient city of U.S.S.R. and now a rapidly developing centre of viticulture for both raisins and wine.

Tastevin: The special vessel used in France, and especially in Burgundy, by the wine tasters. It is a shallow polished silver dish with embossed mounds to reflect colour. A cherished article, kept in silk or chamois and highly polished, it is more effective as an adjunct to eye and nose than might be thought.

Tastevin, Confréries des Chevaliers du: A noted French society of gourmets. See also Vougeot.

Tastins-Malecot: French (Médoc) red wine.

Tatachilla: South Australian wine centre.

Tatja: Ethiopian mead (q.v.) stated to be the principal indigenous alcoholic beverage of that country.

Taubenberg: German (Ruwer, q.v.) white wine.

Taubenberg: German white-wine estate of Casel (q.v.).

Taupine: French (Côte-d'Or) red wine.

Tauzia: French (Graves) red wine.

Tavannes: French (Santenay, q.v.) red wine.

Tavel: This small French town near Avignon is the centre of the district which produces the celebrated *vin rosé* of the same name. The wine of the neighbouring commune of Lirac is also sold as Tavel. Tavel is made from the grenache grape and generally reckoned the best French *rosé* (q.v.).

Tavern: Traditional English name for a public house for the supply of food and drink. See also Licensed Premises.

Taverners, The: A company formed in 1937 for the production of plays and the reading of poetry in pubs. They have performed plays by Shakespeare, Shaw, Galsworthy and many modern authors, chiefly in the London suburbs and the Home Counties.

Tavern Keeper: The landlord or licensee (q.v.).

Tavern Song: One of the many colourful ditties which have sprung up from such an historic meeting-place.

Tavern Tale: Anecdote told over a glass of liquor and generally not too reliable.

Tawny Port: Port wine, a blend of different years and matured in cask at Vila Nova (q.v.). After several years in wood the red pigment becomes changed to a brownish or tawny colour, hence the name. See also Port.

Taxco Fizz: Mixed drink of sweetened tequila, lime, egg white and soda.

Taylor, Fladgate & Yeatman: A great name in port (q.v.). Though the original firm was founded by Job Bearsley in the Douro region in 1692, the present title (the twenty-third in a series of evolutionary changes) dates only from 1844. Rupert Croft-Cooke writes (*Port*, Putnam, 1957), 'There are nonagenarians who still go to their lodges or offices, and octogenarians are not in the least uncommon. One of them, the late Frank Yeatman, attended fifty consecutive wine harvests'.

Tazza: Bronze or silver drinking-vessel in shape of a modern champagne-glass. The name is said to be derived from the French *tasse*, meaning 'cup'. (See also Kylix.) Also a saucer-shaped glass mounted on a foot, especially used for sparkling wines.

T.C.: Abbreviation of the French wine term *très coloré*, (highly pigmented).

Tea, Cream of: Tea-flavoured liqueur. Fr. Crème de Thé.

Teacher: Old-established Scotch whisky distillers, outside the D.C.L. combine.

Tears of Wine: The drops which roll down the inner surface of a glass containing strong wine. The cause is the evaporation of alcohol from the surface. This surface layer then increases in tension and creeps up the side. The phenomenon is more marked in a sweet, fortified wine.

Teddy Bear: Another name for Brown Velvet (q.v.).

Teetotal: A term denoting complete abstinence from beverage alcohol. The origin of the term is arguable. The best theory is that it was first used about 1836 at a meeting of the United States Temperance Union at Hector, N.Y., where two classes of members were recognized, those abstaining only from spirits, whose names were marked O.P. (Old Pledge) and those who included wine in their pledge. The latter were identified on the roll with the capital letter T for 'Total'. Another less likely theory states that the word originated in England in 1833 at a temperance meeting in Preston, when a stammering member advocated 't-total' pledge. There is little or no ground for the belief that it ever meant restriction to tea-drinking.

Teetotalism: Another of those crackpot terms (see also Temperance) beloved of the prohibitionists. The word used to be T-totalism, with the suggestion that adherents of the cult completely avoided alcoholic beverages and that they drank only tea. Brandy, stout and a few more were 'medicines' and some of the patent medicines that teetotallers regularly and copiously drank contained 30% or more of alcohol and little else but sugar and caramel. They were actually cocktails (q.v.).

Tegea: Greek pink wine from Arcadia.

Tej or **Tedj:** The reported national beverage of Ethiopia. It is mead (q.v.) flavoured with a native plant of the same name. It is difficult to obtain reliable information but there is also apparently a spirit distilled from it. A special brew of *tej* is reported to be used at the coronation of Ethiopian emperors and was in evidence for the use of Haile Selassie in 1930. Also known as *tatja*.

Tembo: Swahilian wine made by fermenting coconut palm sap and the 'milk' of the nut.

Temperance: Next to patriotism, this is probably the most abused word in the English language. Instead of meaning of reasonable or of moderate usage, it has been corrupted to become a synonym of total abstinence from alcoholic beverages. A temperance hotel is thus the very opposite to its face meaning. The truly temperate people are not the teetotallers but the moderate drinkers of light wines and ales with food and the imbibers of small alcoholic appetizers with tid-bits of food before meals.

Temperance Drink (or Soft Drink): A beverage, usually carbonated, that is supposed not to contain alcohol, but the supposition is not always correct. See also Ginger Beer.

Temperate Races: Sociologists and pharmacologists point to the clear fact that certain national or ethnic groups are noted for their temperate use of alcoholic beverages and others, of course, for the reverse. For the correct meaning of the adjective *temperate* see the entry Temperance.

Obviously the word temperance has no application to national groups such as those of the Muslim world, to whom alcohol is wholly forbidden. Amongst the truly temperate groups, sociologists consider that the outstanding examples are the southern Italians and the Jews. No conclusive reason has been suggested for this but it may be significant that the Roman Catholic and Jewish religions both employ wine in their services (Communion and Kiddush respectively), their adherents both accustom their children to social drinking (accompanied by food) from early age and both groups frown upon intoxication.

Probably to be classed as temperate are certain American Indian tribes who deliberately aim at intoxication as part of religious ceremonies but who are quite restrained or even teetotal for the greater part of the year.

Temperature: The correct temperature for the service of alcohol is a matter of nationality and custom. It should be remembered that the characteristic flavour of food is largely concealed at very low temperature. Beer is usually served at a much lower temperature in America than in Europe and elsewhere. American custom is gaining the day over the world. With regard to beverage wines, it is widely taught that white wines should be served chilled and red wines at normal room temperature. There is probably good gastronomic sense behind this but the rules should not be applied too rigidly. For example, in hot weather it is quite permissible to serve chilled red wine of ordinary quality.

Sparkling wines should obviously be served really cold to avoid the rapid loss of the precious gas.

Tempter: Cocktail of port and apricot liqueur.

Tenant: The landlord or licensee of a licensed house held under a tenancy.

Tenedos: Ancient-Greek name for Bozcaada; this richly-storied island is still one of the principal centres of Turkish wine-growing.

Ténerèze: District of Armagnac (q.v.).

Tenerife: Wine is still made on this Spanish island of the Canary group but the industry is no longer important.

Tennent: A name associated with brewing in Glasgow since the 16th century. The present company of J. & R. Tennent Ltd. of Wellpark Brewery, Glasgow, was established in 1745.

Tent: The obsolete English name (derived from the Spanish *tinto*, 'deep-coloured') for Spanish red table wine from Alicante. Howell (q.v.) writing in 1634, says of Spain 'the vinteners have Tent, which is a name for all Wines in Spain except white'.

Tequila: Mexican spirit (q.v.) distilled from the fermented sap of a special agave (q.v.), *A. tequilana*. It is a more expensive and refined spirit than mezcal (q.v.). It is the basis of many mixed drinks, e.g. margarita and devil's blood (q.v.).

Tequila Cocktail: Mixture of dry vermouth, tequila and vanilla.

Tequila Sunrise: Mixed drink of tequila, lemon juice, grenadine and cinnamon liqueur.

Teran: Red table wine from Yugoslavia.

Tercios, Los: District of Jerez (q.v.) where *fino* sherry (q.v.) is grown.

Terlano: Italian white wine from Bolzano. Also called Terlaner.

Termo: Portuguese (Lisbon) dry white wine.

Terrano: Italian good black-wine grape. Also the name of a red table wine from Istria.

Tertre: French (Médoc) red wine. The name is also borne by several other Bordeaux red wine estates. Some of the wine is legally sold as Margaux (q.v.).

Tessiner: Swiss wine from canton of same name.

Tetley: English old-established (1823) brewery of Leeds.

Têtu, Le: 'The Stubborn One', the name given to the vast Vougeot (q.v.) timber wine press constructed over 400 years ago.

Teufelskeller: Steinwein vineyard at Randersacker (q.v.).

Teurons: French (Côte-d'Or) red burgundy wine.

Thann: French (Vosges) white wine.

Thasian: Greek wine mentioned in classical writings.

Thé, Crème de: French liqueur flavoured with tea. More pleasant than it sounds.

Theakston: Old-established (1827) Yorkshire brewery.

Theologicum: A term said to have been attached to the strongest wines in medieval times because these were reserved for the clergy.

Theurons, Les: French red wine of Beaune (q.v.).

Thief: A tube for taking a sample of liquor from a cask or other container. The term is synonymous with vellinch and pipette (q.v.).

Third: 15th-century liquid measure.

Third Rail: Cocktail of applejack, rum, cognac and absinthe.

Thistle Cup: Scottish drinking-vessel, usually of silver with single handle, the lower portion decorated by a calyx of applied lobs.

Thorins: French (Beaujolais) red burgundy wine. The name is borne by a large collection of vineyards but the lofty title *Thorins Grand Cru* is legally restricted to the produce of 46 designated vineyards in the Commune of Romanêche-Thorins.

Thornish: German (Moselle) white wine.

Thouarcé: French (Anjou) white wine.

Thrace: A region often mentioned in classical literature as a centre of sound wine.

Thrale: Any student of the work of Samuel Johnson knows of his friendship with the Thrales. At the sale of Thrale's brewery Johnson said, 'We are not here to sell a parcel of boilers and vats, but the potentiality of growing rich beyond the dreams of avarice'.

Thrawl: See Stillion.

Three Heads: Term originally used for a mixture of ale, beer and twopenny (q.v.) drawn from separate casks. It was superseded in 1722 by the production of a single brew called Entire (q.v.) and, later, Porter (q.v.).

Throat-Scraper: Obsolete Australian term for an early morning drink in goldrush days.

Throw: Australian slang term for a serving of liquor, especially spirits.

Thunderclap: Cocktail of equal parts whisky, brandy and gin.

Thüngersheim: German (Franconian, q.v.) white wine.

Thürgau: Swiss wine, mainly red, from Worth.

Tichanères: French (Basque) red wine.

Ticino: Swiss red and white table wines.

Tied House: The opposite to Free House (q.v.).

Tiefental: German (Gau-Odernheim, q.v.) white-wine district.

Tiélandry: French (Côte-d'Or) red wine.

Tierce: An old measure of capacity, also a cask, equivalent to one-third of a pipe (q.v.). The French *tierçon* and the German *Tierze* are equivalent.

Tiergarten: German (Friedelsheim, q.v.) white wine.

Tierra de Lebrija: See Spanish Clay.

Tiffon: Old-established brand of cognac (q.v.).

Tiflis: The chief centre of the Russian sparkling wine industry.

Tiger's Milk: Alleged pick-me-up consisting of a mixture of brandy, rum, milk and cream.

Time, Gentlemen, Please: A sad occasion, necessary but never welcome.

Timolean: Roman wine of antiquity.

Tincture: An alcoholic extract of a vegetable substance. Tinctures are still widely used in medicine. (See also Simple.) The word is mentioned here because many of the flavourings used in liqueurs, gins and other beverages are actually tinctures. In one sense gin itself is a tincture.

Tinetos: The small, shallow timber boxes with handles used in Spain to hold grapes for sherry. A *tineto* holds about one *arroba* or 25 lb.

Tinta: A group of red grapes widely planted in Portugal and Madeira, especially for the production of dark-red dessert wines. Amongst the varieties are cao, carvalha, francisca, and madeira.

Tinta Francisca: Grape resembling the pinot noir of France, widely grown for the production of port (q.v.). It is said to have been brought to Portugal from France in the 18th century by a Scot named Archibald who built a shooting-lodge in the Upper Douro and then became an enthusiastic wine-grower.

Tintara: South Australian century-old vineyard. Beverage and fortified types.

Tintilla de Rota: Spanish red dessert wine from Jerez, near Cadiz.

Tinto: Spanish for red and the origin of the old English name 'tent' (q.v.).

Tio Pepe: Despite the general rule of this glossary that trade-names are avoided, this widely-known Spanish one ('Uncle Joe') for a *fino* (q.v.) sherry demands exception. Tio Pepe was the uncle of the original Manuel Gonzalez (q.v.). A lover of *manzanilla* (q.v.), he asked the founder of the firm to produce a similar *fino* for him. A little *solera* was specially set up and the old gentleman would regale his cronies with this very dry wine and slices of a special heavily-smoked raw ham. The fame of the wine spread and in time Uncle Joe's *bodega* (q.v.) overshadowed all the rest.

Tipling House (*sic*): Medieval term for ale-house.

Tipperary: Cocktail of Irish whiskey, sweet vermouth and green chartreuse.

Tipple: Syn. for 'alcoholic liquor', now slightly contemptuous but not so in original use. It first meant to drink slowly and repeatedly. A tippler is, of course, one who suits the action to the verb. See also Tipling House.

Tiquira: Brazilian spirit made by fermenting sago, tapioca or arrowroot.

Tire-Bouchon: French for corkscrew.

Tirosh: A Biblical term for wine and often taken as a synonym for *yayin* (q.v.). Tirosh is mentioned 38 times, some of them scathingly as creating poverty and taking away understanding.

Tisane (also **Ptisane):** A decoction, originally of barley but later of a wide variety of herbs and aromatics. Tisanes were once highly regarded as medicinal and nutritive agents. They are mentioned here because they had something in common with cordials, known today as liqueurs.

Tischwein: German for run-of-the-mine table wine, the equivalent of the French *vin ordinaire*. It can vary from wholesome to terrible.

TNT: Cocktail of whisky and absinthe.

Toast: An alcoholic salutation to a person, object or sentiment, whose health or advancement is invoked by drinking. Steele wrote in 1709, 'Toast was a new word found by the wits for a Lady' whose name was delightfully supposed to flavour the wine like the spiced toast commonly used for the purpose. A chapter could be written on this word. The early 18th-century toasting glasses were exceedingly beautiful objects of delicate and elaborate workmanship, drawn with a stem so narrow ($\frac{1}{8}$th inch) that the drinkers could snap them between finger and thumb to prevent them ever being used for a lesser toast.

Toastmaster: Person who announces toasts at a public dinner.

Tobermory: Scottish centre for production of highland malt whisky.

Toblino: Wine district of Italian Tyrol.

Toby Jug: The vessel, made in the shape of a man's head, which has been used to dispense beer in England for at least 150 years. It is said to commemorate Toby Philpott, a Yorkshire farmer and mighty drinker and the subject of O'Keefe's bacchanalian songs.

Tocornal: Chilean esteemed red wine.

Toddy: A beverage made by fermenting the sweet sap of various species of palm, including the coconut. The name is also applied to hot, sweetened and flavoured drinks made with whisky and other spirits.

Toeak: Balinese palm-juice 'beer'.

Tokay: A town in the Hegyalia district of the Carpathian foothills in Hungary, and the name of the wine produced in the district. Tokay wines include several types and grades, from dryish to sweet, and ordinary beverage-wines are also made. However, the finest of the sweet tokays are among the most highly esteemed wines in the world, and probably the most expensive. The grape used is the local furmint. In the making of the best grades of tokay the grapes, which are gathered overripe, are carefully selected, and extreme care is taken in the making of the wine. The rarest and richest wine is known as essence (essenz), produced only in small quantities from the juice that oozes from the mass of grapes through no other pressure than their own weight. The important wine is the sweet ausbruch, known as aszu; other grades are szamorodni, forditas, and maslas.

One peculiarity of the wine of Tokay is the designation of quality in terms of Butten or Puttonyo. A *butto* is about 30 lb. For the lesser grades of Tokay a certain amount of the luscious, overripe bunches are added to the ordinary ripe grapes. Two to five Butten or Puttonyos are added to a cask of capacity about 30 gallons. The resulting wine is described by the number of Butten added to the cask.

Certain of the vineyards are part of the original Hapsburg domains, hence the term Imperial Tokay. The great prestige of Tokay wine has led to the manufacture of imitations, and also to the unwarranted use of the name outside Hungary.

It is reported that in late years there has been no general sale of essenz. What is not needed for topping up the lesser wines has been bought by Soviet Russia. Saintsbury calls the essenz 'no more a wine but a prince of liqueurs'.

Tokay, Californian: The name applied indiscriminately in California to almost any sweet, fortified wine.

Tokkuri: Japanese bottle for warming sake (q.v.).

Tolerance, Margin of: The variation allowed by British law of not more than half a degree of proof spirit (q.v.) below that stated on the label of a bottle of spirits.

Tolim: Wine-growing region of merit mentioned in the Bible as suited for the service of the sanctuary.

Tom and Jerry: American hot mixed drink, a type of egg nog (q.v.), made of rum, brandy, eggs and nutmeg. The origin of the beverage is hotly argued. One version has it that the inventor was one 'Professor' Jerry Thomas, a New York bartender. Another is that it was named from two characters in an English novel. As an adjective, Tom-and-Jerry indicates a low type of drinking-house; as a verb, it means roistering.

Tom Collins: Highball (q.v.) of sweetened gin, with lime or lemon juice. Other spirits may be used, e.g. Rum Collins.

Tomson & Wotton: Operators of a British (Ramsgate) brewery established before 1634.

Tonel: Portuguese huge cask used in making port wine (q.v.). The tonel is partly filled with brandy into which the partly fermented must from the lagar (q.v.) is run. After about two weeks in the tonel, the young port is transferred to pipes (q.v.).

Tonelada: The Portuguese tun (q.v.).

Tonic Water: Term applied to mineral water (q.v.) either sparkling or still, natural or artificial, but especially if 'medicated'. The most common addition is a small amount of a soluble quinine salt, just enough to impart an agreeable bitterness. 'Gin and tonic' is perhaps the commonest modern mixed drink.

Tonneau: French container equivalent to a tun or 4 hogsheads, about 200 gallons. It is the standard Bordeaux measure of four *barriques* (q.v.) or nearly 100 cases. Also *tonne*.

Tonnerre: The Lower Burgundy town which is the centre of white-wine estates.

Toodyay: Australian (W.A.) wine centre.

Toohey: Old-established Australian (Sydney) brewery.

Tooth: Old-established large Australian (Sydney) brewery.

Toro: Spanish (Zamora) red wine.

Torpedo: Cocktail of applejack, brandy and gin.

Torrebreba: A chalky district of Jerez (q.v.) which produces manzanilla (q.v.), a sherry of distinctive character.

Torredos: Greek red table wine.

Torre Giulia: Italian (Foggia) golden dry wine.

Torres Vedras: Portuguese inexpensive and plain but wholesome beverage wines grown near Lisbon. Red and white.

Toso: Japanese beverage consisting of sake (q.v.) mixed with four medicinal herbs. Toso is always served at New Year to induce a long life free from evil. It is the Japanese drinking ceremony for the prevention of disease. The name is now also given to ordinary sake drunk at New Year.

Tosspot: A toper, a drunkard, a sot.

Tot: A dram (q.v.), a small drink, especially of spirits.

Total Abstainer: This refers to alcoholic beverages, and without further qualification. Why the term is never considered applicable to love, Elizabethan poetry, hashish, roast pork, swimming or mustard is a mystery.

Toto: Spanish (Zamora) red wine.

Totsäufer: H. L. Mencken, writing of Baltimore, U.S., states: 'Literally dead-drinker, a totsäufer is a brewery customer's man. One of his most important duties is to carry on in a wild and inconsolable manner at the funerals of saloon-keepers.'

Tour, La: Also Latour. This name alone or in combination is borne by nearly 100 vineyards in the Bordeaux (q.v.). A few are merely brand-names, not vineyards. For example, the wine bearing the lofty name Château La-Tour-du-Roi is not really so regal for it denotes the wine of Ch. Lagrange which the proprietor considers not good enough to bear the estate name. Many a Château La Tour this or that is merely a simple country house or small winery where no tower has ever existed.

There are, however, true French red wine estates or vineyards bearing the title La Tour, situated at Saint-Martin-du-Puy, Bazadais, Gabarnac, Fargues, Salleboeuf, Sainte-Foy and Graves.

Touraine: 'The gentle, perfumed vintages of Touraine are among the glories of France. Even the shape of Touraine resembles a leaf from the vine.' (Chamberlain.) Amongst the better-known wines are Vouvray, Chinon and Bourgueil. The whites include Joué, Rochecorbon and Montlouis.

Tour-Ballet, La: French (Côtes Fronsac) red wine.

Tour-Bicheau, La: French (Portets) red wine.

Tour-Blanche, La: Celebrated French vineyard of Bommes, in the Bordeaux, where sauternes, the luscious sweet table wine, is made to perfection.

Tour Boyrein, La: French (Graves) red and white wines.

Tour-Caillet, La: French (Brannes) red and white wines.

Tour-Canon-Horeau, La: French (Fronsac) red and white wines.

Tourne: A bacterial disease of wine characterized by cloudiness and the development of an objectionable and flat taste. Gas is generated and the resulting pressure may force the bung from the container, hence the alternative name *pousse* (push). Tourne usually results from using mildewed grapes.

Tournon: French (Rhône) red and white wines.

Tournus: French (Burgundy) red-wine centre.

Tours: French (St. Émilion) red wine.

Tourteau: French (St. Émilion) red wine.

Toussaints, Les: French red wine of Beaune (q.v.), Côte-d'Or.

Tovarich: Mixture of vodka, kümmel and lime juice. Why the Americans invent these violent mixtures and pretend they are Russian is puzzling.

Tower: A name (La Tour this, that or the other) borne by some hundreds of French vineyards. Fifty or so of these are specifically noted herein. (See the list commencing Latour.) Some few of these estates do indeed possess imposing towers which were erected in medieval times as fortifications. Some again are humble chimneys called towers by courtesy only. But any towers that may have been erected on many of these vineyards or châteaux have long ago disappeared. Before the romantically-minded visitor interested in buildings decides to visit some château, *Tour* or *Schloss*, it would be advisable first to make discreet inquiries, remembering that some of the most disappointing estates architecturally are those with the most extravagant titles.

Traben-Trarbach: Two German villages on opposite points of the Moselle in the Zell district. White wines. Amongst the best vineyards of Traben are Schlossberg, Königsberg, Würzgarten and Kräuterhaus. Trarbach vineyards include Hühneberg and Halsberg.

Trabhaldores: The men who tread Portuguese wine.

Trade, The: The Licensed Trade, collective term for the wholesalers and retailers of beer, wines and spirits.

Trade Arrangement: The innocent term for the association formed in Scotland in 1856 by the patent-still (q.v.) distillers of grain whisky for the purpose of controlling prices. This body was the eventual begetter of the powerful present Distillers Company Ltd. or D.C.L. (q.v.).

Traiskirchen: Austrian wine region near Vienna.

Trakia: Bulgarian red table wine.

Traminer: The name of a fine white grape grown widely in Germany and Alsace. Much of the Alsatian wine is called by the grape name. Some traminer wine has an astonishingly marked perfume or bouquet, prized by many but rather despised by some connoisseurs. Strains of the traminer vine include the frankischer, savagnin (in the Jura) and roter traminer. The traminer grape is now largely grown outside Europe for fine white wines of marked character.

Trance: The technical term of an American bartender for a drunken client.

Trani: Italian (Apulian) red wine.

Traubengarten: German (Niederemmel, q.v.) white wine.

Treading: The operation of smashing or pulping grapes prior to pressing out the juice (must) by walking on them while contained in a vat or other suitable container. Originally the feet were bare. Today mechanical equipment has mainly replaced feet, though some purists contend there is no effective substitute for sensitive soles and toes. The Portuguese have a saying: 'We could not make port without the Gallegan foot.' In Spain the treaders wear special boots (Botas de Jerez, q.v.).

Treating: See Shouting.

Trebbiano: Alternative name for the white Ugni grape, also an Italian (Emilian) white wine.

Trebizond: One of the important Turkish wine regions.

Treis: German (Lower Moselle) white wine.

Tremper son Vin: Fr., 'dilute one's wine'.

Trencherman: A hearty eater, one who appreciates the pleasures of the table. Though usually directed to a lover of food, the term obviously should include the disciple of Bacchus. There is an ardent Fellowship of Trenchermen in Melbourne.

Trendle: An old-fashioned shallow tub used for cooling beer.

Treppchen: German (Erden, q.v.) white wine.

Trester: German term equivalent to Marc (q.v.).

Z

Tresterbranntwein: The sub-quality brandy made in Germany from Tresterwein, which in turn is made from the marc left after pressing. See also Grappo and Eau-de-Vie-de-Marc.

Tresterwein: German crude, cheap wine made from *marc* or residues. Also known as Nachwein or Haustrunk. See also Piquette.

Treuenfels: German (Palatinate) vineyard.

Treux, Les: French (Côte-d'Or) red wine.

Treytorrens: Swiss (Dézaley) white wine.

Tricoche: Old-established (1820) brand of cognac (q.v.).

Trie: The French term for a partial picking of grapes.

Trier: German wine city, the most important centre for the Saar, Moselle and Ruwer areas. It is extremely old and a veritable haven for the wine-lover, with its Wine Museum and trim surrounding white wine estates. (Fr. Trèves.)

Trift: German (Kallstadt, q.v.) wine centre.

Trimmer: A senior cooper who examines each faulty cask thoroughly on its arrival in the cooperage, collects the materials required for its repair and allocates the cask to a cooper. He is responsible for keeping records of all repair work carried out in the cooperage.

Trinidad: Centre for rum production.

Trinkbranntwein: General German term for potable brandy of not less than 35% alcohol by volume.

Triple Sec: Orange-flavoured colourless liqueur. The name is manifestly absurd for a very sweet beverage.

Trittenheimer: Moselle wine from the village of that name near Piesport. Vineyards include Neuberg, Falkenberg and Laurentinusberg.

Trockenbeerenauslese: German wine term ('chosen dried berries (grapes)'). This is the maker's term of highest praise. If the words on the label speak the truth, they mean that the wine was made from the final picking, so that the grapes are so much dried and shrivelled that they are nearly raisins. The sugar content of the resulting must (q.v.) is so high that the wine is sweet. Such wine can only be made in years of exceptionally long, dry, hot autumns and is always expensive. Some oenophiles regard such wine as vulgar. See also Labels, German Wine.

Trois-Moulins: French (St. Émilion) red wine.

Trollinger: Known also under many other names. Black grape giving wine of no special quality. Apparently identical with Black Hamburg table grape.

Trompette: French (Médoc) red wine.

Troplong-Mondot: French (St. Émilion) red wine.

Trotanoy: French (Pomerol) red wine.

Trottevielle: French (St. Émilion) red wine.

Trotzenberg: German (Ahr) red wine estate.

Trotzenberg: German (Marienthal) red wine.

Trou: French for gap or hole. A glass of neat spirit gulped down in the middle of a meal in the pious hope of making room for the second half. A *trou normand* is of calvados (q.v.), a *trou charentais* of cognac. There are also other *trous*.

Trousseau: A grape and a wine. The grape used for red wine is grown in the Jura at Arbois and is said to be indigenous. The name trousseau 'port' is given to a fortified Californian sweet wine of no particular merit, not because it had any relevance to a bride's array but because it was supposed originally to have been made from the French trousseau grape.

Trub: German wine term for the deposit of tartar and vegetable material (lees) which is found in bottles and casks on maturing.

Truss: Expression used in coopering, meaning to bend the staves of a cask into the characteristic elliptical shape. In hand coopering this is achieved by heating the cask over an oak chip fire and hammering down different sizes of ashen hoops. In the saw mills mechanically-made casks are trussed by an hydraulic trusser after being steamed.

Trusser: Operator of an hydraulic truss.

Trussing the Cooper: The ceremony performed in England of placing the newly-qualified young cooper in a cask, dousing and rolling him and finally toasting him on admittance to the ranks of this ancient, romantic and skilled but dying craft. See also Cooper.

Trussing Up: The process in cooperage of drawing the staves together.

Try-box: An adjunct to a still, for the purpose of ascertaining the course of the distillation.

Tsau Leung: The Chinese (Cantonese) term for liquor capacity. Though the Chinese are a sober race, they have many merry drinking-games for social occasions to test *tsau leung*.

Tschirpan: Bulgarian dessert wine.

Tuak: Balinese smoky palm toddy.

Tuica: Romanian term for slivovitz (q.v.) thus the plum brandy of that country.

Tulare: Californian wine centre, mainly for sweet fortified.

Tulbagh: South African wine-producing area.

Tulip: Cocktail of applejack, sweet vermouth, apricot liqueur and lemon juice.

Tulipe: The tulip-shaped wine glass which is, by common consent of the knowledgeable, good for universal use. See also Glass.

Tumbler: A drinking-vessel, usually of glass, without handle or stem, so named because the original tumbler had a rounded bottom and could not be set down until it was emptied.

Tun: Large beer cask, formerly used as a measure of capacity (252 wine gallons); the word is now generally used to describe many vessels in a brewery, e.g., mash tun (q.v.).

The 'tonnage' of a merchant ship was originally the number of tuns or *tonnes* of Bordeaux wine she could carry. Naval ships, which carry no merchandise, are measured in displacement. The weight of a tun of water or wine is in the vicinity of one ton avoirdupois.

Tunis: A region of growing importance for red table wine production. France is a major buyer. It is said some of the best goes to Burgundy for some mysterious purpose!

Tun Room: Department of brewery where fermenting takes place.

Tuquet: French (Graves) red and white wines.

Turckheim: French (Alsatian) centre for both red and white wines.

Turilains: French red wine of Beaune (q.v.).

Turin (Torino): Stated to be the birthplace of vermouth. Antonio Carpano is supposed to have invented the pleasant stuff in 1786.

Turkey: As a Moslem country, one does not ordinarily think of Turkey as a wine-producer, but the output is considerable. The general quality, however, is low. The government has registered the name Kanyak (whose origin is hardly a subtle secret) for Turkish brandy. Though statistics for wine-production are not readily available the amount must be large.

Turkish Blood: Mixed drink of English ale and Burgundy red wine, preferably vintage. A gastronomic insult to both beverages.

Turpeau: French (Graves) red wine.

Tuscany: This Italian wine province, often praised from classical times, is the home of chianti, montepulciano, aleatico and other esteemed beverage wines. Stated by some to be the source of the finest wines of the country. This is the only true home of chianti (q.v.).

Tusculum: Roman wine praised by Horace. Frascati (q.v.) is supposed to be the modern equivalent. The vineyard was near Rome and the wine was also called Albanum.

Twann: Swiss (Berne) esteemed white wine.

Twickheim: Alsatian hamlet, centre for esteemed white and red table wines.

Twist: American term for a long, chilled drink of spirit base with citrus juice and fruit.

Twopenny: A pale, small beer introduced into London from the country and sold, in the 18th century, at 4d. per quart (2d. per pint).

Twos: Colloquial term in general use in Norfolk, for mild and bitter, mixed half-and-half.

Tybur: Vineyard close to Rome in classical times, producing Setinum wine. It was called 'light but by no means weak'.

Tyg (or Tig): Medieval receptacle holding about a quart of liquor, essentially the same as a loving-cup (q.v.).

Tyre, Wine of: A medieval decoction of fennel, thyme, cloves, pepper, nutmeg, cinnamon and ginger, esteemed as a remedy for respiratory diseases.

Tzuica: The Romanian equivalent of slivovitz (q.v.) — plum brandy.

Übig: German (Ahr Valley) red table wine.

Ugni Blanc: White grape from Hermitage district of France, known as White Hermitage in Australia. It is said to be the same grape called St. Émilion (no connection with claret) in the Cognac, Maccabeo in NE. Spain and Trebbiano in Italy. This is a typical example of the confusion resulting from the many names of the one vine. Viticulture appears to be the worst offender in multiple-naming. See also Preface.

Uhlbach: German (Württemberg) Schillerwein (q.v.) centre.

Uhlen: German (Kobern, q.v.) white wine estate.

Ullage: The amount by which a cask or bottle lacks being full, i.e. the amount of air space. A cask is said to be 'on ullage' when it is only partially filled. The term 'ullaged' means, in general, 'short of contents' but in the case of wine it implies deterioration through the container being on ullage. It should be noted, however, that in trade and customs usage the term 'ullage' may be used in a reverse sense, as meaning, not the air space, but the volume of the actual liquid contents.

In France it is sometimes the practice to make up the vacant space with pebbles as the wine is withdrawn, instead of using more wine for the purpose.

Umbria: Italian wine-growing province, the home of the noted Orvieto.

Unctuous: Oily. Applied to a defective wine.

Underback: A control vessel in the brewery through which the wort (q.v.) flows and from which samples are taken by the brewer and chemist. See also Try-Box.

Underletting: A means of heating the contents of the mash tun (q.v.) by admitting hot liquor (q.v.) through the bottom of the tun.

Under-Proof: See Proof Spirit.

Undurraga: Chilean wine estate of quality.

Ungeheuer: German (Forst, q.v.) fine white wine.

Ungstein: German (Palatinate) red and white wines.

Union: A trunnioned cask used in burtonization (q.v.).

United States: As might be expected, so huge a country with 400 years of tradition of consuming alcoholic beverages has evolved a large and interesting list of alcoholic specialities and drinking *mores*. Here was invented the cocktail (q.v.) and many other categories of mixed drinks. The special types of spirit (bourbon and rye whiskey, applejack and Medford rum, for example) are noted alphabetically. Beer of excellent quality is brewed in every state and every sizeable city. Indeed, despite the cocktail hour and the great consumption of Scotch and local whiskies, the U.S., like Australia and New Zealand, retains its Anglo-Saxon tradition as a beer-consuming country.

Applejack (q.v.) is made chiefly in the old-established eastern orchard areas of New Jersey, New York and New England, though the manufacture is spreading.

More brandy is made in the U.S., indeed in California alone, than in France. The best is of good quality.

See the various entries commencing American.

Uno Santo: Sweet wine from the Greek island of Santorin. Also the name applied by Italian owners of small vineyards to the wine they make for local drinking, mainly from semi-dried grapes.

Unterberg: German (Canzem) white wine.

Urbau: Czechoslovakian table wines.

Urlay: Moselle vineyard near Uerzig (q.v.).

Urna: Roman liquid measure containing half an amphora (q.v.).

Ur of the Chaldees: Modern excavations are stated to reveal that 5,000 years ago there were government breweries. According to inscriptions, the citizenry complained that the beer was not strong enough and not so good as it used to be. Moralists were debating the advisability of employing barmaids.

Ürzig: Moselle wine centre where production has been continuous since classical times. Amongst the vineyards are Schwarzlay, Würzgarten, Kranklay, Urlay and Michelslay.

Usquebaugh: Also Uisquebeatha, etc. The old Irish-Gaelic name for whiskey. The literal meaning is 'water of life' and thus an exact translation of *aqua vitae*, *eau de vie*, akvavit, etc. The word whisky is itself a Scots version of *usquebaugh*.

The word is also the name of a liqueur of predominantly coriander flavour.

Valais: One of the most important of the Swiss wine-growing cantons. The wines are mainly whites but the well-known Dôle de Sion is red.

Valdelsa: Italian (Tuscanian, q.v.) wine of the chianti family.

Valdepeñas: Spanish wine centre in the province of La Mancha, north of Malaga. The wines are 'big' and in general of excellent quality. This is Don Quixote country. The name means Stony Valley. It is also applied to a grape in California.

Valencia: Spanish wine centre in the province of Levante, producing heavy-bodied, dark red wines much appreciated, especially in England, for blending with weaker growths.

Valley Tan: Obsolete American term of the 1850's for whiskey made at the original Mormon distillery at Salt Lake City, Utah. Also the opprobrious American term for any low-grade (or supposedly low-grade) spirits (q.v.).

Vallier: French (Médoc) red wine.

Valmur: French (Chablis, q.v.) wine of good quality.

Valpantena: Italian (Veneto) red wine. Also a Spanish white table wine of moderate quality.

Val Polcevera: Italian (Ligurian) white wine.

Valpolicella: Prized red Italian table wine from Lake Garda in the Verona district, including the villages of Negrar, Valgatara and Fumane. See also Amarone and Recioto. Probably no other Italian table wine occurs so often in literature.

Valrose: French (Médoc) red wine.

Valtellin: Hungarian sweet yellow wine from Sopron.

Valtellina: Italian red and white table wines from the Sondrio region in the Lombardy Valley. The region was previously Swiss. While the generic name Valtellina is applied to all the wines of the area, the best of them have individual names — Sasella, Inferno, Grumello and Frecciarossa.

Valwig: German white wine district of Moselle.

Vanderbilt: Cocktail of brandy, grenadine, cherry brandy and bitters.

Van der Hum: South African liqueur of brandy base and mandarin flavour modified with spices. To some palates rather sickly. The translation is, roughly, 'what's his name' or 'thingumabob'.

Vanilla: This delectable seedpod of a gorgeous orchid has a deserved place in modern gastronomy. However, it is a pity that it is so widely used throughout the world to sophisticate brandy. It is reported that even in Cognac it is common for certain lesser merchants to add a trace to give a simulated smoothness, bouquet and age.

Vanille: Liqueur of that flavour.

Varietal: The naming of wine from the variety of grape from which it is made, e.g., Cabernet, Grenache, Traminer. The system is to be commended as an attempt to break down the frequently absurd and always unjust habit of usurping foreign geographical names such as tokay, burgundy, port and cognac. However, a grenache vine in California (the principal user of the varietal system) may produce quite a different wine from the same vine in France or Italy. There is, in truth, no real substitute for geographical nomenclature.

Varietal naming is also applicable to other alcoholic beverages, e.g., rye (whiskey).

Varna: One of the important Bulgarian wine-producing districts.

Vassar: The venerated women's college of New York which is one of many institutions of learning throughout the world whose foundation arises from the benevolence of a maker or purveyor of alcoholic beverages. Matthew Vassar's Poughkeepsie Brewery was in operation until 1899.

Vat: In general, a vessel in which chemical and manufacturing processes involving the use of liquids are carried out. In relation to alcoholic beverages, a vat is a large container, often constructed in the form of a huge cask, in which liquors are fermented, blended, compounded, or matured, in the earlier stages of production. As a measure, vat is obsolete in Britain and U.S.A., but in Belgium and Holland a vat equals one hectolitre (q.v.).

Vat, Fermenting: See Cuve and Tun.

Vatting: This means blending.

Vaucrains: French (Nuits-St.-Georges) red burgundy.

Vaud: Swiss wine-growing canton, generally believed to be the district which produces the finest wines of the country. Those include the Dezaley and Yvorne.

Vaudésir: French (Chablis) fine white wine. See also Chablis Grand Cru.

Vaudieu, Château de: One of the Châteauneuf (q.v.) wines.

Vaulorent: French (Chablis) fine white wine.

Vault: A word redolent of romance. It means an arched structure of masonry, usually underground and hence a large cellar. It is used especially of a storehouse for wine and spirits, both for security and for maturing. The vaults of the Port of London Authority are celebrated. The Crescent Wine Vault has an area of 6½ acres and can hold 12,000 butts, mainly of sherry. The One-to-Five Vaults are even larger.

Vault: The traditional name for the control-room of an English pub. Also called the 'pint-hole'.

Vaumorillons: French (Yonne) white wine.

Vaux: Red wine of Beaujolais, France.

Vaux: English brewery established at Sunderland in 1830.

V.D.N.: *Vins doux naturels* (q.v.).

Védrines: French sweet white wine. See also Barsac.

Veldenz: German (Moselle) white wine.

Veldt: South African red table wine.

Vellinch: A tubular appliance for drawing samples of liquid from a cask. Also valenche. See also Thief and Venencia.

Veltliner: Austrian grape for white wine.

Vendange: French for vintage or grape harvest. The time of *La Vendange* is, of course, in the great tradition of jollity of all sorts. Wherever the grape is grown the vintage is a time for loving and feasting.

Vendimia: Spanish for vintage (q.v.). See also Vendange.

Vendôme: Pink wine from Orléans.

Venencia: Spanish sampling device consisting of silver cup at end of a flexible rod, used for withdrawing sherry from cask. It is used with elaborate ceremony. See also Tastevin and Vellinch.

Veneto: North Italian wine province producing many fine wines, including Valpolicella, Bardolino and Soave (q.v.).

Ventura: Californian wine-growing county.

Verbessert: A German term applied to wines which have been 'improved' by the addition of a legally-permitted amount of ordinary sugar. The French term *sucrage* refers to the permitted addition of sugar to Burgundy wines, usually limited to reds. It should be understood that the sugar is not added to the wine but to the grape-juice before it is fermented into wine. It is a process readily subject to abuse. Some countries prohibit the practice.

Verdelho: Originally a white grape grown in Madeira. A sweet fortified wine of the island still bears the name though the vine is no longer grown there to any extent. It is lighter in colour and less sweet than Bual (q.v.).

Verdicchio de Jesi: Italian (Ravenna) white wine.

Verdignan: French (Médoc) red wine.

Verdiso: Italian (Veneto) white wine.

Verdot: Prolific French grape grown in the Gironde for lesser quality claret.

Verduno: See Barolo.

Vergelesses: French (Côte-d'Or) red wine.

Vergennes: One of the interesting indigenous American white wine grapes, supposed to be native to Vermont.

Verjuice: The juice of unripe grapes. It was once a much-used ingredient of cookery but was supplanted in English kitchens by the lemon. This is rather a pity. Verjuice has its own character and there is room for both as acidifiers.

Vermentino: Italian (Ligurian) white wine.

Vermont: Cocktail of applejack, maple syrup and lemon juice.

Vermouth: A compounded sweetish wine containing aromatic herbs and other flavouring. The French type is pale and 'dry'; the Italian is darker and rather sweet. Vermouths are taken largely as apéritifs and are much used in cocktails and other mixed drinks.

The word is the French variant of the German *Wermut*, the name of a common European shrub. See also Wormwood.

Vermouth Cassis: The universal non-proprietary apéritif (q.v.) of France. It is vermouth (q.v.) to which is added black-currant syrup and usually some soda-water or spa. It effectively disposes of the myth that the French are not consumers of sweet alcoholic beverages. Why so highly and characteristically flavoured a liquid as vermouth should require the addition of so highly and characteristically flavoured a liquid as black-currant juice is still another gastronomic mystery.

Vernaccia: Sardinian white and red table wines. There is also an Italian (Tuscanian) white wine.

Vernage: A wine of Elizabethan times, mentioned by Holinshed, apparently from Tuscany.

Vernas: French (Bressan) red wine.

Vernissons: Commune in Burgundy noted for white wine.

Veronica: Cocktail of applejack, orange juice and bitters.

Versailles: Cocktail of gin, dry vermouth, cinnamon liqueur and lime juice.

Verschnittwein: German term for blended wine.

Verseuil: French (Côte-d'Or) red wine.

Vertheuil: French (Médoc) red wine which is usually legally sold as St. Estèphe.

Verticillium Wilt: A wasting virus disease which affects and wilts hops. Although it had been known for many years among strawberries and tomatoes, it is only since 1938 that it has attacked hops. It is highly contagious and can spread very rapidly through a hop garden, wiping out several acres in a few days. Control is effected by growing wilt-resistant varieties of hops.

Vertus: French (Champagne) white wine.

Verzenay: A French village near Reims long known for still and sparkling wines. See also Sillery.

Verzy: French white wine centre of Reims.

Vespetro: Liqueur with faint caraway flavour.

Vesuvio: Italian wine from Naples district, mainly dry white.

Veyrin: French (Médoc) red wine.

Vianna: An ancient town in North Portugal, about 50 miles north of Oporto, of great historical interest as once the centre of a flourishing wine trade and the scene of a settlement of English merchants about the 16th century. Later Oporto supplanted Vianna as a wine centre.

Vidonia: The recognized best type of canary wine (q.v.) which was once held in high esteem in England. See also Canary.

Vienna Beer: Intermediate between Pilsener and Munich beer. Very good.

Vienne: Ancient French town of the Rhône, the Vienna of Roman Gaul and centre of some interesting wines.

Vierzehnmorgen: German (Meckenheim, q.v.) white wine.

Viesch: Swiss (Upper Rhône) white wine.

Vieux Château Certan: Large and good French red wine (claret) vineyard of Pomerol.

Vieux Moulin-du-Cadet: French (St. Émilion) red wine.

Vigneau: An esteemed sauternes wine. See also Sauternes.

Vigne au Saint, Clos de la: Notable red wine of Burgundy.

Vigne Blanche: French (Côte-d'Or) white wine.

Vigne du Diable: Swiss (Cortaillod) red wine.

Vigneron: A wine-grower, a viticulturist. His produce is sold by a vintner.

Vignes Franches: French (Côte-d'Or) red wine.

Vignoble: The bald meaning is vineyard, but amongst wine-lovers the term is restricted to an establishment, whatever the size, of some antiquity and distinction. It is often used to include all the vineyards of one defined area.

Vikarei: German (Gau-Bischofsheim, q.v.) white wine.

Vila Nova de Gaia: The Portuguese town on the Douro opposite Oporto which is the principal centre for the port shippers' warehouses. By Portuguese law all port must be stored here before shipment.

Villafranca del Panades: Spanish (Barcelona) wine region for good red and white table wines.

Villa Rica: Paraguayan wine centre.

Villány-Pécs: Perhaps the most important wine-growing district of Hungary for both reds and whites.

Villedommange: French white wine centre of the Champagne.

Villemaurine: French (St. Émilion) red wine. The cellar buildings of stone are renowned.

Villenave-d'-Ornon: French (Graves) table wines.

Villers-Marmery: French wine-growing commune of Reims.

Villié: Red wine of Beaujolais, France.

Vin: French for wine. The word can legally only be applied to the beverage produced exclusively from the fermentation of fresh grapes or their juice. Raisins are excluded but not passulated grapes which have been allowed partially to dry on the stem.

Vinacea: Latin for pressed grape residue. Fr. *marc*.

Vinade: See Piquette.

Vinage: French for the act of adding spirit to wine.

Vinasse: The residue left in a pot-still (q.v.) after distilling.

Vin Blanc Cassis: A typical apéritif (q.v.) consisting of white wine flavoured with black currant liqueur. The French understand these things to perfection but the Anglo-Saxon 'gin and two' (q.v.) is equally good in its own way. See also Vermouth Cassis.

Vin Blanc Citron: The light and delightful appetizer of France consisting of common white wine with a dash of syrup, a little soda water, and, of course, a slice of lemon.

Vin Bourru: This is the name, described as 'a rolling Burgundian *r*, probably indicating the contented sound you make after drinking', which is given to the young Beaujolais red wine sold in barrels and bottled up for drinking by Paris café owners. The term is also used for any wine before clarification.

Vin Brûlé: Burnt wine. A French mixed winter drink of red wine, brandy, sugar, lemon and spices. (Very nice in cold weather.)

Vincent: French (Médoc) red wine.

Vin Coupé: French for diluted or cut wine.

Vin Cuit: French term for grape must concentrated by heating; used mainly for sweetening wines. See also Vino Cotto.

Vincent-Margaux: French (Médoc) red wine.

Vin Chaud: French for mulled (q.v.) wine.

Vin de Côtes: French term for wine grown on a hillside (slope) and hence believed to be superior to *vin de plaine* or *vin de palus*. This is often grossly wrong.

Vin de Coule: First-pressed wine.

Vin de Deux Feuilles: French for wine two years old.

Vin de Garde: French wine term of high praise, meaning a wine worthy of being laid down.

Vin de Goutte: The French term for the finest wine fraction, that made from the first pressings. See also Suites.

Vin de Liqueur: French term for a heavy, sweet fortified wine. See also Dessert.

Vin de Messe: The mass or altar wine.

Vin de Paille: See Straw Wine.

Vin de Palus: See Vin de Côtes.

Vin de Paysan: Much the same as *vin ordinaire* (q.v.), but lower in quality than *vin du pays* (q.v.). Originally it meant the poor stuff made for the workmen.

Vin de Plaine: Wine from the plains as opposed to *vin de côtes* (q.v.).

Vin de Tête: The French term for the very best portion of the vintage, especially applied to sauternes. For something abnormally fine *'crème de tête'* may be applied. *'Vin du centre'* or *'vin de milieu'* is sauternes of moderate quality while *'vin de queue'* is comparatively inferior.

Vin Doux: French for unfermented grape juice.

Vin du Pays: The French term for local wine, the wine of the country or district, with a purely local appeal. Such wines are often, indeed usually, excellent and the rational traveller will follow regional custom and avoid wine-snobbery by drinking them to the advantage of his palate and his purse. Of course, the sturdy provincial Frenchman who is ordinarily quite content with his *vin du pays* is capable, on unusual occasions, of paying for and appreciating a princely importation from Bordeaux or Burgundy or even the Rhine.

Vine: The word standing alone is usually taken to mean a grape vine.
- (a) The plant that produces grapes. Latin: *Vitis*. Italian: *Vite*. Spanish: *Vid*. Portuguese: *Videira*. French: *Vigne*.
- (b) Quality and kind of vine. Latin: *Vinea*. Italian: *Vitigno*. Spanish: *Veduño*. Portuguese: *Vidonho*. French: *Cépage*.
- (c) A vine-trellis. Latin: *Pergula*. Italian: *Pergola*. Spanish: *Parral* Portuguese: *Parreiral*. French: *Treille*.
- (d) A vine branch. Latin: *Sarmentum*. Italian: *Sermento*. Spanish: *Sarmiento*. Portuguese: *Sarmento*. French: *Sarment*.
- (e) A vine layer. Latin: *Propago*. Italian: *Propaggine*. Spanish: *Proveña*. Portuguese: *Mergulhão*. French: *Provin*.
- (f) A vine leaf. Latin: *Pampinus*. Italian: *Pampano*. Spanish: *Pampana*. Portuguese: *Parra*. French: *Feuille de vigne*.

Vinegar: Derived from the French *vinaigre*, meaning 'sour wine'. Vinegar results from the acetic fermentation of light alcoholic liquids, the alcohol being oxidized to acetic acid through action of a micro-organism. Beer, cider, and wine are the liquors most commonly used, the vinegar in each case having its own distinctive qualities. The sourness that develops in light wines, when continuously exposed to the air, is due to the formation of acetic acid.

Vinegar: See Jailer.

Vinelli: Italian crude cheap wine made from marc or residues. See also Piquette.

Vin en Cercles: French for wine in the cask or wood.

Vineus: Latin for belonging to or consisting of wine. There are many off-shoots. Thus a *vineus porticus* was an arbour formed by a vine and that name was given, because of the supposed resemblance, to a war-machine or roof used at sieges to protect the assailants from the missiles of the enemy.

Vineyard: An orchard planted with grape vines. The natural result of viti-culture. The vineyard is one of the oldest and, to many people, quite the most romantic form of all agriculture.

Vin Gris: The uncomplimentary name given to a wine made from mixed red and white (a sort of cheap *rosé*), especially in Lorraine.

Vinho: Portuguese for wine. *Vinho Claro* is unfortified (natural wine, *Vinho Generoso* is fortified wine and *Vinho Verde* (lit. 'green') is the Portuguese term for new or young wine, cheap and pleasant with simple food.

Vinho de Roda (travelled wine): The special name applied to Madeira wines which had been matured by sending them for a long return voyage as ballast on a sailing-ship.

Vinho Estufado: Madeira wine after it has been heat-treated.

Vinho Generoso: Portuguese term for fortified sweet wines.

Vinho Spumoso: Portuguese for sparkling wine.

Vinho Verde: Literally, 'green wine'. The new, but wholesome wine that is largely consumed as a beverage in Portugal. Specially applicable to the light white wines of the north, undistinguished but pleasant and whole-some and sold in bulk.

Vinicola da Madeira: Old-established shippers of madeira (q.v.).

Vini di Lusso: Italian term for dessert-wines.

Vinification: The process of converting grape or other fruit juice to wine. It is a pompous term for wine-making.

Vini Forzati: Italian term for wines made from overripe grapes. See also Vin Pourri.

Vin Jaune: Syn. for 'straw wine' (q.v.).

Vin Negru: Generic native name for the very dark-red table wines of Romania.

Vin non-Mousseux: Still (i.e. non-sparkling) wine.

Vino: Italian for wine. See also Vin and Vine.

Vino Corriente: Spanish term for ordinary or beverage wine. On the whole it is superior to the French *vin ordinaire*.

Vino Cotto: Italian name of must (q.v.) concentrated to a syrup by evapora-tion (boiling) and used for sweetening marsala (q.v.) and similar fortified dessert wines. See also Vino de Color and Vin Cuit.

Vino de Añada: The Spanish name of young wine destined to become sherry but before the flor (q.v.) has developed.

Vino de Arrosto: Italian term for a wine of fine quality or 'breeding' (q.v.).

Vino de Color: Spanish for concentrated grape juice used for colouring and sweetening wines. See also Vino Cotto and Arrope.

Vino de Cuarte: Spanish (Valencian) *rosé* wine (q.v.).

Vino de la Tierra: Spanish term for local wine, the exact equivalent of the French *vin du pays*.

Vino della Riviera: Italian (Lake Garda) table wines.

Vino de Pasto: This Spanish term, literally 'pasture wine', is variable in meaning. It can stand for a family wine, one for everyday use, a plain wine of no nonsense. But it is also used by English wine merchants for a mediocre type of sherry, pale and not too dry. It would seem that the price of such sherry is not always commensurate with quality. The term is also used in Spain for an ordinary dessert wine.

Vino di Arrosto: Italian for well-bred wine.

Vino di Lusso: The Italian name for the more luscious and expensive fortified sweet dessert wines.

Vino Dulce: Sherry whose fermentation has been arrested with brandy at an early stage to produce a very sweet blending wine. See also Angelica.

Vino Frizzante: The Italian sweetish, pink, gassy wine put up for cheap entertaining. See also Carbonated.

Vino Generoso: Spanish term for fortified wine (q.v.).

Vino Maestro: Spanish name of the extra sweet and alcoholic wines used to top up the lesser breeds. Especially used in compounding malaga (q.v.).

Vin Ordinaire: The ordinary beverage-wine of France. Cheap but whole-some, and consumed in large quantity. Sold without distinctive label — simply as *'vin rouge'* or *'vin blanc'*. ('Australia needs a *vin ordinaire'* — Castella.)

Vino Rosato: Italian for rose or pink wine, equivalent to the French *vin rosé*.

Vino Santo: Greek sweet white wine, mainly from Santorin.

Vinosity: The essential quality of wine.

Vinos Viejos: Lit. 'old wines'. The term is applied to amontillado (q.v.) wines stored in wood until they become dark brown and acquire a bitter taste. They are then of value for blending. See also Sherry.

Vino Tierno: Spanish wine made from partially dried grapes. Used in compounding malaga (q.v.). See also Passulated.

Vino Tipico: The official Italian term for an established wine, one that conforms to standard. When a wine has been admitted to this status and meets approved standards of quality, a government seal of authenticity will be issued. Already the system has greatly uplifted the quality of Italian wines.

Vin Pourri: Wine made from overripe (lit. almost rotten) grapes.

Vin Pur: French for neat or straight wine.

Vin Rosé (Vino Rosato): Pink-coloured wine made in France, North Africa and Italy in various ways. That of Tavel in France is generally regarded as the best.

Vins de Garde: French term for wines intended to be stored to mature, hence superior, as opposed to *vin ordinaire*, common wine to be drunk young.

Vins Doux Naturels: Abbreviated to V.D.N.: The curious French term 'natural sweet wines' for the dessert wines produced in and near Roussillon. They are no more natural than port, madeira or sherry for they also are made by adding spirit to partly fermented wine. Despite their sweetness they are widely used as apéritifs by the French. Amongst regions making these wines are Banyuls, Rivesaltes, Maury, Frontignan, Lunel, Rasteau and Agly.

Vins Liquoreux: French term for wines such as *vins de paille* which are higher than average in alcohol but are not fortified (q.v.). See also Vins de Liqueur.

Vintage: Originally the word simply meant the yield of the vine, but it has now acquired a special significance. As a rule, the year of the vintage is quoted only when the wine of that particular year shows great promise; hence, a 'vintage wine' is presumed to be one of outstanding merit. As in the case of port, 'vintage' also implies that the wine is from one particularly good crop, kept separate and unblended on account of its own special quality.

Vintage Charts: Classification of qualities of wines according to years. They probably do more harm than good, especially in the hands of the uninformed. A little consideration will verify this. A good vintage is primarily a function of weather. A sudden spell of humid or frigid weather at the wrong time may ruin what might otherwise have been a good vintage. But these natural disasters are often of the most limited occurrence and effect. A good vintage in one district may be accompanied by a bad one in another a few miles away.

Again, even adjoining vineyards may experience radically differing results according to altitude, time of ripening and, of course, individual skill.

Finally, some fortunate areas such as California, Australia and South Africa, are not usually subject to capricious changes of weather. For these wines, almost every year is likely to be good.

Perhaps the only good general rule for vintages is that there is no general rule.

Vintage Port: Port blended from the best wines of the *quintas* (vineyards), normally bottled in the second year in the country where it is to be drunk though sometimes kept in wood another year for earlier maturing. Vintage port throws a crust and must be decanted carefully. See also Port.

Vintner: A wine merchant. He sells the produce of a vigneron.

Vinum de Cupa (Cicero): See Cupa. Whether this meant bulk wine or wine of special quality fit for storage is uncertain.

Vinum Rusticum: See Vinum Vetus.

Vinum Vetus: Latin name for the matured wine of the Romans, in two qualities, costing 24 and 16 *denarii* the pint. While it was not fine wine, it was a cut above the *vinum rusticum* or country wine, the Roman *vin ordinaire* drunk well-diluted with water.

Vinzelles: French wine-growing commune of Burgundy. The wines are mainly white and are sold under other names.

Viognier: Grape grown in Rhône Valley which tradition holds was first planted in the district by a Roman general who brought it from Dalmatia.

Violette, Crème de: Sickly-sweet liqueur of violet flavour.

Viré: French (Burgundy) red wine.

Virelade: French (Graves) red and white wines.

Virginia Eggnog: Mixture of whisky, rum, eggs, milk and cream.

Virgin Isles: Centre for rum production.

Vispthal: This Swiss (Valais) area is said to be the highest wine-producing valley in Europe.

Vitamin: The generic name for a group of substances occurring naturally in small amount in foodstuffs, now known to be essential to health. Previously included in the term 'accessory food factors'. The vitamin content of some undistilled alcoholic beverages is now known to be significant.

Viterbo: Italian (Latium) white wine.

Viticulture: The cultivation of the grape-vine (*Vitis*).

Vitis: The ancient Latin name for a vine and the modern botanical name of the huge *Vitaceae* family, which includes all the many genera of grape vines. Some of these are separately noted herein.

Vitis Apiana: Old name for the muscat grape of Alexandria, so named because its excessive sweetness attracted bees.

Vitis Labrusca: The large collection of native American grape vines. They hybridize freely with the so-called European grape vines, *Vitis vinifera*. Because the *labrusca* vines are resistant to *Phylloxera* (q.v.) almost all vineyards are composed of *vinifera* scions grafted on *labrusca* stocks. The taste and yield of the *vinifera* grapes are not affected.

There are many varieties of American *labrusca* grapes and wine is made from most of these except in California, which uses only *vinifera* species. These *labrusca* species are noted alphabetically, including Noah, Delaware, Catawba.

Vitis Rupestris: Native vine of the S.E. and Central United States, also called the bush grape. It is a remarkably hardy dwarf vine used both for its round, black grapes of distinctive flavour and for stock in grafting.

Vitis Silvestris: A variety of the European grape wine (*Vitis vinifera*, q.v.) which occurs wild in the Mediterranean region and is usually regarded as the parent of the cultivated vine.

Vitis Vinifera: The genus of grape vine from which the overwhelming bulk of the world's wine is made. (The only significant exception is the *Vitis labrusca*, the native grape of North America.) There are at least two hundred recognized and listed varieties of *Vitis vinifera* in Europe alone and there is some justification for naming the species the European grape vine. In Australia, South Africa and South America there are many imported varieties which have local names and are supposed to be local productions but some at least are merely European importations which have lost their origin. The original home of *Vitis vinifera* is supposed to have been between Samarkand and the Caucasian mountains.

Some of the more important varieties of *Vitis vinifera* are noted separately in these pages.

Vizetelly, Henry: This turbulent writer and publisher, b. London 1820, deserves to be remembered for his championship of sherry (q.v.) though his other books, including *Wines of the World*, are long forgotten. In 1876 he wrote *Facts about Sherry*, a vigorous defence of that wine, especially the process of plastering (q.v.) based upon his tour of the Jerez district.

V.O.: These initials were originally confined to the labels of cognac brandy (q.v.) but are now widely used for spirits generally and also occasionally on the labels of port and other dessert wines. The letters mean 'very old' but actually their true significance may be nil. They have, indeed, become so common that many respected distillers and merchants disdain to use them. There are many variants and extensions of V.O. For example, V.V.O. is 'very, *very* old' or, if you prefer it, '*very* very old'. V.S.O. is 'very special old' and V.S.O.P. is 'very special old pale'. There is even a V.V.S.O.P., which the reader can translate without much effort.

There used to be a trade convention, not too rigidly observed, that V.S.O. was reputed to be 12 to 17 years old, V.S.O.P. 18 to 25 years and V.V.S.O.P. up to 40 years.

There is a somewhat similar but even greater mumbo-jummery involved in the stars on brandy labels. See also Stars and Pale.

Vodka, Vodki or Wodky: The national spirituous beverage of the U.S.S.R. and also, to some extent, of other Slavonic countries. The name is stated to be derived from the Russian *voda*, water. Vodka, the diminutive, is said to mean 'little water'. Presumably this is an affectionate term, for vodka is actually a spirit (q.v.) of heroic proportions.

Though a certain amount of flavoured vodka is made (and the resulting beverage is therefore to be classed technically as a gin, q.v.), most vodka is essentially merely rectified spirit suitably diluted with water. In other words, it is a fairly pure alcohol, a white spirit, broken down with water to potable strength. Such vodka, made by re-distillation followed by filtration through charcoal or activated carbon to remove coloured constituents and perfumed congenerics (q.v.), is free from taste, colour and odour. It will therefore blend with anything. It reminds one of the Australian politician Deakin, who dubbed the policy of his opponent 'a necklace of negatives'. In recent years the sale of vodka outside Russia, and especially in the U.S., has grown enormously.

Vodka can be made from grain, potatoes or any other source of fermentable carbohydrate. Why people have proved willing to pay a high price for neutral spirit under a fancy name is one of the romances of modern commerce and a tribute to the mysterious power of the advertising agent.

Vodka Cocktail: Mixture of vodka, cherry brandy and lemon juice. American, of course.

Vodkatini: Mixture of vodka and dry vermouth. This clever American invention merely boils down to vermouth of increased alcohol.

Vogelsang: There are a number of German vineyards bearing this pretty name but despite the presumed birdsong on the estates nobody seems to sing the praises of the wines very loudly. There are Vogelsangs situated on the Rheingau, Moselle and Saar.

Voiteur: French (Jura) white wine, usually sold as Château Chalon (q.v.).

Volnay: Celebrated wine-growing commune of the Côte-d'Or, Burgundy. Here are made some of the quick-maturing red perfumed table wines that are considered typical of the finest French art. Amongst the best vineyards are Fremiet, Champans, Caillerets, Clos des Ducs, Chevret, Les Angles, La Barre En Verseuil, Bousse d'Or and (legally although not geographically within the commune) Les Santenots.

Volrads: Celebrated hock (q.v.) from Schloss Volrads, Winkel, Rheingau. Owned by the one family for over five hundred years. Also Vollrads.

Vomitorium: The annexe to a Roman dining-room provided for the use of revellers. Who shall say we have not advanced in 2,000 years?

Voskeat: Sherry-type grape of Lake Sevan (q.v.) said to be indigenous.

Voslau: Austrian table wine, red and white. Some consider red voslau the premier wine of Austria.

Vosne-Romanée: A name capable of bringing tears to the eyes of lovers of French wines in general and those of Burgundy in particular. It is a commune of the French Côte-d'Or containing about fifty of the most renowned wine estates of the world. The commercial value of these vineyards, mostly ancient, is beyond computation. A few of these are Richebourg, La Tâche, La Romanée, Romanée-Conti, Romanée-St.-Vivant, Les Gaudichots, Les Malconsorts, Les Suchots, Clos des Réas, Chaumes and Les Beaumonts.

Vougeot, Clos de: This celebrated Burgundian (Côte-d'Or) vineyard is situated in the commune of the same name. There are now over 50 owners for the varying-sized bits of the 130 or so acres and in consequence the red wine which can be sold legally under this proud name shows wide variation. It is a picturesque site. The buildings were first erected by Cistercian monks eight hundred years ago. The main one, after a chequered career, including a spell as a prisoner-of-war camp, is now owned and has been restored by the Chevaliers du Tastevin, the Burgundian boosting organization of growers, merchants and others interested in wine. Here are held the vast monthly meals that are already renowned.

Some of the better Vougeot vineyards are separately noted. There is also a good white wine, the Clos Blanc de Vougeot, grown just outside the walls of the castle from the chardonnay (q.v.) grape.

Vouvray: This is the most important wine-growing district of the Loire Valley (Touraine) and produces some distinctive and highly esteemed types. The whites are by far the more important and are both still and sparkling. Some is in-between (*pétillant*). Contrary to the widely printed statement, Vouvray does travel and has a valuable market in the U.S.A. Vouvray enthusiasts seem to be very constant.

Wachauer: Austrian table wine from Danube.

Wachenheim: German hock (q.v.) region in the Palatinate. The vineyard records are reported to reach back to the 8th century.

Wachstum: German for 'the property of' or 'the growth of'. The best hocks and moselles are always labelled thus, followed by the name of the owner of the vineyard. *Gewachs, Eigengewachs* and *Kresenz* mean much the same. It is to some extent an indication of authenticity and quality.

Wager-Cup: Any vessel used to hold liquor intended to be drunk at one draught. Some of the most elaborate ones were the windmill cups of the 17th-century Dutch, which had mechanical attachments to be set in motion by the breath of the drinker.

Wahgunyah: Australian (Victorian) wine centre on Murray River near Rutherglen. The principal vineyard is All Saints, where fine dessert wines and sherries are produced.

Waikerie: Australian (S.A.) wine centre.

Waist-Banding: The hopgrower's term for the process of tying each group of strings about four feet from the ground. See also Stringing.

Wake: The spiritual (and usually highly spirituous) guard over an Irish corpse before burial.

Wak Shee: Tibetan spirit, reputed to be especially fiery.

Waldböckelheim: German (Nahe) white wine centre.

Waldrach: German white wine centres of Ruwer (q.v.) and Saar (q.v.).

Waldulm: German (Baden) red wine.

Walkenburg: German (Nieder-und-Oberwalluf, q.v.) white wine.

Wallangarra: Australian (Queensland) wine centre.

Wallhausen: German (Kreuznach) white wine.

Wallis: Swiss wine district which contains one of the highest vineyards in Europe.

Wallop or **Wallup:** Cockney slang for mild beer.

Walnut Mead: Old beverage brewed from honey and walnut leaves.

WAL-WAS

Walporzheimer: Red wine of the Ahr Valley, Germany. The wine is said to resemble a burgundy.

Walsheim: German (Palatinate) red and white wines.

Walterberg: German white wine estate of Casel (q.v.).

Waltham Cross: Also known as rosaki. Prolific white grape used, especially in Australia, as dual-purpose wine and table variety.

Wanneroo: Australian (W.A.) wine centre.

Ward Eight: Cocktail of whisky, lemon juice and bitters, decorated with fruit.

Warham, William: When he was enthroned as archbishop at Canterbury he provided for his clergy and guests 'four tuns of London ale, six of Kentish ale and twenty of English beer', in addition to 'six pipes of red wine, four of claret, one of choice wine, one of white for the kitchen, one butt of Malmsey, one pipe of wine of Oysey and two tierces of Rhenish wine'.

Warmara: Turkish wine region.

Warna: Bulgarian centre for wine production; also a dessert wine.

Warre & Co.: Old-established (1670) shippers of port. There are still members of the Warre family in the business. A sister firm is Silva & Cosens (q.v.). The firm owns a vat holding 244 pipes (q.v.) of port, possibly the largest piece of cooperage in the world.

Warte: German (Nierstein, q.v.) white wine.

Wasenweiler: German (Baden) white wine.

Wash: The curious trade name for the alcoholic beverage resulting from the fermentation of wort (q.v.) in the production of whisky (q.v.). This resembles strong beer of about 10% alcohol. It is then distilled.

Washington: This American state (not the political capital city) grows superb pome and berry fruits but is a little too northerly for an extensive wine industry. There are, however, some pleasant light wines grown in the Yakima Valley.

From the berry fruits, so-called wines are made after the addition of sugar.

Perhaps Washington may some day become a great world centre for applejack (q.v.).

Washington, George: The first President of the U.S. was a keen judge of the quality of ale and beer, and was particularly fond of porter (q.v.). In 1760 he was ordering porter from England and later was a loyal customer of Robert Hare, the first brewer of porter in Philadelphia. Washington was also a home-brewer and a recipe for small beer appears in a notebook (still preserved) that he kept as a Colonel in the Virginia Militia. He also grew barley at Mount Vernon. See also Franklin, Jefferson and Rush.

Wash Still: The pot-still (q.v.) for the production of low wines (q.v.) in Scotch whisky manufacture.

Wassail: Liquor for a festive occasion. The word is Old English. Also wassail cup, bowl, etc. The word is especially applied to a hot English beverage of brandy or other spirit heavily spiced and containing baked apples. Some ruin the result by setting the brandy alight and losing the alcohol. See also Blue Blazer.

Wasserrose: German (Kiedrich, q.v.) white wine.

Water: A 19th-century Frenchman is reported as stating that the drinking of water as a beverage is an almost obscene operation. James Howell (q.v.) wrote in 1634 of the drought-stricken Italian peasant-farmer who said 'For want of water I am forc'd to drink water: If I had water I would drink wine.' The quality of water is of paramount importance in the production of alcoholic beverages and high purity is not necessarily high suitability. See also Burton. Brewers term water 'liquor'.

Waterford: The celebrated glassware of Ireland which for generations has enclosed choice beverages, thus elevating container, contained and consumer.

Waterloo: Australian (W.A.) wine centre.

Watervale: South Australian wine-growing district north of Adelaide. Here some of the finest wines of Australia are grown, especially light wines and flor sherries.

Watney Mann Ltd.: Large British company resulting from the amalgamation of many old-established breweries.

Wawern: German white wine vineyard on Saar (q.v.).

Weeper: A defectively-corked bottle showing leakage, especially in the bin (q.v.).

Wehlen: German (Moselle Valley) white-wine centre. Here wine records go back a thousand years. Amongst the celebrated estates are the Wehlener Sonnenuhr ('sundial'). Other fine vineyards are Nonnenberg, Rosenberg, Feinter and Klosterlay.

Wehlener Sonnenuhr: One of the outstanding Moselle wines. See also Wehlen.

Wehling: German (Gau-Bischofsheim, q.v.) white wine.

Weid: German (Hochheim, q.v.) white wine.

Weihenstephan: The Department of Brewing (and a full-scale brewery) of Munich University.

Wein: German for wine. See also Vin.

Weinbach: German (Deidesheim, q.v.) white wine. There is also a vineyard of that name at Ruppertsberg (q.v.).

Weinbauer: German for wine-grower.

Weinberg: German for vineyard.

Weinbrand: General German term for brandy (q.v.) made from wine.

Weingeist: German term for alcohol distilled from wine ('spirits of wine').

Weingrube: German (Reil, q.v.) white wine.

Weingut: Often seen on German wine labels, this word has somewhat the same connotation as *Wachstum* (q.v.). It means vineyard or wine estate when followed by the owner's name.

Weinhändler: German for wine merchant.

Weinlese: German for vintage (q.v.).

Weinrebe: German for grape vine. Also Weinstock.

Weinsberg: German (Württemberg) red wines.

Weinstein: German for tartar ('winestone').

Weinstock: German for grapevine, almost the same as *Weinrebe*.

Weinstrasse: Hallowed name! The road from the French border to Deidesheim and Forst through the celebrated wine-producing regions of the Palatinate or Pfalz (q.v.).

Weisert: German (Nittel, q.v.) white wine.

Weissbier: Acid-flavoured beer, made chiefly in Berlin, containing both alcohol and lactic acid, formed by a special yeast and bacterial fermentation of a mash of wheat with a little barley malt. As the name ('white beer') suggests, it is almost colourless.

Weissenberg: German (Kobern, q.v.) white wine estate.

Weisserberg: German white wine. See also Briedel.

Weissmauer: German (Königsbach, q.v.) white wine.

Weiss mit Schuss: Berlin beer made from wheat malt and served with a dash of raspberry syrup.

Wellington: South African wine-growing district.

Welsh: Old-established shippers of madeira (q.v.).

Wente: Californian winery near San Francisco. Good white wines.

Werdelstück: German (Burg, q.v.) white wine.

Werribee: Australian wine centre, almost a suburb of Melbourne. The wine is made by Italians for local consumption.

Wertheim: German (Baden) white wines of Steinwein type.

Westerberg: German (Niedersaulheim, q.v.) white wine.

Westhofen: German wine-growing parish of Rheinhessen. Good white wine.

West Swan: Australian (W.A.) wine centre.

Wet One's Whistle: (Colloquial.) To slake one's thirst.

Wettolsheim: Alsatian dry white wine centre.

Weyersborn: German (Nackenheim, q.v.) white wine.

Weyher: German (Palatinate) white wines.

What's Yours?: An invitation which sums up the companionable atmosphere of the public house.

Whiskin: 17th-century drinking vessel.

Whisky: A spirituous beverage made by distilling fermented cereals. The word is derived from the original Gaelic name *uisquebeatha*, *uisguebeath* or *usquebaugh*, which is in turn a literal translation of the Latin *aqua vitae* or water of life, the medieval synonym for alcohol. The word is spelt 'whisky' in Scotland and all other English-speaking countries with the exception of Ireland and the United States, which employ the variant 'whiskey'.

Exactly what constitutes whisky is difficult to say. The opening sentence is true enough but the statement would also apply to other spirits. These include the German Kornbranntwein, the Oriental rice spirit of many names made from sake, and so on. It is not even a question of the predominant use of one cereal, for though barley may be the chief ingredient of one type of whisky, rye and maize (corn) may be equally important in others. Again, it is not a question of technique, for either a pot-still, a continuous still (both q.v.) or a combination of both may be employed. Moreover, even flavour is not the criterion. There may be as marked a difference in taste and bouquet between a good Scotch and an equally good bourbon whiskey as between either and a fine cognac.

Whiskies are usually classified according to their geographical source, e.g., Scotch, Irish, American, Canadian, Australian, but while this is broadly useful the only real distinction lies in the nature and amount of the secondary constituents or 'congenerics' such as esters, aldehydes and higher alcohols.

By general consent Scotch whisky is the most prized and consumption has steadily increased. However, there is much more whisky made in the U.S. than in Scotland.

Irrespective of nationality or type, all whisky is manufactured in a basically similar manner and the process involves four stages:

(1) Mashing or the production of the solution called wort.
(2) Fermenting the wort to produce a liquor like strong ale called wash. (The principal difference between wash and ale is the absence of hops.)
(3) Making the spirit from the wash by distillation.
(4) Maturing or ageing the spirit as required by law or custom, both before and after blending.

All the technical terms (wort, wash, distillation, etc.) used in this note are the subjects of separate entries.

Scotch whisky (except for singles, q.v.) is a judicious blend usually of about equal quantities of whiskies made by the pot-still and the continuous still.

The pot-stilled whisky of Scotland is made almost entirely from malted barley and the experts distinguish four main types:

(1) **Highland malts:** Scotch pot-stilled whisky from Speyside and Glenlivet districts, greatly prized for its full and peaty flavour.
(2) **Lowland malts:** Scotch pot-stilled whisky from the south, of less distinction than the above.
(3) **Islay:** Scotch pot-stilled whisky of particularly full flavour, hence prized for blending.
(4) **Campbeltown:** Scotch pot-stilled whisky of even fuller flavour than Islay.

As in the case of brewing (q.v.) the barley is cleaned by screening and blowing. It is then malted, dried and ground. The drying is accomplished over open peat fires and it is beyond doubt that much of the characteristic flavour of Scotch whisky is derived from the acrid smoke that impregnates the barley malt, though the nature of the water and of the processes may also contribute. After mashing the wash contains about 10% of alcohol, more than twice that of most beer.

Scotch malt whisky is made from the wash by double distillation in pot stills. These are of quite simple construction without a *chauffe-vin* or heat-exchanger, as in the case of a cognac still. They are also usually much larger, even more than 10,000 gallons in the largest distilleries. After the first distillation, the product, called low wines, and which contains about 20% of alcohol, is distilled again in a smaller pot-still called the spirit-still. The first distillate collected is called the 'foreshots' and is a complex mixture of alcohol and other constituents. This is put aside and added to the next lot of low wines. Next comes the principal fraction or distillate, the whisky itself, which contains between 60% and 70% of alcohol. After the whisky has been collected, there is a further and final fraction called the 'feints', containing alcohol, 'fusel oil' and numerous other constituents. Like the foreshots, the feints are returned to a new batch of low-wines for re-distillation. Sometimes the term 'heads and tails' is used to include both foreshots and feints. The foreshots may contain a little of the poisonous methyl alcohol (q.v.). Many Scots distillers contend, apparently with sound foundation, that perhaps the most important skill in making whisky is to decide at what stage to change the collection from whisky to feints.

In Lowland distilleries it is common practice to carry out a third distillation of malt whisky. This is standard procedure in Ireland, where the pot-stills are usually very large, even more than 20,000 gallons capacity of wash.

Whisky made in a continuous or patent or Coffey still (the terms are synonymous) is derived from a mixture of grains and is usually called grain whisky. Of course, the name is not logical, as the barley of the pot-still is also a grain. Grain whisky can be made from any mixture of malted and unmalted cereals. Some malted grain (usually barley) must be included to saccharify (q.v.) the rest. For details of distillation see Patent Still. This grain whisky is much less flavourous and distinctive than malt whisky.

Some connoisseurs of Scotch whisky prize an all-malt, unblended pot-stilled spirit, a 'single', but, as stated, the general taste is for something milder and more constant. The blender is a person of great power and prestige. To maintain a regular and constant produce he mixes many constituent spirits. Some technologists contend that more than simple mixing is involved and that some form of true chemical combination occurs.

Freshly made whisky of either type is colourless and very harsh in taste. The familiar colour of whisky is due to the addition of caramel. Contrary to popular belief, very little colour is extracted from the storage casks.

The English law (Customs and Excise Act 1952) requires whisky in the cask to be matured or aged for not less than three years before sale but in practice this period is almost always greatly exceeded. Much is aged for ten years. The whisky is stored in oak barrels in cool warehouses. Old sherry casks are much prized for storage purposes and complex chemical actions take place. In the process the harsh new spirit becomes mellow and agreeable. It is impossible here to enter into detail.

Irish whiskey has a history older than that of Scotland itself. Until comparatively recently Irish whiskey was wholly pot-stilled but today it is a blend approximating to Scotch. The bulk of both Scotch and Irish whiskies is exported, mainly to the United States.

Canada makes much whisky, the bulk of it either from rye or maize (bourbon). The flavour is milder than that of Scotch or Irish. Strict laws control the quality. Australia has a growing local whisky-distilling industry and the product is wholesome and agreeable. Some Australian firms import peat from Scotland to approximate to traditional practice. However, the fact remains that Scotch whisky cannot be made outside Scotland. It is certain that it would be if it could!

American whiskey means little beyond 'made within the United States'. The fact is that this whiskey can range legally from a superb spirit such as a straight full-proof bourbon to a dull mixture of alcohol and water flavoured with as little as a fifth genuine whisky. America was the pioneer of pure-food legislation and it seems curious that although it makes possibly more whisky than the rest of the world combined, that there alone it is possible to sell such a mixture as whisky. Certainly the mixture must be labelled 'blended' but this also applies to Scotch, Irish and all other whiskies which are not wholly of one type.

Three-quarters or more of the total production of American whiskey is blended with neutral spirits. Legally this is required to be a mixture of a minimum of 20% of 100-proof (i.e. 50% alcohol) straight whisky with *neutral spirits*, the common term for flavour-free alcohol usually made from grain but sometimes from molasses (sugar residue), potatoes or any other suitable source. This spirit does not need to be matured.

It should be emphasized that a mixture of whisky and plain alcohol is in no sense unwholesome. The objection is only that it is not really whisky. After all, high prices are paid for vodka, which is merely a fancy name for alcohol and water alone. See Vodka.

Varietal American whiskies, as stated, may be and often are, distinctive and delicious. The chief of these whiskies are corn (bourbon) and rye. To bear the varietal name, the whiskey must be distilled at not higher strength than 160% proof (80% alcohol) from a fermented mash of not less than 51% of the named grain. Bourbon whiskey is made from corn (maize) and gets its name from Bourbon County in Kentucky, where this whiskey is supposed to have been first made. There are legal requirements as to the method and time of maturing.

One characteristic of the American industry is the use of internally-charred white oak barrels for storage. The origin of this custom is said to be a hangover of the old practice of burning out the tainted surface from old barrels which had previously contained molasses or salt fish. Today it does produce a distinctive spirit. Some enthusiasts contend that a fine Bourbon is the best of all whisky. The U.S. term 'bottled in bond' means that the whiskey can be bottled and held in a government store until duty is paid provided it is not less than 4 years old and the bottling strength is not below 100% proof (50% alcohol). 'Bottled in bond' is not a guarantee of quality.

There is an increasing production in Japan of true whisky of good quality.

Whiskey, Irish: See Irish Whiskey and Whisky.

Whisky, Japanese: This is a large industry operated on modern principles. One brand, however, is described by the maker as 'squeezed from clearest Scottish grapes'.

Whisky Money: The vernacular name for the proceeds of a duty on whisky in the U.K. introduced in the Local Taxation (Customs and Excise) Act of 1890. This provided local authorities with a fund to be expended on technical education. In 1901, out of £1 million of public money so spent, over £850,000 was 'whisky money'. The logic of the tax has never been satisfactorily explained.

Whitbread: One of the chief names in English brewing. The brewery was founded in London in 1742. A number of descendants of the founder are still active in Whitbread & Co., Ltd.

White Ale: A somewhat mysterious 'hot and rebellious' brewed beverage produced in Devon and Cornwall until comparatively recent times and said to be compounded from eggs, salt and wheaten flour in addition to rum, beer and malt. It bore an almost mystical reputation as a tonic. See also Eggy-Hot.

White Cloud: Cocktail of orange liqueur, lime juice, egg white, and nutmeg.

White Horse: Old-established (1742) firm of Scotch whisky distillers, now part of D.C.L. (q.v.).

White Lady: Cocktail of gin, cointreau and orange juice.

Also Australian slang for a tot of methylated spirit (q.v.) when used by the depraved as beverage. See also Lunatic Soup.

White Lightning: Opprobrious American term for low-grade (or supposedly low-grade) spirits (q.v.). See also Moonshine, Valley Tan and Tarantula Juice.

White Mule: Moonshine (q.v.) straight from the still.

White Port: A wine often maligned by the extremists but a true port nevertheless. In other words it is legally entitled to the name port. Made from white grapes, it is much drier than other port and is prized by some as an apéritif wine. The true white port of Portugal must not be confused with the sweet, heavy dessert wine of Australia and California which can also double as 'sweet sherry' at the whim of the maker.

White Wings: Cocktail of gin and crème de menthe.

Whittington, Richard: Mayor of London in 1419, Dick Whittington was no beloved, romantic figure to brewers and publicans. On the contrary he was regarded by them as an enemy of the craft. From contemporary accounts of his domineering and eccentric behaviour, such as compelling brewers for some fancied slight to sell their ale at a penny a gallon for so many days or inflicting severe fines on hucksters for some trifling real or imagined infraction of his rules, the reputation seems to have been thoroughly merited.

Widow: A term applied colloquially to a certain bottling of champagne in which the word 'veuve' is part of the title.

Widow's Kiss: Cocktail of applejack, benedictine, chartreuse and bitters.

Wiener Geschichten: Austrian table wine from Vienna.

Wiesbaden: Noted German wine region of Rheingau (q.v.).

Wieshell: German (Rauenthal, q.v.) white wine.

Wild Irish Rose: Cocktail of Irish whiskey, grenadine and lime juice.

Willborn: German (Hattenheim, q.v.) white wine.

Williams and Humbert: Old-established (1877) firm of sherry shippers (q.v.) founded by two young Englishmen, brothers-in-law. It is still a family concern.

Willmes Press: German invention for pressing grapes consisting of perforated cylinder with inflatable rubber inner tube.

Wilt: See Verticillium Wilt.

Wiltingen: German (Saar Valley) white wine centre. This is the chief wine district of the Saar and vineyards have been tended here for a thousand years. The white wines of fine quality are noted for their delicacy and are sold as moselles. Many ancient vineyards, including Schlossberg, Schlangengraben, Scharzhofberg, Rosenberg, Klosterberg, Johannislay, Gottesfuss, Braune Kupp and Brauenfels.

Wiltringer Riesling: White table wine of Luxembourg.

Wincheringen: German (Moselle) white wine centre.

Winchester Quart: Glass bottle much larger than a quart and usually glass-stoppered. The capacity is customarily about five pints.

Windesheim: German (Nahe) white wine centre.

Wine, American: See American wine.

Wine, Beverage: See Beverage Wine.

Wine, Dessert: See Dessert wine.

Wine, Dilution of: In hot climates where wine is drunk as a beverage, it is common sound practice to dilute it with water especially as a thirst-quencher after exertion. Much peasant wine (*vin ordinaire*) is so acid that dilution is necessary to make it drinkable. There is some evidence that in classic times a Greek or Roman who drank undiluted wine was regarded with disfavour. Alcaeus, born 620 B.C., wrote a drinking-song of which the following is a fragment:

> Wine the great son of Zeus
> And Semele gave to men
> To make them forget their cares.
> Pour out the mixture, then,
> Twice water to one of wine
> And let cup follow cup around
> Each on the heels of the other.

Wine, Diseases of: Wine, if really sound and healthy at time of bottling, is surprisingly and gratifyingly resistant to disease. However, the slightest defect may open the way to attack by many malign agents. Such diseases as 'breaks', the 'yellows', the 'blues', the 'fat', 'bitterness' and many more are grim enemies of the wine-maker.

Wine, Dry: Not sweet. A dry wine should contain less than 0·25% sugar (1 part in 400).

Wine, Wormwood: See Wormwood.

Wine and Soda: Pleasant, light summer drink of about equal parts wine and chilled soda or lemonade. See also Spritzer.

Winebag: A wine-bibber, a drunkard.

Wine-card: The table of wines available at a restaurant.

Wine-Carriage: Small wheeled object for circulating wine at the dining-table.

Wine-Cask Borer: The ambrosia beetle that destroys wine-casks.

Wine-conner: A taster or tester of wine (obs.).

Winefat: Obsolete term for winepress.

Wine-Ferment: Wine yeast, *Sacch. ellipsoideus*. See also Yeast.

Wine-Grape: Any grape used for wine-making, as distinct from table grapes which are used exclusively for fresh consumption. The term is also, but rather unfairly, used generally for the European grape, *Vitis vinifera*, although the American grape, *V. labrusca*, also yields some excellent local wines which only the snobs despise. A large number of the more important wine varieties are separately noted.

Wine-Making: Although we speak loosely of elderberry, parsnip, cowslip and other wines, the only true wine is that made from grapes. The essential process has hardly altered in more than 3,000 years of recorded history. (See Bible.) The first stage consists in picking the ripe grapes and crushing them to release the juice. Usually sulphur dioxide is then added. Next, the juice (now called 'must') is run into a suitable container where it soon starts to 'ferment' (q.v.) from the action of the yeast (q.v.) naturally present as the 'bloom' on the skin of the ripe grapes. After fermentation is completed the new wine is run off ('racked') free from skins, pips and debris. If worth the effort, it is then stored in an air-free and air-tight vessel to mature. Later it may be bottled and tightly corked.

However, there are many differences in detail according to the nature of the wine desired. Most modern wineries have mechanical equipment to remove stalks, pips and skins where white wine is the aim, for it is not commonly known that the tint of red wines is derived wholly from the skins. (There is little or no pigment in the pulp and juice, hence it is possible and common to make white wine from red or black grapes. The French call this process *blanc de rouge*.) If especially luscious and sweet wine is the aim the grapes may be allowed to overripen and be attacked by a grey mould. (See Pourriture noble.) If a strong wine which will keep after the bottle is opened is desired, the fermentation is stopped (arrested) by adding brandy. This leaves the wine quite sweet because much unchanged sugar remains. If a wine of the special character called *fino* sherry is the aim, the wine is dosed with brandy and stored in special casks to allow the film called flor (q.v.) to grow and produce the highly characteristic *fino* flavour.

A large winery, especially in California, Australia or South Africa, would operate along the following lines for the production of red table wine. A week or so prior to vintage (picking or harvesting) a load of grapes is brought in, crushed, the juice sterilized and a special culture of yeast added. This fermenting juice is called a 'starter' and is used to inoculate the main mass of grapes as crushed. Picking time is important. If too early the wine may be 'green' and unduly acid. Fermentation may be carried on in large cement or glass tanks. Temperature of the fermenting mass must be carefully controlled, mainly by cooling, though sometimes warming may be needed. The density, which measures the sugar content, must be systematically tested; this tells the degree of 'attenuation' or removal of sugar (q.v.). The amount of colour and tannin being extracted from the skins must be watched and the wine run away as soon as the fermentation has gone far enough. The wine will subsequently receive several rackings (q.v.). The fining process varies greatly both with the country and the type of wine. After a suitable period of 'storage in wood' (i.e. maturing in oak or other suitable timber vessels) which may vary for red table wine from a few months to about three years, the wine is bottled and, if of sufficient promise, aged in bottle for a further period of one to five years.

If the juice is not sweet enough because the grapes have not fully ripened, owing to sustained cold weather or other cause, some countries permit the addition of concentrated grape juice or of cane sugar. Tannin may also be added if the must is deficient in this.

The subject is a vast one and a specialized text-book must be consulted for fuller information. Numerous special types of wine are separately noted in these pages, e.g., port, sherry, champagne.

Wine of (Opium, Ipecac, Antimony, etc.): An old term in pharmacy denoting a medicinal agent containing alcohol but originally made with actual wine, usually sherry.

Wine-Palm: Any palm from whose sap an alcoholic beverage is made.

Winepress: Any equipment for expressing the juice from grapes. Obviously a misnomer, as the liquid expressed is not wine but fresh fruit juice.

Winery: A place where wine is made.

Wines, Low: — Strong: The illogical but time-honoured terms used to designate fractions (q.v.) obtained in the distillation of whisky (q.v.).

Wineskin: The whole skin of a sheep or a goat sewn up to act as a holder for wine (or for that matter milk or water). Still in use in the East.

Winestone: The deposit of *acid potassium tartrate*. See also Argol, Tartar.

Wine-Vault: A cellar for the storage of wine. The term is also used for a bar (q.v.) at which wine is retailed for immediate drinking.

Wine Whey: The whey of milk prepared by coagulating milk with wine.

Winkel: German wine district of the Rheingau. Amongst the finest vineyards are Schloss Vollrads, Dachsberg, Hasensprung, Oberberg, Erntebringer, Steinchen, Ansbach, Rheinpflicht and Lett.

Winningen: German wine district of Moselle.

Wino: The American (Californian) slang and opprobrious term for an alcohol addict who specializes in the consumption of fortified sweet (dessert) wine. Such wine is cheap in America, Australia and South Africa, and is the easiest way of getting drunk at low cost. Unhappily, it is a rather damaging method. The irony is that it is not the alcohol so much as the sugar that does the harm for the human body cannot usefully cope with large amounts of immediately available soluble carbohydrate. A further trouble is that sweet wine has high calorific value but is almost wholly lacking in minerals and vitamins. Thus appetite is satisfied but the body is not adequately nourished.

Wintrich: Also Winterich. German wine district of Moselle. Amongst the fine white wine estates are Sonnseite, Ohligsberg and Geierslay. Wintricher is widely praised. So is the orchestra of the town.

Wintriger: Dry white wine from Luxembourg.

Winzenheim: German (Nahe, q.v.) white wine.

Winzerverein or Winzergenossenschaft: German wine-growers' association, especially of the Palatinate (q.v.) often with own presses, cellars and trade mark.

Wirges: German (Klotten, q.v.) white wine estate.

Wisdom and Warter: Old-established (1855) shippers of sherry (q.v.). *Punch* is supposed to have printed 'Wisdom sells the wine, Warter makes it'. The firm long ago passed into Spanish hands.

Wisselbrunnen: German (Hattenheim, q.v.) white wine.

Withdrawals: The term used for the amount of beer and spirits upon which excise tax is paid, and thus a measure of sales.

Witzenberg: South African white table wine of merit from Tulbagh.

Wodky: See Vodka.

Wolfenweiler: German (Baden) white wine.

Wolfsdarm: German white wine from Wachenheim (q.v.).

Wolfshoele: See Bacharach.

Wollmesheim: German (Palatinate) white wine.

Wölm: German (Ostofen, q.v.) white wine.

Wolxheim: French (Alsatian) white wine.

Wompo: Local name for ale, used particularly in the East End of London.

Wong Dzao: Chinese (Pekinese) term for rice wine.

Wood: British general term for casks, barrels and all timber containers. 'In the wood' means unbottled. 'Rum in the wood' is thus equivalent to bulk. 'Beer from the wood' may mean that served direct from the cask, instead of being pumped from the cellar by beer-engine or merely not bottled, i.e. draught (q.v.).

Woodruff, or Sweet Woodruff: *Asperula odorata*, small scented European herb used for flavouring wine. See also Maybowl.

Woody: A vague term applied to wine and to a lesser extent to spirits to indicate that the beverage has acquired an unwanted taste of the timber. Fully seasoned oak should not transmit a taste but if young or defective timber is used there may be a solvent action. Not infrequently the diagnosis 'woody' is wrongly applied. Indeed, the term is used to cover a multitude of faults.

Worcester: South African wine-producing area.

Working: A common synonym for fermenting (q.v.).

Wormeldinger: Dry white wine from Luxembourg.

Worms: This river city of Rheinhessen is a German commercial wine centre rather than one of production and therefore unlike Bordeaux. There are some very fair vineyards around the famous old city but they are not in the category of the really fine sources of hock. At Worms is the church that has the vineyard around its grounds, whence the true Liebfraumilch (now legally allowed to be any fairly good hock) originally came. See also Liebfraumilch.

Wormwood: The popular name of the small shrub *Artemisia absinthium*, a native of Europe but now widely grown. It has a bitter, aromatic, characteristic taste and its medicinal properties have long been known. It is a vermifuge and is supposed to have tonic properties. It is, or was, used as a flavouring in the beverage absinthe (q.v.). Wormwood wine and ale were popular in England about 1660 and are mentioned more than once by Pepys.

Worn: Descriptive term applied to wine or other beverage on downgrade through age.

Wort: The sweet liquid obtained by extracting malt and ready to undergo fermentation. The process of producing the wort (pronounced 'wert') is called mashing.

Wulfen: German (Rauenthal, q.v.) white wine.

Würzburg: German (Franconian) city, the centre of Steinwein (q.v.). Notable vineyards are Stein, Homburger Kallmuth, Innere Leiste, Rossberg, Harfe, Randersackerer Lämmerberg, Casteller Schlossberg, Eschendorfer Lump and Eschendorfer Hengtsberg. This is also a centre for superb beer.

Würzgarten: German (Detzem, Moselle) white wine. Also a vineyard near Ürzig (q.v.) and another of the Rheingau. All fine hocks.

Würzweine: German term for spiced wine.

Wüst: German (Eibingen, q.v.) white wine.

Wynberger: South African white table wine.

Wynllan: The Celtic word for vineyard. It still survives in parts of Wales as the name of wine-growing places of many centuries past.

X: The mysterious letter sign applied to ale and beer, especially in England. There are two theories of origin:

(1) A sign used by monks during the Middle Ages as a guarantee of quality when each monastery was also a brewery.

(2) The sign originally placed on the cask by Excise officers to denote it had been examined and graded for duty.

Today the sign may mean as little as the stars on cognac, though in truth some good breweries do use the 'X' system as a reliable indication of quality and type. Thus, X or XX is mild beer and up to XXXX (strong ale). Sometimes 'K' is used in place of 'X'.

Xalello: Spanish table wine from Barcelona.

Xérès: French form of Jerez or sherry.

Xtabentun, Crema de: Mexican liqueur of aromatic flavour. The name is Mayan and is said to mean 'sweet grass'.

Yale: Cocktail of gin and orange bitters.

Yalumba: The trade name of a range of South Australian wines of merit. Yalumba Carte d'Or is riesling.

Yardarm, Over the: Originally a nautical but now a universal Anglo-Saxon term for congregating for a social drink.

Yard of Ale or Beer: Known also as a 'long glass', an old form of practical joke, companion of the puzzle jug of earlier centuries. Although the length varied, the yard of ale was approximately 3 feet long, shaped like a horn with a glass bulb at one end and open at the other. It held between $2\frac{3}{4}$ and $3\frac{1}{2}$ pints and needed to be drained in one steady drink; if tilted too steeply, the beer ran out over the drinker's face. 'Flooring the long glass' at Eton was a test of drinking capacity. Some glasses were designed suddenly to expel the beer in an unexpected direction. Other trick glasses were the boots, cocked hats and frogs.

Yard of Flannel: Old English hot drink of ale, brandy or rum, beer, brown sugar, ginger and other spices, lemon peel and beaten whole eggs. Mix until creamy and smooth. Possibly worth revival.

Yarmouth: Cocktail of brandy, cranberry juice and grenadine.

Yashioro No Sake: The traditional Japanese origin of alcoholic beverages, fermented by Prince Susanoono, younger brother of the Goddess Amaterasu.

Yayin: The Biblical term for wine, obviously related to *vinum, wine, wein, vin, vino, vinho, oinos*, etc. It is the commonest word for wine in the Bible. It is not a Hebrew root but a loan-word, presumably from the Greek *oinos*, wine. Yayin occurs 143 times in the Bible. It cheers God and man (Judges 9:13), makes glad the heart of man (Ps. 104:15), repentant and returning Israel is to be rewarded by again drinking the wine of her vineyards (Amos 9:14), it was to be given to them of heavy heart (Prov. 31:6), and is a mocker (Prov. 20:1). See also Bible.

Yeast: The *sine qua non* of alcoholic beverages, German *hefe*, French *levure*. Also barm, godesgood, leavening.

To the scientist and technologist the word yeast (*Saccharomyces*, meaning 'sugar-splitter') is applied to a large group of microscopic, simple, single-celled plants many or most of which are able to act upon sugars and some other carbohydrates to form common (ethyl) alcohol, together with carbon dioxide gas and usually small amounts of glycerin and many other organic compounds. Until 1897 it was believed that fermentation could only occur by the action of living yeast cells but in that year Büchner made the momentous discovery that the agent was an enzyme (q.v.) or ferment he called zymase. This could be extracted from the yeast cells after killing them by grinding with sand and filtering off the liquid containing the enzyme. The non-living extract could then set up fermentation on addition to a solution of suitable sugar. The process is, of course, only of academic interest and in practice fermentation (Latin *fervere*, to boil, from the bubbling appearance of the liquid on the way to wine or beer) is always effected by growing yeast in the sugary solution or dough in the case of bread.

As grapes ripen, the beautiful 'bloom' on the skin collects a mixed mass of various yeasts, bacteria and other micro-organisms. These yeasts are of several kinds. For example there are the wild yeasts (*Saccharomyces apiculatus*) with cells shaped like lemons and the elliptic-shaped wine yeast (*Saccharomyces ellipsoideus*). The latter are the valued friends of the wine-maker, the former his enemy. The fermentation of grape juice (must, q.v.) consists largely of adjusting temperature and adding sulphur dioxide so that the wild yeasts are restrained and the wine yeasts flourish. The practice is now common to add pure cultures of the desired wine yeasts. Special yeasts are used for brewing, breadmaking and many other alcoholic fermentations as well as for industrial purposes. The subject is a large one and there is an extensive literature.

Commercial yeast for alcoholic fermentation and breadmaking is a yellowish-white thick liquid or a soft mass, according to water content. This consists of innumerable cells and/or spores of yeast organisms. Yeast is known as 'bottom' or 'top' yeast according to whether it multiplies and ferments at the bottom or the surface of the liquid.

Yecla: Spanish (Murcian) pink beverage-wine.

Yekeb: The Biblical name for the first pressing of grape juice in wine-making, which was offered to God.

Yelarbon: Australian (Queensland) wine centre.

Yellow Daisy: Cocktail of gin, dry vermouth and orange liqueur.

Yellows: The practically incurable disease that will probably appear in champagne (q.v.) if any mildewed grapes are used.

Yellow Texas Rose: Cocktail of brandy, yellow chartreuse and orange juice.

Yenda: Australian (N.S.W.) wine centre.

Yering: Now defunct vineyard in the Yarra Valley of Victoria. Here Swiss vignerons in the seventies and eighties produced wine of superlative quality. The longevity of these wines was phenomenal. They gained many prizes at European wine fairs. The cause of the decline was low yield and not, as commonly believed, *Phylloxera* (q.v.).

Yeso: Crude Spanish plaster of paris used in making sherry to increase the active acidity of the must (q.v.). The process is ancient. The mineral and process are mentioned by Howell in 1635 ('Letter to Lord Cliff'). See also Howell.

Yeuk Tsau: General Chinese (Cantonese) term for medicinal spirits.

Yeuk Ts Oi Po Yeung: Chinese (Cantonese) soup made from wine, herbs and mutton, highly esteemed as a medicine.

Yin: Chinese liquid measure of about 46 imperial gallons.

Yintsieu: Chinese sweet wine.

Yoghurt: Fermented milk product, made mainly by Bulgarians; is always acid, but may or may not contain alcohol.

Yolo: Californian wine-growing county.

Yon-Figeac: French (Graves) red wine.

Yonne: French (Burgundian) wine-growing region. Here are some superb white wines, including chablis.

York: Cocktail of dry vermouth, maraschino and orange bitters.

Yorkshire Stone Square System: The distinctive process of brewing adopted exclusively in northern England, employing closed slate or stone vessels of special 'back flow' construction.

Younger: Old-established (1749) Scottish brewery. There are several separate concerns of this name.

Yquem, Château d': A magic name. This is the French wine estate of the Sauternes (q.v.) area of the Bordeaux that produces the sweet white table wine that gains the salute of every knowledgeable wine-maker of the world. This is a large estate (about 230 acres) and the wine is made from a blend of $\frac{2}{3}$ sémillon and $\frac{1}{3}$ sauvignon grapes. For process of wine-making see Sauternes. Yquem is probably the most consistently costly wine in the world.

Yuba: North Californian wine-growing county producing some wines of merit. 'Crossing the Yuba' used to be a toast in the Californian gold-rush days.

Yugoslavia: This country acquired much of the Austrian wine-growing land after the First World War, but the general quality is not notably high. There are, however, some wines of good repute. These include Lju-tomer, Radgona, Kraski Teran and Zilavka. The plum brandy (slivovitz) of the country is famous.

Yull-Cawp: Ale-bowl, in the central Ayrshire dialect of Robert Burns.

Yungas: Bolivian centre for rum production.

Yvorne: Swiss (Lake Geneva) region for esteemed white table wine. Amongst the good vineyards are Maison Blanche, Crosère-Guillé, and Clos du Rocher.

Zaco: Spanish white wine from Rioja (q.v.), stated to be the best of the region and certainly a table wine of great merit.

Zahnacker: Alsatian wine from Ribeauville, esteemed for pronounced bouquet.

Zahr-e-Khoosh: Persian for the 'pleasant poison', i.e. wine.

Zante: Currant indigenous to Greek island of that name. The vine is widely-grown on the Greek mainland in the district of Corinth, hence the name currant. The name is also that of a heavy, very sweet Ionian dessert wine.

Zapekenka: Ukrainian variety of nalivka (q.v.).

Zell: German town of lower Moselle, centre for much publicized white wines, including the Schwartze Katz (black cat). The name Zell is also that of a white wine district of the Palatinate.

Zellemberg: French (Alsatian) white wine.

Zeller Schwartze Katz: A vague name lacking legal significance used for Moselle wines from the central region. The only common characteristic is the 'black cat' on the label.

Zeltingen: German wine region on the Moselle. Amongst the most esteemed vineyards are Kirchlay, Rotlay, Sonnenuhr, Himmelreich, Kirchenpfad and Steinmauer. White wines of high quality.

Zichus: According to Howell (q.v.) this was the Latin name for an alcoholic beverage 'which was no other than decoction of Barley and Water', i.e. beer. This lacks confirmation but so probably does much else of Howell's artless prattle.

Ziegler: White wine from Forst, Palatinate (q.v.).

Zilavka: Yugoslavian (Sarajevo) wine area reputed to produce the best white wine of the country.

Zimmuk: Biblical term for raisins compressed into cakes. The best grapes were sun-dried for this purpose.

Zinfandel: This Californian grape is possibly the principal American contribution to the art of wine. Schoonmaker and Marvel state that the vine is definitely a *vitis vinifera* and therefore transplanted from Europe, but the true origin of the vine, like that of its name, remains wholly problematical, despite a great deal of research. Widely planted, productive, and dependable, the Zinfandel may well turn out to be a sort of fountainhead of *vin ordinaire* in America. The quality of the wine it gives varies enormously from one district to another. On hillside vineyards in Sonoma and Napa and in the Santa Cruz Mountains, the Zinfandel yields something quite extraordinary, a wine which matures quickly, is fine and fruity, like young Beaujolais, and sound.

The grape was presumably introduced by Spanish missionaries. Zinfandel is one of the few distinctive American table wines not made from indigenous grapes or from known European vines.

Zizerser: Pink table wine of Switzerland.

Zobing: Austrian wine centre.

Zollhaus: German (Rüdesheim, q.v.) fine white wine.

Zombie: Long mixed drink of rum with assorted fruits and much ice.

Zonnebloem: South African red table wine from near Paarl.

Zornheim: German (Rheinhessen) fine white wine centre.

Zubrowka: A central Russian spirit said to resemble vodka, but with the addition of herb flavouring, hence technically a gin (q.v.).

Zucco: The best-known Sicilian dessert-wine after marsala. It is said to have a vogue in France amongst Royalists, because it is made on estates belonging to the House of Orléans.

Zuckerberg: German (Oppenheim, q.v.) white wine.

Zumzammin: The Semitic name for the 'bottles' or large containers for wine made from a goat skin. The hair was left on the outer face, the skin sewn up except for the neck and then tanned. When filled the neck hole was tied with a thong. There are numerous Biblical references. A synonym is *mattaru*.

Zürich: Swiss wine-producing area.

Zwetschkengeist: Also Zwetschken. German term for plum brandy (slivovitz, q.v.), usually farm-distilled. See also Quetsch.

Zwicker: Also Zevicker. This curious Alsatian wine term is sometimes found on the label and indicates that the contents are a hotch-potch, i.e. made from a nondescript blend of grapes. The term is often regarded as derogatory, meaning that the contents of the bottle have no particular merit, but this is arguable. Some believe that the title Zwicker is a manifestation of strict commercial honesty and may conceal very good value.

Zymase: The ferment or enzyme produced by yeast, which is responsible for the conversion of fermentable carbohydrate to ethyl alcohol and carbon dioxide gas.

Zythus: A strong mead (q.v.) alleged to have been the common beverage of the Norsemen in Gaul.

PRINTED IN GREAT BRITAIN BY ROBERT MACLEHOSE AND CO. LTD
THE UNIVERSITY PRESS GLASGOW

Inauguration of a monster wine tun at Dieppe 1853